Z

Bibliography. Library Science. Information Resources

Library of Congress Classification
2009

LIBRARY OF CONGRESS

Prepared by the Policy and Standards Division

LIBRARY OF CONGRESS
Cataloging Distribution Service
Washington, D.C.

This edition cumulates all additions and changes to Class Z through Weekly List 2009/21, dated May 27, 2009. Additions and changes made subsequent to that date are published in weekly lists posted on the World Wide Web at

<http://www.loc.gov/aba/cataloging/classification/weeklylists/>

and are also available in *Classification Web*, the online Web-based edition of the Library of Congress Classification.

Library of Congress Cataloging-in-Publication Data

Library of Congress.
    Library of Congress classification. Z. Bibliography. Library science. Information resources / prepared by the Policy and Standards Division. — 2009 ed.
        p. cm.
    "This edition cumulates all additions and changes to Class Z through Weekly list 2009/21, dated May 27, 2009. Additions and changes made subsequent to that date are published in weekly lists posted on the World Wide Web ... and are also available in *Classification Web*, the online Web-based edition of the Library of Congress classification" — T.p. verso.
    Includes index.
    ISBN: 978-0-8444-1232-0
    1. Classification, Library of Congress. 2. Classification—Books—Bibliography. 3. Classification—Books—Library science. 4. Classification—Books—Information resources. I. Library of Congress. Policy and Standards Division. II. Title. III. Title: Bibliography. IV. Title: Library science. V. Title: Information resources.

    Z696.U5Z 2009   025.4'602—dc22   2009024436

For sale by the Library of Congress Cataloging Distribution Service, 101 Independence Avenue, S.E., Washington, DC 20541-4912.
Product catalog available on the Web at **www.loc.gov/cds**.

PREFACE

The first edition of Class Z, *Bibliography and Library Science*, was published in 1902, the second in 1910, the third in 1926, the fourth in 1959 (reprinted with supplementary pages in 1965), and the fifth in 1980. A 1995 edition cumulated all additions and changes that had been made since 1980. The 2001 edition, which cumulated changes made between 1995 and 2001, was the first to be published under the expanded title *Bibliography. Library Science. Information Resources*, and the first to include subclass ZA, *Information Resources (General)*, which was approved for use at the Library of Congress in 1996. The 2006 edition cumulated changes made between 2001 and 2006. This 2009 edition cumulates changes made since 2006.

Classification numbers or spans of numbers that appear in parentheses are formerly valid numbers that are now obsolete. Numbers or spans that appear in angle brackets are optional numbers that have never been used at the Library of Congress but are provided for other libraries that wish to use them. In most cases, a parenthesized or angle-bracketed number is accompanied by a "see" reference directing the user to the actual number that the Library of Congress currently uses, or a note explaining Library of Congress practice.

Access to the online version of the full Library of Congress Classification is available on the World Wide Web by subscription to *Classification Web*. Details about ordering and pricing may be obtained from the Cataloging Distribution Service at:

<http://www.loc.gov/cds/>

New or revised numbers and captions are added to the L.C. Classification schedules as a result of development proposals made by the cataloging staff of the Library of Congress and cooperating institutions. Upon approval of these proposals by the weekly editorial meeting of the Policy and Standards Division, new classification records are created or existing records are revised in the master classification database. Weekly lists of newly approved or revised classification numbers and captions are posted on the World Wide Web at:

<http://www.loc.gov/aba/cataloging/classification/weeklylists/>

Libby Dechman, subject cataloging policy specialist in the Policy and Standards Division, is responsible for coordinating the overall intellectual and editorial content of class Z. Kent Griffiths, assistant editor of classification schedules, is responsible for creating new classification records, maintaining the master database, and creating index terms for the captions.

Barbara B. Tillett, Chief
Policy and Standards Division

June 2009

OUTLINE

Libraries

Library science. Information science - Continued

OUTLINE

Z4-115.5

	Writing
	Typewriters. Typewriting. Keyboards. Keyboarding --
	Continued
49.4.A-Z	Machines using non-Roman characters, A-Z
49.4.A7	Arabic
49.4.B4	Bengali
49.4.B8	Burmese
49.4.C4	Chinese
49.4.H5	Hindi
49.4.J3	Japanese
49.4.K6	Korean
49.4.O7	Oriya
49.4.R8	Russian
49.4.S55	Sindhi
49.4.U73	Urdu
50.A-Z	Individual machines, A-Z
	e. g.
50.C8	Corona
50.R7	Royal
50.U5	Underwood
50.2	Art typing
50.7	Tabulation
	Stenotypy. Phonotypy
	Including shorthand for writing machines
51	General works
51.5	Computer-aided transcription systems
	Abbreviations see P365+
	Word processing
	Cf. HF5548.115 Office practice
52	Periodicals. Societies. Serials
52.2	Bibliography
52.25	Dictionaries
52.3	Examinations, exercises, etc.
52.4	General works
52.5.A-Z	Individual programs, machines, etc., A-Z
52.5.A32	Adam (Computer)
52.5.A34	AES word processors
52.5.A63	Apple computer
52.5.A64	Apple Writer (Computer program)
52.5.A65	Apple Writer II (Computer program)
52.5.A66	Apple Writer IIe (Computer program)
52.5.A68	AppleWorks (Computer program)
52.5.A77	ASTRA (Computer program)
52.5.B35	Bank street writer (Computer program)
52.5.B38	BBC Microcomputer
52.5.C54	Clean Slate (Computer program)
52.5.C65	CP/M (Computer operating system)

Writing
  Word processing
    Individual programs, machines, etc., A-Z -- Continued

52.5.C73	Creative writer (Computer file)
52.5.D57	DisplayWrite (Computer program)
52.5.D59	DisplayWrite 3 (Computer program)
52.5.D6	DisplayWrite 4 (Computer program)
52.5.D62	DisplayWrite 5 (Computer program)
52.5.E27	EasyWriter (Computer program)
52.5.E28	EasyWriter II (Computer program)
52.5.E52	Enable/OA (Computer program)
52.5.E67	Epson printers
52.5.E95	EXP (Computer program)
52.5.E97	Expert writer
52.5.F84	FullWrite professional (Computer program)
52.5.H35	Han'gŭl (Computer file)
52.5.H65	HomeWord (Computer program)
52.5.I24	IBM Displaywriter
52.5.I26	IBM PCjr (Computer)
52.5.I27	IBM Personal Computer
52.5.K39	Kaypro computers
52.5.L47	LetterPerfect
52.5.L63	LocoScript PC
52.5.M28	Macintosh (Computer)
52.5.M32	MacWrite (Computer program)
52.5.M47	Mercury (Computer program)
52.5.M52	Microsoft Word (Computer program)
(52.5.M523)	Microsoft Word for Windows (Computer program)
	see Z52.5.M52
52.5.M53	Microsoft Write (Computer program)
52.5.M58	MicroUSE-WORD (Computer program)
52.5.M84	MultiMate (Computer program)
52.5.M85	MultiMate Advantage (Computer program)
52.5.N57	Nisus Writer
52.5.N67	Norton Textra
52.5.P35	PC-Write (Computer program)
52.5.P47	Perfect Writer (Computer program)
52.5.P48	PFS:WRITE (Computer program)
52.5.P55	Philips/Micom
52.5.P56	Philips P5020 (Word processor)
52.5.Q2	Q-ONE (Computer program)
52.5.Q55	QL Quill (Computer program)
52.5.R4	Ready, set, go! (Computer program)
52.5.R46	Reportpack (Computer program)
52.5.S25	Samna (Computer program)
52.5.S37	SCRIPSIT (Computer program)
52.5.S39	SCRIPT (Computer file)

	Writing
	Word processing
	Individual programs, machines, etc., A-Z -- Continued
52.5.S45	Select Write (Computer program)
52.5.S55	Sinclair ZX (Computer)
52.5.S57	SITAR (Computer program)
52.5.S6	SmartWRITER (Computer program)
52.5.S63	SpeedScript (Computer program)
52.5.S65	Spellbinder (Computer program)
52.5.S67	Sprint (Computer program)
52.5.S94	Superscripsit (Computer program)
52.5.T48	TEXTEDIT (Computer program)
52.5.T49	ThinkTank (Computer program)
52.5.T53	TI Professional Computer
52.5.T55	TV (Computer file)
52.5.U54	UNIX (Computer operating system)
52.5.V6	VNIW
52.5.V64	Volkswriter
52.5.W36	Wang OIS 140
52.5.W365	Wang Professional computer
52.5.W37	Wang 30 (Word processor)
52.5.W38	Wang word processors
52.5.W63	Word writer
52.5.W632	Word writer PC
52.5.W65	WordPerfect (Computer program)
(52.5.W655)	WordPerfect for Windows (Computer program)
	see Z52.5.W65
52.5.W67	WordStar (Computer program)
52.5.W676	WordStar professional (Computer program)
52.5.W68	WordStar 2000 (Computer program)
52.5.W72	WPS-plus (Computer program)
52.5.W74	Write for kids
52.5.W75	Write-Now (Computer program)
52.5.X47	Xerox 860
52.5.X94	XyWrite (Computer program)
	Shorthand. Stenography. Phonography
53	General works
53.12	Bibliography
53.15	Periodicals, societies, congresses, etc.
	Biography
53.2.A1	Collective
53.2.A2-Z	Individual
	e.g.
53.2.G8	Gregg, John Robert
53.2.P5	Pitman, Sir Issac
53.2.T6	Towndrow, Thomas

Writing
   Shorthand. Stenography. Phonography -- Continued
     By subject
       see the subject, e. g. KF320.S4 Law; R728.8 Medicine; etc.
     By language
      English

54	Periodicals. Yearbooks
55	Societies. Congresses
55.5	Dictionaries
	Class here works cataloged before 1978
55.7	Directories
56	Manuals
	Class here works cataloged before 1978
56.2.A-Z	Special systems. By name, A-Z
	Class here works cataloged after 1977
56.2.A35	AgiliWriting (Table Z13)
56.2.A44	Alpha hand (Table Z13)
56.2.A45	Alphabet (Table Z13)
56.2.A9	Avancena American language (Table Z13)
56.2.F67	Forhner (Table Z13)
56.2.G7	Gregg (Table Z13)
56.2.P18	PS (Table Z13)
56.2.S58	Speedee-Write (Table Z13)
56.2.S6	Speedwriting (Table Z13)
56.2.S87	Stenoscript ABC (Table Z13)
56.2.S94	SuperWrite (Table Z13)
56.2.T33	Tabor (Table Z13)
56.2.W47	Wesley (Table Z13)
	Other languages
58.5	Afrikaans
58.8	Arabic
58.85	Armenian
59	Bohemian (Czech)
59.2	Burmese
59.3	Catalan
59.5	Chinese
60	Chinook
60.9	Czech
61	Danish. Norwegian
62	Dutch
62.5	Esperanto
63	Finnish
	French
65	General works. History
67	Periodicals. Serials
67.5	Dictionaries
68	Manuals

Writing
   Shorthand. Stenography. Phonography
     By language
      Other languages
       French -- Continued

68.5	Transcriptions of literary works
	German
70	General works. History
71	Periodicals. Serials
72	Societies
73	Manuals
73.5	Transcriptions of literary works
	Greek
73.9	Ancient
74	Modern
74.7	Hebrew and Yiddish
75	Hungarian
76.A-Z	Indic, A-Z
76.A1	General
76.G83	Gujarati
76.H5	Hindi
76.K3	Kannada
76.M27	Malayalam
76.M3	Marathi
76.P3	Panjabi
76.S5	Sinhalese
76.T3	Tamil
76.T4	Telugu
76.U7	Urdu
76.5	Indonesian
	Italian
77	General works. History
78	Periodicals. Serials
79	Societies
80	Manuals
80.5	Japanese
80.7	Korean
81	Latin
	Including Tironian notes
	Cf. Z111 Paleography
	Cf. Z114+ Paleography
83	Malagasy
	Norwegian see Z61
85	Polish
87	Portuguese
89	Romanian
	Slavic

Manuscripts. Paleography
Special alphabets, etc.
Other, A-Z -- Continued

115.5.A94	Azerbaijani
115.5.B44	Belarusian
115.5.B84	Bulgarian
115.5.C54	Chinese
115.5.C57	Church Slavic
115.5.C6	Coptic
115.5.C95	Czech
115.5.E39	Egyptian
115.5.E85	Ethiopic
115.5.G46	Georgian
115.5.G55	Glagolitic
115.5.G6	Gothic
115.5.J3	Japanese
115.5.M42	Malayalam
115.5.P45	Persian
115.5.P64	Polish
115.5.R8	Russian
115.5.S45	Serbo-Croatian
115.5.S53	Slavic
115.5.S68	Southern Slavic
115.5.T38	Tatar
115.5.T45	Thai
115.5.U4	Ukrainian
115.5.U73	Urdu

Cuneiform writing see PJ3191+
Facsimiles of particular manuscripts
see classes B-Z

Z116-659

Printing
  History
    Origin and antecedents of printing. History of the invention
     Celebrations of the invention -- Continued
      Individual celebrations

127.A4	1640
127.B1	1740
127.C1	1823
127.C3	1840
127.C4	1900
127.C5	1940
127.C7	1968

    By region or country
      Cf. Z1201+ National bibliography
     Europe
      For general works on Europe see Z124.A5+
      Austria

133	General works
134.A-Z	By province, city, etc., A-Z
	e.g.
134.V7	Vienna

      Czechoslovakia. Czech Republic

135	General works
136.A-Z	By place, A-Z
	Including works on the product of the presses
136.5	Slovakia

      Hungary

137	General works
138.A-Z	By place, A-Z
	Including works on the product of the presses

      France

144	General works
145.A-Z	By place, A-Z
	Including works on the product of the presses

      Germany
       Including West Germany

147	General works
148.A-Z	By place, A-Z
	Including works on the product of the presses
149	Germany (East)

      Great Britain

151	General works
	By period
151.2	15th century
151.3	16th century
151.4	17th-18th centuries
151.5	19th-20th centuries

Z116-659

Printing
  History
    By region or country
      Asia
        By country, island, etc., A-Z -- Continued

186.I5	Indonesia
186.J3	Japan
186.K67	Korea
186.L4	Lebanon
186.M65	Mongolia
186.P5	Philippines

Africa

195	General works
196.A-Z	By region or country, A-Z
	e.g.
196.E3	Egypt
196.M2	Madagascar
196.M67	Morocco
196.S7	South Africa

America

205	General works
	North America (General). Canada
206	General works
207.A-Z	By place, A-Z
	Including works on the product of the presses
	United States
208	General works
209.A-Z	By place, A-Z
	Including works on the product of the presses
	Mexico
210	General works
211.A-Z	By place, A-Z
	Including works on the product of the presses
	South and Central America. West Indies
212	General works. Latin America
213.A-Z	By country, city, etc., A-Z
	e.g.
213.A69	Argentina
213.B22	Barbados
213.B5	Bermuda Islands
213.B7	Bogota
213.B8	Brazil
213.B92	Buenos Aires
213.C53	Chile
213.L5	Lima
213.V45	Venezuela
213.W46	West Indies

Printing
History
By region or country -- Continued
Australia and Oceania

221	General works. Australia
222.A-Z	By province, island, etc., A-Z
	e.g.
222.H2	Hawaiian Islands
222.M3	Mascarene Islands
222.N5	New Zealand
225.A-Z	Special isolated islands, A-Z
	e.g.
225.S24	St. Helena
228.A-Z	By language, A-Z
	e.g.
228.H4	Hebrew

Printers and printing establishments

231	Collective biography
231.5.A-Z	Classes of presses, A-Z
231.5.C3	Catholic presses
231.5.L5	Little presses. Small presses
231.5.P7	Private presses
	Small presses see Z231.5.L5
231.5.U6	University presses
	Cf. Z286.U54 Bookselling and publishing
	Vanity presses see Z285.5
232.A-Z	Individual printers and establishments, A-Z
	Including catalogs, etc., of their productions
	Including individual public printers
	For inventors and supposed inventors see Z126+
232.A115	Aå, Pieter van der, 1659-1773
	Ad Insigne Pinus see Z232.P962
232.A148	Adam z Veleslavína, Daniel, 1546-1599
	Aḥim Kats see Z232.K22
	Aḥim Shulzinger see Z232.S556
232.A44	Allen Press
232.A5	Amerbach, Johannes, 1441?-1513
232.A63	Athoensen, Fred, 1882-
232.A76	Ashendene Press
232.A862	Audin, Marius
232.A89	Avramenko, Inessa
232.B147	Baĭnov, Pavel Marinov, 1870-1943
232.B23	Basson, Govert, ca. 1581-1643
232.B29	Bauersche Giesserei
232.B33	Baumgart, Konrad, 15th/16th cent.
	Benítez, Imprenta see Z232.I316
232.B469	Bentley, Wilder, 1900-

Printing
  Printers and printing establishments
    Individual printers and establishments, A-Z -- Continued

232.B498	Berliner Handpresse
232.B556	Bertoni, Moisés Santiago
232.B5815	Bianchino, dal Leone, ca. 1475-1544
232.B585	Bieler Press (Minneapolis, Minn.)
232.B6	Bird & Bull Press
232.B652	Blinn, Carol J.
232.B654	Blumenthal, Joseph
232.B66	Bodoni, Giovanni Battista
232.B687	Bonducci, Andrea
232.B79	Bowyer, William
232.B797	Bradbury & Evans
232.B8	Bradford, William
232.B812	Bradley, Will, 1868-1962
232.B83	Brazil. Departamento de Imprensa Nacional
232.B848	Brewer (Breyer) family. Breyer, Lucas, I and II
232.B85	Brewhouse Press
232.B87	Bringhurst, John, fl. 1680-1685
232.B897	Brumen, Thomas, 1532?-1588
232.B927	Bulkley, Stephen, d. 1680
232.B93	Bulmer, William, 1757-1830
232.B945	Burgert, Hans-Joachim
232.B948	Burov, K.M. (Konstantin Mikhạilovich)
232.C14	Caflisch, Max
232.C146	Caliban Press
232.C17	Cambridge University Press
232.C21	Canada. Dept. of Public Printing and Stationery
232.C28	Carter, Will, 1912-
232.C35	Casa Literária do Arco do Cego
232.C354	Caseg Press
232.C37	Cavellat, Guillaume, d. 1576 or 7
232.C38	Caxton, William
232.C55	Clark, Willard (Willard F.)
232.C65	Cobden-Sanderson, Thomas James
232.C7933	Corvinus Press
232.C794	Cossee, Piet C.
232.C835	Crampton's Printing House
232.C84	Cranach Presse
232.C92	Crespin, Jean, d. 1572
232.C927	Crnojević, Đurđe, ca. 1460-ca. 1514
232.C93	Cromberger family
232.C94	Crutchley, Brooke
232.C962	Cuala Press
232.C978	Curwen, Harold
232.D16	Dahlstrom, Grant Edward

Printing
Printers and printing establishments
Individual printers and establishments, A-Z -- Continued

232.D1615	Dai Nihon Insatsu Kabunshiki Kaisha
232.D163	Daiichi Insatsujo
232.D165	Dalla Volpe, Lelio and Petronio
232.D18	Daniel Press
232.D19	Daragnès, J.-G. (Jean-Gabriel), 1886-1950
232.D2	Darantière, Maurice. Imprimerie Darantière
232.D25	Davison, William, 1780-1858
232.D27	Dawks, Ichabod, 1661-1730
232.D277	Day, John, 1522-1584
232.D278	Day Moon Press
232.D285	De Montfort Press
232.D287	Dean, Mallette, 1907-
232.D343	Degotardi, John, 1860-1937
232.D375	Denique, Aegidius
232.D43	Derrydale Press
232.D52	De Vinne, Theodore Low, 1828-1914
232.D58	Diovatelli, family of printers
232.D65	Doesborch, Jan van, d. 1536
232.D66	Dolet, Etienne, 1509-1546
232.D68	Donnelley (R.R.) and Sons Company
	Doves Press see Z232.C65
232.D73	Draeger frères
232.D78	Druckerei Wallau
232.D84	Duensing, Paul Hayden, 1929-
232.E14	E.H. Walton Group (Port Elizabeth, South Africa)
232.E42	Edizioni Pulcinoelefante
232.E424	Eede, Louis van den
232.E43	Egenolff, Christian
232.E45	Ellandi, Otto, 1912-
232.E47	Ellis, Richard Williamson, 1894-1982
232.E5	Elsevier, family of printers
232.E56	Ema Insatsu Kabushiki Kaisha
232.E58	Emser, Hieronymus, 1478-1527
232.E63	Enitharmon Press
	Eragny Press see Z232.P65
232.E77	Espinosa, Antonio de, d. 1578
232.E8	Estienne, family of printers
232.E92	Everson, William
	Ex Ophidia Press see Z232.R94
232.F34	Fedorov, Ivan, ca. 1510-1583
232.F36	Ferretti family
232.F49	Finfgeld, Richard K.
232.F5	Finland. Valtion painatuskeskus
232.F52	Fiol, Szwajpolt, d. 1525 or 6

Printing
Printers and printing establishments
Individual printers and establishments, A-Z -- Continued
Fischer, G.L. see Z232.P975

232.F55	Florence. Sant' Jacopo di Ripoli (Dominican convent)
232.F56	Florian, Josef
232.F58	Flying Paper Press
232.F62	Fonseca, Arthur Arezio da, 1873-1940
232.F67	Forsberg, Vidar
232.F72	Foulis Press
232.F74	France. Imprimerie nationale
232.F8	Franklin, Benjamin, 1706-1790
232.F86	Fredericks, Claude
232.F96	Fu dan da xue (Shanghai, China). Chu ban she
232.G23	Galeati, Paolo, d. 1903
232.G25	Garnett, Porter, 1871-1951
232.G26	Garth, William W., 1915-1975
232.G458	Gilbert & Rivington
232.G486	Ginammi, Marco
232.G55	Giunti, family of printers
232.G565	Gliwa, Stanisław, 1910-1986
232.G567	Glykys, family of printers
232.G58	Göbl, Carol, 1845-1916
232.G63	Golden Cockerel Press
232.G635	Golden Hind Press
232.G638	Goltzius, Hubertus, 1526-1583
232.G68	Goudy, Frederic William
232.G72	Grabhorn Press. Grabhorn, Edwin E. and Jane Bissell
232.G73	Gráfico Amador
232.G87	Great Britain. Her/His Majesty's Stationery Office
232.G8753	Grefwe, Amond
232.G87535	Grégr, Eduard, 1900-1986
232.G8754	Gregynog Press. Gwasy Gregynog
232.G8755	Grenfell Press
232.G8756	Grenzius, Michael Gerhard
232.G876	Gröll, Michal
232.G878	Grover, James, d. 1700
232.G933	Gullanders bogtrykkeri
	Gwasg Gregynog see Z232.G8754
232.H114	Haas, Robert, 1898-
232.H145	Haiman, György
232.H148	Hamady, Walter
232.H2	Hansard, Luke
232.H358	Hatch Show Print (Firm)
232.H4344	Hele, Rudolf
232.H54	Hertzog, Carl
232.H613	Hijar, Gabriel de, fl. 1563-1576

Z116-659

Printing
  Printers and printing establishments
    Individual printers and establishments, A-Z -- Continued

232.H72	Hoffman, Richard J.
232.H73	Hogarth Press
232.H796	Hoply, Wolfgang, d. 1522
232.H836	Hrushivskyĭ monastyr (Hrushovo, Ukraine)
232.H87	Hutegger (Firm)
232.I14	İbrahim Müteferrika, 1674?-1745
232.I26	Iliazd, 1894-1975
232.I313	Imprensa Nacional de Lisboa
232.I3134	Imprensa Nacional de Moçambique
232.I316	Imprenta Benítez
232.I323	Imprenta del Monasterio de Nuestra Señora de Prado (Valladolid, Spain)
232.I325	Imprenta Federal de William P. Griswold y John Sharpe, Montevideo
	Imprimerie Darantière see Z232.D2
232.I47	Infante, family of printers
232.I83	Istituto poligrafico dello Stato (Italy)
232.J37	Japan. Ōkurasho. Insatsukyoku
232.J54	Jenson, Nicholas, ca. 1420-1480
232.J56	Joh. Enschedé en Zonen
232.J72	Jones, George William, 1860-1942
232.J73	Jones, Thomas, 1648-1713
232.J78	Jou, Louis
232.K22	Kats (Aḥim)
232.K32	Keimena (Firm)
232.K34	Kennedy, Lawton, 1900-
232.K66	Kner, family of printer. Kner, Imre, 1890-1945
232.K676	Kníhtlačiareň Václava a Jána K. Jelínka v Trnave
232.K7953	Kongstad, Kristian, 1867-1929
232.K7954	Kožičić, Šimun, ca. 1460-1536
232.K82	Kraszewski, Józef Ignacy, 1812-1887
232.K86	Kuhn, family of printers. Kühn, Balthasar
232.K94	Kyōdō Insatsu Kabushiki Kaisha
232.L15	Lagos State Printing Corporation
232.L17	Laguna Verde Imprenta
232.L184	Laichter, Jan
	Lakeside Press see Z232.D68
232.L29	Landen, Johann, ca. 1462-ca. 1521
232.L313	L'Angelier, Abel, d. fl. 1572-1609
232.L393	Lavagna, Filippo da
232.L398	Leers, Reinier, 1654-1714
232.L399	Leeu, Gerard, ca. 1445-1493
232.L62	Leslie, Robert L., 1885-
232.L75	Lone Goose Press

Printing
  Printers and printing establishments
    Individual printers and establishments, A-Z -- Continued

232.L77	Long Shop Printing Office
232.L89	Ludwig, von Renchen, 15th/16th cent.
232.L95	Lyons, T.J. (Thomas Joseph)
232.M195	Mahiḷōŭskae Bohaḯaŭlenskae bratstva
232.M242	Malaysia. Jabatan Cetak Kerajaan (Sabah)
232.M3	Manuzio, family of printers
232.M322	Marcus Ward & Co.
232.M33	Marion Press
232.M34	Marlborough College Press
232.M38	Martínez, Enrico, d. 1632
232.M45	Mauritius. Government Printing Office
232.M454	Maverick Press
232.M477	Mažvydas, Martynas
232.M482	McCollam Printers, Ltd.
232.M485	McGarth, Harold P.
232.M55	Mentelin, Johann, ca. 1410-1478
232.M57	Merrymount Press
232.M585	Metaxas, Nikodēmos, 1585-1646
232.M627	Middle Hill Press
232.M67	Minkman, J.
232.M74	Monasch, Bar Loebel
232.M82	Morano family
232.M85	Morison, Stanley, 1889-1967
232.M87	Morris, William. Kelmscott Press
232.M886	Mosher, Thomas Bird, 1851-1923
232.M8862	Moskovskaḯa sinodal'naḯa tipografiḯa
232.M88624	Moskovskiĭ pechatnyĭ dvor
232.N243	Nakata Insatsujo
232.N247	Narodiczky's Press
232.N25	Nash, John Henry
232.N54	Never Mind the Press (Firm)
232.N62	Nhà xuất b'an Chính trị quốc gia
232.N69	Nirṇayasāgara Presa
232.N82	Nonesuch Press
232.O18	Ocharte, Pedro, ca. 1532-1592
232.O33	Officina Bodoni
232.O333	Officina Chimerea
	Otto Rohse Presser see Z232.R674
232.O87	Overbrook Press
232.O98	Oxford University Press
232.P12	Pablos, Juan, d. 1561?
232.P14	Paganino, Alessandro, 1509-1538
232.P154	Paltasîchis, Andreas de, fl. 1476-1493
232.P33	Pavoni, Giuseppe, 1551-1641

Z116-659

Printing
  Printers and printing establishments
    Individual printers and establishments, A-Z -- Continued

232.P432	Perger, Sandor
232.P436	Perna, Pietro, 1519-ca. 1582
232.P44	Perrin, Louis, 1799-1865
232.P46	Petrejus, Johannes, 1497-1550
232.P47	Petri, Johannes, 1441-1511
232.P475	Petrunev, I.
232.P52	Pfeil, Johann
232.P57	Pichon, Léon, 1876-
232.P65	Pissarro, Lucien, 1863-1944. Eragny Press
	Plain Wrapper Press see Z232.R94
232.P71	Plantin, family of printers. Plantin, Christophe
232.P73	Plantin Press (Los Angeles, Calif.)
232.P793	Półtawski, Adam, 1881-1952
232.P795	Poltroon Press
232.P94	Preller, Carl, 1802-1877
232.P945	Press at Colorado College
232.P962	Privatbuchdruckerey Ad Insigne Pinus in Augsburg
232.P97	Pulman (George) & Sons Ltd. Pulman, George Frederick
232.P975	Pump Press. G.L. Fischer
	Quadflieg, Roswitha see Z232.R12
232.R12	Raamin Presse. Quadflieg, Roswitha
232.R17	Rampant Lions Press
232.R23	Ratdolt, Erhard
232.R29	Red Ozier Press
232.R318	Reflection Press
232.R353	Remondini (Firm)
232.R354	Renildis Handpers
232.R61	Ritchie, Ward, 1905-
232.R62	Riva, Franco, 1922-
232.R63	Robertson, George
232.R67	Rogers, Bruce
232.R674	Rohse, Otto
232.R68	Rollins, Carl Purington, 1880-1960
232.R682	Ross, Sjoerd de, 1877-
232.R8	Roycroft Shop
232.R94	Rummonds, Richard-Gabriel
232.S15	Saga-ken (Japan). Insatsukyoku Imprensa
232.S184	Samurai Press
	San Jacopo di Ripoli (Convent: Florence, Italy) see Z232.F55
232.S186	Sancha, Antonio de, 1720-1790
232.S22	São Paulo (Brazil: State). Imprensa oficial do Estado
232.S253	Schmied, François-Louis, 1873-1941
232.S397	Seihan Insatsu Kabushiki Kaisha

Z116-659

Printing
   Printers and printing establishments
      Individual printers and establishments, A-Z -- Continued

232.S47	Sessa, Melchiorre, fl. 1506-1549
232.S525	Shakespeare Head Press
232.S556	Shulzinger (Aḥim)
232.S56	Siberch, John, 1475 or 6-1554?
232.S57	Sichowsky, Richard von
232.S615	Skaryna, Frantsysk Heorhiĭ, ca. 1490-ca. 1535
232.S643	Sleepeck, William, 1871-1941
232.S67	Snell, Johann
232.S753	Squires, Roy A.
232.S759	Stadsdrukkerij van 'Amsterdam
232.S769	Stamperia reale di Torino
232.S784	Stanislao, Polono, fl. 1491-1514
232.S8298	Stanley, Joe, 1889-1950
232.S84	Stent, Peter, fl. 1640-1667
232.S863	Stinehour Press
232.S877	Stone House Press
232.S9	Strawberry Hill Press
232.S918	Struck, Michael Anton, 1676-1744
232.S965	Sweynheim, Konrad, d. 1477
232.S976	Szántó, Tibor
232.T178	Taller Martín Pescador
232.T185	Tanaka Insatsu Kōgyō Kabushiki Kaisha
232.T195	Tarasiev, Nikifor
232.T198	Tarousopoulos family
232.T218	Taylor, Edward DeWitt
232.T22	Taylor & Taylor
232.T38	Thejils, Henry
232.T4	Thomas, Isaiah, 1749-1831
232.T43	Thompson, Nathaniel
232.T588	Tipografia dell'Oratorio (Rome, Italy)
232.T594	Tipografia medicea orientale
232.T596	Tipografia Zanetti
232.T64	Tokuda, Kinsen, 1897-
232.T69	Toppan Insatsu Kabushiki Kaisha
232.T7	Torrentino, Lorenzo, d. 1563
232.T74	Torresani, Gian Francesco, 1498-1557 or 8
232.T8	Tory, Geoffroy, ca. 1480-ca. 1533
232.T814	Tótfalusi Kis, Miklós, 1650-1702
232.T85	Tragara Press
232.T853	Treebus, K.F. (Karel F.)
232.T863	Tschichold, Jan, 1902-1974
232.T97	Typografia Agnelli
232.U6	U.S. Government Printing Office
232.V32	Vardi, Ari'el

Z116-659

Printing
Practical printing
Type and type founding. Specimen books -- Continued
Data processing. Computerized type and type founding.
Computer fonts

250.7	General works
250.8.A-Z	By special language or system, A-Z
250.8.A23	Adobe Type Manager
250.8.A25	Adobe TypeAlign
250.8.F65	Fontographer
250.8.M46	METAFONT
250.8.P68	PostScript
250.8.T78	TrueType
251.A-Z	By language, A-Z
251.A6	Arabic
251.A7	Armenian
251.B45	Bengali
251.C5	Chinese
251.C56	Church Slavic
251.D4	Devanagari
251.G45	Georgian
251.G7	Greek
251.H4	Hebrew
251.H6	Hieroglyphic
251.I7	Irish
251.J3	Japanese
251.K65	Korean
251.O6	Oriental
251.R9	Russian
251.S68	South Asian
251.S97	Syriac
251.T45	Thai
251.U47	Ukrainian
251.U73	Urdu
252	Stereotyping. Electrotyping
252.5.A-Z	Other processes, A-Z
252.5.A87	Autotype process printing
252.5.C47	Cerography
252.5.D54	Digital printing
	Including digital printing presses
252.5.F6	Flexography
252.5.I48	Ink jet printing
252.5.I49	Instant printing
252.5.I5	Intaglio printing
252.5.L37	Laser printing
252.5.L5	Lithography
	For offset lithography see Z252.5.O5

Z116-659

	Printing
	Practical printing
	Other processes, A-Z -- Continued
252.5.M8	Multiple printing
252.5.N64	Nonimpact printing
252.5.O5	Offset printing. Offset lithography
	For waterless printing see Z252.5.W37
252.5.O55	On-demand printing
252.5.P5	Plate printing
252.5.R4	Relief printing
252.5.W37	Waterless printing
	Composition, typesetting, makeup. Style manuals
253	General works
253.2	Phototypesetting
	Computerized typesetting
253.3	General works
253.4.A-Z	By special language or system, A-Z
253.4.A65	AMS-LaTeX
253.4.L38	LaTeX systems
253.4.L43	LEFT language
253.4.M53	MicroTeX system
253.4.P34	PAGE-1 System
253.4.T47	TeX System
253.4.U47	ULTRA-X language
253.4.U53	UNIX System
253.5	Makeup
	Desktop publishing
	Class here works on desktop publishing software and its use
	For works on desktop publishing as a business see Z244.64+
253.53	General works
253.532.A-Z	Individual programs, machines, etc., A-Z
	Adobe Framemaker see Z253.532.F7
253.532.A34	Adobe InDesign
	Adobe PageMaker see Z253.532.P33
	Aldus PageMaker see Z253.532.P33
253.532.A54	Ami pro
253.532.D48	DeScribe
253.532.E94	Express publisher
253.532.F7	FrameMaker
(253.532.F73)	FrameMaker for Windows see Z253.532.F7
253.532.I58	Interleaf publisher
253.532.M34	MacWrite Pro
253.532.M53	Microsoft Publisher
253.532.P33	PageMaker

Printing
  Practical printing
    Composition, typesetting, makeup. Style manuals
      Desktop publishing
        Individual programs, machines, etc., A-Z -- Continued
        PageMaker for Windows see Z253.532.P33

253.532.P34	PagePlus
253.532.Q37	QuarkXPress
(253.532.Q375)	QuarkXPress for Windows
	see Z253.532.Q37
253.532.S37	Serif Publishing power-suite
	Ventura see Z253.532.V45
253.532.V45	Ventura Publisher. Ventura. Xerox Ventura Publisher
253.532.W67	Word Pro
	Xerox Ventura Publisher see Z253.532.V45
254	Proofreading
255	Imposition and locking up
	Presswork
256	General works
257	Printing of pictures, illustrations, etc.
	Cf. NE2800+ Printing of engravings
258	Color printing
260	Drying
261	Folding
	Including folding of blank stationery, bags, boxes, and other
	unprinted paper products
262	Machines for paging
264	Stencils. Stamps. Rubber type
	Printing for the blind see HV1667.A1+
	Printing of catalogs see Z695.87
264.5	Printing of documents. Public printing
264.7	Security printing

      Representation or reproduction of books, documents, etc., by
        photography, microphotography, and other means
        For technical aspects of photographic reproduction see
          TR824+
        Cf. Z48 Processes of duplicating
        Cf. Z110.R4 Reproduction of manuscripts
        Cf. Z681+ Photography and other methods of
          reproduction in library science
        Cf. Z1033.M5 Microform editions

265	General works
265.5.A-Z	Special means, A-Z
	Micrographics see Z265.5.M53

Printing
    Representation or reproduction of books, documents, etc., by
        photography, microphotography and other means
      Special means, A-Z -- Continued

265.5.M53	Microphotography. Micrographics

           Class here works on the design and use of books,
              documents, computer-output data, etc., in a microform
              format
           For technical aspects of microphotography and
              microfilming, including standards see TR835
           For micropublishing see Z286.M5

Z116-659

Bookbinding
    Including topics and forms not elsewhere provided for, e. g. hand
        bookbinding, rebinding, addresses
    For commercial bookbinding see Z269.5
    For library bookbinding see Z700

266	General works
266.5	Bibliography
266.7	Dictionaries
267	Periodicals. Serials
268	Societies
	History. Biography of bookbinders

        Including exhibitions and collections of facsimiles, etc.,
           illustrating history, styles, etc.

269	General works
269.2.A-Z	Individual bookbinders, A-Z
269.3.A-Z	Special types of bindings, A-Z
269.3.A34	Adhesive bindings
269.3.A75	Armorial
269.3.B37	Baroque
	Blind tooled see Z269.3.S73
269.3.C58	Cloth
269.3.D78	Drum leaf
269.3.D87	Durable
269.3.E42	Embossed
269.3.E43	Embroidered
269.3.F55	Fine bindings. Ornamental bindings
269.3.G68	Gothic
269.3.I95	Ivory
269.3.J48	Jeweled
269.3.L43	Leather
	Library bindings see Z700
269.3.M44	Medieval
269.3.M67	Mosaic
(269.3.O75)	Ornamental
	see Z269.3.F55
269.3.P37	Paper

Z116-659

276	Book decoration and ornamentation (General)
	Cf. NC960 Book illustration
	Cf. ND2370 Fore-edge painting
	Cf. Z4+ Books and bookmaking (History)
	Cf. Z116.A2 The modern printed book (General)
	Cf. Z250.3 Type ornaments
	Cf. Z269+ Bookbinding (History, etc.)
	Cf. Z1023 Illustrated books (Bibliography)
	Bookselling and publishing
	Including book industries and trade in general
278	General works
279	Bibliography
	History. Biography of booksellers
280	General works
281	Antiquity and Middle Ages
	Class here works primarily on the selling of manuscripts
282	Directories
	By country, area, etc., see Z289+
282.5	Dictionaries. Encyclopedias
283	Handbooks, manuals, etc.
284	Periodicals. Societies. Congresses
285	Collections
	Study and teaching
285.3	General works
285.35.A-Z	By region or country, A-Z
285.5	Self-publishing. Subsidy publishing. Vanity publishing
	Cf. Z231.5.P7 Private presses
	Cf. Z1028 Private printed books
285.6	Marketing
	Including Internet marketing
286.A-Z	Special lines of business, A-Z
	For classification by place see Z289+
286.A35	Africa
286.A5	Anthropology
286.A55	Antiquarian booksellers
286.A73	Archaeology publishing
286.A77	Art publishing
	Associations see Z286.T7
286.A83	Audiobook publishing
286.B56	Biography publishing
286.B88	Business literature
286.C35	Catalogs, Commercial
	CD-ROM publishing see Z286.O68
286.C48	Children's literature
286.C53	Classical literature
286.C6	College bookstores
286.C63	College publications

Bookselling and publishing
  Special lines of business, A-Z -- Continued
    College textbooks see Z286.T48

286.C64	Comic books, strips, etc.
	Commercial catalogs see Z286.C35
286.C65	Computer science literature
286.C67	Cookery
286.C68	Corporation reports
(286.D47)	Desktop publishing
	see Z244.64+
286.D57	Directories
286.E3	Education
286.E43	Electronic publishing
	Cf. Z286.I57 Internet publishing
286.E74	Erotic literature
286.F3	Fantastic fiction. Science fiction
286.F45	Feminist literature
286.G46	Genealogy
	Government dissemination of information see Z286.G69
286.G69	Government publishing. Government dissemination of information. Public printing for public distribution
286.H34	Handbooks, vade-mecums, etc.
286.H47	High interest-low vocabulary books
286.H5	History (Sources) publishing
	Interactive multimedia see Z286.O68
286.I56	International agencies
286.I568	Internet bookstores. Online bookstores
286.I57	Internet publishing
286.L44	Legal publishing
286.L58	Literature
	Cf. Z286.C53 Classical literature
286.L59	Lithographed books
286.M27	Mail-order bookselling
	Cf. Z549 Book clubs
286.M29	Management literature
286.M3	Maps
286.M4	Medical publishing
	Microform publishing see Z286.M5
286.M5	Micropublishing. Microform publishing
286.N46	Newsletters
286.N48	Newspapers
	Online bookstores see Z286.I568
286.O63	Open access publishing
286.O68	Optical publishing. CD-ROM publishing
	Including interactive multimedia
286.P35	Paperback books

Bookselling and publishing

    Special lines of business, A-Z -- Continued

286.P4	Periodicals. Serials
	Including serials subscription agencies
286.P46	Philology
286.P48	Physics
286.P53	Picture-books
286.P63	Poetry
	Professional associations see Z286.T7
	Public printing for public distribution see Z286.G69
286.R37	Reference books
286.R4	Religious literature
	Cf. BM496.8 Publication of rabbinical literature
	Cf. BP131.18.A+ Publication of the Qur'ān
	Cf. BQ1117+ Publication of the Tripitaka
	Cf. BV2369+ Publication of the Bible
286.S37	Scholarly publishing
286.S4	Science
	Science fiction see Z286.F3
	Serials see Z286.P4
286.S55	Slavic books
286.T4	Technology
286.T48	Textbooks
	Including college textbooks
286.T5	Theatrical publishing
286.T7	Trade, professional, or other associations
286.U54	University presses
	Cf. Z231.5.U6 Printing
	Cf. Z286.C63 College publications
286.Y43	Yearbooks
286.Z54	Zines
	By region or country
289	Developing countries
	Europe
291-291.8	General works (Table Z12)
292-292.8	Eastern Europe (Table Z12)
293-300	Austria (Table Z7)
301-301.86	Czechoslovakia. Czech Republic (Table Z8)
	For Slovakia see Z447.S54+
302-302.86	Hungary (Table Z8)
303-310	France (Table Z7)
313-320	Germany (Table Z7)
	Including West Germany
321-321.86	Democratic Republic of Germany (Table Z8)
323-330	Great Britain (Table Z7)
331-331.86	Ireland (Table Z8)
333-333.86	Greece (Table Z8)

Z116-659

Bookselling and publishing
  By region or country
    Europe -- Continued
338-345   Italy (Table Z7)
                  Benelux countries
347-347.8   General works (Table Z12)
348-355   Belgium (Table Z7)
356-363   Netherlands (Table Z7)
365-365.86   Poland (Table Z8)
366-373   Soviet Union. Russia (Federation) (Table Z7)
                  Baltic States
375   General works
375.E7-.E786   Estonia (Table Z9)
375.L3-.L386   Latvia (Table Z9)
375.L7-.L786   Lithuania (Table Z9)
                  Scandinavia
376   General works
                      Including topics and forms not otherwise provided for
377   Bibliography
378   History
379   Special lines of business (not A-Z)
380   Directories
381   Handbooks, manuals, etc.
382   Collections
384-391   Denmark (Table Z7)
392-399   Norway (Table Z7)
400-407   Sweden (Table Z7)
408-408.86   Finland (Table Z8)
410-417   Spain (Table Z7)
418-425   Portugal (Table Z7)
428-435   Switzerland (Table Z7)
439-439.86   Bulgaria (Table Z8)
441-441.86   Romania (Table Z8)
443-443.86   Yugoslavia (Table Z8)
444-444.86   Albania (Table Z8)
                  Turkey see Z464.T89+
447.A-Z   Other, A-Z
447.A53-.A5386   Andorra (Table Z9)
447.B44-.B4486   Belarus (Table Z9)
447.B67-.B6786   Bosnia and Hercegovina (Table Z9)
447.C76-.C7686   Croatia (Table Z9)
447.I5-.I586   Iceland (Table Z9)
447.M33-.M3386   Macedonia (Republic) (Table Z9)
447.M35-.M3586   Malta (Table Z9)
447.M64-.M6486   Moldova (Table Z9)
447.M66-.M6686   Monaco (Table Z9)
447.S54-.S5486   Slovakia (Table Z9)

Bookselling and publishing
By region or country
Europe
Other, A-Z -- Continued

447.S56-.S5686	Slovenia (Table Z9)
447.U35-.U3586	Ukraine (Table Z9)

Asia

448-448.8	General works (Table Z12)
449-449.86	Israel. Palestine (Table Z8)
450-450.86	Iran. Persia (Table Z8)
451-458	India (Table Z7)
459-459.86	Pakistan (Table Z8)
460-460.86	Indonesia (Table Z8)
461-461.86	Philippines (Table Z8)
462-462.86	China (Table Z8)
463-463.86	Japan (Table Z8)
464.A-Z	Other, A-Z
464.A67-.A6786	Armenia (Table Z9)
464.A93-.A9386	Azerbaijan (Table Z9)
464.G45-.G4586	Georgia (Republic) (Table Z9)
464.I7-.I786	Iraq (Table Z9)
464.J6-.J686	Jordan (Table Z9)
464.K39-.K3986	Kazakhstan (Table Z9)
464.K6-.K686	Korea (Table Z9)
464.K94-.K9486	Kyrgyzstan (Table Z9)
464.L43-.L4386	Lebanon (Table Z9)
464.M34-.M3486	Malaysia (Table Z9)
464.S33-.S3386	Saudi Arabia (Table Z9)
	Siam see Z464.T5+
464.S72-.S7286	Sri Lanka (Table Z9)
464.S9-.S986	Syria (Table Z9)
464.T35-.T3586	Taiwan (Table Z9)
464.T43-.T4386	Tajikistan (Table Z9)
464.T5-.T586	Thailand. Siam (Table Z9)
464.T89-.T8986	Turkey (Table Z9)
464.T92-.T9286	Turkmenistan (Table Z9)
464.U93-.U9386	Uzbekistan (Table Z9)
464.V5-.V586	Vietnam (Table Z9)
464.Y4-.Y486	Yemen (Republic) (Table Z9)

Africa

465-465.8	General works (Table Z12)
466.A-Z	Egypt and North Africa, A-Z
466.A35	Africa, North
466.A4	Algeria (Table Z9)
466.E4	Egypt (Table Z9)
466.L53	Libya (Table Z9)
	North Africa see Z466.A35

Bookselling and publishing
  By region or country
    Africa
      Egypt and North Africa, A-Z -- Continued

466.T8	Tunisia (Table Z9)
467.A-Z	East Africa, A-Z
467.A353	Africa, East
	East Africa see Z467.A353
467.E65	Eritrea (Table Z9)
467.E88	Ethiopia (Table Z9)
467.K4	Kenya (Table Z9)
467.M33	Madagascar (Table Z9)
467.R4	Réunion (Table Z9)
467.T36	Tanzania (Table Z9)
467.U33	Uganda (Table Z9)
468.A-Z	West Africa, A-Z
468.B45	Benin (Table Z9)
468.B87	Burkina Faso (Table Z9)
468.C68	Côte d'Ivoire (Table Z9)
468.G5	Ghana (Table Z9)
468.L5	Liberia (Table Z9)
468.N5	Nigeria (Table Z9)
469-469.86	South Africa (Table Z8)
470.A-Z	Central and Southern Africa, A-Z
470.A356	Africa, Southern
470.A5	Angola (Table Z9)
470.C66	Congo (Democratic Republic). Zaire (Table Z9)
470.N36	Namibia (Table Z9)
	South Africa see Z469+
	Southern Africa see Z470.A356
	Zaire see Z470.C66
470.Z33	Zambia (Table Z9)
470.Z55	Zimbabwe (Table Z9)
	United States
471	General works
472	Bibliography
473	History
	Arrange histories of individual firms by name of firm, A-Z
	Including histories of individual firms, and including
	collective and individual biography
	For catalogs see Z1217.A+
475	Directories
476	Handbooks, manuals, etc.
477	Periodicals. Societies. Congresses
478	Collections
	Local
478.3.A-Z	By state or region, A-Z

Bookselling and publishing
  By region or country
    United States
      Local -- Continued

478.6.A-Z	By city, A-Z
(479)	Special lines of business
	see Z480
480.A-Z	Special lines of business, A-Z
	For list of Cutter numbers see Z286.A+
481-488	Canada (Table Z7)
490-490.8	Latin America (Table Z12)
491-498	Mexico (Table Z7)
501-501.86	Central America (Table Z8)
508-515	West Indies. Caribbean Area (Table Z7)
	South America
517-517.8	General works (Table Z12)
519-519.86	Argentina (Table Z8)
520-520.86	Bolivia (Table Z8)
521-521.86	Brazil (Table Z8)
522-522.86	Chile (Table Z8)
523-523.86	Colombia (Table Z8)
524-524.86	Ecuador (Table Z8)
525-525.86	Guianas (Table Z8)
528-528.86	Paraguay (Table Z8)
529-529.86	Peru (Table Z8)
530-530.86	Uruguay (Table Z8)
531-531.86	Venezuela (Table Z8)
	Australia
533	General works
	Including topics and forms not otherwise provided for
533.2	Bibliography
533.3	History
	Arrange histories of individual firms by name of firm, A-Z
	Including histories of individual firms, and including
	collective and individual biography
	For catalogs, see Z4013
533.4	Special lines of business (not A-Z)
533.5	Directories
533.6	Handbooks, manuals, etc.
533.7	Periodicals. Societies. Congresses
533.8	Collections
536-536.86	New South Wales (Table Z8)
(537-537.86)	New Zealand
	see Z543.9+
538-538.86	Northern Territory (Table Z8)
539-539.86	Queensland (Table Z8)
540-540.86	South Australia (Table Z8)

Z116-659

Bookselling and publishing
　By region or country
　　Australia. Oceania -- Continued
541-541.86　　　　Tasmania (Table Z8)
542-542.86　　　　Victoria (Table Z8)
543-543.86　　　　Western Australia (Table Z8)
　　　　New Zealand
543.9　　　　　General works
　　　　　　　　Including topics and forms not otherwise provided for
543.92　　　　　Bibliography
543.93　　　　　History
　　　　　　　　Arrange histories of individual firms by name of firm, A-Z
　　　　　　　　Including histories of individual firms, and including
　　　　　　　　　　collective and individual biography
　　　　　　　　For catalogs, see Z4103
543.94　　　　　Special lines of business (not A-Z)
543.95　　　　　Directories
543.96　　　　　Handbooks, manuals, etc.
543.97　　　　　Periodicals. Societies. Congresses
543.98　　　　　Collections
　　　　　　Local
543.983.A-Z　　　　By region or state, A-Z
543.986.A-Z　　　　By city, A-Z
　　　　Pacific Ocean islands. Oceania
543.99　　　　　General works
544.A-Z　　　　　Individual Pacific islands, A-Z
544.S2　　　　　Samoan Islands (Table Z9)
549　　　　Book-buying organizations
　　　　　Including organization and management, book clubs, etc.
　　　　　For periodical book lists see Z1007
　　Copyright
　　　　Class here works dealing with nonlegal aspects of copyright,
　　　　　　including catalogs of copyright entries
　　　　For legal aspects, see class K
551　　　General works
552　　　International copyright
　　　By region or country
553.8　　　Africa
554　　　Argentina
554.5　　　Asia
555　　　Australia
557　　　Austria
561　　　Belgium
563　　　Bolivia
564　　　Brazil
　　　　Bulgaria see Z638.3
565　　　Canada

Copyright
 By region or country -- Continued
  Ceylon see Z567

567	Sri Lanka. Ceylon
569	Chile
570	China
570.5	Colombia
572	Cuba
573	Czechoslovakia
575	Denmark
578	Dominican Republic
	East Germany see Z587
579	Ecuador
580	Egypt
581	Europe
582	Finland
584	France
586	Germany
	Including West Germany
587	Germany, East
587.4	Ghana
589	Great Britain
590	Greece
591	Guatemala
591.3	Haiti
591.5	Honduras
593	Hungary
594	India
594.3	Indonesia
595	Ireland
595.5	Israel
596	Italy
598	Japan
600	Korea
605	Latin America
606	Lebanon
608	Malaysia
609	Mexico
615	Netherlands
620	New Zealand
620.5	Nicaragua
623	Norway
623.5	Pakistan
624	Philippines
625	Poland
627	Portugal
	Romania see Z638.5

Z116-659

Copyright
   By region or country -- Continued
630   Soviet Union
632   Scandinavia
635   Spain
           Sri Lanka see Z567
636   Sweden
637   Switzerland
638   Turkey
638.3   Bulgaria
638.5   Romania
638.7   Yugoslavia
639   Taiwan
639.5   Thailand
           United States
642   General works
645   Confederate States
647   Uruguay
648   Venezuela
648.4   Vietnam
           Yugoslavia see Z638.7
648.8   Zaire
649.A-Z   Special topics, A-Z
649.C38   Cataloging
(649.D4)   Deposition of copies. Legal deposit
              see class K
649.F35   Fair use
              Including fair use of photocopying processes
649.L53   Library copyright policies
(649.M6)   Moral rights
              see class K
(649.P4)   Perpetual copyright
              see class K
649.P5   Piracy (Literary)
(649.P7)   Pseudonyms
              see class K
649.P83   Public lending rights of authors
649.R68   Royalties
649.T5   Title
(649.T7)   Transfer
              see class K
(649.T8)   Translations
              see class K
652.A-Z   Special classes of literary work, A-Z
652.C45   Children's literature
652.D7   Drama
652.L4   Letters

Copyright
  Special classes of literary work, A-Z -- Continued
652.N4   Newspaper articles
  Other branches of copyright and physical forms that can be
      copyrighted
        Including special topics and copyright issues related to these
            branches
653   Music
653.7   Electronic information resources. Databases
654   Designs and models
654.5   Artistic performance
655   Motion pictures
655.5   Radio broadcasting. Television broadcasting
655.6   Sound recordings
656.A-Z   Other printed formats, A-Z
656.L2   Labels
656.M3   Maps
  Freedom of the press. Censorship
        Class here works dealing with nonlegal aspects of censorship, or
            censorship outside the law
        For legal aspects of censorship, see class K
        Cf. BV4730 Precepts of the church
        Cf. PN156 Censorship (Authorship)
        Cf. PN4735+ Government and the periodical press
        Cf. Z1020+ Index librorum prohibitorum
657   General works
658.A-Z   By region or country, A-Z
659   Destruction of books and libraries. Book burning

Libraries
   Collections
      Cf. Z674 Library science
      Cf. Z720.5 Historiography
      Cf. Z729+ Library reports
      Cf. Z881+ Library catalogs and bulletins

Z662-1000.5

662	General
	Individual libraries
	Library of Congress

Under each department, division, etc.:

.A1-.A6	*Serials*
.A7-.Z	*Nonserials. By title or keyword, A-Z*

Class here complete sets of Library of Congress publications
Class publications according to the responsibility for the publication as author
Class works about a division or description of its activities or contents of its collections with the division
For individual publications, serial or nonserial, see classes B-Z, by subject or form
For catalogs not confined to the collections of a particular division, see Z663.7+ , Library Services

General

663.A1-.A6	Serials. By title
	e. g.
663.A2	Annual report
663.A3	Departmental and divisional manuals
663.A35	Information bulletin
663.A4	Library of Congress series in American civilization
663.A5	Quarterly journal of current acquisitions
663.A6	United States quarterly book review
663.A7-Z	Nonserials. By title
663.113	Office of the Librarian
663.115	American Revolution Bicentennial Office
	American Folklife Center
663.116	General works
663.117	Archive of Folk Song. Archive of American Folk Song
	Including the former Folklore Section of the Music Division
	Associate Librarian for Management see Z663.9+
663.118	The Center for the Book
663.1185	National Digital Library Program
663.119	National Library Service for the Blind and Physically Handicapped
663.12	Network Development and MARC Standards Office. Network Development Office
663.121	Children's Literature Center. Children's Book Section
663.13	Committee on Bibliography and Publications

Collections
   Individual libraries
      Library of Congress
         Research Services. Reference Department
            Humanities and Social Sciences Division. Director for
               General Reference. General Reference and
               Bibliography Division -- Continued

663.293	Gertrude Clarke Whittall Poetry and Literary Fund
663.295	International Organizations Section
663.315	Reading rooms of the Humanities and Social Sciences Division. General Reading Rooms Division
663.32	Hispanic Division. Hispanic Foundation
663.33	Loan Division
	Manuscript Division
663.34	General works
	e. g.
663.34.J6	Journals of Continental Congress
663.341	Poetry Office
663.35	Geography and Map Division. Map Division
663.36	Motion Picture, Broadcasting and Recorded Sound Division
	Music Division
663.37.A1-.A6	Serials. By title
663.37.A7-Z	Nonserials. By title
663.372	Elizabeth Sprague Coolidge Foundation
(663.373)	Folklore Section
	see Z663.117
663.375	Gertrude Clarke Whittall Foundation
663.378	Recording Laboratory
(663.379)	National Referral Center for Science and Technology
	see Z663.42
	Asian Division. Orientalia Division
663.38	General works
663.382	Chinese and Korean Section
(663.384)	Hebraic Section
	see Z663.252
663.385	Japanese Section
663.389	South Asia Section
663.39	Prints and Photographs Division. Fine Arts Division
	Preservation Office
663.395	General works
663.396	Binding Office
663.397	National Preservation Program Office
663.398	Preservation Microfilming Office
663.4	Rare Book and Special Collections Division. Rare Book Division. Rare Book Collection

Z662-1000.5

Collections
Individual libraries
Library of Congress
Library Services. Collections Services. Processing
Services. Processing Department -- Continued

663.7345	Cataloging Policy and Support Office
	For Library of Congress classification schedules see Z663.78.C5+
663.7347	Collections Policy Office
663.735	Decimal Classification Division
	Descriptive Cataloging Division. Catalog Division
663.74	General works
663.745	Cooperative Cataloging Section
663.746	Descriptive Cataloging Policy, Office for
663.75	Exchange and Gift Division
663.756	MARC Editorial Division
(663.757)	MARC Development Office
	see Z663.172
663.7575	NACO. National Coordinated Cataloging Operation
	Network Development and MARC Standards Office see Z663.12
	Order Division. Division of Accessions. Acquisitions Department
663.76	General works
663.765	Library of Congress Mission
	Overseas Operations Division
663.766	General works
663.7665	Library of Congress Office, Brazil
663.7666	Library of Congress Office, Egypt
663.7667	Library of Congress Office, Kenya
	Public Law 480 Project
663.767.A1	General works
663.767.A2-Z	By region or country, A-Z
663.768	Regional and Cooperative Cataloging Division
663.7689	SACO. Subject Authority Cooperative Program
	Serial Record Division
663.77	General works
663.773	CONSER Program
663.775	National Serial Data Program Section
663.778	Shared Cataloging Division
663.78	Subject Cataloging Division. Classification Division
	e. g.
663.78.A4	L.C. Classification--Additions and Changes
663.78.C5-.C5Z	Classification (Classes A-Z)
	Subarrange by class
	e.g.
663.78.C5G	Class G

Collections
   Individual libraries
    Library of Congress
     Library Services. Collections Services. Processing
      Services. Processing Department
      Subject Cataloging Division. Classification Division
      Classification [Classes A - Z] -- Continued

663.78.C5P2	Class P-PA
663.78.C5P3	Class PB-PH
663.78.C5Z	Class Z
663.78.C52	Outline of the Library of Congress Classification
663.78.M8	Music subject headings
663.78.S7	Subject headings--a practical guide, by D.J. Haykin
663.78.S8	Subject headings used in the dictionary catalogs of the Library of Congress

Z662-1000.5

663.785	Subject Cataloging Policy, Office for

        For Library of Congress classification schedules
         see Z663.78.C5+

663.79	Union Catalog Division
	Copyright Office
663.8	General works
663.81	Acquisitions and Processing Division
663.82	Cataloging Division
663.84	Examining Division
663.86	Information and Reference Division. Reference Division
663.87	Licensing Division
663.88	Records Management Division. Service Division
	Associate Librarian for Management. Administrative Department
663.9	General works
	Accounts Office see Z663.91
	Automated Systems Office see Z663.172
663.91	Financial Management Office. Budget and Management Office
663.92	Building Management Division. Buildings and Grounds Division
	Disbursing Office see Z663.91
	Information Technology Services see Z663.172
663.94	Special police. Guard Division
	Personnel and Labor Relations Office. Personnel Division
663.95	General works
	e. g.
663.95.L5	The Library of Congress and you
663.951	Employee Relations Office
663.953	Labor Relations Office
663.955	Personnel Operations Office

	Collections
	Individual libraries
	Library of Congress
	Associate Librarian for Management. Administrative Department
	Personnel and Labor Relations Office. Personnel Division -- Continued
663.957	Training Office
663.96	Photoduplication Service
	Central Services Division. Secretary's Office
663.97	General works
663.975	Mail Receipt and Delivery Unit. Mail and Delivery Service
663.976	Procurement and Supply Division
663.99.A-Z	Other, A-Z
	Including staff organizations
	e. g.
663.99.L5	Library of Congress Welfare and Recreation Association. Library of Congress Beneficiary Association
664.A-Z	Other libraries, A-Z
	Library science. Information science
	Cf. ZA3038+ Information resources
	Collected works (nonserial) see Z674
665	General works
	Including topics and forms not elsewhere provided for
665.2.A-Z	By region or country, A-Z
665.5	Juvenile works
	Dictionaries see Z1006
666	Bibliography
	Information organization
666.5	General works
666.6	Functional Requirements for Bibliographic Records. FRBR (Conceptual model)
666.7	Metadata
	Including metadata harvesting
	Information storage and retrieval systems
	Class here works on automated or manual systems for the retrieval of information other than bibliographic information
	For works on information retrieval systems on a specific topic, see the topic
	For works on structured databases see QA76.9.D26
	For works on automated systems for the storage and retrieval of bibliographic information see Z699+
667	General works
667.5	Cross-language information retrieval
	Cf. P307+ Machine translating

Library science. Information science
Information storage and retrieval systems -- Continued
Information filtering systems
667.6   General works
667.63   Recommender systems
Library education
For training and education of specific groups of library
personnel see Z682.4.A+
668   General, and United States
668.2   Audiovisual aids
668.3   Examinations, questions, etc.
668.5   In-service training
669.A-Z   Individual schools in the United States, A-Z
Other countries
669.1   Canada. British North America
669.3   Great Britain
669.5.A-Z   Other, A-Z
669.7   Research. Authorship
669.8   Statistical methods
Including bibliometrics and informetrics
Cf. Z711.3 Reference statistics
Cf. Z721+ Library reports. History. Statistics
Handbooks, manuals, etc.
670.A2   Early through 1800
670.A3-Z   1801-
670.5   Charts, diagrams, etc.
671   Periodicals
Class here periodicals of general interest
For periodicals pertaining to libraries of particular places
or individual libraries (United States) see Z731+
Library cooperation and coordination
Cf. Z672.3 International librarianship
672   General works
672.13.A-Z   By region or country, A-Z
Subarrange each country by Table Z15
672.2   Comparative librarianship
672.3   International librarianship
672.5   Congresses
For congresses of individual library associations see
Z673.A1+
Library associations
673.A1   General works
673.A5-.A52   American Library Association
Cf. Z675.W2 A.L.A. war service
673.A54-Z   Other associations. By name, A-Z
(673.5)   Library exhibits
see Z717

Z662-1000.5

Library science. Information science -- Continued

674	Collected works (nonserial)
	Information services. Information centers
	see ZA3150+
(674.2)	Periodicals. Societies. Congresses
(674.25)	Bibliography
(674.3)	Directories
(674.4)	General works
(674.5.A-674.Z)	By region or country, A-Z
	Library information networks
	Class here works on networks not limited by topic
	Including library applications of general computer networks
	For works on networks limited to specific topics see
	Z699.5.A+
674.7	General works
674.73	Security measures
674.75.A-Z	Individual international networks, projects, etc., A-Z
674.75.I58	Internet
674.75.W67	World Wide Web
	Including library Web sites
	By region or country
	United States
674.8	General works
674.815.A-Z	By region or state, A-Z
674.82.A-Z	Individual networks, projects, etc. A-Z
674.82.A53	Amigos
674.82.F43	FEDLINK (network)
674.82.F55	Florida Library Information Network
674.82.I52	ILLINET
674.82.I53	Illinois Valley Library System
(674.82.I59)	Internet
	see Z674.75.I58
674.82.K37	Kansas Library Network
674.82.L56	Linked Systems Project
674.82.M54	Minitex (Program)
674.82.N48	New Jersey Library Network
674.82.O15	OCLC, Inc.
674.82.O36	Ohio Regional Library and Information System
674.82.O42	Oklahoma Telecommunications Interlibrary System
674.82.O48	OLTN (Library information network)
674.82.R47	Research Libraries Group
674.82.S24	Sailor (Computer network)
674.82.S42	Seymour (Library information network)
674.82.S65	South Dakota Library Network
674.82.S68	Southeastern Library Network
674.82.T47	Texas State Library Communications Network
674.82.W37	Washington Library Network

Library science. Information science
　Library information networks
　　By region or country
　　　United States
　　　　Individual networks, projects, etc. -- Continued
674.82.W47　　　　　Western Pennsylvania Buhl Network
674.83.A-Z　　　　Other regions or countries, A-Z
　　　　　Under each country:
　　　　　.x　　　　　　　*General works*
　　　　　.x2A-.x2Z　　　　*Individual networks. By name, A-Z*
675.A-Z　　Classes of libraries, A-Z
　　　　Class special school libraries with the special class of libraries,
　　　　　e. g. class law school libraries in .L2, Law libraries
　　　　For works about an individual library in one of these
　　　　　classes see Z729+
　　　　Cf. Z1039.A+ Books for special classes, institutions, etc.

Z662-1000.5

675.A2　　　Special libraries
　　　　Academic libraries see Z675.U5
675.A5　　　Aeronautical
675.A55　　　African libraries
675.A8　　　Agricultural
675.A815　　　Anthropological libraries
675.A817　　　Aquarium
675.A818　　　Aquatic sciences
675.A82　　　Arabic libraries
675.A83　　　Architectural
675.A84　　　Area studies
675.A85　　　Art
　　　　Asia see Z675.O75
675.A87　　　Association
675.B5　　　Biological libraries
675.B53　　　Biotechnology
675.B55　　　Birth control
675.B6　　　Blind, The (Libraries for)
675.B67　　　Botanical libraries
　　　　Branch libraries see Z686
675.B8　　　Business
675.C3　　　Catholic libraries
　　　　Charities libraries, see Z675.S63
　　　　Children's libraries see Z718.1+
675.C47　　　Chemical libraries
675.C48　　　Chiropractic libraries
675.C49　　　Christian libraries
675.C5　　　Church libraries. Parish libraries
　　　　　For Sunday school libraries see Z675.S9
675.C55　　　City planning libraries
　　　　College libraries, see Z675.U5

	Library science. Information science
	Classes of libraries, A-Z -- Continued
(675.C7)	Commercial
	see Z675.B8
	Community college libraries see Z675.J8
675.C75	Community development
675.C76	Construction industry libraries
675.C77	Cooperative society libraries
675.C778	Corporate libraries
675.C78	Costume design libraries. Fashion design libraries
(675.C8)	County libraries
	see Z729+
675.C83	Criminal justice
675.D28	Demography
675.D3	Dental
675.D4	Depository libraries
675.D63	Documents libraries
	Cf. Z675.D4 Depository libraries
675.E22	East Asian libraries
675.E25	Economics libraries
	Education see Z675.P3
	Elementary school see Z675.S3
675.E6	Engineering
675.E75	Environmental
675.F3	Factory
	Fashion design libraries see Z675.C78
675.F5	Financial
675.F57	Fishery
675.F67	Forestry libraries
675.F7	Fraternity
675.G44	Genealogical libraries
675.G46	Geological libraries
675.G7	Government
	Cf. Z675.N2 National libraries
	Cf. Z675.S7 State and provincial libraries
	Cf. Z675.V7 Village libraries. Rural libraries
	High school see Z675.S3
675.H5	Historical
675.H7	Hospital
	For patients' libraries see Z675.P27
675.H8	Hotel
675.H86	Humanities
675.I53	Industrial relations
675.I6	Institution
675.I7	Insurance
675.I75	International agency libraries
675.I84	Islamic

Library science. Information science
Classes of libraries, A-Z -- Continued

675.J4	Jewish
675.J64	Joint-use libraries
675.J8	Junior college
	Including community college libraries
	Junior high school see Z675.S3
675.L17	Latin Americanist libraries
675.L2	Law
675.L45	Legislative libraries
675.L48	Lesbian libraries
675.L5	Library science libraries
675.L54	Life sciences libraries
675.L58	Literary libraries
	Map see GA192+
675.M35	Marine science libraries
675.M37	Mathematics libraries
675.M4	Medical
	Membership libraries see Z675.S8
675.M43	Mental health
675.M44	Metallurgical
675.M45	Meteorological
675.M48	Middle East libraries
	Middle school see Z675.S3
675.M5	Military
675.M6	Military post libraries
	Cf. Z675.W2 War libraries
675.M7	Monastic libraries
675.M72	Mosque libraries
675.M9	Municipal reference
	Municipal university and college see Z675.J8
675.M94	Museum
	Music see ML111
675.N2	National
675.N24	Natural history
675.N25	Natural resources
675.N3	Naval
675.N37	Newspaper and periodical libraries
675.N4	News libraries. Newspaper office libraries
675.N8	Nursing
	Including nursing school libraries
675.O22	Occupational health
675.O23	Oceanographic
675.O75	Orientalia
675.O76	Ornithological
675.O78	Orthodox Eastern libraries
	Package libraries see Z716.1

Z662-1000.5

Library science. Information science
Classes of libraries, A-Z -- Continued
Packhorse libraries see Z716.15
Parish libraries see Z675.C5

675.P27	Patients' libraries
675.P3	Pedagogical. Education
	Including teachers colleges
675.P45	Performing arts
675.P46	Personnel management libraries
675.P48	Pharmacology libraries. Pharmacy libraries
	Phonorecords see ML111.5
675.P49	Physics
675.P56	Polar
675.P568	Polish libraries
675.P57	Political science
675.P6	Postal libraries
	Presidential libraries see CD3029.82
675.P8	Prison
675.P85	Proprietary
	Public libraries see Z729+
675.P9	Publishers' libraries
675.P94	Puerto Rican studies libraries
675.R15	Railroad
675.R27	Rare book libraries
675.R33	Real estate
675.R35	Regional
675.R37	Religious
675.R4	Rental
675.R45	Research
	Rural libraries see Z675.V7
675.S3	School
	Scientific see Z675.T3
	Ship see Z675.N3
675.S57	Small libraries
675.S6	Social science
675.S63	Social service
675.S67	South Asian libraries
675.S7	State and provincial
675.S75	Storage
675.S8	Subscription. Membership
675.S9	Sunday school
	Synagogue see Z675.J4
	Teachers college libraries see Z675.P3
675.T3	Technical. Scientific
675.T33	Telecommunication
675.T36	Theater

Library science. Information science
Classes of libraries, A-Z -- Continued

675.T4	Theological
	Including theological seminary libraries
(675.T58)	Toy lending libraries
	see GV1218.6+
	Trade school see Z675.V8
675.T6	Trade-union
675.T7	Transportation libraries
675.U37	Ukrainian
675.U5	University and college. Academic libraries
	For directories of academic libraries in specific places see Z730+
	For junior college see Z675.J8
	For teachers college see Z675.P3
	For statistics of academic libraries in specific places see Z729+

Z662-1000.5

675.V47	Veterinary libraries
675.V7	Village libraries. Rural libraries
675.V8	Vocational school. Trade school
675.V84	Volunteer
675.W2	War libraries
	Including libraries in camps, stations, hospitals, etc.
	Cf. Z675.M6 Military post libraries
675.W57	Women's studies libraries
675.W6	Workingmen's libraries
675.Y7	Young Men's Christian Association
	Young adults' libraries see Z718.5
675.Z66	Zoological libraries

Library administration and organization
Including library planning
For works on administration of specific types of libraries see Z675.A+
For works on government aid to libraries see Z683.3+
Cf. Z670.A2+ Handbooks, manuals, etc.

678	General, and United States
678.2	National
	State boards, commissions, etc.
	Cf. Z716+ Library extension, etc.
678.3	General
678.4.A-.W	By state, A-W
	Cf. Z732.A+ Library reports
678.6	Local administration
	For works on individual library systems see Z733.A+
678.8.A-Z	Other countries, A-Z
678.82	Library records
678.83	Meetings

	Library science. Information science
	Library administration and organization -- Continued
678.85	Evaluation. Rating. Standards
678.88	Use studies
	Cf. Z711.3 Reference statistics
	Library service agencies
678.89	General works
678.892.A-Z	By region or country, A-Z
	Automation
	Including information technology in libraries
	Cf. Z674.7+ Library information networks
	Cf. Z695.92 Automatic indexing. Punched card systems
	Cf. Z699+ Machine-readable bibliographic data.
	Information storage and retrieval systems
678.9.A1	Periodicals. Societies. Congresses
678.9.A2	Bibliography
678.9.A3	Directories
678.9.A4A-.A4Z	By region or country, A-Z
678.9.A5-Z	General works
678.93.A-Z	Special topics, A-Z
678.93.A48	ALS (Computer system)
678.93.A65	Apple computer
	CD-ROMs see Z678.93.O7
678.93.C62	COBOL (Computer program language)
678.93.C65	Computer programs
	Including individual multifunction programs other than
	integrated library systems
678.93.C67	Contracting out
	Including application service providers
678.93.D33	Database management
	Including individual database management
	Cf. Z678.93.I57 Integrated library systems
678.93.D35	Data Research System
678.93.D46	Desktop publishing
678.93.D85	Dynix (Computer system)
678.93.E44	Electronic mail systems
678.93.E46	Electronic spreadsheets
	Including individual electronic spreadsheet programs
678.93.E93	Expert systems
678.93.F65	Forms
678.93.G43	Geac Library Information System
678.93.G73	Graphics
	Including individual graphics programs
678.93.H94	Hypertext systems
678.93.I55	INMAGIC
678.93.I56	INNOPAC
678.93.I57	Integrated library systems

Library science. Information science
　　Automation
　　　Special topics, A-Z -- Continued
　　　　Laser disks see Z678.93.O7

678.93.L63	Local area networks (Computer networks)
678.93.L68	Lotus 1-2-3 (Computer program)
678.93.M53	Microcomputers
678.93.M57	Microsoft Windows
678.93.M73	MS-DOS (Computer operating system)
678.93.O25	OCLC M300 Workstation
678.93.O64	On-line data processing
678.93.O68	Optical character recognition devices
678.93.O7	Optical disk or storage. Laser disks. CD-ROMs
678.93.P35	Pascal (Computer program language)
678.93.P74	Printers
678.93.P83	Public access computers in libraries
678.93.S32	SABINI
678.93.S43	Sebina Produx
678.93.S53	Shared virtual environments
678.93.S6	Small libraries
	Spreadsheets see Z678.93.E46
678.93.T87	Turnkey computer systems
678.93.U73	UNIX (Computer operating system)
678.93.U74	URICA (Computer system)
678.93.V54	Videotex systems
678.93.W53	Wide area networks (Computer networks)
	Windows, Microsoft see Z678.93.M57
678.93.W67	Word processing

　　　　　　　Including individual word processing programs

678.93.X54	XML (Document markup language)

　　Library buildings. Library architecture
　　　Including design, construction, etc.

679	General works
679.2.A-Z	By region or country, A-Z
679.5	Planning. Furnishing

　　　　　Including hiring of consultants or architects, choosing a site,
　　　　　　fittings, etc.
　　　　　Cf. Z684 Supplies

679.55	Space utilization

　　　　　Cf. Z685 Shelving. Bookstacks

679.57	Signs
679.6	Security measures

　　　　　Including security guards, crime prevention in libraries, etc.
　　　　　Cf. Z702.A3+ Thefts and losses of books

679.7	Safety measures
679.8	Library architecture for people with disabilities. Barrier-free design

Z662-1000.5

	Library science. Information science
	Library buildings. Library architecture -- Continued
680	Heating and ventilation. Lighting
	Library communication systems
	Cf. Z674.7+ Library information networks
680.3	General works
680.5	Teletype. Telecommunication
	For computer networks see Z674.7+
680.6	Image transmission
	Including facsimile transmission
	Reproduction of library materials. Storage media of library materials
(681)	General works
	see Z701
(681.3.A-Z)	Special storage media, materials stored, methods, etc., A-Z
	see Z701.3.A+
	Trustees. Library boards, committees, etc.
	Including friends of the library
681.5	General works
681.7.A-Z	By region or country, A-Z
	Personnel
	Including librarian, staff, etc.
	For education of librarians see Z668+
	For biography and directories of librarians see Z720.A1+
682	General works
682.2.A-Z	By region or country, A-Z
682.25	Job descriptions
682.28	Evaluation. Rating of employees
682.3	Salaries. Pensions, etc.
682.35.A-Z	Other special, A-Z
682.35.A45	Affirmative action
682.35.C47	Certification
682.35.C58	Civil service
682.35.C64	Collective bargaining
682.35.C66	Conflict (Psychology)
682.35.E63	Employee orientation
682.35.E65	Employment
682.35.H67	Hours of labor
682.35.L52	Librarians' unions
682.35.M35	Manpower planning
682.35.M43	Meetings
682.35.P75	Professional ethics
682.35.P82	Psychology
682.35.R42	Recruiting
682.35.S75	Statistics
682.35.S95	Supply and demand
682.35.T43	Technological literacy

	Library science. Information science
	Personnel
	Other special, A-Z -- Continued
682.35.T55	Time management
682.35.V62	Vocational guidance
682.4.A-Z	Special groups, A-Z
	Academic librarians see Z682.4.C63
682.4.A25	Acquisitions librarians
682.4.A34	Administrators. Directors
682.4.A37	African Americans
682.4.A83	Asian Americans
682.4.B87	Business librarians
682.4.C38	Catalogers
682.4.C49	Children's librarians
682.4.C63	College librarians. College library employees
	College library employees see Z682.4.C63
682.4.C64	Computer specialists
682.4.C65	Consultants
	Directors see Z682.4.A34
682.4.G39	Gay men and lesbians
682.4.H58	Hispanic Americans
682.4.I58	Interns
682.4.L37	Law librarians
	Lesbians see Z682.4.G39
682.4.L49	Library pages
682.4.L52	Library technicians
682.4.M56	Minorities
682.4.P37	Part-time employees
682.4.P82	Public librarians
682.4.R44	Reference librarians
682.4.S34	School librarians
682.4.S35	Science and technology librarians
682.4.S37	Serials librarians
682.4.S65	Special librarians
682.4.S89	Student library assistants
682.4.S94	Systems librarians
682.4.T42	Teacher-librarians
	Technology librarians see Z682.4.S35
682.4.V64	Volunteer workers
682.4.W65	Women
682.4.Y68	Young adult librarians
682.5	Library humor, anecdotes, etc.
	Finance
	Including bookkeeping, the budget, cost accounting, etc.
	For financial statistics of individual libraries and groups of libraries see Z729+
683	General works

Z662-1000.5

Library science. Information science

Finance -- Continued

683.2.A-Z	By region or country, A-Z
	United States
683.2.U6	General works
683.2.U62A-.U62W	By state, A-W
	Government aid to libraries
683.3	General works
	By region or country
	United States
683.35	General works
683.36.A-Z	By region or state, A-Z
683.37.A-Z	Other regions or countries, A-Z
683.5	Insurance. Risk management
684	Supplies
	Cf. HF5741 Business files and indexes
685	Shelving. Bookstacks
686	Branches. Bookmobiles
	The collections. The books
	Including collection development
	Cf. ZA4080.5 Digital library collection development
687	General works
687.15	Cooperative collection development
687.2.A-Z	By region or country, A-Z
	Special collections
	Including collections of books on special subjects and
	collections of classes of materials, e. g. maps, music, etc.
	For thefts from special collections see Z702.A3+
	Cf. Z675.A+ Classes of libraries
688.A1	Bibliography
688.A2	General works
688.A3A-.A3Z	By region or country, A-Z
	For works on collections in a special subject or format, see
	the subject or format
688.A5-Z	Special. By subject, A-Z
	Cf. Z691+ Special classes of materials
688.A54	Africa
688.A55	African Americans
688.A58	Aging
688.A66	Arab countries
688.A68	Area studies
688.A7	Art books
688.A75	Asia
688.A93	Audiobooks
688.A95	Australia
688.B49	Bible
688.B52	Big books (Children's books)

Library science. Information science
The collections. The books
Special collections
Special. By subject, A-Z -- Continued

688.B54	Biochemistry
688.B55	Birth control
688.B7	Bookplates
688.C28	Canada
688.C34	Caribbean Area
	CD-ROMs see Z692.C39
688.C47	Children's literature
688.C5	Chinese literature
688.C53	Christian fiction
(688.C55)	Clippings
	see Z691
688.C64	Comic books, strips, etc.
688.C66	Commonwealth of Nations
688.C663	Communication
	Computer files see Z692.C65
688.C667	Conference proceedings
688.C67	Conservative literature
	Culture, Popular see Z688.P64
688.D46	Detective and mystery stories
688.E25	East Asia
688.E28	Ecology. Environment
688.E3	Economics
688.E6	English literature
	Environment see Z688.E28
	Ephemera see Z688.P74
688.E76	Erotic literature. Sex-oriented literature
688.E87	Europe
(688.F53)	Fiction
	see Z711.5
688.F54	Film literature
688.F56	Fine editions
688.F6	Foreign publications
688.G3	Genealogy
688.G33	Geography
	Including geographic information systems
688.G35	German imprints
688.G6	Government publications
	Including electronic government information, and
	including municipal documents
688.H27	Haitian publications
	Hebrew literature see Z688.J48
688.H57	Hispanic Americans
688.I5	Indonesia

Z662-1000.5

Library science. Information science
The collections. The books
Special collections
Special. By subject, A-Z -- Continued
Interactive multimedia see Z692.I57

688.I57	International agencies
	Including United Nations' publications
688.I85	Israel
688.J29	Japan
688.J3	Japanese literature
688.J48	Jews and Judaism. Hebrew and Yiddish literature
688.K65	Korea
688.L36	Languages
688.L4	Latin America
688.L58	Literacy
688.L59	Literature
	Cf. Z711.5 Fiction in libraries
	Little press books see Z688.S57
688.L8	Local history
688.M4	Medicine
688.M42	Medieval civilization
	Middle Ages see Z688.M42
	Middle East see Z688.N43
688.M84	Multicultural materials
	Mystery stories see Z688.D46
688.N43	Near East. Middle East
688.N6	Nonbook library materials
	Cf. Z692.A+ Other classes of materials
688.O52	Oral history
688.O55	Oriental literature
688.P35	Panjabi imprints
688.P37	Peace
688.P38	Performing arts
	Periodicals. Serials see Z692.S5
688.P45	Philippines
688.P6	Political science
688.P64	Popular culture
688.P74	Printed ephemera
688.R3	Rare books
	Reference books see Z711+
688.R4	Religious literature. Theology
688.R8	Russia
688.S3	Science. Technology
688.S32	Science fiction
688.S45	Sex instruction
	Sex-oriented literature see Z688.E76
688.S47	Sexual minorities

Library science. Information science
The collections. The books
Special collections
Special. By subject, A-Z -- Continued

688.S5	Shakespeare
688.S56	Slavic countries
688.S57	Small press books
	Software see Z692.C65
688.S6	South Asia
688.S65	Southeast Asia
688.S68	Spanish imprints
	Technology see Z688.S3
688.T6	Theater
688.U53	Underground press
	Video tapes, videocassettes, etc. see Z692.V52
688.W65	Women's studies
	Yiddish literature see Z688.J48

Processing. Technical services

688.5	General works
688.6.A-Z	By region or country, A-Z
	Acquisition (selection, purchase, gifts, duplicates)
	Including incorporation, bill-checking, collation, accessioning, replacements
	Class here general works only
	For works dealing with the acquisition of materials on a specific topic, in a special language or of a special class, see Z688.A5-Z or Z691-Z692
689.A1	Bibliography
689.A15	Periodicals. Societies. Congresses
689.A2	History
689.A3-Z	General works
689.5.A-Z	By region or country, A-Z
(689.8)	By type of library
	see Z675
690	Exchanges
	Special classes of materials
	Including treatment, handbooks, etc.
	For thefts of special classes of materials see Z702.A3+
	Cf. Z688.A5+ Materials on special subjects
691	Pamphlets, leaflets, broadsides, clippings
	Including vertical files
692.A-Z	Other classes, A-Z
692.A72	Art works
692.A93	Audiovisual materials
692.C36	Catalogs, Commercial
692.C39	CD-ROMs
692.C63	Community information files

Library science. Information science
The collections. The books
Special classes of materials
Other classes, A-Z -- Continued

692.C65	Computer files. Software. Electronic information resources

      Including computer programs and data files
      Cf. Z692.E43 Electronic journals
      Cf. Z692.R47 Electronic reserve collections

692.D38	Databases
692.E42	Electronic dissertations
692.E4215	Electronic games
	Electronic information resources see Z692.C65
692.E43	Electronic journals
692.E82	Examinations
692.F5	Filmstrip collections
692.F73	Free material
692.G7	Graphic novels
692.H6	House organs
692.I57	Interactive multimedia
692.M28	Manuscripts
692.M3	Maps
692.M5	Microforms
692.M9	Motion picture film collections

      Cf. Z688.F54 Film literature collections

692.N38	National
692.N4	Newspapers
	Nonbook materials (General) see Z688.N6
692.O68	Optical disks
692.O95	Out-of-print materials
692.P37	Paperbacks
692.P5	Photograph and picture collections
692.P65	Postcards
692.R45	Reports
692.R47	Reserve collections

      Including electronic reserves

692.S5	Serials. Periodicals

      Cf. Z692.E43 Electronic journals

692.S65	Slides (Photography)
	Software see Z692.C65
692.S72	Sound recordings

      Cf. ML111.5 Music

692.V52	Video tapes, videocassettes, etc.

      Cf. Z701.3.M34 Video storage media

Library science. Information science
The collections. The books -- Continued
Cataloging
Including materials on indexing, abstracting, etc.
Cf. Z699+ Machine-readable bibliographic data.
Information storage and retrieval systems

693.A1	Bibliography
693.A15	Periodicals. Societies. Congresses
693.A2	History
693.A3-Z	General works
693.3.A-Z	Special topics, A-Z
693.3.A52	Analytical entry
693.3.A55	Annotating, Book
693.3.A88	Authority files
693.3.C37	Catalog cards
	Cataloging errors see Z693.3.E76
693.3.C38	Cataloging in publication
693.3.C55	Classified catalogs
693.3.C63	Collection level cataloging
693.3.C65	Contracting out
693.3.C66	Cooperative cataloging
693.3.C67	Copy cataloging
693.3.C68	Costs
693.3.E76	Errors
693.3.H65	Holdings (Bibliographic data)
693.3.L52	Library catalogs
693.3.N68	Notes
693.3.S63	Special collections
693.3.S65	Specimens
693.3.S72	Standards
693.3.T47	Terminology
693.3.U53	Union catalogs
693.5.A-Z	By region or country, A-Z
	Descriptive cataloging
	For descriptive cataloging of special subjects see Z695.1.A+
694.A1	Bibliography
694.A15	Periodicals. Societies. Congresses
694.A3-.Z4	General works
694.15.A-Z	By system, A-Z
694.15.A42	A.L.A. (American Library Association) cataloging rules
	Anglo-American cataloguing rules
694.15.A5	General works
	Individual editions
	Class here both texts of, and works about, specific editions of the rules

Z662-1000.5

Library science. Information science
The collections. The books
Cataloging
Descriptive cataloging
By system, A-Z
Anglo-American cataloguing rules
Individual editions -- Continued

694.15.A54	1967 edition (British text)
694.15.A55	1967 edition (North American text)
694.15.A56	Second edition, 1978
	Including subsequent revisions
694.15.B74	British Library Dept. of Printed Books
694.15.H34	Han'guk mongnok kyuch'ik (Korea)
694.15.I58	International Standard Bibliographic Description (ISBD)
694.15.R44	Regeln fur die alphabetische Katalogisierung
694.15.R46	Reglas de catalogación (Spain)

Subject cataloging. Subject headings
Including form headings or genre terms
For subject cataloging of special subjects see Z695.1.A+

695.A1	Bibliography
695.A3-.Z4	General works
(695.Z5A-.Z5Z)	By language, A-Z
695.Z8A-.Z8Z	Individual lists, thesauri, etc., A-Z

Class here general subject heading lists or thesauri
For individual subject heading lists or thesauri on special subjects see Z695.1.A+
ASCIS see Z695.Z8S35

695.Z8B52	Biblioteca nazionale centrale di Firenze
695.Z8B53	Biblioteka Narodowa (Poland)
695.Z8B55	Blanc-Montmayeur, M. and Danset, F. Choix de vedettes matières à l'intention des bibliothèques
695.Z8B912	BUB thesaurus. Thesaurus de la Universitat de Barcelona
695.Z8C35	Canadian thesaurus
695.Z8G48	Getty thesauri
695.Z8L44	Legislative indexing vocabulary
695.Z8L5	Library of Congress
695.Z8L713	Liburutegi publikoetako gaien izenburuen zerrenda
695.Z8L73	Lietuvos Nacionalinė Martyno Mažvydo biblioteka
695.Z8N54	NICEM thesaurus
695.Z8S35	SCIS. Schools for Catalogue Information Service
695.Z8S43	Sears
695.Z8S74	STEBIS. System tezaurusów Biblioteki Sejmowej

Thesaurus de la Universitat de Barcelona see Z695.Z8B912

	Library science. Information science
	The collections. The books
	Cataloging
	Subject cataloging. Subject headings
	Individual lists, thesauri, etc., A-Z -- Continued
695.Z8U54	Universitat Bar-Ilan
695.1.A-Z	By subject, A-Z
	Including descriptive cataloging, subject cataloging, or both
	Academic dissertations see Z695.1.D57
695.1.A25	Aeronautics
695.1.A37	African literature
	African Americans see Z695.1.B57
695.1.A376	Aging
695.1.A38	Agricultural machinery
695.1.A4	Agriculture
695.1.A5	Air pollution
695.1.A56	Anesthesiology
695.1.A6	Anonymous classics
695.1.A63	Anthropology
695.1.A67	Archaeology
695.1.A68	Architecture
695.1.A69	Archival materials
695.1.A7	Art, Visual
695.1.A8	Asia
695.1.A86	Atomic energy. Nuclear energy
695.1.A9	Automation
695.1.A93	Automobiles
695.1.B3	Banks and banking
695.1.B44	Benedictines
695.1.B5	Biology
695.1.B55	Birth control
695.1.B57	Blacks. African Americans
695.1.B65	Bookbinding
695.1.B74	Brewing
695.1.B78	Buddhist literature
695.1.B8	Building
695.1.C3	Canada
695.1.C32	Caribbean Area
695.1.C34	Cassava
	Catalogs of exhibitions see Z695.1.E95
695.1.C36	Catalonia (Spain)
695.1.C5	Chemistry
	Children, Exceptional see Z695.1.E93
695.1.C6	Children's material
695.1.C62	Chinese imprints
695.1.C625	Chiropractic
695.1.C63	Cities and towns. City planning

Z662-1000.5

Library science. Information science
The collections. The books
Cataloging
By subject, A-Z -- Continued
Civil law see Z695.1.L3

695.1.C68	Commerce
695.1.C7	Communism
695.1.C75	Concrete
695.1.C76	Conservation of natural resources
695.1.C77	Consumers
695.1.C78	Corporate body names
695.1.C8	Cosmetics
695.1.C82	Credit
695.1.C84	Criminal justice administration
695.1.C85	Cultural property
695.1.C86	Culture
695.1.D4	Decoration and ornament
695.1.D45	Demography
695.1.D46	Design
695.1.D47	Developing countries
695.1.D55	Diffusion
695.1.D56	Diplomatics
695.1.D57	Dissertations, Academic
695.1.E17	East Asian publications
	Economic integration, International see Z695.1.I577
695.1.E2	Economics
695.1.E3	Education
695.1.E36	Electric engineering
695.1.E4	Electronic data processing
695.1.E5	Engineering
695.1.E57	Entomology
695.1.E59	Environmental protection
695.1.E62	Environmental sciences
695.1.E84	Ethics
	European War (World War I), 1914-1918 see Z695.1.W7
695.1.E93	Exceptional children
695.1.E95	Exhibition catalogs
695.1.F47	Fiction
695.1.F5	Finance
	Fire prevention see Z695.1.F55
695.1.F55	Fires. Fire prevention
695.1.F66	Foreign language publications
695.1.F67	Founding
695.1.F8	Freemasons
695.1.G38	Genetics
695.1.G4	Geographic names

Library science. Information science
The collections. The books
Cataloging
By subject, A-Z -- Continued

695.1.G42	Geography
695.1.G43	Geology
695.1.G44	Geometry
695.1.G7	Government publications
695.1.G75	Greek imprints
695.1.G77	Groundwater
695.1.H26	Handicapped. People with disabilities
695.1.H3	Harbors
	Health see Z695.1.M48
	Hebrew literature see Z695.1.J48
695.1.H6	History
	Including oral history
695.1.H67	Homosexuality
695.1.H7	Hospitals
695.1.H8	Housing
695.1.H86	Human engineering
695.1.H87	Human settlements
695.1.I28	Industrial relations
695.1.I3	Industry. Business
695.1.I56	Information science
695.1.I57	Instrument manufacture
695.1.I575	International agency publications
695.1.I577	International economic integration
695.1.I58	International law
695.1.I74	Islam
695.1.I77	Italian literature
695.1.J33	Japan
695.1.J34	Japanese imprints
695.1.J48	Jews and Judaism. Hebrew and Yiddish literature
695.1.J88	Justice, Administration of
695.1.K67	Korean imprints
695.1.L12	Labor
695.1.L19	Land use
695.1.L2	Language and languages
695.1.L26	Lasers
695.1.L28	Latin America
695.1.L3	Law
695.1.L52	Library science
695.1.L55	Life sciences
	Linguistics see Z695.1.L2
695.1.L58	Lisbon (Portugal)

Z662-1000.5

Library science. Information science
The collections. The books
Cataloging
By subject, A-Z -- Continued

695.1.L6	Literature
	Cf. Z695.1.I77 Italian literature
	Cf. Z695.1.O7 Oriental literature
695.1.L65	Livestock
695.1.L69	Local government
695.1.L7	Local history
695.1.M35	Marketing
695.1.M39	Materials
695.1.M42	Mathematics
695.1.M48	Medicine. Health
695.1.M55	Metallurgy
695.1.M57	Mexican Americans
695.1.M6	Military science
695.1.M63	Mineralogy
695.1.M64	Mines and mineral resources
695.1.M65	Mining engineering
	Music see ML111
695.1.N3	Naval art and science
	Negroes see Z695.1.B57
	Nuclear energy see Z695.1.A86
695.1.N78	Nuclear reactors
695.1.N8	Nursing
695.1.N84	Nutrition
695.1.O29	Occupational training
695.1.O3	Occupations
695.1.O54	Oil well drilling, Submarine
	Oral history materials see Z695.1.H6
695.1.O68	Ore dressing
	Organic compounds see Z695.1.C5
695.1.O7	Oriental literature
695.1.P3	Packaging
695.1.P35	Paint
695.1.P36	Paleontology
695.1.P364	Paper industry
695.1.P366	Paraguay
695.1.P368	Pastures
695.1.P37	Patents
695.1.P38	Peace
	People with disabilities see Z695.1.H26
695.1.P39	Persian materials
695.1.P4	Personal names
695.1.P43	Petroleum
695.1.P46	Pharmacy

Library science. Information science
The collections. The books
Cataloging
By subject, A-Z -- Continued

695.1.P463	Philology
695.1.P465	Philosophy
695.1.P477	Photogrammetry
695.1.P495	Physical education and training
695.1.P5	Physics
695.1.P55	Pictures
695.1.P63	Political science
695.1.P65	Polymers and polymerization
695.1.P67	Postage stamps
695.1.P68	Power resources
695.1.P7	Psychology
695.1.P79	Public administration
695.1.P83	Puerto Rico
695.1.R32	Race relations
695.1.R34	Railroads
695.1.R4	Recreation
695.1.R42	Recycling (Waste, etc.)
695.1.R424	Refugees
695.1.R43	Regional planning
695.1.R44	Rehabilitation literature
	Religion see Z695.1.T3
695.1.R46	Research grants
695.1.R6	Roads
695.1.R63	Rock mechanics
695.1.R85	Russian imprints
695.1.S3	Science and technology
695.1.S4	Sex
695.1.S43	Sexual minorities
695.1.S5	Slavic literature
695.1.S6	Social sciences
695.1.S62	Social service
695.1.S63	Sociology
695.1.S65	Soviet Union
695.1.S68	Soyfoods
695.1.S7	Sports
695.1.S74	Standardization
695.1.S83	Substance abuse
695.1.T23	Technical education
	Technology see Z695.1.S3
695.1.T236	Telecommunication
695.1.T24	Television
695.1.T26	Textiles
695.1.T27	Theater

Library science. Information science
The collections. The books
Cataloging
By subject, A-Z -- Continued

695.1.T3	Theology. Religion
	Including denominations and sects
695.1.T52	Tibetan literature
695.1.T73	Transportation
(695.1.U5)	Underdeveloped areas
	see Z695.1.D47
695.1.U55	Uniform titles
695.1.U73	Urdu literature
695.1.V4	Veterinary medicine
	Vocational education see Z695.1.O29
695.1.V6	Vocational rehabilitation
	Vocational training see Z695.1.O29
695.1.W3	Water resources development
695.1.W315	Water supply
695.1.W32	Waterpower
695.1.W45	Welding
695.1.W47	Wetlands
695.1.W65	Women
695.1.W7	World War I, 1914-1918
695.1.W8	World War II, 1939-1945
	Yiddish literature see Z695.1.J48
695.1.Z55	Zionism
	By form
695.2	Archival material
	Including records, documents (manuscript and printed), charters, deeds, etc.
	Cf. Z695.1.G7 Government publications
	Cf. Z695.1.L3 Law, legal records
	Cf. Z695.5 Manuscripts
695.214	Artists' books
	Atlases see Z695.6
	Audiovisual materials see Z695.66
	Cartographic materials see Z695.6
	Computer files see Z695.615
695.24	Computer network resources. Electronic information resources
	Including Internet resources
695.25	Conference proceedings
	Data files see Z695.615
	Continuing resources see Z695.7+
	Electronic information resources see Z695.24
	Engravings see NE60
695.255	DVDs

Library science. Information science
The collections. The books
Cataloging
By form -- Continued

695.27	Graphic materials
695.3	Incunabula. Early printed books
695.35	Integrating resources
	Including updating loose-leafs, updating online databases, and updating Web sites
695.37	Interactive multimedia
695.4	Lantern slides. Photographic slides
(695.44)	Loose-leaf publications
	see Z695.35
(695.47)	Machine-readable data files
	see Z695.615
695.5	Manuscripts
695.6	Maps. Atlases. Cartographic materials
695.615	Microcomputer software. Computer programs. Data files
	Cf. Z695.37 Interactive multimedia
695.62	Microforms
	Monographic series see Z695.78
695.64	Motion pictures and video recordings
	Music see ML111
695.655	Newspapers
695.66	Nonbook materials
	Periodicals. Continuing resources
695.7	General works
695.712	Electronic journals
695.715	Phonorecords. Sound recordings
	For sound recordings of music see ML110+
	Photographic slides see Z695.4
695.718	Photographs and pictures
	Cf. N440 accessioning, cataloging, and classification of works of art
695.7184	Preloaded audio players
695.719	Printed ephemera
695.7196	Radio programs
695.72	Raised characters, Books in
695.74	Rare materials
	Record material (manuscript and printed) see Z695.2
695.75	Reproductions
	Slides (Photography) see Z695.4
695.78	Series. Monographic series
695.8	Publications of societies and other corporate bodies
	Software see Z695.615
695.82	Trade literature

Z662-1000.5

Library science. Information science
The collections. The books
Cataloging
By form -- Continued
Sound recordings see Z695.715
695.83 Union catalogs
Cf. Z881+ Library catalogs and bulletins
695.85 Library handwriting
695.87 Printing of catalogs
695.88 Catalog management. Catalog maintenance
Indexing. Abstracting
For abstracts of value for subject content, and for abstracting
and indexing of special topics, see the topic in classes A-
Z
For abstracts chiefly of bibliographic value, e. g. annotated
bibliographies, see Z5051+
For serial indexes see AI1
For abstracting and indexing of materials in special
formats see Z695.2+
Cf. Z6293 Lists of indexes
695.9 General works
695.915.A-Z Special indexing systems, A-Z
695.915.N48 NEPHIS
695.915.P73 PRECIS
695.92 Automatic indexing. Automatic abstracting. Punched card
systems
Abstracting and indexing services
695.93 General works
695.94.A-Z By region or country, A-Z
695.95 Alphabetizing. Filing
695.98 Recataloging. Reclassification
Classification and notation
696.A1 Periodicals. Societies. Serials
696.A2 Congresses
696.A3 Bibliography
696.A4 General works. Theory
696.A5-Z Individual general classification schemes. By name, A-Z
For schemes limited to a single subject, see the subject in
Z697
696.B2 BBK Classification
696.B6 Bliss Bibliographic classification
696.B782 Broad System of Ordering
696.C5517 Chung-kuo t'u shu kuan t'u shu fen lei fa
696.D48 Deutsche Nationalbibliographie classification system
Dewey Decimal Classification
696.D5 Periodicals. Serials
696.D52 Decimal Classification. By date

Library science. Information science
The collections. The books
Classification and notation
Individual classification schemes. By name, A-Z
Dewey Decimal Classification -- Continued

696.D54	Abridged Decimal Classification. By date
696.D56A-.D56Z	Translations. By language, A-Z, and date
	Including translations of abridged editions, tables, etc.
(696.D6)	History
	see Z696.D7
696.D62	Summaries. By date
(696.D64)	Tables
	see Z696.D52
696.D7	General works on Dewey Decimal Classification
	Including history
696.D72A-.D72Z	By subject, A-Z
	Class here the schemes themselves, including unofficial expansions, and works on the application of DDC to a specific subject
696.D8933	Double uniform notation classification
696.G66	Gosudarstvennai͡a avtomatizirovannai͡a sistema nauchno-technicheskoi informat͡sii (GASNTI)
	Library of Congress Classification see Z696.U4+
696.M596	Mezinárodní system vĕdeckých a technickych informací (MSVTI)
696.R43	Regensburger Verbundklassifikation (RVK)
696.S24	SAB classification. Klassifikationssystem for svenska bibliotek
696.S4542	Schema voor de Indeling van de Systematische katalogus in Openbare bibliotheken (SISO)
696.S92	Superintendent of Documents Classification
	U.S. Library of Congress. Classification
	For works on the application of LC Classification to a specific subject see Z697.A+
696.U4	General works
696.U42	Outline of the Classification. By date
696.U45	Indexes to LC Classification
	Official editions
696.U48	Comprehensive. By date
696.U5A-.U5Z	Indivdual classes and subclasses. By class, A-Z, and date
696.U5A	A
696.U5B1	B-BJ
696.U5B2	BL-BX
696.U5B25	BL-BQ
696.U5B7	BR-BV
696.U5B9	BX

Z662-1000.5

Library science. Information science
The collections. The books
Classification and notation
Individual classification schemes. By name, A-Z
U.S. Library of Congress. Classification
Official editions
Individual classes and subclasses. By class, A-Z,
and date -- Continued

696.U5C	C
696.U5D2	D
696.U5D25	D-DR
696.U5D3	D-DJ
696.U5D35	DJK-DK
696.U5D4	DL-DR
696.U5D5	DS
696.U5D53	DS-DX
696.U5D6	DT-DX
696.U5E3	E-F
696.U5G	G
696.U5H	H
696.U5H3	H-HJ
696.U5H5	HM-HX
696.U5J	J
696.U5K23	K
696.U5K25	KB
696.U5K3	KD
696.U5K34	KDZ, KG-KH
696.U5K4	KE
696.U5K55	KF
696.U5K64	KJ-KKZ
696.U5K65	KJV-KJW
696.U5K7	KK-KKC
696.U5K75	KL-KWX
696.U5K77	KZ
696.U5K78	K Tables
696.U5L	L
696.U5M	M
696.U5N	N
696.U5P6	P-PA
696.U5P63	PB-PH
696.U5P635	PG (Russian)
696.U5P64	PJ-PM
696.U5P7	PJ-PK
696.U5P73	PL-PM
696.U5P74	PN, PR, PS, PZ
696.U5P75	PN
696.U5P77	PQ

Library science. Information science
The collections. The books
Classification and notation
Individual classification schemes. By name, A-Z
U.S. Library of Congress. Classification
Official editions
Individual classes and subclasses. By class, A-Z,
and date -- Continued

696.U5P8	PQ (Part 1)
696.U5P82	PQ (Part 2)
696.U5P83	PR, PS, PZ
696.U5P84	PT
696.U5P85	PT (Part 1)
696.U5P87	PT (Part 2)
696.U5P88	P-PZ Tables
696.U5P9	P-PM Supplement (Index to Languages and Dialects)
696.U5Q	Q
696.U5R	R
696.U5S	S
696.U5T	T
696.U5U	U-V

Including editions of Class U published separately

696.U5V	V
696.U5Z	Z

Unofficial editions

696.U6	Comprehensive
696.U7A-.U7Z	Individual classes and subclasses. By class, A-Z, and date

For Cutter numbers see Z696.U5A+

Universal Decimal Classification (UDC)

696.U86	Periodicals. Serials
696.U862	Universal Decimal Classification: English editions. By date
696.U864A-.U864Z	Universal Decimal Classification: Foreign language editions. By language, A-Z, and date
696.U866	Tables. By date
696.U87	General works on Universal Decimal Classification
696.U875A-.U875Z	By subject, A-Z

Class here only classification schedules authorized by
the International Federation for Documentation,
e.g. Z696.U875M4 Medicine

	Library science. Information science
	The collections. The books
	Classification and notation -- Continued
697.A-Z	By subject or form, A-Z

For classification schedules issued by the Library of
Congress see Z696.U48+

For classification schedules authorized by the
International Federation for Documentation see
Z696.U875A+

697.A23	Accounting
697.A25	Adult education
697.A33	African languages
697.A35	African literature
697.A4	Agriculture
697.A43	Aichi, Japan
697.A45	Alcohol
697.A76	Archives
697.A78	Area studies
697.A8	Art
697.A87	Automation
697.B4	Bees
697.B55	Birth control
697.B7	Brighton, Australia
697.B8	Building
697.B9	Business
697.C32	Canada
697.C47	Cerebral palsy
697.C5	Chemistry
697.C515	Children's literature
697.C52	Chinese literature
697.C53	City planning
697.C6	Clippings
697.C68	College catalogs
697.C69	Commerce
697.C72	Community life
697.C74	Cooperation. Cooperative societies
697.C8	Correspondence
697.C9	Current events
697.D4	Deafness
697.D48	Detective and mystery stories
697.D73	Drawings
697.E38	Economics
697.E4	Education
697.E45	Electric engineering
697.E8	Ethnology
697.F29	Fantastic literature. Science fiction
697.F45	Fiction

Library science. Information science
The collections. The books
Classification and notation
By subject or form, A-Z -- Continued

697.F58	Folklore
697.F6	Forestry
697.F86	French-Canadian literature
697.F9	Fuel
697.G22	Games
697.G3	Gas industry
697.G35	Geodesy
697.G4	Geography
697.G42	Geology
697.G5	Glass
697.G7	Government publications
	Including international agency publications
697.H6	History
	History, Local see Z697.L66
697.H8	Hospitals
697.H84	Housing
697.H86	Human services
697.H87	Humanities
697.H9	Hydrology
697.I37	Industrial hygiene. Industrial safety
	International agency publications see Z697.G7
697.I5	International law
697.I52	International relations
697.I7	Iranian literature
697.I77	Islam
697.J3	Japanese
697.J53	Jews
697.L37	Language and languages
697.L4	Law
697.L5	Leyden
697.L6	Library science
697.L63	Literature
697.L66	Local history
697.L7	London
697.M15	Malawi
697.M17	Maps
697.M18	Marathi literature
697.M2	Mathematics
697.M4	Medicine
697.M5	Metallurgy
697.M52	Metalwork
697.M6	Military art and science
697.M7	Mining engineering

Z662-1000.5

Library science. Information science
The collections. The books
Classification and notation
By subject or form, A-Z -- Continued

697.M8	Municipal government
697.M82	Museums
	Music see ML111
	Mystery stories see Z697.D48
697.N64	Nonbook materials
697.N66	Norway
697.N77	Nursing
697.O2	Oceanography
697.P44	Performing arts
697.P53	Philately
697.P538	Philology
697.P54	Philosophy
697.P545	Phonorecords
697.P548	Photographs and pictures
697.P57	Physics
697.P7	Political science
697.P88	Printing
697.P95	Public health
697.P97	Public relations
697.R25	Radio
697.R38	Recreation
697.R6	Roads
697.S5	Science
	Science fiction see Z697.F29
697.S52	Semiconductors
697.S53	Sewage disposal
697.S57	Slides (Photography)
697.S6	Social sciences
697.S62	Sociology
697.S64	Speleology
697.S7	Standards, Engineering
697.T4	Technology
697.T45	Telecommunication
697.T49	Textbooks
	Theology
697.T5	General
697.T51A-.T51Z	By religion, denomination, etc., A-Z
697.T6	Tourism
697.T7	Transportation
697.T73	Trentino-Alto Adige, Italy
697.V35	Venezuelan literature
697.V4	Veterinary medicine
697.W45	West Indian literature

Library science. Information science
The collections. The books
Classification and notation
By subject or form, A-Z -- Continued

697.W47	Western stories
698	Shelflisting. Author notation
	Machine-readable bibliographic data. Information storage and retrieval systems
699.A1	Periodicals. Societies. Congresses
699.A2-Z	General works
699.2	Bibliography
699.22	Directories of machine-readable bibliographic data bases
699.35.A-Z	Special topics, A-Z
699.35.C38	Catalogs, Online
699.35.C48	Character sets (Data processing)
	Including diacritics
699.35.C65	Computer output microfilm devices
	Data formats see Z699.35.M28
	Diacritics see Z699.35.C48
699.35.E94	Exchange of bibliographic information
699.35.F54	Filing systems
699.35.M28	Machine-readable bibliographic data. Data formats
	MARC formats see Z699.35.M28
699.35.M84	Multiple versions (Cataloging)
699.35.O55	Online bibliographic searching
	Online catalogs see Z699.35.C38
699.35.P85	Punched card systems
699.35.Q35	Quality. Quality control
699.35.R48	Retrospective conversion
699.35.S92	Subject access
699.35.U74	User interfaces (Computer systems)
699.355.A-Z	By region or country, A-Z
699.4.A-Z	By special project or system, A-Z
	Prefer classification by subject, Z699.5
699.4.A13	ADLIB System
699.4.A16	AMY system
699.4.B17	BALLOTS project
699.4.B2	BASIS-E
699.4.B22	BIBDATA Network
699.4.B23	BIBLIOS System
699.4.B26	BIOSIS Connection (Information retrieval system)
699.4.B33	BLAISE System
699.4.B87	BURK III System
699.4.C15	CATS System
699.4.C17	CDS/ISIS
699.4.C2	CISS System
699.4.C23	CLAP System

Library science. Information science
The collections. The books
Machine-readable bibliographic data. Information storage
and retrieval systems
By special project or system, A-Z -- Continued

699.4.C25	CONSER Project
699.4.D18	DIALOG System
699.4.D62	DOBIS System
699.4.E15	EPIC System
699.4.E17	ESTC Project
699.4.E19	EUREKA System
699.4.F23	FAUST System
699.4.G34	GALILEO
699.4.G55	GIPSY System
699.4.H3	Hand-printed Book Project
699.4.H36	Harmonie system
699.4.I13	IBAS System
699.4.I15	INNOPAC System
699.4.I18	ISDS (International Serials Data System)
699.4.I19	ISIS (Information retrieval system)
699.4.J18	JPTRS System
699.4.K14	KOBAS System
699.4.K2	KONKAT System
699.4.L15	LCS System
699.4.L17	LFP System
699.4.L2	LIBRIS System
699.4.L23	LITSYS System
699.4.L25	LOC System
699.4.L26	LOCIS (Information retrieval system)
699.4.M16	MADOK System
(699.4.M2)	MARC formats
	see Z699.35.M28
699.4.M22	MELVYL System
	Micro CDS/ISIS see Z699.4.C17
699.4.M226	Microsoft Access
699.4.M23	MINICS project
699.4.M25	MONOCLE project
699.4.M5	Minsk-Ardis system
699.4.N48	NEXIS (Information retrieval system)
699.4.O29	OCLC Cataloging Subsystem
699.4.O43	Okapi (Information retrieval system)
699.4.P2	PADIS (Information retrieval system)
699.4.P23	PICA Project
699.4.P73	Pro-cite
699.4.Q2	QUERY system
699.4.R45	REMARC (Information retrieval system)
699.4.R47	Research Library Resources Access Project (N.Y.)

Library science. Information science
The collections. The books
Machine-readable bibliographic data. Information storage
and retrieval systems
By special project or system, A-Z -- Continued

699.4.R55	RLIN System. RLIN II system
699.4.S12	SAMKAT System
699.4.S14	SATIN 1 system
699.4.S16	SERaT (Information retrieval system)
699.4.S17	SESAM System
699.4.S173	SICLaC (Information retrieval system)
699.4.S175	SIPORbase (Information retrieval system)
699.4.S18	SISMAKOM (Information retrieval system)
699.4.S2	SMART system
699.4.S23	SOKRATUS System
699.4.S25	STAIRS system
699.4.S7	STATUS (Information retrieval system)
699.4.T12	TAUBIPE (Information retrieval system)
699.4.T14	3RIP system
699.4.T16	Tramps system
699.4.U216	UNDIS system
(699.4.U22)	UNIMARC System
	see Z699.35.M28
699.4.U74	UTLAS System
699.5.A-Z	By subject or form, A-Z
699.5.A25	Accounting
699.5.A29	Acupuncture
699.5.A4	Aeronautics
699.5.A45	Africa
699.5.A5	Agriculture
699.5.A53	Agroforestry
699.5.A57	Air pollution
699.5.A67	Arabic materials
699.5.A69	Archaeology
699.5.A7	Archival material
699.5.A72	Arctic regions
699.5.A75	Art. The arts
699.5.A85	Atomic energy
699.5.A9	Audiovisual materials
699.5.B5	Biochemistry
699.5.B53	Biology
699.5.B6	Botany
699.5.B8	Building
699.5.C27	Canada
699.5.C3	Cartography. Maps
699.5.C44	Census
699.5.C48	Chemical industries

Library science. Information science
The collections. The books
Machine-readable bibliographic data. Information storage
and retrieval systems
By subject or form, A-Z -- Continued

699.5.C5	Chemistry
699.5.C53	Chinese language
699.5.C55	City planning
699.5.C57	Coal mines and mining
699.5.C573	Conference proceedings. Congresses
	Congresses see Z699.5.C573
699.5.C575	Consumer protection
699.5.C576	Consumers
699.5.C58	Corporations
699.5.C6	Corrections
699.5.C7	Crime and criminals
699.5.D37	Data bases
699.5.E16	Early printed books
699.5.E18	Earthquakes
699.5.E23	Ecology
699.5.E24	Economic development
699.5.E25	Economics
699.5.E3	Education
699.5.E48	Electric utilities
699.5.E5	Electronics
699.5.E56	Employee fringe benefits
699.5.E6	Engineering
699.5.E62	Engineering geology
699.5.E63	English philology
699.5.E67	Entomology
699.5.E7	Environmental engineering
699.5.E73	Environmental protection
699.5.F49	Finance
699.5.F5	Finance, Public
699.5.F55	Fluoro-organic compounds
699.5.F67	Foreign language publications
699.5.F68	Forestry
699.5.G38	Geography
699.5.G4	Geology
699.5.G44	Geophysics
699.5.G6	Government publications
699.5.H6	Home economics
699.5.H8	Humanities
699.5.H9	Hydrogeology
699.5.H93	Hydrology
699.5.H95	Hydrometeorology
	Image files see Z699.5.P53

Library science. Information science
The collections. The books
Machine-readable bibliographic data. Information storage
and retrieval systems
By subject or form, A-Z -- Continued

699.5.I47	Indic periodicals
699.5.I5	Industrial relations
699.5.I52	Industry
699.5.I54	International relations
699.5.K65	Korea
699.5.L25	Labor economics
699.5.L28	Land
	Law
	see class K
699.5.L34	Law enforcement
	Legislation
	see class K
699.5.L44	Legislative documents
699.5.L54	Linguistics
699.5.L56	Livestock
699.5.L6	Local government
699.5.M25	Management
699.5.M26	Manufacturing engineering
699.5.M27	Manuscripts
	Maps see Z699.5.C3
699.5.M28	Marine biology
699.5.M29	Marine ecology
699.5.M3	Marine sediments
699.5.M34	Marketing management
699.5.M352	Mass media
699.5.M36	Materials
699.5.M37	Mathematics
699.5.M38	Mechanical engineering. Machinery
699.5.M39	Medicine
699.5.M4	Metallurgy
699.5.M45	Meteorology
699.5.M48	Military art and science
699.5.M5	Mines and mineral resources
699.5.M6	Molecular spectra
699.5.M65	Monuments
699.5.M67	Motion pictures
699.5.N3	Naval art and science
699.5.N47	Newspapers
	Non-wage payments see Z699.5.E56
699.5.N6	Nonmetallic minerals
699.5.N7	Nursing
699.5.O3	Oceanography

Z662-1000.5

Library science. Information science
The collections. The books
Machine-readable bibliographic data. Information storage
and retrieval systems
By subject or form, A-Z -- Continued

699.5.O7	Organic chemistry
699.5.P3	Patents
699.5.P4	Petroleum engineering
699.5.P47	Photographs, Conservation of
699.5.P5	Physics
699.5.P53	Pictures
	Including image files
	Plastics see Z699.5.P65
699.5.P56	Police personnel management
699.5.P6	Political science
699.5.P65	Polymers and polymerization. Plastics
699.5.P72	Psychology
699.5.R3	Railroads
699.5.R38	Raw materials
699.5.R39	Recreation
699.5.R394	Refugees
699.5.R4	Regional planning
699.5.R44	Religion. Theology
699.5.R47	Research
699.5.S3	Science
699.5.S45	Serial publications
699.5.S57	Siouan languages
699.5.S6	Slavic literature
699.5.S65	Social sciences
699.5.S653	Social services
699.5.S66	Soil science
699.5.S74	Special collections
699.5.S8	Standards, Engineering
699.5.S83	Statistics
699.5.T4	Technology
699.5.T45	Terrestrial magnetism
699.5.T73	Transportation
699.5.U47	United Nations
699.5.U5	United States
699.5.U7	Urban renewal
699.5.V5	Vision
699.5.V63	Vocational guidance
699.5.W3	Water supply
699.5.Z66	Zoology

Inventory control
For inventory control of special types of materials see
Z692.A+

Library science. Information science
The collections. The books
Inventory control -- Continued

699.7	General works
699.75	Radio frequency identification systems
700	Bookbinding
	Including repairing, and including works on library bindings

Preservation, conservation, and restoration of books and
other library materials
Including reproduction and storage of library materials
Cf. Z265+ Reproduction of books, documents, etc.

700.9	Periodicals. Societies. Congresses
701	General works
701.2	Bibliography
701.3.A-Z	Special topics, A-Z
	Audiotapes see Z701.3.M34
701.3.B56	Biodeterioration
701.3.B64	Book boxes
701.3.B65	Book covers
701.3.B66	Book worms
701.3.B75	Brittle books
701.3.C45	Children's libraries
701.3.C65	Computer files
	Computer tapes and magnetic disks for computers see Z701.3.M34
701.3.D4	Deacidification
	Digital preservation see Z701.3.C65
701.3.D53	Digitally printed materials
701.3.D54	Digitization
701.3.D57	Dissertations
701.3.E38	Education
701.3.E44	Electronic journals
701.3.F53	Fine editions
701.3.F55	Floods
701.3.H85	Humanities libraries
701.3.I45	Illustrated books and illustrations
	Illustrations see Z701.3.I45
	Machine-readable files see Z701.3.C65
701.3.M34	Magnetic media
	Including magnetic tapes and magnetic disks
	Manuscripts see Z110.C7
701.3.M53	Microforms. Microphotography
	Including preservation microfilming
701.3.M64	Molds (Fungi)
701.3.N48	Newspapers
701.3.N65	Nonbook materials

Z662-1000.5

Library science. Information science
The collections. The books
Preservation, conservation, and restoration of books and
other library materials
Special topics, A-Z -- Continued

701.3.O66	Optical disks
	Including compact discs, CD-ROMs, and DVDs
701.3.P38	Paper
701.3.P47	Pest control
701.3.P48	Photocopying processes
	Including preservation photocopying
	Photographs see TR465
701.3.P64	Polyester films
701.3.P74	Private libraries
701.3.R37	Rare books
701.3.R48	Research libraries
701.3.S35	Scientific libraries
701.3.S38	Selection for preservation
701.3.S53	Small libraries
701.3.S76	Storage conditions
701.3.T75	Tropical conditions
	Video recordings see Z701.3.M34
701.3.W43	Web pages. Web archiving
701.4.A-Z	By region or country, A-Z
701.5	Specimens of books injured by bookworms, etc.
	Thefts and losses of books and other library materials
	Cf. Z992.8 Bibliokleptomania
702.A3	General works
702.A6-Z	Cases
	Including cases not confined to an individual library, e. g. Z702.L557 Libri affair
	For cases confined to an individual library (United States) see Z733.A+
703.5	Stack management. Disposition of books on shelves, etc.
	Including library moving
703.6	Discarding. Weeding
	Regulations
704	General works
704.3	Food and beverage regulations
708	Hours of opening. Sunday opening
710	Aids. Guides
	For manuals for readers in individual libraries (United States) see Z733.A+
	Public services. Reference services
	Including consultations, access to books, etc.
711	General works

	Library science. Information science
	Public services. Reference services -- Continued
	Library orientation. Study and teaching of the use of libraries
711.2	General works
711.25.A-Z	Special groups, A-Z
711.25.C65	College students
711.25.H54	High school students
711.25.S36	School children
711.3	Statistics. Use studies
711.4	Restrictions on use. Intellectual freedom. Direction of use
711.45	Electronic reference services
711.47	Internet in library reference services
711.5	Fiction in libraries
	Cf. Z675.L58 Literary libraries
	Cf. Z688.L59 Special collections
711.55	Readers' advisory services
711.6.A-Z	Reference work in special topics, A-Z
711.6.A76	Art
711.6.G46	Genealogy
711.6.L58	Literature
711.6.S64	Social sciences
	Library service to special groups
711.7	General works
711.75	Business and industry
	Cf. Z675.B8 Business libraries
711.8	Ethnic minorities. Linguistic minorities
	Including immigrants
	For African Americans or Blacks see Z711.9
	For other individual minority groups see Z711.92.A+
	Industry see Z711.75
711.85	Labor
711.9	Blacks. African Americans
711.92.A-Z	Other, A-Z
711.92.A25	Abused women
711.92.A32	Adults
711.92.A35	Aged. Older people
711.92.A84	Asian Americans
711.92.D4	Deaf. Hearing impaired
711.92.F34	Families
711.92.G37	Gays
711.92.G73	Graduate students

<table>
<tr><td></td><td>Library science. Information science</td></tr>
<tr><td></td><td>Public services. Reference services</td></tr>
<tr><td></td><td>Library service to special groups</td></tr>
<tr><td></td><td>Other, A-Z -- Continued</td></tr>
<tr><td>711.92.H3</td><td>Handicapped. People with disabilities</td></tr>
</table>

	Library science. Information science
	Public services. Reference services
	Library service to special groups
	Other, A-Z -- Continued
711.92.H3	Handicapped. People with disabilities
	Including children with disabilities
	Cf. Z679.8 Library architecture for people with disabilities
	Cf. Z711.92.M4 People with mental disabilities
	Cf. Z711.92.P5 People with physical disabilities
	Hearing impaired see Z711.92.D4
711.92.H56	Hispanic Americans
711.92.H67	Hospital patients
711.92.H85	Hungarian Americans
711.92.I58	Intellectuals
	Linguistic minorities see Z711.8
711.92.M4	Mental disabilities, People with
	Including children with mental disabilities
711.92.M42	Mentally ill
711.92.M47	Mexican Americans
	New literates see Z716.45
	Older people see Z711.92.A35
711.92.P5	Physical disabilities, People with
711.92.P66	Poor
711.92.S49	Sexual minorities
711.92.S54	Shut-ins
711.92.S6	Social disabilities, People with
	Students see Z718.7
711.92.U53	Unemployed persons
711.92.V57	Visual disabilities, People with
	Cf. Z675.B6 Libraries for the blind
711.92.W65	Women
711.95	Document delivery
	Information services, information centers see ZA3150+
	Clipping bureaus see AG500+
	Circulation. Loans
712	General works
	Interlibrary loans
713	General works
713.5.A-Z	By region or country, A-Z
714	Charging systems
	Including photocharging
715	Forms, blanks, etc. used in libraries
	Library extension. Library commissions. Traveling libraries, etc.
	Cf. Z686 Branches, bookmobiles
716	General works

Library science. Information science

Library extension. Library commissions. Traveling libraries, etc. -- Continued

716.1   Package libraries
716.15   Packhorse libraries
716.2   Libraries and metropolitan areas
716.25   Libraries and rural areas

Public relations. Advertising and marketing. Publicity
Cf. Z1003.15 Book talks

716.3   General works
716.33   Activity programs
716.35   Bulletin boards

Libraries and community. Libraries and society. Social aspects of libraries

Z662-1000.5

716.4   General works
716.43   Library etiquette
716.45   Libraries and new literates. Libraries and the illiterate
716.5   Endowments. Bequests
716.6   Libraries and publishing. Libraries and bookselling
Including electronic publishing

Audio-visual library service
716.65   General works
716.7   Libraries and radio
716.8   Libraries and television
Cf. Z692.V52 Video tape and videocassette collections
716.9   Libraries and museums

Exhibitions of books, etc., in libraries
717   General works
717.5   Environmental management of library exhibits
718   Libraries and schools. Libraries and colleges
Cf. Z675.S3 School libraries
Cf. Z675.U5 University and college libraries

Children's libraries. Children's departments in public libraries, etc.
718.1   General works
718.2.A-Z   By region or country, A-Z
718.3   Activity programs
Including storytelling
718.5   Libraries and teenagers. Young adults' libraries
718.7   Libraries and students
718.75   Libraries and home schooling
718.8   Libraries and adult education
Including continuing education
718.85   Libraries and distance education

Libraries (General)
719   Bibliography
Including bibliographies of directories

Libraries (General) -- Continued
    Biography of librarians
      Collective

720.A1	International
	By region or country
	United States
720.A4	General works
720.A45A-.A45Z	By region or state
720.A46A-.A46Z	Other regions or countries, A-Z
720.A5-Z	Individual
720.5	Historiography

      History and statistics
        Including directories of libraries
        For history and statistics of libraries in individual regions
          or countries see Z729+

721	General works
	By period
	To 400
722	General works. Greece and Rome
722.5	Egypt
722.7	Assyria. Babylonia. Persia (Iran)
722.9.A-Z	Other, A-Z
723	400-1600

        Including scriptoria
        For individual regions or countries see Z729+
        Cf. Z6601+ Manuscripts

(725)	Individual libraries

          see numbers for individual libraries under specific
            countries in Z729+
        1600- see Z721
    Library reports. History. Statistics
      Including public libraries

729	United Nations libraries
730	Developing countries
730.5	Tropics
	North America
730.7	General works
	United States
731	General works. History

        Including directories of libraries

732.A-Z	By region or state, A-Z
733.A-Z	Individual libraries. By name, A-Z

        Including bibliography of their publications
      Canada. British North America

735.A1	General works. History
735.A2-Z	By region or place, A-Z
736.A-Z	Individual libraries. By name, A-Z

Library reports. History. Statistics -- Continued
  Latin America. Spanish America
738   General works
                Mexico
739.A1   General works. History
739.A2-Z   By region, state, or place, A-Z
740.A-Z   Individual libraries. By name, A-Z
                Central America
743.A1   General works. History
743.A2-Z   By region, state, or place, A-Z
744.A-Z   Individual libraries. By name, A-Z
                West Indies
753.A1   General works. History
753.A2-Z   By region, state, or place, A-Z
754.A-Z   Individual libraries. By name, A-Z
                Bermuda Islands
759.A1   General works. History
759.A2-Z   By region, state, or place, A-Z
760.A-Z   Individual libraries. By name, A-Z
                South America
763   General works
                Argentina
765.A1   General works. History
765.A2-Z   By region, state, or place, A-Z
766.A-Z   Individual libraries. By name, A-Z
                Bolivia
767.A1   General works. History
767.A2-Z   By region, state, or place, A-Z
768.A-Z   Individual libraries. By name, A-Z
                Brazil
769.A1   General works. History
769.A2-Z   By region, state, or place, A-Z
770.A-Z   Individual libraries. By name, A-Z
                Chile
771.A1   General works. History
771.A2-Z   By region, state, or place, A-Z
772.A-Z   Individual libraries. By name, A-Z
                Colombia
773.A1   General works. History
773.A2-Z   By region, state, or place, A-Z
774.A-Z   Individual libraries. By name, A-Z
                Ecuador
775.A1   General works. History
775.A2-Z   By region, state, or place, A-Z
776.A-Z   Individual libraries. By name, A-Z
                Guianas
777.A1   General works. History

	Library reports. History. Statistics
	South America
	Guianas -- Continued
777.A2-Z	By region, state, or place, A-Z
778.A-Z	Individual libraries. By name, A-Z
	Paraguay
779.A1	General works. History
779.A2-Z	By region, state, or place, A-Z
780.A-Z	Individual libraries. By name, A-Z
	Peru
781.A1	General works. History
781.A2-Z	By region, state, or place, A-Z
782.A-Z	Individual libraries. By name, A-Z
	Uruguay
783.A1	General works. History
783.A2-Z	By region, state, or place, A-Z
784.A-Z	Individual libraries. By name, A-Z
	Venezuela
785.A1	General works. History
785.A2-Z	By region, state, or place, A-Z
786.A-Z	Individual libraries. By name, A-Z
	Europe
789	General works
789.5	Eastern Europe
789.7	Western Europe
790	British Commonwealth
	Great Britain
791.A1	General works. History
791.A2-Z	By region, state, or place, A-Z
792.A-Z	Individual libraries. By name, A-Z
	Ireland
792.5.A1	General works. History
792.5.A2A-.A2Z	By region, state, or place, A-Z
792.5.A3-Z	Individual libraries. By name, A-Z
	Austria
	For Bosnia and Hercegovina see Z841.2.A1+
	For Croatia see Z841.25.A1+
	For Slovenia see Z841.8.A1+
793.A1	General works. History
793.A2-Z	By region, state, or place, A-Z
794.A-Z	Individual libraries. By name, A-Z
	Hungary
794.3.A1	General works. History
794.3.A2A-.A2Z	By region, state, or place, A-Z
794.3.A3-Z	Individual libraries. By name, A-Z
	Czechoslovakia. Czech Republic
795.A1	General works. History

Library reports. History. Statistics
  Europe
    Czechoslovakia -- Continued
795.A2-Z   By region, state, or place, A-Z
796.A3-Z   Individual libraries. By name, A-Z
    Slovakia
796.5.A1   General works. History
796.5.A2-Z   By region, state, or place, A-Z
796.6.A-Z   Individual libraries. By name, A-Z
    France
797.A1   General works. History
797.A2-Z   By region, state, or place, A-Z
798.A-Z   Individual libraries. By name, A-Z
    Germany
        Including West Germany
801.A1   General works. History
801.A2-Z   By region, state, or place, A-Z
802.A-Z   Individual libraries. By name, A-Z
    East Germany
803.A1   General works. History
803.A2A-.A2Z   By region, state, or place, A-Z
803.A3-Z   Individual libraries. By name, A-Z
    Greece
805.A1   General works. History
805.A2-Z   By region, state, or place, A-Z
806.A-Z   Individual libraries. By name, A-Z
    Italy
809.A1   General works. History
809.A2-Z   By region, state, or place, A-Z
810.A-Z   Individual libraries. By name, A-Z
    Vatican City
811   General works
812.A-Z   Individual libraries. By name, A-Z
    Malta
812.2   General works
812.3.A-Z   By region, state, or place, A-Z
812.5.A-Z   Individual libraries. By name, A-Z
    Belgium
813.A1   General works. History
813.A2-Z   By region, state, or place, A-Z
814.A-Z   Individual libraries. By name, A-Z
    Netherlands
815.A1   General works. History
815.A2-Z   By region, state, or place, A-Z
816.A-Z   Individual libraries. By name, A-Z
    Luxembourg
816.3.A1   General works. History

	Library reports. History. Statistics
	Europe
	Luxembourg -- Continued
816.3.A2A-.A2Z	By region, state, or place, A-Z
816.3.A3-Z	Individual libraries. By name, A-Z
	Liechtenstein
816.4.A1	General works. History
816.4.A2A-.A2Z	By region, state, or place, A-Z
816.4.A3-Z	Individual libraries. By name, A-Z
	Poland
817.A1	General works. History
817.A2-Z	By region, state, or place, A-Z
818.A-Z	Individual libraries. By name, A-Z
	San Marino
818.5.A1	General works. History
818.5.A2A-.A2Z	By region, state, or place, A-Z
818.5.A3-Z	Individual libraries. By name, A-Z
	Russia
819.A1	General works. History
819.A2-Z	By region, state, or place, A-Z
820.A-Z	Individual libraries. By name, A-Z
	Belarus
820.3.A1	General works. History
820.3.A2A-.A2Z	By region, state, or place, A-Z
820.3.A3-Z	Individual libraries. By name, A-Z
	Ukraine
820.4.A1	General works. History
820.4.A2A-.A2Z	By region, state, or place, A-Z
820.4.A3-Z	Individual libraries. By name, A-Z
	Baltic States
821	General works
	Estonia
821.3.A1	General works. History
821.3.A2A-.A2Z	By region, state, or place, A-Z
821.3.A3-Z	Individual libraries. By name, A-Z
	Latvia
821.5.A1	General works. History
821.5.A2A-.A2Z	By region, state, or place, A-Z
821.5.A3-Z	Individual libraries. By name, A-Z
	Lithuania
821.7.A1	General works. History
821.7.A2A-.A2Z	By region, state, or place, A-Z
821.7.A3-Z	Individual libraries. By name, A-Z
	Scandinavia
822	General works
	Denmark
823.A1	General works. History

Library reports. History. Statistics
Europe
Scandinavia
Denmark -- Continued
823.A2-Z   By region, state, or place, A-Z
824.A-Z   Individual libraries. By name, A-Z
Iceland
824.2   General works. History
824.3.A-Z   By region, state, or place, A-Z
824.5.A-Z   Individual libraries. By name, A-Z
Norway
825.A1   General works. History
825.A2-Z   By region, state, or place, A-Z
826.A-Z   Individual libraries. By name, A-Z
Sweden
827.A1   General works. History
827.A2-Z   By region, state, or place, A-Z
828.A-Z   Individual libraries. By name, A-Z
Finland
829.A1   General works. History
829.A2-Z   By region, state, or place, A-Z
830.A-Z   Individual libraries. By name, A-Z
Spain
831.A1   General works. History
831.A2-Z   By region, state, or place, A-Z
832.A-Z   Individual libraries. By name, A-Z
Portugal
833.A1   General works. History
833.A2-Z   By region, state, or place, A-Z
834.A-Z   Individual libraries. By name, A-Z
Switzerland
837.A1   General works. History
837.A2-Z   By region, state, or place, A-Z
838.A-Z   Individual libraries. By name, A-Z
Albania
838.5.A1   General works. History
838.5.A2A-.A2Z   By region, state, or place, A-Z
838.5.A3-Z   Individual libraries. By name, A-Z
Bulgaria
839.A1   General works. History
839.A2A-.A2Z   By region, state, or place, A-Z
839.A3-Z   Individual libraries. By name, A-Z
Moldova
839.5.A1   General works. History
839.5.A2A-.A2Z   By region, state, or place, A-Z
839.5.A3-Z   Individual libraries. By name, A-Z
Romania

Z662-1000.5

	Library reports. History. Statistics
	Europe
	Romania -- Continued
840.A1	General works. History
840.A2A-.A2Z	By region, state, or place, A-Z
840.A3-Z	Individual libraries. By name, A-Z
	Serbia and Montenegro. Yugoslavia
841.A1	General works. History
841.A2A-.A2Z	By region, state, or place, A-Z
841.A2M6	Montenegro
841.A2S46	Serbia
841.A3-Z	Individual libraries. By name, A-Z
	Bosnia and Hercegovina
841.2.A1	General works. History
841.2.A2A-.A2Z	By region, state, or place, A-Z
841.2.A3-Z	Individual libraries. By name, A-Z
	Croatia
841.25.A1	General works. History
841.25.A2A-.A2Z	By region, state, or place, A-Z
841.25.A3-Z	Individual libraries. By name, A-Z
	Macedonia (Republic)
841.4.A1	General works. History
841.4.A2A-.A2Z	By region, state, or place, A-Z
841.4.A3-Z	Individual libraries. By name, A-Z
	Montenegro
	see Z841.A2M6
	Slovenia
841.8.A1	General works. History
841.8.A2A-.A2Z	By region, state, or place, A-Z
841.8.A3-Z	Individual libraries. By name, A-Z
	Turkey see Z845+
	Near East
843.A1	General works. History
843.A2-Z	By region or country, A-Z
844.A-Z	Individual libraries. By name, A-Z
	Asia
845.A1	General works. History
845.A2-Z	By region or country, A-Z
846.A-Z	Individual libraries. By name, A-Z
848	Arab countries
	Africa
857.A1	General works. History
857.A2-Z	By region or country, A-Z
858.A-Z	Individual libraries. By name, A-Z
	Australia
870.A1	General works. History
870.A2-Z	By region, state, or place, A-Z

Library reports. History. Statistics
    Australia. Oceania
871.A-Z   Individual libraries. By name, A-Z
        New Zealand
872.A1   General works. History
872.A2-Z   By region, state, or place, A-Z
873.A-Z   Individual libraries. By name, A-Z
        Oceania. Pacific islands
            For Hawaii see Z732.A+
874.A1   General works. History
874.A2-Z   By region or country, A-Z
875.A-Z   Individual libraries. By name, A-Z
Library catalogs
    Class here library catalogs not limited to a particular topic or
        format
    For catalogs of private libraries see Z997+
    For catalogs limited to a particular topic or format see
        Z1201+
    By region or country
        United States
881.A1A-.A1Z   Catalogs of collections not confined to one region or state
                        e. g.
881.A1C3-.A1C39   Catalog of books represented by Library of Congress
                            printed cards
881.A1U52   National Union catalog in the Library of Congress
881.A12A-.A12Z   By region or state, A-Z
881.A13A-.A13Z   By city or county, A-Z
881.A14-Z   Individual libraries. By place, A-Z
                        e. g.
                    U.S. Library of Congress
881.U49A-.U49Z   Serials
881.U5   Catalogs, etc. By date
881.U52   Online catalog
881.W92   Worcester, Mass. Free Public Library
883   Canada (Table Z10)
885   Mexico (Table Z10)
        Central America
887.A1   Catalogs of collections not confined to one country
887.A2-Z   Individual countries, A-Z
                    Subarrange each by Table Z11
        West Indies
897.A1   Catalogs of collections not confined to one country
897.A2-Z   Individual countries, A-Z
                    Subarrange each by Table Z11
        Atlantic Ocean Islands
902   Bermuda (Table Z10)

	Library catalogs
	By region or country
	Atlantic Ocean Islands -- Continued
903.A-Z	Other, A-Z
	Subarrange each by Table Z11
	South America
907.A1	Catalogs of collections not confined to one country
907.A2-Z	Individual countries, A-Z
	Subarrange each by Table Z11
	Europe
918	Catalogs of collections not confined to one country
921	Great Britain and Ireland (Table Z10)
925	Austria (Table Z10)
925.3	Hungary (Table Z10)
926	Czechoslovakia. Czech Republic (Table Z10)
926.5	Slovakia (Table Z10)
927	France (Table Z10)
929	Germany (Table Z10)
931	Greece (Table Z10)
933	Italy (Table Z10)
933.5	Malta (Table Z10)
	Benelux (Low Countries)
935	Belgium (Table Z10)
936	Netherlands (Holland) (Table Z10)
937	Luxembourg (Table Z10)
938	Poland (Table Z10)
939	Russia. Former Soviet Union (Table Z10)
939.3	Belarus (Table Z10)
939.5	Moldova (Table Z10)
939.7	Ukraine (Table Z10)
940	Finland (Table Z10)
940.3	Estonia (Table Z10)
940.5	Latvia (Table Z10)
940.7	Lithuania (Table Z10)
	Scandinavia
941	Denmark (Table Z10)
941.5	Iceland (Table Z10)
942	Norway (Table Z10)
943	Sweden (Table Z10)
945	Spain (Table Z10)
946	Portugal (Table Z10)
949	Switzerland (Table Z10)
949.5	Albania (Table Z10)
950	Bulgaria (Table Z10)
951	Romania (Table Z10)
952	Yugoslavia (Table Z10)
	Including Serbia and Montenegro

	Library catalogs
	By region or country
	Europe -- Continued
952.2	Bosnia and Hercegovina (Table Z10)
952.4	Croatia (Table Z10)
952.6	Macedonia (Table Z10)
	Montenegro see Z952
	Serbia see Z952
952.8	Slovenia (Table Z10)
953	Turkey (Table Z10)
	Asia
	For Russia in Asia see Z939
	For Turkey see Z953
955.A1	Catalogs of collections not confined to one country
955.A2-Z	Individual countries, A-Z
	Subarrange each by Table Z11
	Africa
965.A1	Catalogs of collections not confined to one country
965.A2-Z	Individual countries, A-Z
	Subarrange each by Table Z11
975	Australia (Table Z10)
976	New Zealand (Table Z10)
977.A-Z	Pacific islands, A-Z
	Subarrange each by Table Z11
	For Hawaii see Z881.A12A+
(979)	Business, commercial, and industrial libraries
	see Z7164.C8+
(980)	Semipublic libraries
	see Z997+
	Book collecting
987	General works
987.5.A-Z	By region or country, A-Z
988	Bibliography
	Biography of book collectors
989.A1	Collective
989.A2-Z	Individual, A-Z
990	Periodicals. Serials
991	Societies
992	Bibliophilism. Bibliomania
	Cf. Z1001+ General bibliography
(992.5)	Poetry. Book verse
	see class P
992.8	Bibliokleptomania
	Cf. Z702.A3+ Thefts from public libraries
	Bookplates. Ex libris
993.A1	Periodicals. Serials

Z662-1000.5

Book collecting
Bookplates. Ex libris -- Continued
993.A2   Societies, A-Z
                              Cf. Z284 Booksellers' and publishers' societies
                              Cf. Z1008.A1+ Bibliographical societies
                              Cf. Z1201+ Societies as subdivision under names of
                                  countries in National bibliography
993.A25   Congresses
993.A3-Z   General works
993.15   General special
993.2   Bibliography
993.4   Superexlibris
994.A-Z   By region or country, A-Z
                              e.g.
                              America. United States
994.A5   General
994.A6A-.A6W   States (U.S.), A-W
994.B7   Brazil
994.F8   France
994.G37   Germany
994.G7   Great Britain
994.H93   Hungary
994.I8   Italy
994.M6   Mexico
994.N4   Netherlands
994.5.A-Z   By subject, A-Z
994.5.A36   Agriculture
994.5.A38   Alps
994.5.A54   Animals
994.5.A76   Art
994.5.B34   Balances (Weighing instruments)
994.5.B84   Bullfights
994.5.C37   Cardiology
994.5.C42   Cervantes Saavedra, Miguel de
994.5.C44   Chess
994.5.D36   Dante Alighieri, 1265-1321
994.5.D42   Death
994.5.D47   Dentistry
994.5.F35   Fantasy
994.5.F37   Fascism
994.5.F57   Fishing
994.5.F74   Freemasonry
994.5.H4   Heraldry
994.5.L4   Lenin, V.I.
994.5.L52   Library
994.5.L54   Lions International
994.5.L57   Literary

Book collecting
Bookplates. Ex libris
By subject, A-Z -- Continued

994.5.M43	Medicine
994.5.M5	Military
994.5.M87	Music
994.5.N8	Nude and erotic
994.5.O28	Ocean
994.5.O94	Owls
994.5.P45	Pharmacy
994.5.P55	Playing cards
994.5.P86	Pushkin, A.S.
994.5.R44	Religion
994.5.S3	Scenic
994.5.S66	Sports
994.5.T9	Typography
994.5.W5	Wine
994.5.W65	Women
995	Specimens
995.5	Imaginary bookplates
995.6	Miniature bookplates
996.A1	Directories
996.A2-Z	Individual designers, A-Z
996.2	Bookmarks
996.3	Booksellers' labels

Private libraries
Including history and catalogs

997.A1	General works
997.A2-Z	Individual libraries. By owner, A-Z
	For catalogs of private libraries on specific topics, see the topic
997.2.A-Z	By region or country, A-Z
	Subarrange each country by Table Z15

Booksellers' catalogs
Including second-hand booksellers' and auction catalogs
For catalogs on specific topics or in specific formats, see the
numbers for the topic or the format in Z1001+

(998)	General works
	see Z999
999	General
999.5	Bibliographies of booksellers' catalogs
1000	Sale records
1000.5	Catalogs of out-of-print books. Lists of books wanted, etc.

Z662-1000.5

General bibliography

1001   Introduction to bibliography. Theory, philosophy, psychology.
        Bibliography. Documentation
            For theory, philosophy, psychology, etc., of bibliography in
                specific countries see Z1201+
            For theory, philosophy, psychology, etc., of bibliography on
                specific subjects see Z5051+

1001.3 History of bibliography
            For history of bibliography by country see Z1201+

1002   Bibliography of bibliographies. Books about books
            For bibliography of bibliography in specific countries see
                Z1201+
            For bibliography of bibliography on specific subjects see
                Z5051+

        Books and reading. Choice of books. Book reviews
            For reviews of books on a special topic, see the topic
            For collections of reviews of recommended ("best") books
                see Z1035.A1
            Cf. Z992 Bibliophilism, bibliomania
            Cf. Z1035.A1+ Best books
            Cf. Z1037+ Books and reading for the young
            Cf. Z1039.A+ Books and reading for special groups

1003   General works
1003.15   Book talks
            By region or country
                United States
1003.2   General works
1003.3A-.3Z   By region or state, A-Z
1003.5A-.5Z   Other regions or countries, A-Z
            Biography of bibliographers
                Including promoters of bibliographical undertakings, etc.
                Cf. Z231+ Biography of printers
                Cf. Z280+ Biography of booksellers
                Cf. Z720.A1+ Biography of librarians
                Cf. Z989.A1+ Biography of book collectors
1003.8   Collective
1004.A-Z   Individual, A-Z
                    e.g.
1004.D95   Dzóban, O. O.
1004.E2   Eames, Wilberforce
1004.M49   Medina, Jose Toribio
1005   Addresses, essays, lectures
                Including collected and single
1006   Dictionaries. Encyclopedias
                Including bibliographical terms, library science, information
                    science, documentation, etc.
                Cf. Z118.A5+ Dictionaries of printing terms

1007	Periodicals
	Cf. Z671 Library periodicals
	Cf. Z1201+ Periodicals as subdivision under names of countries in National bibliography
	Societies. Congresses, etc.
	Cf. Z549 Book-buying organizations
	Cf. Z673.A1+ Library associations
1008.A1	General works
1008.A2	Congresses
1008.A4-Z	Individual societies. By name, A-Z
	e. g.
1008.G886	Grolier Club
(1008.4-.5)	Museums. Exhibitions
	see Z121
1009	Collections
	Cf. Z674 Collections on library science
	Cf. Z1005 Addresses, essays, lectures (Collected and single)
1010	Bio-bibliography
	General bibliographies
	Including dictionaries, catalogs, etc., of books
	Cf. Z118.A5+ Dictionaries of typographical terms
	Cf. Z1006 Dictionaries of bibliographical terms
1011	General
	Early (ca. 1500-1800). Notable books
	Including bibliographies dealing with books of that period, and general bibliographies published during the period
	Class here general works and works on early printed books in Europe
	For early printed books in a specific country or in a region other than Europe see Z1201+
1012	General
	Incunabula see Z240.A1
1014	16th century
1015	17th century
1016	18th century
1017	19th century
	Special classes of books
	Condemned books. Prohibited books. Challenged books. Expurgated books
	Cf. BV4730 Precepts of the Church
1019	General
	Index librorum prohibitorum
1020	Pre-2000 editions
	Subarrange by using a Cutter number consisting of the letter "I" and the final three digits of the year of publication, e. g. .I570 for the year 1570

Z1001-1121

	Special classes of books
	Condemned, prohibited, expurgated books
	Index librorum prohibitorum -- Continued
1020.2	2000- editions. By date
1021	Eccentric literature, curiosa, etc.
	Cf. Z1034 Bibliographical notes and queries
	Cf. Z5865+ Erotica
	Cf. Z7291 Riddles
1021.3	Emblem books
1022	High-priced books
1023	Illustrated books. Extra illustrated books
	Cf. ND2889+ Illumination of books and manuscripts, miniature painting, etc.
	Cf. NE890+ Artists' illustrated books
	Cf. Z5948.M6 Bibliography of miniatures, etc.
1024	Imaginary books. Lost books. Forgeries, etc.
1026	Livres à clef. Romans à clef. Drames à clef
1028	Privately printed books. Limited editions
	Cf. Z285.5 Self-publishing
1029	Rare books
	For prices of rare books see Z1000
1029.3	Street literature
1029.5	Printed ephemera
	Cf. NC1280+ Drawing. Design. Illustration
1030	Vellum printed books
1033.A-Z	Other special classes, A-Z
	Alphabet books. ABC's see Z1033.H8
1033.A84	Books interesting through their associations
1033.A87	Autographed editions
1033.B3	Best sellers
1033.B35	Big little books
1033.C3	Cazin editions
	CD-ROM books see Z1033.E43
1033.C4	Books with changed editions
1033.D85	Dummies
	Easy reading books see Z1033.H53
1033.E43	Electronic books. CD-ROM books
1033.F3	Facsimile editions
1033.F4	Festschriften
1033.F5	Fine editions
1033.F53	First editions
1033.G73	Grey literature
1033.H35	Hand-printed books
1033.H53	High interest-low vocabulary books
1033.H8	Hornbooks. Alphabet books. Primers
(1033.I4)	Immoral literature (Pornography)
	see Z7164.P84

	Special classes of books
	Other special classes, A-Z -- Continued
1033.L4	Leaf books
1033.L6	Library editions
1033.L7	Linked books
1033.L73	Little press books. Small press books
1033.M5	Microform editions. Books on microfilm, etc.
1033.M6	Microscopic and miniature editions
1033.P3	Paperbacks
1033.P52	Picture books
1033.P63	Pocket editions
	Primers see Z1033.H8
1033.R4	Reprints
1033.S5	Books issued in series
	Small press books see Z1033.L73
1033.T68	Toy and movable books
	Translations see Z6514.T7
1033.U58	Underground press publications
1033.U6	Unfinished books
1033.U64	University press publications
1033.Y44	Yellowback books
1034	Notes and queries. Bibliographical problems, etc.
	Class here works that deal with bibliographical information only
	For general compilations of questions and answers see AG305+
	Best books
	For primarily bibliographical works see Z1002
1035.A1	Book selection, reviews, etc.
	For general collections of book reviews see Z1003
1035.A2	Prize books
	Lists, catalogs, etc.
1035.A24	Through 1800
1035.A25-Z	1801-
1035.1	Reference books (General, and English)
	Reference books and best books in languages other than English
1035.2	French
1035.3	German
1035.4	Italian
1035.5	Scandinavian
1035.6	Slavic and Hungarian
1035.7	Spanish and Portuguese
1035.8.A-Z	Other, A-Z
	e. g.
1035.8.T8	Turkish

Z1001-1121

	Best books -- Continued
1035.9	Minor lists of best books
	Including lists of books for leisure hours, pleasure, self-education, choice of hobbies, etc.
1036	Booksellers' general catalogs of modern books
	Cf. Z1201+ Publishers' catalogs as subdivision under names of countries in National bibliography
	Books for the young
	Including works on reading interests of children and young people
	Cf. Z5784.C5 Children's plays
1037.A1	General works
1037.A2	Prize books
	Class here bibliographies only
	For discussions of prizes for children's literature see classes PA-PT
	Lists, catalogs, etc.
1037.A24	Early children's books through 1800
1037.A25-Z	Modern children's books 1801-
1037.1	Reference books for children
	Children's books in languages other than English
	Including children's books and reading interests of children in non-English speaking countries
1037.2	French
1037.3	German
1037.4	Italian
1037.5	Scandinavian
1037.6	Slavic and Hungarian
1037.7	Spanish and Portuguese
1037.8.A-Z	Other. By language, or by region or country for multilingual regions or countries, A-Z
1038.A-Z	Individual libraries. By name, A-Z
1039.A-Z	Books for other special classes, institutions, etc., A-Z
	Including works on reading interests of special groups
	African Americans see Z1039.B56
1039.A35	Aged. Older people
1039.A77	Artists
1039.A87	Authors
1039.B56	Blacks. African Americans
	Blind see HV1721+
1039.B67	Boys
1039.B87	Businesspeople
1039.C28	Capuchins
1039.C32	Catholics
1039.C45	Celebrities
	Children of minorities see Z1039.M56
1039.C47	Christians
1039.C65	College students

	Books for other special classes, institutions, etc., A-Z -- Continued
1039.C66	Conservatives
1039.D4	Deaf
1039.D5	Disabilities, People with
	Including children with disabilities
	Cf. Z1039.M4 People with mental disabilities
	Cf. Z1039.S55 People with social disabilities
1039.D94	Dyslexic readers
	Including dyslexic children
1039.E44	Elementary school graduates
1039.G55	Gifted children
1039.G57	Girls
1039.H54	High school students
	Including junior high school students
1039.H7	Hospital libraries
	Indians of North America see E97.8
1039.I56	Intellectuals
1039.J48	Jews
1039.L3	Laborers
1039.L4	Legislative bodies
1039.M4	Mental disabilities, People with
	Including children with mental disabilities
1039.M5	Mexican Americans
1039.M56	Minorities
	Including children of minorities and minority teenagers
	Negroes see Z1039.B56
1039.N47	New literates
1039.N76	Nuns
	Older people see Z1039.A35
	People with disabilities see Z1039.D5
	People with mental disabilities see Z1039.M4
	People with social disabilities see Z1039.S55
1039.P8	Prison libraries
1039.R8	Rural libraries
1039.S5	Slow learning children
1039.S55	Social disabilities, People with
	Including children with social disabilities
1039.S6	Soldiers
1039.T43	Teachers
1039.V63	Vocational school students
1039.W65	Women
(1040)	Databases
	see ZA4450+
	Anonyms and pseudonyms
1041	General bibliography
	Including bibliography of early works to 1800

Z1001-1121

Anonyms and pseudonyms -- Continued
   By region or country
      If classification by country is not applicable, class by language

1045	America (General). United States
1047	Canada
	Latin America
1049.A1	General works
1049.A3A-.A3Z	By region or country, A-Z
	e.g.
1049.A3B8	Brazil
1049.A3C7	Colombia
1049.A3C9	Cuba
1049.A3D6	Dominican Republic
1049.A3M6	Mexico
1049.A3U8	Uruguay
1049.A3V4	Venezuela
1065	Great Britain and Ireland
1066	Austria
1066.5	Czechoslovakia
	France
1067	General works
1067.2	Breton
1067.5	Langue d'oc
1068	Germany
1069	Greece
1069.5	Israel
1069.7	Hungary
1070	Italy
	Benelux (Low Countries)
1071	General and Belgium
1072	Netherlands (Holland)
1073	Russia. Former Soviet Union
1073.25	Ukraine
1073.3	Finland
1073.5	Poland
1073.6	Estonia
1073.7	Latvia
1073.8	Lithuania
	Scandinavia
1074	General and Denmark
1075	Norway
1076	Sweden
	Spain and Portugal
1077	General and Spain
1078	Portugal
1079	Switzerland

Anonyms and pseudonyms
   By region or country -- Continued
1080.A-Z　　　　Turkey and Balkan states, A-Z
      e.g.
1080.B8　　　　 Bulgaria
   Asia
1087.A1　　　　 General works
1087.A3-Z　　　 By region or country, A-Z
1097　　　　　Africa
1107　　　　　Australia
1121　　　Books with chronograms

National bibliography
> For each country, national bibliography includes:
> Books printed and published in that country; books by natives or
>> resident authors;
> Books written in the language of that country by foreigners (if not
>> confined to authors of one foreign country), i. e., a bibliography
>> of French literature produced by Belgian, Canadian, Italian,
>> Romanian, Russian, and Swiss authors would class under
>> France; but a bibliography of French-Canadian literature would
>> class under Canada;
> That country as subject: General bibliographies, and special having
>> to do with literature, biobibliography, history, and description.
>> Other special, as art, music, agriculture, geology, etc, are
>> classed with subject bibliography in Z5051+

America

1201	General bibliography
	Including Sabin's Bibliotheca americana
	Printed books
1202	1492-1600
	Including Harrisse's Bibliotheca Americana vetustissima
1203	1492/1600-1800
	1801- see Z1201
1206	Biobibliography of Americanists
1207	Private libraries, and booksellers' catalogs of Americana
	Including Americana in public libraries
	American archaeology
1208.A1	Periodicals
1208.A2	General works. History
1208.A3-Z	By region or country, A-Z
	American ethnology
1208.5	General works
	Indians
	For bibliography of Indian language see Z7116+
1209	General bibliography
1209.2.A-Z	By region or country, A-Z

Under each country:

.x	*General works*
.x2.A-Z	*By region, province, state, etc., A-Z*

1210.A-Z	Individual tribes, A-Z
	e.g.
1210.M4	Mayas
1210.N3	Navajo
1210.S5	Seminole
1211.A-Z	Other individual elements in the population, A-Z
1211.P64	Poles
1211.R87	Russian Germans
1211.S68	South Asians

Z1201-4980

America -- Continued

1212	Discovery of America
	United States
1215.A2	Bibliography of bibliography
1215.A3-Z	General bibliography
	Including the American catalogue
	For early works see Z1202+
1216	History of bibliography
1217.A-Z	Publishers' catalogs. By publisher, A-Z
1219	Periodicals
	Including the Publishers' weekly
1220	Societies. Publishing clubs
1221	Collections
1223	Government publications
	For bibliographies of government publications on specific
	topics, see the topics in Z5051+
1223.5	State publications
1223.5.A1	General bibliography
	Including Bowker's State publications
1223.5.A2	History, theory, method
1223.5.A3-.W	By state
1223.6	Municipal publications
1223.6.A1	General bibliography
1223.6.A2	History, theory, method
1223.6.A3-Z	By city, town, etc.
1224	Biobibliography
	Including Adams' Dictionary of American authors
	American literature
1224.2	Bibliography of bibliography
1224.5	Theory, method, etc.
1225	General bibliography
	Including bibliographies not otherwise provided for
	For local see Z1250+
1227	By period
1229.A-Z	Special classes or groups of writers, A-Z
	African American see Z1229.N39
1229.A75	Asian-American
1229.C3	Catholic
1229.G25	Gays
1229.G3	German-American
1229.G7	Greek-letter
1229.I52	Indians
1229.I8	Italian-American
1229.M48	Mexican-American
1229.N39	Negro. African American
1229.N44	Newspaper carriers
1229.P6	Polish-American

Z1201-4980

	America
	United States
	American literature
	Special classes or groups of writers, A-Z -- Continued
1229.P74	Prisoners
1229.W8	Women
1231.A-Z	Special topics, A-Z
	Prefer Z1232 for all forms of children's literature
1231.A39	Adventure stories
1231.A6	Almanacs
1231.B2	Ballads
1231.B4	Beat generation. Bohemianism
	Bohemianism see Z1231.B4
1231.B7	Broadsides
1231.C4	Chapbooks
1231.D47	Detective and mystery stories
1231.D55	Dime novels
1231.D7	Drama
1231.F32	Fantastic literature
1231.F4	Fiction
1231.F5	First editions
1231.G66	Gothic revival
1231.H57	Historical fiction
	Humor see Z1231.W8
1231.L68	Love stories
1231.M5	Minorities
	Mystery stories see Z1231.D47
1231.O7	Orations
1231.P2	Pamphlets
	Cf. AG600 Lists of free material
1231.P45	Periodicals
1231.P7	Poetry
1231.P74	Popular literature
1231.P8	Prose
1231.S66	Sports stories
1231.S87	Suspense fiction
1231.T7	Translations of American works
1231.W58	Western stories
1231.W8	Wit and humor
1231.W85	Women
1232	Children's literature. Juvenile literature
	English language in the United States
1233	General works
1234.A-Z	Special topics, A-Z
1234.D5	Dialects
	Orthography and spelling see Z1234.S67
1234.S67	Spellers. Orthography and spelling

America
United States -- Continued
History and description
1236   General bibliography
By period
1237   Colonial period, 1492/1607-1775
1238   Revolution, 1775-1783
1239   1783-1809
1240   War of 1812
1815-1861
1240.5   General works
1241   Mexican War, 1845-1848
1242   Civil War, 1861-1865
1242.5   Confederate States publications (imprints)
Including all books, etc., printed within the territory of the
C.S.A., 1861-1865
1242.8   1865-1900
1243   War of 1898 (Spanish-American War)
1244   1900-1945
1245   1945-
1247   General special
1249.A-Z   Special topics, A-Z
Congress
1249.C65   Organization, committees, etc.
1249.C67   Senate
1249.C7   House
1249.C74   Conservatism
1249.C75   Constitutional history
1249.D29   Declaration of Independence
Diplomatic history see Z6465.U5
1249.E9   Executive departments
1249.F5   Flags
Foreign relations see Z6465.U5
1249.F9   Frontier, The
Historic monuments. Historic sites see Z6465.U5
1249.I5   Independent regulatory commissions
1249.K8   Ku Klux Klan
1249.L67   Lewis and Clark Expedition
1249.M5   Military history
1249.N3   Naval history
1249.P7   The presidency
Relations (General) see Z1361.R4
1249.S6   Slavery
1249.S9   Supreme Court
1249.T74   Treasure troves
Wars see Z1249.M5
Local

Z1201-4980

America
United States
Local -- Continued

1250	General bibliography
	Including Ludewig's Literature of American local history
1251.A-Z	By region or section, etc., A-Z
	e.g.
1251.A2	National parks. Landmarks. Historic monuments
	Including preservation
1251.A7	Appalachian Mountains
1251.C6	Colorado River
1251.E1	The East
	Including New England
1251.G8	Great Lakes
	Great Smoky Mountains see Z1251.A7
1251.L8	Louisiana Purchase
	Middle West see Z1251.W5
1251.M6	Mississippi River and Valley
1251.N5	New Sweden
	Northwest (Old) see Z1251.W5
1251.N7	Northwest (Pacific)
1251.N72	Northwestern States
1251.O4	Ohio River and Valley
1251.P2	Pacific States
1251.R7	Rocky Mountains
1251.S7	The South
1251.S8	Southwest (New)
1251.W5	The West. Middle West. Old Northwest
	By state
1253-1254	Alabama (Table Z14)
1255-1256	Alaska (Table Z14)
1257-1258	Arizona (Table Z14)
1259-1260	Arkansas (Table Z14)
1261-1262	California (Table Z14)
1263-1264	Colorado (Table Z14)
1265-1266	Connecticut (Table Z14)
1267-1268	Delaware (Table Z14)
	District of Columbia. Washington (City)
1269	General bibliography
1270.A-Z	City sections, buildings, etc., A-Z
	e.g.
1270.C2	Capitol
1270.G4	Georgetown
1270.W3	White House
1271-1272	Florida (Table Z14)
1273-1274	Georgia (Table Z14)
	Hawaii see Z4701+

America
  United States
    Local
      By state -- Continued

1275-1276	Idaho (Table Z14)
1277-1278	Illinois (Table Z14)
1279-1280	Indian Territory (Table Z14)
1281-1282	Indiana (Table Z14)
1283-1284	Iowa (Table Z14)
1285-1286	Kansas (Table Z14)
1287-1288	Kentucky (Table Z14)
1289-1290	Louisiana (Table Z14)
1291-1292	Maine (Table Z14)
1293-1294	Maryland (Table Z14)
1295-1296	Massachusetts (Table Z14)
1297-1298	Michigan (Table Z14)
1299-1300	Minnesota (Table Z14)
1301-1302	Mississippi (Table Z14)
1303-1304	Missouri (Table Z14)
1305-1306	Montana (Table Z14)
1307-1308	Nebraska (Table Z14)
1309-1310	Nevada (Table Z14)
1311-1312	New Hampshire (Table Z14)
1313-1314	New Jersey (Table Z14)
1315-1316	New Mexico (Table Z14)
1317-1318	New York (Table Z14)
1319-1320	North Carolina (Table Z14)
1321-1322	North Dakota (Table Z14)
1323-1324	Ohio (Table Z14)
1325-1326	Oklahoma (Table Z14)
1327-1328	Oregon (Table Z14)
1329-1330	Pennsylvania (Table Z14)
1331-1332	Rhode Island (Table Z14)
1333-1334	South Carolina (Table Z14)
1335-1336	South Dakota (Table Z14)
1337-1338	Tennessee (Table Z14)
1339-1340	Texas (Table Z14)
1341-1342	Utah (Table Z14)
1343-1344	Vermont (Table Z14)
1345-1346	Virginia (Table Z14)
1347-1348	Washington (Table Z14)
1349-1350	West Virginia (Table Z14)
1351-1352	Wisconsin (Table Z14)
1353-1354	Wyoming (Table Z14)
1357	Territories and possessions
1361.A-Z	Special topics (not otherwise provided for), A-Z
	African Americans see Z1361.N39

Z1201-4980

	America
	United States
	Special topics (not otherwise provided for), A-Z --
	Continued
1361.A51	Americanization
1361.A73	Arabs
1361.A75	Asians in the United States
1361.B3	Basques in the United States
1361.B74	British Americans
1361.C4	Chinese in the United States
1361.C6	Civilization. Intellectual life
1361.C85	Cuban Americans
1361.C94	Czech-Americans in the United States
1361.D3	Danes in the United States
1361.D4	Defenses (National)
1361.D64	Dominican Americans
1361.D8	Dutch in the United States
1361.E37	East Indians in the United States
1361.E4	Elements in the population. Ethnic groups (General)
	Including foreign population, minorities, etc.
1361.E97	European Americans
1361.F48	Filipinos
1361.F5	Finns in the United States
1361.F8	French in the United States
1361.F83	Friends, Society of. Quakers
1361.G37	Germans in the United States
1361.H83	Huguenots in the United States
	Cf. Z7845.H8 Huguenots (Religious sect)
1361.H84	Hungarians in the United States
	Indians see Z1209+
1361.I53	Indochinese in the United States
	Intellectual life see Z1361.C6
1361.I7	Irish in the United States
1361.I8	Italians in the United States
1361.J2	Japanese in the United States
1361.K65	Koreans in the United States
1361.L87	Luxembourg Americans
1361.M4	Mexicans in the United States
	National defense see Z1361.D4
1361.N39	Negroes. African Americans
1361.N67	Norwegians in the United States
(1361.O7)	Orientals in the United States
	see Z1361.A75
1361.P34	Pacific Islanders
1361.P6	Poles in the United States
1361.P65	Portuguese
1361.P8	Puerto Ricans in the United States

America
United States
Special topics (not otherwise provided for), A-Z --
Continued
Quakers see Z1361.F83
1361.R4   Relations (General) with other countries
1361.R65   Romanian Americans
1361.R86   Russian Germans in the United States
1361.S35   Scots-Irish
1361.S4   Serbs in the United States
1361.S47   Sikhs
1361.S5   Slavs in the United States
1361.S56   Slovenes in the United States
Society of Friends see Z1361.F83
1361.S7   Spanish-Americans in the United States
1361.S9   Swedes in the United States
1361.S94   Swiss in the United States
1361.U4   Ukrainians in the United States
1361.V53   Vietnamese in the United States
1361.W3   Welsh in the United States
1361.W45   West Indians in the United States
1361.Y8   Yugoslavs in the United States
1363   Private libraries' and booksellers' catalogs of U.S.
                 Americana
Canada. British North America
1365.A1   Bibliography of bibliography
1365.A2   Theory, method, etc.
1365.A3-Z   General bibliography
1367.A-Z   Publishers' catalogs. By publisher, A-Z
1369   Periodicals
1370   Societies
1371   Collections
Government publications
                     For bibliographies of government publications on specific
                     topics, see the topics in Z5051+
1373   General works
Publications of the provinces
1373.3   General works
1373.5.A-Z   By province, A-Z
                         e.g.
1373.5.B8   British Columbia
1373.5.N4   New Brunswick
1373.5.N6   Northwest Territories
1373.5.O7   Ontario
1374   Biobibliography
Canadian literature
1375   General bibliography

Z1201-4980

	America
	Canada. British North America
	Canadian literature -- Continued
1376.A-Z	Special classes or groups of writers, A-Z
1376.B55	Black authors
1376.C37	Caribbean authors
1376.W65	Women authors
1377.A-Z	Special topics, A-Z
1377.D7	Drama
1377.F4	Fiction
1377.F8	French-Canadian
1377.P7	Poetry
1377.R68	Royal Canadian Mounted Police
1377.T73	Translations
1378	Children's literature. Juvenile literature
1379	English language in Canada
1380	French language in Canada
	History and description
1382	General bibliography
1383	New France
1385	Recent
1387.A-Z	Special topics, A-Z
1387.M54	Military history
	Local
1391	General bibliography
1392.A-Z	Regions, provinces, cities, A-Z
1392.A2	National parks. Landmarks. Historic monuments
	Including preservation
1392.A3	Acadians
1392.A4	Alberta
1392.B78	Bruce County, Ont.
1392.C68	Côte-Nord
1392.E37	Eastern Townships (Québec)
1392.E39	Edmonton (Alta.)
1392.G54	Glengarry
1392.H38	Le Haut-Saint-Laurent
1392.L35	Lanaudière
1392.M35	Manitoba
1392.M37	Maritime Provinces
1392.N6	Northern regions of Canada (General). Arctic regions
1392.N7	Northwest (Canadian)
1392.N75	Nova Scotia
1392.O6	Ontario
1392.P5	Pittsburgh (Ont.)
1392.Q3	Quebec (Province)
1392.S15	Saquenay-Lac-Saint-Jean-Chibouqamau
1392.W37	Waterloo (Ont. : County)

America
  Canada. British North America
    Local
      Regions, provinces, cities, A-Z -- Continued

1392.Y9	Yukon Territory
1395.A-Z	Special topics (not otherwise provided for), A-Z
1395.B55	Blacks
1395.E4	Elements in the population. Ethnic groups (General)
1395.F7	French-Canadians
1395.G45	Germans
1395.H9	Hudson's Bay Company
1395.H94	Hungarians
1395.I43	Icelanders
1395.I82	Italians
1395.M45	Mennonites
1395.P57	Poles
1395.U47	Ukrainians
1395.W47	West Indians
1401	Private libraries' and booksellers' catalogs of Canadiana

  Latin America see Z1601+
  Mexico

1411.A1	Bibliography
1411.A3-Z	General bibliography
	Including Medina's La imprenta en México (1539-1821)
1412	Bibliography of early works
	Including Garcia Icazbalceta's Bibliografia mexicana del siglo XVI
1413.A-Z	Publishers' catalogs. By publisher, A-Z
1415	Periodicals
1416	Societies
1417	Collections
1419	Government publications
	For bibliographies of government publications on specific topics, see the topics in Z5051+
1420	Biobibliography
	Literature
1421	General bibliography
1424.A-Z	Special topics, A-Z
	e.g.
1424.D7	Drama
1424.F4	Fiction
1424.P7	Poetry
1424.5	Spanish language in Mexico
	History and description
1425	General bibliography
	By period
1426	Early to 1810

Z1201-4980

America
  Mexico
    History and description
      By period -- Continued

1426.1	1810-1821 (Revolution against Spain)
1426.2	1821-1860 (Internal revolution and war with the United States)
	Cf. Z1241 Mexican War, 1845-1848
1426.3	1861-1867 (European intervention)
1426.4	1867-1910 (Díaz)
1426.5	1910- (Revolution)
1427.A-Z	Local, A-Z
	e.g.
1427.B3	Baja California
1427.C3	Campeche (State)
1427.M6	Mexico (City)
1427.N8	Nuevo León (State)
1429.A-Z	Special topics (not otherwise provided for), A-Z
	e.g.
1429.G9	Guadalupe, Nuestra Señora de
1431	Catalogs
	Central America
1437	General bibliography
	Belize
1441	General bibliography
1443	Periodicals
1445	Government publications
	For bibliographies of official publications on specific topics, see the topics in Z5051+
1447.A-Z	Special topics in history, literature, etc., A-Z
1448.A-Z	Local, A-Z
1449	Catalogs
	Costa Rica
1451	General bibliography
1453	Periodicals
1455	Government publications
	For bibliographies of government publications on specific topics, see the topics in Z5051+
1457.A-Z	Special topics, A-Z
1457.L57	Literature
1458.A-Z	Local, A-Z
1459	Catalogs
	Guatemala
1461	General bibliography
1463	Periodicals

	America
	Central America
	Guatemala -- Continued
1465	Government publications
	For bibliographies of government publications on specific topics, see the topics in Z5051+
1467.A-Z	Special topics, A-Z
1467.L5	Literature
1468.A-Z	Local, A-Z
1469	Catalogs
	Honduras
1471	General bibliography
1473	Periodicals
1475	Government publications
	For bibliographies of government publications on specific topics, see the topics in Z5051+
1477.A-Z	Special topics, A-Z
1477.L57	Literature
1478.A-Z	Local, A-Z
1479	Catalogs
	Nicaragua
1481	General bibliography
1483	Periodicals
1485	Government publications
	For bibliographies of government publications on specific topics, see the topics in Z5051+
1486	History
1487.A-Z	Special topics, A-Z
1487.L36	Language
1488.A-Z	Local, A-Z
1489	Catalogs
	Salvador
1491	General bibliography
1493	Periodicals
1495	Government publications
	For bibliographies of government publications on specific topics, see the topics in Z5051+
1497.A-Z	Special topics, A-Z
1497.P66	Politics and government
1498.A-Z	Local, A-Z
1499	Catalogs
1500	Panama
	West Indies
1501	General bibliography
1502.A-Z	Special groups of islands, A-Z
	e.g.
1502.B5	British

Z1201-4980

	America
	West Indies
	Special groups of islands, A-Z -- Continued
	Danish see Z1561.V8
1502.D7	Dutch
1502.F5	French
	Bahamas
1503	General bibliography
1504.A-Z	Special topics, A-Z
1507.A-Z	Local, A-Z
1509	Catalogs
	Cuba
1511.A1	Bibliography of bibliography
1511.A3-Z	General bibliography
1513	Publishers' catalogs
1515	Periodicals
1516	Societies
1517	Collections
1519	Government publications
	For bibliographies of government publications on specific topics, see the topics in Z5051+
1520	Biobibliography
	Literature
1521	General bibliography
1524.A-Z	Special topics, A-Z
1524.D7	Drama
1524.P6	Poetry
1524.3	Children's literature. Juvenile literature
1525	History
1527.A-Z	Local, A-Z
	e.g.
1527.H2	Havana
1529.A-Z	Special topics (not otherwise provided for), A-Z
1529.C58	Civilization. Popular culture
	Popular culture see Z1529.C58
1530	Catalogs
	Hispaniola
1530.5	General works
	Haiti
1531	General bibliography
1532.A-Z	Special topics, A-Z
1532.H57	History
1532.L56	Literature
1533.A-Z	Local, A-Z
1534	Catalogs
	Dominican Republic. Santo Domingo
1536	General bibliography

America
West Indies
Dominican Republic. Santo Domingo -- Continued

1537.A-Z	Special topics, A-Z
1537.L56	Literature
1538.A-Z	Local, A-Z
1539	Catalogs
	Jamaica
1541	General bibliography
1543	Periodicals
1545	Government publications

For bibliographies of government publications on specific topics, see the topics in Z5051+

1547.A-Z	Special topics, A-Z
1548.A-Z	Local, A-Z
1549	Catalogs
	Puerto Rico
1551	General bibliography
1553	Periodicals
1555	Government publications

For bibliographies of government publications on specific topics, see the topics in Z5051+

1556	Biobibliography
1557.A-Z	Special topics, A-Z
1557.H57	History
1557.L56	Literature
1557.S54	Short stories
1558.A-Z	Local, A-Z
1559	Catalogs
1561.A-Z	Other islands, A-Z
	e.g.
1561.V8	Virgin Islands of the United States
1591	Bermuda
1595	Spanish Main. Caribbean Area
	South America. Latin America
1601.A2	Bibliography of bibliography
1601.A3-Z	General bibliography
1602.5	History of bibliography
1605	Periodicals
1605.5	Societies
1606	Collections
1607	Biobibliography
1609.A-Z	Special topics, A-Z
1609.B6	Biography
1609.B65	Blacks as an element in the population
1609.B7	Boundaries
1609.C5	Children's literature

Z1201-4980

	America
	South America. Latin America
	Special topics, A-Z -- Continued
1609.C54	Chinese as an element in the population
1609.C57	Civilization. Popular culture
1609.D47	Description and travel
1609.D7	Drama
1609.E79	Essays
1609.E87	Europeans as an element in the population
1609.F4	Fiction
1609.G7	Government documents
1609.H5	Historical geography
1609.H53	History
1609.I5	Inter-American conferences
1609.L3	Language
1609.L7	Literature
	Negroes see Z1609.B65
1609.P6	Poetry
1609.P63	Poles as an element in the population
1609.P64	Politics and government
	Popular culture see Z1609.C57
1609.R4	Relations (General)
1609.T7	Translations
1610	Catalogs
	By region or country
1611-1639	Argentina (Table Z1)
1641-1669	Bolivia (Table Z1)
1671-1699	Brazil (Table Z1)
1701-1729	Chile (Table Z1)
1731-1759	Colombia (Table Z1)
1761-1789	Ecuador (Table Z1)
	Guianas
1791-1799	Guyana. British Guiana (Table Z2)
1801-1809	Suriname. Dutch Guiana (Table Z2)
1811-1819	French Guiana (Table Z2)
1821-1849	Paraguay (Table Z1)
1851-1879	Peru (Table Z1)
1881-1909	Uruguay (Table Z1)
1911-1939	Venezuela (Table Z1)
1945	Falkland Islands
1946	Saint Helena. Tristan da Cunha. Ascension Island
1975	Eastern Hemisphere
	Europe
2000	General bibliography
2000.6	European Defense Community
2000.7	Fascism
2000.9	Commonwealth of Nations

	Europe -- Continued
2001-2029	Great Britain and Ireland. England (Table Z1 modified)
	Language. Philology
	For English language in the United States see Z1233+
	For English language in Canada see Z1379
2015.A1	General
(2015.A2)	This number not used
2015.A3-Z	Special topics, A-Z
	For special topics, see Table Z1 14
	Local
2024.A-Z	Special, A-Z
	e.g.
2024.L8	London
2024.M15	Isle of Man
2024.Y6	Yorkshire
	Ireland. Eire. Irish Free State
2031	General bibliography
2032	Bibliography of early works
2033	Publisher's catalogs
2034	Periodicals. Societies. Collections
2035	Official publications
	For bibliographies of official publications on specific topics, see the topics in Z5051+
2036	Biobibliography
	Literature
2037	General works
	Early see Z2032
2039.A-Z	Special topics, A-Z
2039.A6	Almanacs
2039.D7	Drama
2039.F4	Fiction
2039.G3	Gaelic imprints
	Humor see Z2039.W57
2039.P6	Poetry
2039.T7	Translations
2039.W57	Wit and humor
	Language see Z7011+
	History and description
2041	General bibliography
2043.A-Z	Local, A-Z
	e.g.
2043.A1	Collective
2043.B4	Belfast
2043.N6	Northern Ireland
2047.A-Z	Special topics, A-Z
2047.N35	Nationalism
2047.P3	Pamphlets

Z1201-4980

Europe
Great Britain and Ireland. England
Ireland. Eire. Irish Free State
History and description -- Continued
2049   Catalogs. Lists, etc.
Scotland
2051   General bibliography
2052   Bibliography of early works
2053   Publishers' catalogs
2054   Periodicals. Societies. Collections
2055   Official publications
             For bibliographies of official publications on specific topics, see the topics in Z5051+
2056   Biobibliography
Literature
2057   General works
         Early see Z2052
2059.A-Z   Special topics, A-Z
2059.A6   Almanacs
2059.D7   Drama
2059.F4   Fiction
2059.G3   Gaelic imprints
2059.P6   Poetry
2059.T7   Translations
         Language see Z7011+
         History and description
2061   General bibliography
2063.A-Z   Local, A-Z
2063.A1   Collective
2063.A3   Aberdeen
2063.A6   Angus
2063.C2   Caithness
2063.C55   Clackmannanshire
2063.D9   Dunfermline
2063.E3   Edinburgh
2063.F53   Fife
2063.G55   Glasgow
2063.H5   Highlands of Scotland
2063.I7   Inverness
2063.O7   Orkney Islands
2063.S13   St. Andrews
2063.S53   Shetland
2067.A-Z   Special topics, A-Z
2067.D2   Darien. Scots' colony
2067.N35   Nationalism
2067.P3   Pamphlets
             Scots' colony see Z2067.D2

Z1201-4980

	Europe -- Continued
2250	East Germany
2260	Mediterranean area
	Cf. Z6207.G7 Greco-Roman civilization
2281-2309	Greece (Table Z1)
	Cf. Z7016+ Classical philology
	Cf. Z7021+ Greek
2340	Rome. Roman Empire
	Cf. Z7026+ Latin language and literature
2341-2369	Italy (Table Z1)
	Cf. Z7016+ Classical philology
	Cf. Z7026+ Latin
2371	San Marino
2373	Vatican City
2375	Malta
2401-2429	Benelux (Low Countries). Belgium (Table Z1 modified)
2401.5	Rare books
2431-2459	Netherlands (Holland) (Table Z1)
2461-2465	Luxembourg (Table Z3)
	Eastern Europe
2483	General works
2491-2519	Soviet Union. Russia (Table Z1 modified)
2491.5	Rare books
2519.5	Belarus
	Ukraine
2519.6.A1	Bibliography of bibliography
2519.6.A2	Theory, method, etc.
2519.6.A6-Z	General bibliography. Imprints (General)
	Including general bibliography of the country as subject
2519.62	Government publications
	For bibliographies of government publications on specific topics, see the topics in Z5051+
2519.63.A-Z	Local, A-Z
	History and description see Z2519.6.A6+
2519.64.A-Z	Special topics, A-Z
	Subarrange like Z2 8.A6+
2519.65	Catalogs
2519.7	Moldova
2520	Finland
2521-2529	Poland (Table Z2)
	Baltic States
2531	General bibliography
2533	Estonia
2535	Latvia
2537	Lithuania
	Finland see Z2520
2540	Baltic Sea region

	Europe -- Continued
	Scandinavia
2551	General bibliography
2552	Bibliography of early works
2553	Periodicals
2554	Biobibliography
2555	Philology
	Icelandic and Old Norse
2556.A2	Runic
2556.A7-Z	Icelandic and Old Norse
2557	History and description
2559.A-Z	Special topics, A-Z
2559.B3	Ballads and songs
2559.D7	Drama
2559.F52	Fiction
2559.G45	Geography
2559.L53	Lapps
2559.L58	Literature
2559.R65	Romances
	Songs see Z2559.B3
2559.T7	Translations
2560	Catalogs
2561-2589	Denmark (Table Z1)
	Iceland
	History and description
2590.A1	Bibliography of bibliography
2590.A3	General bibliography
2590.A4	Periodicals
	Printed books
2590.A5	Early
2590.A7-Z	Modern
2590.7.A-Z	Local, A-Z
2591-2619	Norway (Table Z1)
2621-2649	Sweden (Table Z1)
2650	Lapland
2681-2709	Spain and Portugal. Spain (Table Z1)
2710	Andorra
2711-2739	Portugal (Table Z1)
2771-2799	Switzerland (Table Z1)
2820	Liechtenstein
	Turkey and the Balkan states
2831-2859	General works (Table Z1)
2881-2889	Albania (Table Z2)
2890	Bosnia and Hercegovina
2891-2899	Bulgaria (Table Z2)
2901-2909	Croatia (Table Z2)
2911-2919	Macedonia (Republic) (Table Z2)

Z1201-4980

	Europe
	Turkey and the Balkan states -- Continued
	Montenegro see Z2951+
2921-2929	Romania (Table Z2)
	Serbia see Z2951+
2931-2939	Slovenia (Table Z2)
2951-2959	Yugoslavia (Table Z2)
	Asia. Africa. Australia
	Cf. Z7046+ Bibliography of languages and literatures of
	countries in Asia, Africa, Australia, and Oceania
	Asia
3001	General bibliography
3002	Bibliography of early works
3004	Biobibliography
3005	Latin Orient
3008.A-Z	Special topics, A-Z
	Antiquities see Z3008.A7
3008.A7	Archaeology. Antiquities
3008.C48	Children's literature. Juvenile literature
3008.C5	Chinese
3008.C55	Civilization. Intellectual life
3008.D7	Drama
3008.E2	Economic conditions
3008.H57	History
3008.H6	Hittites
3008.H65	Hmong (Asian people)
	Intellectual life see Z3008.C55
	Juvenile literature see Z3008.C48
3008.L58	Literature
3008.M54	Minorities
3008.P6	Portuguese as an element in the population
3008.Y87	Yuruks (Turkic people)
3009	Catalogs
	Middle East. Near East. Arab countries
	For Turkey see Z2831+
	For North Africa see Z3515
	For Egypt see Z3651+
	For Sudan see Z3665
3013	General bibliography. Imprints (General)
3013.2	Bibliography of early works
3013.3	Theory, method, etc.
3013.5	Periodicals
3013.6	Societies. Institutions
3013.7	Collections
3013.8	Government publications
	For bibliographies of government publications on specific
	topics, see the topics in Z5051+

Asia. Africa. Australia
   Asia
      Middle East. Near East. Arab countries -- Continued

3014.A-Z	Special topics, A-Z
	Antiquities see Z3014.A72
3014.A72	Archaeology. Antiquities
3014.A77	Assyrians (Nestorians). Chaldean Catholics. Nestorians
3014.B43	Bedouins
	Chaldean Catholics see Z3014.A77
3014.C48	Children's literature
3014.C57	Civilization. Intellectual life
3014.D45	Description and travel
3014.D78	Druzes
3014.E85	Ethnology
3014.H55	History
	Intellectual life see Z3014.C57
	Kurdistan see Z3014.K85
3014.K85	Kurds. Kurdistan
3014.L56	Literature
3014.M55	Military history
3014.M56	Minorities
	Nestorians see Z3014.A77
3014.P64	Politics
3014.R44	Relations with other countries
3014.S64	Social life and customs
3015	Catalogs
3015.3	Persian Gulf region
3015.6	Red Sea region
3016-3020	Afghanistan (Table Z3)
3026-3030	Arabia, Saudi Arabia (Table Z3)
	Including Persian Gulf States in general
3028.A-Z	Local, A-Z
	Aden see Z3028.Y39
3028.B34	Bahrain
3028.K87	Kuwait
	Muscat and Oman see Z3028.O5
3028.O5	Oman. Muscat and Oman
3028.Q3	Qatar
	Southern Yemen see Z3028.Y39
	Trucial States see Z3028.U54
3028.U54	United Arab Emirates. Trucial States
3028.Y39	Yemen (People's Democratic Republic). Southern Yemen. Aden
3028.Y4	Yemen (Yemen Arab Republic)
	Armenia see Z3461+
3036-3040	Iraq (Table Z3)
	Cf. Z7055 Assyriology

Z1201-4980

	Asia. Africa. Australia
	Asia -- Continued
3041-3045	Baluchistan (Table Z3)
3101-3109	China (Table Z2)
3111-3119	Taiwan (Table Z2)
3121-3125	Mongolian People's Republic. Outer Mongolia (Table Z3)
(3126-3130)	Central Asia
	see Z3411+
	Indian subcontinent. South Asia
3185	General bibliography
3186-3190	Bangladesh (Table Z3)
3191-3199	Pakistan (Table Z2)
3201-3209	India (Table Z2)
	Including Republic of India and India to 1947
3210	Nepal
3210.5	Bhutan
3211-3215	Sri Lanka (Table Z3)
3216-3220	Burma. Myanmar (Table Z3)
	Southeast Asia
3221	General bibliography
	Indochina
3222	General works
3226-3230	Vietnam (Table Z3)
3232	Cambodia
3233	Laos
3236-3240	Thailand (Table Z3)
3246-3250	Malaysia (Table Z3)
3261-3265	Brunei (Table Z3)
3271-3279	Indonesia (Table Z2)
3285	Singapore
3291-3299	Philippines (Table Z2)
3301-3309	Japan (Table Z2)
3316-3320	Korea (Table Z3)
	Including South Korea
3321-3325	North Korea (Table Z3)
3366-3370	Iran (Table Z3)
3401-3409	Soviet Union in Asia. Siberia (Table Z2)
	Central Asia (General)
3411.A1	Bibliography of bibliography
3411.A2	Theory, method, etc.
3411.A6-Z	General bibliography. Imprints (General)
	Including general bibliography of Central Asia as subject
3411.A6-Z	General bibliography. Imprints (General)
	Including general bibliography of Central Asia as subject
	History and description see Z3411.A6+
3414.A-Z	Special topics, A-Z
	For subarrangement see Table Z2 8.A6+

Asia. Africa. Australia
    Asia
        Central Asia (General) -- Continued

3415	Catalogs
3416-3420	Kazakhstan (Table Z3)
3421-3425	Kyrgyzstan (Table Z3)
3426-3430	Tajikistan (Table Z3)
3431-3435	Turkmenistan (Table Z3)
3436-3440	Uzbekistan (Table Z3)
	Arabia see Z3026+
3461-3465	Armenia (Table Z3)
	Including Armenia (Republic)
3465.5	Azerbaijan
3465.6	Georgia (Republic)
3466-3470	Lebanon (Table Z3)
3471-3475	Jordan (Table Z3)
3476-3480	Israel (Table Z3)
	Including Pilgrimages to Palestine
3481-3485	Syria (Table Z3)
	Islands of the Aegean see Z2281+
3496	Cyprus
	Indian Ocean Region
3499	General bibliography
3499.3	Comoros
3499.49	Maldives
3499.5	Mauritius
3499.7	Seychelles
3499.9	Islamic countries
	Africa
3501	General bibliography
3502	Bibliography of early works
3502.5	History of bibliography
3503	Periodicals
3504	Societies. Institutions
3507	Collections
3507.5	Government publications
	For bibliographies of government publications on specific topics, see the topics in Z5051+
3508.A-Z	Special topics, A-Z
3508.A73	Archaeology. Antiquities
3508.C5	Children's literature
3508.C58	Civilization
3508.C7	Colonization
3508.D7	Drama
3508.H5	History
3508.L5	Literature
3508.P35	Pan-Africanism

Z1201-4980

Asia. Africa. Australia
Africa
Special topics, A-Z -- Continued
3508.P6	Politics
3508.P8	Psychology
3508.R4	Relations (General) with other countries
	Cf. Z6465.A36 Foreign relations
3508.S35	Scots as an element in the population
3508.T4	Theater
3509	Catalogs
3511	Ancient Africa
3513	Carthage
3515	North Africa
	Including the Barbary States and Sahel
3516	East Africa
	West Africa
3516.5	General works
3516.55	Ghana Empire
	Cf. Z3785 Ghana
3517	Central Africa
3518	Southern Africa
	Cf. Z3601+ South Africa
3520	Former Italian Africa (Collective)
3521-3525	Ethiopia. Abyssinia (Table Z3)
3526	Somalia
	Including former British and Italian Somaliland
	British Africa
3551.A1	Bibliography of bibliography
3551.A2	Theory, method, etc.
3551.A6-Z	General bibliography. Imprints (General)
	Including general bibliography of the region as subject
3554.A-Z	Special topics, A-Z
	Antiquities see Z3554.A8
3554.A8	Archaeology. Antiquities
	Drama see Z3554.L5
3554.E74	Ethnology
	Including individual ethnic groups
3554.H5	Historiography
	Juvenile literature see Z3554.L6
	Language see Z3554.L5
3554.L5	Literature, language, poetry, drama, etc.
3554.L6	Children's literature. Juvenile literature
	National characteristics see Z3554.P7
	Poetry see Z3554.L5
3554.P7	Psychology. National characteristics
3554.R3	Race relations
3555	Catalogs

Asia. Africa. Australia
    Africa
        British Africa -- Continued
3558   Lesotho. Basutoland
3559   Botswana. Bechuanaland
3560   Swaziland
                Central and South (General) see Z3518
3576   Rhodesia. Federation of Rhodesia and Nyasaland
3577   Malawi. Nyasaland
3578   Zimbabwe. Southern Rhodesia
3579   Zambia. Northern Rhodesia
                East (General) see Z3516
3586   Uganda
3587   Kenya
                Tanzania. Tanganyika. Former German East Africa
                    For former German colonies in Africa (General) see
                        Z3751+
3588   General bibliography
3589   Zanzibar
3597   Nigeria
3598   Sierra Leone
3601-3609   South Africa (Table Z2)
3631-3635   Zaire. Congo (Democratic Republic). Belgian Congo (Table
                    Z3)
3651-3659   Egypt (Table Z2)
3665   Sudan
3671-3675   French Africa (Table Z3)
3681-3685   Algeria (Table Z3)
3685.2   Tunisia
3686   Benin. Dahomey
3687   Djibouti (Republic). French Territory of the Afars and
                        Issas
3688   Guinea
3689   Côte d'Ivoire. Ivory Coast
3690   Burkina Faso
                    French-speaking Equatorial Africa
3691   General bibliography
3694   Central African Republic
3695   Chad
3696   Congo (Brazzaville)
3697   Gabon
                    French Sudan see Z3716
3701-3705   Madagascar (Table Z3)
3706   Mauritania
3707   Niger
3708   Réunion
3709   Sahara

Z1201-4980

	Asia. Africa. Australia
	Africa
	French Africa -- Continued
3711-3715	Senegal (Table Z3)
3716	Mali
3717	Ruanda-Urundi
3719	Burundi
3721	Rwanda
3735	Gambia
	German Africa (Former)
	For Tanganyika and the former German East Africa see Z3588+
3751-3755	General (Table Z3)
3761-3765	Cameroon (Table Z3)
3771-3775	Namibia. South-West Africa (Table Z3)
3778	Togo
3785	Ghana
	Cf. Z3516.55 Ghana Empire
	Italian Africa (Former) see Z3520
3821-3825	Liberia (Table Z3)
3836-3840	Morocco (Table Z3)
	Orange Free State see Z3601+
3871-3875	Portuguese Africa (Table Z3)
3877	Cape Verde
3878	Guinea-Bissau. Portuguese Guinea
3879	Sao Tome and Principe
3881-3885	Mozambique (Table Z3)
3891-3895	Angola (Table Z3)
	Spanish Africa
3931	General works
	Canary Islands see Z2681+
	Ifni see Z3836+
	Spanish Morocco see Z3836+
3933	Spanish West Africa. Spanish Sahara. Rio de Oro
3937-3941	Equatorial Guinea (Table Z3)
3971-3975	Libya (Table Z3)
	Australia. Oceania
4001	General bibliography
4008.A-Z	Special topics, A-Z
4009	Catalogs
	Australia
4011-4039	General (Table Z1)
4041-4069	New South Wales (Table Z1)
4101-4129	New Zealand (Table Z1)
4161-4169	Northern Territory (Table Z2)
4191-4219	Queensland (Table Z1)
4251-4279	South Australia (Table Z1)

	Asia. Africa. Australia
	Australia. Oceania
	Australia -- Continued
4311-4339	Tasmania (Table Z1)
4371-4399	Victoria (Table Z1)
4431-4439	Western Australia (Table Z2)
4501-5000	Oceania
	Including Melanesia, Micronesia, Polynesia
4501	General bibliography
4651	Fiji
4671	Gilbert Islands. Kiribati
4701-4709	Hawaiian Islands (Table Z2)
4741	Mariana Islands. Ladrone Islands
4781	Marshall Islands
4805	New Caledonia
4811-4815	New Guinea. Papua New Guinea (Table Z3)
4816	Irian Barat
4820	New Hebrides
4891	Samoan Islands
4898	Solomon Islands
4941	Tonga
4980.A-Z	Other islands, A-Z

Z1201-4980

Subject bibliography
    Subjects are arranged in an alphabetical sequence; however, since
        a large number of the subjects are broad in scope and supplied
        with subtopics, it is suggested that the general index to the
        schedule be used in locating any subject
    For abstracts giving substantive information, see the subject in
        classes A-Z
    For mechanized bibliographic control of subject bibliography
        see Z699.5.A+
Academies. Societies. Universities. Museums
    Including only bibliography of the learned publications whether
        official, faculty, or graduate
    Including conference proceedings in general, not limited to a
        specific topic, whether explicitly associated with an
        organization or not
    For bibliographies of society publications relating to a special
        subject, see the bibliography of that subject
    For bibliographies of universities or schools as subject see
        Z5816.A+
    Cf. Z6940+ Periodicals

5051	General bibliography
5051.5	International associations, congresses, conferences, etc.
	Museums
5052	General bibliography
5052.5.A-Z	By region or country, A-Z
	Dissertations. Theses
	Class here general bibliographies not confined to one country
5053.A1	Bibliography of bibliography
5053.A2	Theory, method, etc.
5053.A3-Z	General bibliography
	University publications (other than theses) see Z5814.U7
	By region or country
	For museums see Z5052.5.A+
5055.A38-.A384	Albania (Table Z16)
5055.A5-.A54	Angola (Table Z16)
5055.A57-.A574	Armenia (Republic) (Table Z16)
5055.A66-.A69	Argentina (Table Z17)
	Australia
5055.A696	General bibliography
5055.A697	Societies
	Universities
5055.A698	Collective
5055.A7A-.A7Z	Individual. By city and institution, A-Z
	Austria
5055.A77	General bibliography
5055.A78	Societies
	Universities

Z5051-7999

Academies. Societies. Universities. Museums
By region or country
Austria
Universities -- Continued
5055.A79	Collective
5055.A8A-.A8Z	Individual. By city and institution, A-Z
5055.B38-.B384	Belarus (Table Z16)
	Belgium
5055.B39	General bibliography
5055.B4	Societies
	Universities
5055.B49	Collective
5055.B5A-.B5Z	Individual. By city and institution, A-Z
5055.B55-.B554	Benin (Table Z16)
5055.B57-.B574	Bolivia (Table Z16)
	Brazil
5055.B77	General bibliography
5055.B78	Societies
	Universities
5055.B79	Collective
5055.B8A-.B8Z	Individual. By city and institution, A-Z
	Bulgaria
5055.B87	General bibliography
5055.B88	Societies
	Universities
5055.B89	Collective
5055.B9A-.B9Z	Individual. By city and institution, A-Z
5055.B94-.B944	Burundi (Table Z16)
5055.C18-.C184	Cameroon (Table Z16)
5055.C2-.C24	Canada (Table Z16)
5055.C52-.C524	Chile (Table Z16)
5055.C53-.C534	China (Table Z16)
5055.C61-.C614	Colombia (Table Z16)
5055.C62-.C624	Congo (Brazzaville) (Table Z16)
5055.C65-.C654	Costa Rica (Table Z16)
5055.C89-.C894	Cuba (Table Z16)
	Czech Republic
5055.C917	General bibliography
5055.C918	Societies
	Universities
5055.C919	Collective
5055.C92A-.C92Z	Individual. By city and institution, A-Z
5055.D3-.D34	Denmark (Table Z16)
5055.D65-.D654	Dominican Republic (Table Z16)
	Egypt
5055.E27	General bibliography
5055.E28	Societies

	Academies. Societies. Universities. Museums
	By region or country
	Egypt -- Continued
	Universities
5055.E29	Collective
5055.E3A-.E3Z	Individual. By city and institution, A-Z
	Estonia
5055.E79	General bibliography
5055.E8	Societies
	Universities
5055.E82	Collective
5055.E83A-.E83Z	Individual. By city and institution, A-Z
5055.E84-.E844	Ethiopia (Table Z16)
5055.F4-.F44	Fiji (Table Z16)
	Finland
5055.F49	General bibliography
5055.F5	Societies
	Universities
5055.F52	Collective
5055.F53A-.F53Z	Individual. By city and institution, A-Z
	France
5055.F69	General bibliography
5055.F7	Societies
	Universities
5055.F79	Collective
5055.F8A-.F8Z	Individual. By city, A-Z
5055.F8M7-.F8M79	Montpellier. Université
5055.G2-.G24	Gabon (Table Z16)
5055.G28-.G284	Georgia (Republic) (Table Z16)
	Germany
5055.G29	General bibliography
5055.G3	Societies
	Universities
5055.G39	Collective
5055.G4A-.G4Z	Individual. By city and institution, A-Z
	Great Britain
5055.G59	General bibliography
5055.G6	Societies
	Universities
5055.G69	Collective
5055.G7A-.G7Z	Individual. By city and institution, A-Z
5055.G8-.G84	Greece (Table Z16)
	Guatemala
5055.G89	General bibliography
5055.G9	Societies
	Universities
5055.G92	Collective

Academies. Societies. Universities. Museums
By region or country
Guatemala
Universities -- Continued

5055.G93A-.G93Z	Individual. By city and institution, A-Z
	Hungary
5055.H69	General bibliography
5055.H7	Societies
	Universities
5055.H79	Collective
5055.H8A-.H8Z	Individual. By city and institution, A-Z
5055.I3-.I34	Iceland (Table Z16)
	India
5055.I57	General bibliography
5055.I58	Societies
	Universities
5055.I59	Collective
5055.I6A-.I6Z	Individual. By city and institution, A-Z
5055.I63-.I66	Indonesia (Table Z17)
5055.I67-.I674	Iran (Table Z16)
5055.I676-.I679	Iraq (Table Z17)
5055.I7-.I74	Ireland (Table Z16)
5055.I75-.I754	Israel (Table Z16)
	Italy
5055.I78	General bibliography
5055.I785	Societies
	Universities
5055.I79	Collective
5055.I8A-.I8Z	Individual. By city and institution, A-Z
5055.J26-.J29	Jamaica (Table Z17)
5055.J3-.J34	Japan (Table Z16)
5055.J64-.J67	Jordan (Table Z17)
	Kazakhstan
5055.K3	General bibliography
5055.K32	Societies
	Universities
5055.K34	Collective
5055.K4A-.K4Z	Individual. By city and institution, A-Z
5055.K42-.K45	Kenya (Table Z17)
	Korea (South)
5055.K59	General bibliography
5055.K6	Societies
	Universities
5055.K62	Collective
5055.K63A-.K63Z	Individual. By city and institution, A-Z
5055.L3-.L34	Latvia (Table Z16)
	Lebanon

Z5051-7999

	Academies. Societies. Universities. Museums
	By region or country
	Lebanon -- Continued
5055.L396	General bibliography
5055.L397	Societies
	Universities
5055.L398	Collective
5055.L4A-.L4Z	Individual. By city and institution, A-Z
5055.L5-.L54	Lithuania (Table Z16)
5055.M25-.M254	Macedonia (Republic) (Table Z16)
	Madagascar
5055.M269	General bibliography
5055.M27	Societies
	Universities
5055.M272	Collective
5055.M273A-.M273Z	Individual. By city and institution, A-Z
5055.M28-.M284	Malawi (Table Z16)
5055.M34-.M37	Malaysia (Table Z17)
	Mexico
5055.M57	General bibliography
5055.M58	Societies
	Universities
5055.M59	Collective
5055.M6A-.M6Z	Individual. By city and institution, A-Z
	Morocco
5055.M69	General bibliography
5055.M7	Societies
	Universities
5055.M72	Collective
5055.M73A-.M73Z	Individual. By city and institution, A-Z
5055.M82-.M85	Mozambique (Table Z17)
5055.N432-.N435	Nepal (Table Z17)
	Netherlands
5055.N49	General bibliography
5055.N5	Societies
	Universities
5055.N59	Collective
5055.N6A-.N6Z	Individual. By city and institution, A-Z
	New Zealand
5055.N68	General bibliography
5055.N69	Societies
	Universities
5055.N7	Collective
5055.N72A-.N72Z	Individual. By city and institution, A-Z
	Niger
5055.N817	General bibliography
5055.N818	Societies

Academies. Societies. Universities. Museums
By region or country
Niger -- Continued
Universities

5055.N82	Collective
5055.N822A-.N822Z	Individual. By city and institution, A-Z
5055.N83-.N834	Nigeria (Table Z16)
	Norway
5055.N88	General bibliography
5055.N89	Societies
	Universities
5055.N9	Collective
5055.N92A-.N92Z	Individual. By city and institution, A-Z
5055.P3-.P34	Pakistan (Table Z16)
5055.P36-.P364	Panama (Table Z16)
5055.P38-.P384	Papua New Guinea (Table Z16)
	Philippines
5055.P47	General bibliography
5055.P48	Societies
	Universities
5055.P49	Collective
5055.P5A-.P5Z	Individual. By city and institution, A-Z
	Poland
5055.P57	General bibliography
5055.P58	Societies
	Universities
5055.P59	Collective
5055.P6A-.P6Z	Individual. By city and institution, A-Z
	Portugal
5055.P7	General bibliography
5055.P72	Societies
	Universities
5055.P75	Collective
5055.P8A-.P8Z	Individual. By city and institution, A-Z
5055.P9-.P94	Puerto Rico (Table Z16)
5055.R4-.R44	Réunion (Table Z16)
	Romania
5055.R58	General bibliography
5055.R59	Societies
	Universities
5055.R6	Collective
5055.R63A-.R63Z	Individual. By city and institution, A-Z
	Russia
5055.R78	General bibliography
5055.R8	Societies
	Universities
5055.R89	Collective

Z5051-7999

	Academies. Societies. Universities. Museums
	By region or country
	Russia
	Universities -- Continued
5055.R9A-.R9Z	Individual. By city and institution, A-Z
5055.R96-.R964	Rwanda (Table Z16)
5055.S33-.S334	Saudi Arabia (Table Z16)
	Scotland
5055.S35	General bibliography
5055.S352	Societies
	Universities
5055.S353	Collective
5055.S36A-.S36Z	Individual. By city and institution, A-Z
	Senegal
5055.S37	General bibliography
5055.S372	Societies
	Universities
5055.S3725	Collective
5055.S373A-.S373Z	Individual. By city and institution, A-Z
5055.S38-.S384	Singapore (Table Z16)
	Slovakia
5055.S39	General bibliography
5055.S395	Societies
	Universities
5055.S4	Collective
5055.S42A-.S42Z	Individual. By city and institution, A-Z
	South Africa
5055.S45	General bibliography
5055.S453	Societies
	Universities
5055.S455	Collective
5055.S46A-.S46Z	Individual. By city and institution, A-Z
	Soviet Union
5055.S465	General bibliography
5055.S466	Societies
	Universities
5055.S467	Collective
	Individual
	see the appropriate country, e.g. Russia, Z5055.R9 ; Ukraine, Z5055.U254
	Spain
5055.S47	General bibliography
5055.S48	Societies
	Universities
5055.S49	Collective
5055.S5A-.S5Z	Individual. By city and institution, A-Z
	Sri Lanka

Academies. Societies. Universities. Museums
 By region or country
  Sri Lanka -- Continued

5055.S66	General bibliography
5055.S662	Societies
	Universities
5055.S67	Collective
5055.S674A-.S674Z	Individual. By city and institution, A-Z
5055.S68-.S684	Swaziland (Table Z16)
	Sweden
5055.S69	General bibliography
5055.S7	Societies
	Universities
5055.S79	Collective
5055.S81A-.S81Z	Individual. By city and institution, A-Z
	Switzerland
5055.S87	General bibliography
5055.S88	Societies
	Universities
5055.S89	Collective
5055.S9A-.S9Z	Individual. By city and institution, A-Z
5055.S96-.S964	Syria (Table Z16)
5055.T25-.T28	Taiwan (Table Z17)
5055.T35-.T354	Tanzania (Table Z16)
5055.T6-.T64	Togo (Table Z16)
	Turkey
5055.T87	General bibliography
5055.T88	Societies
	Universities
5055.T89	Collective
5055.T9A-.T9Z	Individual. By city and institution, A-Z
5055.U2-.U24	Uganda (Table Z16)
5055.U25-.U254	Ukraine (Table Z16)
	United States
5055.U39	General bibliography
5055.U4	Societies
5055.U49	Doctoral dissertations
5055.U5A-.U5Z	Universities, etc., A-Z
5055.U5H3-.U5H39	Harvard University
5055.U9-.U94	Uzbekistan (Table Z16)
5055.V3-.V6	Venezuela (Table Z17)
5055.W3-.W34	Wales (Table Z16)
5055.Z25-.Z28	Zaire (Table Z17)
5055.Z33-.Z334	Zambia (Table Z16)
5056	Catalogs
	Aerospace technology
5060.A1	Bibliography of bibliography

Z5051-7999

	Aerospace technology -- Continued
5060.A2	Periodicals. Societies
5060.A3-Z	General bibliography
	Astronautics
5061.A1	Bibliography of bibliography
5061.A2	Periodicals
5061.A3-Z	General bibliography
	Aeronautics
5063.A1	Bibliography of bibliography
5063.A2	Periodicals. Societies
5063.A3-Z	General bibliography
5064.A-Z	Special topics, A-Z
5064.A2	Aerodynamics
5064.A25	Aeroplanes (Airplanes)
5064.A26	Air cushion vehicles
5064.A27	Airlines
	Airplanes see Z5064.A25
5064.A28	Airports
5064.A32	Airships
5064.A7	Artificial satellites
	Astronautics in meteorology see Z6683.A7
5064.B3	Batteries
	Charts, Aeronautical see Z6026.A2
5064.C7	Commercial aviation
5064.C8	Communication systems (Astronautics)
5064.D4	Design and construction of airplanes
5064.E4	Education
5064.F5	Flying saucers
5064.F8	Freight and express service. Air cargo
5064.F9	Fuel and fuel systems
5064.G55	Gliders
5064.H44	Heliports
5064.L8	Lunar bases
5064.M3	Materials
	Medical aspects see Z6664.3
5064.M47	Meteorology in aeronautics
5064.N3	Navigation. Aids to navigation
5064.N6	Noise
5064.O7	Orbital rendezvous
5064.P3	Parachutes. Parachuting
5064.P6	Pilots
5064.P62	Planetary quarantine
5064.P64	Politics. Air power. Space power
5064.P7	Aeronautics as a profession
5064.R2	Radio in aeronautics
5064.R6	Rockets
	Cf. Z6724.G8 Guided missiles

	Aerospace technology
	Special topics, A-Z -- Continued
5064.S3	Safety measures
5064.S5	Shock waves
5064.S68	Space colonies. Space communities
	Space communities see Z5064.S68
5064.S7	Space flight to Mars
5064.S8	Space vehicles
5064.S89	Study and teaching
5064.T7	Traffic control
	UFO's see Z5064.F5
	Unidentified flying objects see Z5064.F5
5064.W4	Weight control engineering
5065.A-Z	By region or country, A-Z
5066	Catalogs
5069	Aesthetics
	Cf. Z5931+ Fine arts
5071-5076	Agriculture (Table Z4 modified)
	Cf. Z5701 Cotton
	Cf. Z5706+ Dairying
	Cf. Z5856+ Entomology
	Cf. Z5991 Forestry
	Cf. Z5996+ Gardening
	Cf. Z6674 Veterinary medicine
	Cf. Z7164.C93 Cooperative agriculture
	Cf. Z7609+ Sugar
	Cf. Z7882 Tobacco
	Cf. Z7971+ Wool
5074.A-Z	Special topics, A-Z
5074.A2	Country life (Amateur farming, etc.)
5074.A4	Aeronautics in agriculture
	Agricultural innovations see Z5074.I55
5074.A6	Agrobiodiversity
	Including agrobiodiversity conservation
5074.A7	Agroforestry
5074.A8	Agrostology (Grasses)
5074.A815	Alternative agriculture
5074.A816	Amaranths
	Including grain and vegetable amaranths
5074.A817	Andropogon gayanus
5074.A82	Annatto tree
5074.A83	Arid regions agriculture
	Cf. Z5074.D8 Dry farming
	Cf. Z5074.I7 Irrigation
5074.A85	Aromatic plants
5074.A87	Asparagus
	Artificial plant growing media see Z5074.P64

Z5051-7999

Agriculture
Special topics, A-Z -- Continued

5074.B33	Bamboo
5074.B35	Barley
5074.B4	Beans
5074.B47	Betel nut
5074.B54	Biotechnology
5074.B8	Buckwheat
5074.B9	Farm buildings
5074.B94	Burning of land. Prescribed burning
5074.C25	Cacao
5074.C27	Camels
5074.C28	Cassava
5074.C3	Castor bean
5074.C33	Cattle

Including beef cattle

5074.C4	Chemistry
5074.C5	Cinchona
5074.C55	Coconut and coconut palm

Coffee see Z5601

5074.C57	Compost
5074.C58	Conservation and agricultural resources

Cf. Z5074.S65 Soil conservation

5074.C6	Corn

Cotton see Z5701

5074.C63	Cowpea
5074.C65	Crambe abyssinica
5074.C7	Credit
5074.C75	Cropping systems
5074.C9	Crops
5074.C95	Cucumber
5074.D37	Data processing
5074.D73	Draft animals (General)

Including animal traction

5074.D75	Drainage
5074.D8	Dry farming
5074.E29	Ecology, Agricultural
5074.E3	Economic aspects

Education see Z5818.A5

5074.E48	Emus
5074.E54	Energy and agriculture

Including energy consumption

5074.E6	Engineering
5074.E63	Ensilage
5074.E8	Extension work
5074.F25	Farm management
5074.F35	Feeds and feeding

Agriculture
  Special topics, A-Z -- Continued
5074.F4   Fertilizers
5074.F55   Fique
5074.F6   Flax
5074.F7   Forage plants
                     Fumigation see Z5074.P4
                     Fur bearing animals see Z5994.6
5074.G45   Geography
5074.G55   Ginseng
5074.G8   Grain
                     Grain amaranths see Z5074.A816
                     Grapes see Z5996.G7
                     Grasses see Z5074.A8
5074.G85   Green manuring
5074.G87   Grevillea robusta
5074.G9   Guar
5074.G92   Guarana
5074.H5   Hemp. Sisal hemp, etc.
5074.H58   Hevea
5074.H6   Hill farming
5074.H63   Historic farms
5074.H64   Hops
5074.H9   Hydroponics
5074.I55   Innovations
                         Including innovation diffusion and technology transfer
5074.I57   International cooperation
5074.I7   Irrigation
5074.J58   Jojoba
5074.J8   Jute
5074.L2   Labor productivity
5074.L24   Laboratory animals (Culture)
5074.L27   Land capability for agriculture
5074.L3   Legumes
5074.L7   Livestock
                         Cf. Z5074.R27 Range management
                         Cf. Z5862.2.A53 Animal waste (Pollution)
                         Cf. Z6674 Veterinary medicine
5074.L75   Location
                     Macadamia nut see Z5996.M3
5074.M18   Machinery
                     Maize see Z5074.C6
5074.M26   Malva
                     Marketing of produce see Z5074.E3
5074.M35   Mathematics
                     Meteorology see Z6683.A4
5074.M5   Millet

Z5051-7999

	Agriculture
	Special topics, A-Z -- Continued
5074.O5	Oil palm
5074.O56	Oilseed plants
5074.O75	Organic farming
5074.O77	Ostriches
5074.P27	Palms
5074.P3	Pastures
	Cf. Z5074.R27 Range management
5074.P34	Peanuts
	Peat see Z6915
5074.P38	Pepper (Spice). Piper nigrum
5074.P39	Peppers (Vegetables)
5074.P398	Pesticide resistance and tolerance
	Including herbicide resistance and tolerance
	Pesticides and environment see Z5322.P43
5074.P4	Pests and diseases. Pest control. Pesticides
	Including treatment, spraying, fumigation, etc.
	Cf. Z5354.P3A+ Diseases and pests of particular plants
	Cf. Z5858.E2 Economic entomology
	Pets see Z6980
5074.P58	Pigeon pea
5074.P6	Pigeons
5074.P63	Piper betle
	Piper nigrum see Z5074.P38
	Plant breeding see Z5354.P7
5074.P64	Plant growing media, Artificial
	Including types of media
5074.P644	Plant regulators
5074.P665	Plastics
	Pollution, Agricultural see Z5862.2.A35
5074.P75	Potatoes
5074.P8	Poultry
	Prescribed burning see Z5074.B94
	Propagation see Z5354.P8
5074.Q5	Quinoa
5074.R2	Radioisotopes
5074.R27	Rangelands
	Including range management
5074.R3	Rape (Plant)
5074.R37	Rattan palms
5074.R4	Reclamation of land
5074.R47	Research
5074.R49	Rhus
5074.R5	Rice
5074.R58	Root and tuber crops
5074.R6	Roselle

	Agriculture
	Special topics, A-Z -- Continued
5074.S2	Safflower
5074.S25	Salt-tolerant crops
5074.S35	Scrapie
5074.S44	Seeds
	Including growing, production, and industry
5074.S49	Sheep
	Cf. Z7971+ Wool
5074.S53	Shifting cultivation
	Sisal hemp see Z5074.H5
5074.S65	Soil conservation
5074.S68	Soil erosion
5074.S7	Soils
	Cf. Z6915 Peat
5074.S714	Solar energy
5074.S72	Sorghum
5074.S73	Soybeans
5074.S75	Spices (General)
5074.S76	Statistics
5074.S78	Sterility in animals
5074.S8	Storage of produce
	Sugarcane see Z7610.S8
5074.S9	Sunflowers
5074.S92	Sustainable agriculture
5074.S94	Sweet potatoes
5074.S96	Swine
5074.T34	Taro
5074.T38	Taxation
5074.T4	Tea
5074.T56	Tillage
	Tobacco see Z7882
5074.T8	Transportation of produce
5074.T84	Tropical crops
	Tuber crops see Z5074.R58
5074.U72	Urban agriculture
5074.W3	Water
5074.W33	Water buffalo
	Weeds see Z5354.W44
5074.W5	Wheat
5074.Z4	Zebus
5095	Almanacs
	Cf. Z1231.A6 American almanacs
	Amusements see Z7511+
5106	Ana
	Cf. Z7191 Proverbs
	Anatomy see Z6662+

Z5051-7999

	Anthropology and ethnology
	For individual tribes see Z1201+
5111	General bibliography
	Including general special
5112	Periodicals. Societies
	Local
5113	Africa
	America see Z1209
5114	Arctic regions
5115	Asia
5116	Australia. Pacific islands
5117	Europe
5118.A-Z	Special topics, A-Z
	Aged. Aging see Z7164.O4
5118.A45	Ainu
5118.A5	Anthropogeography
5118.A53	Anthropometry
5118.A54	Applied anthropology
5118.A6	Archaeology. Prehistoric man
	Cf. Z5131+ Archaeology (Antiquities)
	Art, Primitive see Z5956.P68
5118.A7	Aryans
5118.B3	Batak
5118.B5	Black race
5118.C44	Celts
5118.C57	Circumcision. Clitoridectomy
	Cf. Z6667.C57 Surgery
	Clitoridectomy see Z5118.C57
5118.C64	Consanguinity. Inbreeding
5118.C9	Crime in pre-literate societies
5118.C93	Csangos
5118.C95	Culture shock
	Including reverse culture shock
5118.D45	Dental anthropology
5118.D47	Dermatoglyphics. Fingerprints
5118.E25	Economics
	Educational anthropology see Z5814.E2
5118.E84	Ethnicity. Ethnic groups (General)
5118.E86	Ethnobotany
5118.E87	Ethnozoology
5118.F2	Family
	Cf. Z7164.M2 Marriage
	Cf. Z7961+ Woman
5118.F27	Farming. Traditional farming. Traditional agriculture
5118.F44	Fieldwork
	Fingerprints see Z5118.D47
5118.F46	Finno-Ugrians

Anthropology and ethnology
Special topics, A-Z -- Continued
5118.F58	Food
5118.F6	Foot
5118.G5	Gypsies. Romanies
5118.H85	Human body (Social aspects)
5118.H86	Hunting and gathering societies
	Inbreeding see Z5118.C64
5118.M3	Maritime anthropology
5118.M36	Masks
5118.M4	Medicine. Medical anthropology
5118.M43	Megalithic monuments
5118.M5	Miscegenation
	Negro race see Z5118.B5
5118.N65	Nomads
5118.P33	Peaceful societies
5118.P5	Philosophy
5118.P54	Physical anthropology
	Cf. Z5118.A53 Anthropometry
5118.P65	Political anthropology
5118.P67	Pottery
5118.P9	Pygmies
	Religion (Primitive) see Z7833
5118.R5	Rites and ceremonies
	Romanies see Z5118.G5
5118.S6	Slavs
5118.S7	Somatology
5118.T7	Totemism
	Traditional agriculture see Z5118.F27
	Traditional farming see Z5118.F27
5118.T87	Turkic peoples
5118.U72	Urban anthropology
5118.V58	Visual anthropology
	Including motion pictures and photography
5118.W3	Warfare, Primitive
5118.W65	Women
5119	Catalogs
	Aquaculture see Z5970
	Archaeology
	For local see Z1201+
	For special subjects see Z5051+
	Cf. Z5118.A6 Prehistoric archaeology
	Cf. Z5931+ Fine arts
5131	General bibliography
5132	Periodicals. Societies
5133.A-Z	Special topics, A-Z
5133.A34	Aerial photography. Remote sensing

Z5051-7999

	Archaeology
	Special topics, A-Z -- Continued
5133.D37	Dating
	Industrial archaeology see Z7914.I48
5133.P48	Petroglyphs
5133.P73	Preservation, restoration, and conservation of antiquities
	Including historic monuments, landmarks, and scenery
	Cf. Z1251.A2 Historic preservation in the United States
	Cf. Z5940 Artistic monuments
5133.R46	Remains of special materials
	Remote sensing see Z5133.A34
5133.U53	Underwater archaeology
5134	Catalogs
	Architecture see Z5941+
5140	Archives. Records
	For inventories, calendars, etc. of individual archives, see subclass CD
	For special archives by subject see Z6611.A+
	For papers of individuals see Z6616.A3+
	Cf. Z6208.A7 History
	Art see Z5931+
	Arts and crafts see Z6151+
	Astrology see Z6878.A88
	Astronautics see Z5061.A1+
5151-5156	Astronomy (Table Z4 modified)
	Cf. Z6651+ Mathematics
5151	General bibliography
5151.5	Atlases. Charts. Diagrams. Maps, etc.
	Including star catalogs
5154.A-Z	Special topics, A-Z
5154.A85	Asteroids
5154.C4	Comets
5154.C7	Constellations
5154.C78	Cosmology
5154.D6	Double stars
5154.G34	Galaxies
5154.G7	Gravity
5154.H2	Halley's comet
5154.H57	History
5154.I5	Interstellar matter
5154.L5	Life on other planets
5154.M3	Magellanic Clouds
5154.M55	Mercury
5154.M7	Moon
5154.N5	Nebulae
5154.O27	Observatories
5154.P53	Planetariums

	Astronomy
	Special topics, A-Z -- Continued
5154.P55	Planets
5154.R3	Radio astronomy
5154.S65	Spectrum analysis
5154.S8	Stars
5154.S9	Sun
5154.T5	Tides
5158	Atmospheric radioactivity
5160-5164	Atomic energy and power. Nuclear engineering (Table Z6 modified)
	Cf. Z7144.N8 Nuclear physics
5162.A-Z	Special topics, A-Z
5162.A26	Accidents
5162.C57	Citizen participation
5162.C68	Costs
5162.R42	Reactors
5165	Authorship (General)
	Autobiography see Z5301+
5167	Automation
	Cf. Z6333.A8 Iron and steel industry
	Automobiles. Automobile travel. Motor vehicles
	Cf. Z7514.M68 Motorsports
5170	General bibliography
5171	Catalogs
5173.A-Z	Special topics, A-Z
5173.A2	Abandoned vehicles
5173.A5	Air conditioning
5173.A54	All terrain vehicles
5173.C6	Cold weather operation
5173.E43	Electric vehicles
5173.F7	Freight
5173.L5	Lighting
5173.M3	Maintenance and repair
5173.M58	Motorcycles
5173.M6	Motors
5173.P3	Parking
5173.P6	Pollution control devices
5173.S2	Safety measures
5173.S65	Spray control
5173.T7	Trailers. Mobile homes
	Aviation see Z5063.A1+
	Bacteriology. Microbiology
	Cf. Z6658+ Medicine
	Cf. Z6704+ Microscopy
5180	General bibliography
5185.A-Z	Special topics, A-Z

Z5051-7999

Bacteriology. Microbiology
  Special topics, A-Z -- Continued
5185.A52   Anaerobic bacteria
5185.B53   Bifidobacterium
5185.F4   Fermentation
                    Cf. Z7914.B6 Brewing
5185.F66   Food microbiology
5185.L3   Lactobacillus
5185.M92   Mycoplasmatales
5185.P36   Pathogenic microorganisms
5185.R5   Rhizobium
5185.S3   Salmonella
5185.V5   Viruses
5185.W37   Water microbiology
5230   Beauty culture
5256   Bees and bee culture
5275   Bells
                Biography. Genealogy. Heraldry
                  Cf. Z1201+ Biobibliography as subdivision under names of
                    countries in National bibliography
5301   General bibliography
                    Cf. Z6824 Names
                    Cf. Z8001.A1+ Personal bibliography
5304.A-Z   By class, A-Z
                    Class here classes not provided for under subjects
                    e.g.
5304.C44   Celebrities
5305.A-Z   By region or country, A-Z
                  Genealogy and heraldry
5311   General bibliography. Genealogy (separately)
5312   Heraldry (separately)
                    Cf. Z5980 Flags
5313.A-Z   By region or country, A-Z
                    Subarrange each country (except the United States) by Table
                      Z15
                    United States
5313.U5   General
5313.U6A-.U6Z   Local, A-Z
5315.A-Z   By family, A-Z
                    Cf. Z8001.A1+ Personal bibliography
5319   Catalogs
                Biology
                  Cf. Z5351+ Botany
                  Cf. Z6662+ Anatomy and physiology
                  Cf. Z6704+ Microscopy
                  Cf. Z7991+ Zoology
5320   General bibliography

Biology -- Continued

5321	Periodicals. Societies
5322.A-Z	Special topics, A-Z
5322.A25	Acid precipitation
5322.A57	Air pollution and the environment
5322.A62	Aquatic biology
5322.A74	Arid regions ecology
5322.B46	Benthos
	Biodiversity see Z5322.B53
5322.B5	Bioethics
5322.B53	Biological diversity. Biodiversity. Biodiversity conservation
5322.B54	Biological invasions
	Biophysics see Z7144.B5
	Biotechnology see Z7914.B33
5322.C3	Cell
5322.C62	Coastal ecology
5322.C67	Coral reef ecology
5322.C9	Cultures
	Death see Z5725
5322.D47	Desert ecology
5322.E2	Ecology
5322.E26	Ecosystem health
5322.E43	Electrophoresis
5322.E85	Eutrophication
5322.E9	Evolution
5322.E95	Exobiology
5322.F57	Fire ecology
5322.F65	Forest ecology
	Cf. Z5354.F75 Botany
5322.F7	Freshwater biology
5322.F73	Freshwater ecology
5322.G4	Genetics
5322.H8	Human genetics
	Cf. Z6675.M4 Medical genetics
	Cf. Z7164.E9 Eugenics (Sociology)
5322.H93	Hybridization
5322.I8	Isotopes
5322.L4	Lead and the environment
	Cf. Z5862.2.L4 Lead pollution
	Cf. Z7891.L4 Toxicology
5322.M27	Mangrove swamp ecology
5322.M3	Marine biology
5322.M32	Marine ecology
5322.M33	Marine radioecology
5322.M66	Mountain ecology
5322.N83	Nuclear warfare and the environment. Nuclear winter
	Nuclear winter see Z5322.N83

Z5051-7999

Biology
   Special topics, A-Z -- Continued
5322.O4   Oil spills and wildlife
5322.O74   Origin of life
5322.O87   Outdoor recreation and the environment
5322.P4   Periodicity
5322.P43   Pesticides and the environment
                        Cf. Z6663.P44 Physiological effect
                        Cf. Z7891.P47 Toxicology
5322.P44   Phenology
5322.P45   Philosophy
5322.P5   Plankton
5322.P64   Pollution and the environment
5322.R2   Radioecology
5322.R3   Regeneration
5322.S47   Shot (Pellets) and the environment
                        Cf. Z5862.2.L4 Lead pollution
5322.S49   Shrubland ecology
5322.S75   Stream ecology
5322.S84   Sulfur and the environment. Sulfur cycle
5322.U72   Urban ecology
5322.W38   Water quality bioassay
5322.W47   Wetland ecology
5323   Catalogs
5331-5335   Birds. Ornithology (Table Z6 modified)
5333.A-Z   Special topics, A-Z
                General
5333.A12   Air sac
5333.A15   Anatomy
5333.A19   Color
                Conservation see Z5333.A42
5333.A22   Eggs
5333.A25   Embryology
5333.A29   Feathers
5333.A33   Food
5333.A37   Migration
5333.A38   Mortality
5333.A42   Protection. Conservation
               Taxonomic
                Anatidae see Z5333.D8
5333.A8   Auk
5333.B55   Blackbirds
5333.C34   Calidris
5333.C6   Condors
5333.C64   Corvidae
5333.D8   Ducks, geese, and swans. Anatidae
5333.E2   Eagles

Birds. Ornithology
   Special topics, A-Z
     Taxonomic -- Continued

5333.E55	Emperor goose
5333.F34	Falcons
5333.G73	Grebes
5333.G85	Guineafowl
5333.H8	Hungarian partridge
5333.L47	Lesser scaup
5333.L7	Limicolae
5333.O8	Ostriches
	Owl, Spotted see Z5333.S66
5333.O97	Owls
5333.P37	Parrots
5333.P45	Penguins
5333.P47	Peregrine falcon
5333.P49	Phalaropes
5333.Q34	Quails
	Including individual species
5333.S24	Sage grouse
5333.S4	Sea birds
5333.S66	Spotted owl
	Swans see Z5333.D8
5333.W64	Woodstock

Blind, The

5346.A2-.A39	Periodicals. Societies
5346.A4-.Z8	General bibliography
5346.Z9	Books in raised type
5347	Talking books
5348	Large type books
5349.A-Z	Special topics, A-Z
5349.A66	Apparatus for the blind
5349.H43	Health
5349.H6	Home economics
5349.S65	Sports
5349.T7	Travel. Mobility
5349.U6	United States history

Botany
   Cf. Z5996+ Gardening
   Cf. Z6033.P2 Paleontology

5351.A1	Bibliography of bibliography
5351.A3-Z	General bibliography
5352	Bibliography of early works
5353	Periodicals. Societies
5354.A-Z	Special topics (General), A-Z
5354.A44	Allelopathy. Allelopathic agents
5354.A5	Anatomy

Botany
　Special topics (General), A-Z -- Continued
5354.B56	Biography
5354.B67	Botanical gardens
5354.B68	Botanical illustrations
5354.C37	Carbon dioxide (Effect on plants)
5354.C44	Cell and tissue culture
5354.C5	Chemistry
5354.C52	Chromosomes. Chromosome numbers
5354.C53	Classification. Taxonomy
5354.E1	Ecology
5354.E2	Economic botany
5354.E33	Edible plants
	Endangered plants see Z5354.P73
	Ethnobotany see Z5118.E86
5354.F6	Fertilization of plants
5354.F66	Flavonoids
5354.F75	Forest ecology
5354.G45	Genetics
5354.G8	Growth
5354.I57	Invasive plants
5354.M42	Medical botany
	Cf. Z6665.H47 Herb therapy
5354.M83	Mucilage
5354.N4	Nectaries
	Pathology
	Cf. Z5074.P4 Pest control
5354.P2	General works
5354.P3A-.P3Z	Diseases and pests of individual plants or trees, A-Z
	e. g.
5354.P3C4	Chestnut blight
5354.P43	Pectins
5354.P46	Phenology
5354.P48	Photoperiodism
5354.P5	Photosynthesis
5354.P53	Phreatophytes
5354.P57	Physiology
5354.P58	Phytochrome
5354.P7	Plant breeding
5354.P72	Plant communities
5354.P73	Plant conservation. Rare plants. Endangered plants
5354.P77	Pollen
5354.P8	Propagation
	Rare plants see Z5354.P73
5354.R6	Roots
5354.S35	Salt (Effect on plants)
5354.S4	Seeds

	Botany
	Special topics (General), A-Z -- Continued
5354.S94	Sulfur dioxide (Effect on plants)
	Taxonomy see Z5354.C53
5354.T4	Temperature (Effect on plants)
	Tissue culture see Z5354.C44
5354.T7	Transpiration
5354.V43	Vegetation monitoring
5354.W44	Weeds
	Including control
	For individual weeds and groups of weeds, see the individual
	or group, e. g. Z5356.I4 Imperta
5354.W64	Wood
	For Technology see Z7914.W8
5356.A-Z	Special topics (Taxonomic), A-Z
5356.A42	Agaricales
5356.A6	Algae
5356.A65	Amaranths
5356.A68	Annonaceae
5356.A8	Asclepiadaceae
5356.A95	Azolla
5356.B3	Bamboo
5356.B38	Beetleweed
5356.B4	Beggar-weed
5356.B55	Bloodroot
5356.B7	Bryophytes
5356.C45	Chrysophyceae
5356.C57	Cirsium arvense
5356.C65	Conifers
5356.C78	Cryptogams
5356.D34	Dalbergia
5356.D47	Desmidiaceae
5356.D5	Diatoms
5356.D52	Dicotyledons
5356.D56	Dinoflagellates
5356.E37	Eastern redcedar
5356.E9	Eucalyptus
	Ferns see Z5356.P75
5356.F97	Fungi
5356.G5	Ginseng
5356.G65	Goldenseal
	Grasses see Z5074.A8
5356.H36	Hemlock
5356.H4	Hepaticae
5356.H64	Hollies
5356.H95	Hypomycetaceae

Z5051-7999

	Botany
	Special topics (Taxonomic), A-Z -- Continued
(5356.I2)	Ilex
	see Z5356.H64
5356.I4	Imperata
5356.I7	Iris
5356.L27	Lantana camara
5356.L3	Lauraceae
5356.L5	Leguminosae
5356.L53	Lichens
5356.L55	Liliales
5356.L57	Liriodendron tulipifera
5356.L58	Liverworts
5356.L93	Lycoperdales
5356.M33	Macrophomina phaseolina
5356.M37	Mentha
5356.M4	Mesquite
5356.M6	Mosses
5356.M95	Myxomycetes
5356.N4	Neurospora
5356.O2	Oak
5356.O8	Orchidaceae
5356.P28	Palms
5356.P3	Papaver
5356.P45	Phallales
5356.P5	Pine
5356.P52	Piperaceae
5356.P6	Poplar
5356.P75	Pteridophyta
5356.P95	Pythium
5356.R42	Red alder
5356.R43	Red rice
5356.S65	Spruce
5356.T4	Teak
5356.T8	Trees and shrubs (General)
	Cf. Z5991 Forestry
	Cf. Z5996.T74 Trees in cities
5356.Y48	Yew
5358.A-Z	Local, A-Z
	e.g.
5358.A18	Africa
5358.A2	Africa, South
5358.A4	America
5358.A7	Arctic regions
5358.A8	Argentina
5358.A82	Asia

	Botany
	Local, A-Z -- Continued
(5358.A83)	Asia, Southeastern
	see Z5358.S64
5358.C2	Canada
5358.C5	China
5358.C9	Czechoslovakia
5358.D3	Denmark
5358.E8	Europe
5358.F8	France
5358.G3	Germany
5358.G7	Great Britain
5358.I8	Italy
5358.K6	Korea
	Melanesia see Z5358.O3
5358.M6	Mexico
	Micronesia see Z5358.O3
5358.N86	North America
5358.N88	Norway
5358.O3	Oceania
	Including Micronesia, Melanesia, Polynesia
5358.P65	Poland
	Polynesia see Z5358.O3
5358.R9	Russia. Soviet Union
	South Africa see Z5358.A2
5358.S5	South America
5358.S64	Southeast Asia
5358.S7	Spain
5358.S9	Sweden
5358.S92	Switzerland
5358.U4	Ukraine
	United States
5358.U49	General works
5358.U5A-.U5Z	By region or state, A-Z
5360	Catalogs
5440	Calendars
	Canals
5451	General bibliography
5452.A-Z	Interoceanic, A-Z
	e. g.
5452.A2	General bibliography
5452.N5	Nicaragua Canal
5452.P2	Panama Canal
5481	Cards and card playing
	Cf. Z7164.G35 Gambling. Casino gaming
	Cartography see Z6021+
	Casino gaming see Z7164.G35

Z5051-7999

5491	Cats
5521-5526	Chemistry (Table Z4 modified)
	Cf. Z6675.P5 Pharmacy
	Cf. Z6678+ Metallurgy
	Cf. Z7890+ Toxicology
	Cf. Z7914.C4 Chemical engineering
5524.A-Z	Special topics, A-Z
5524.A31	Aceto acetic ester
5524.A33	Acetylene
5524.A335	Acids
5524.A337	Adenylic acid
5524.A34	Aerosols
5524.A35	Alchemy
	Cf. Z6876+ Occult sciences
	Cf. Z8658 Paracelsus
5524.A37	Alkali metal halides
5524.A38	Alkaloids
5524.A4	Alloys
5524.A5	Aluminum
5524.A52	Analysis
5524.A55	Aniline
5524.A75	Aromatic compounds
5524.B37	Barium
5524.B5	Beryllium
5524.B54	Biochemistry
	Cf. Z6662+ Physiology
5524.B56	Bioorganic chemistry
5524.B58	Bituminous materials
5524.B7	Boron
5524.B9	Butines
5524.C25	Cadmium
5524.C27	Camphor
5524.C3	Carbides
5524.C32	Carbohydrates
5524.C33	Catalysis
5524.C38	Centrifuges
5524.C41	Cerium
5524.C47	Chemical bonds
5524.C49	Chitin
5524.C5	Chloropicrin
5524.C55	Chromatography
5524.C58	Chromium
5524.C6	Cigarette smoke
5524.C65	Cobalt
5524.C68	Collagen
5524.C7	Colloids
5524.C72	Columbium

	Chemistry
	Special topics, A-Z -- Continued
5524.C8	Crystallography
5524.C94	Cyclic compounds
5524.D45	Deuterium
5524.D55	Didymium
5524.D58	Distillation
	Earths, Rare see Z5524.R4
5524.E36	Electrochemistry
5524.E39	Electrolysis
5524.E43	Electrophoresis .
5524.E5	Enzymes
5524.E8	Ethylene and ethylene compounds
5524.E9	Extraction
5524.F35	Fermentation
5524.F55	Flame
5524.F6	Fluorine
5524.F84	Fullerenes
5524.F9	Furocoumarins
5524.F93	Fused salts
5524.G2	Gallium
5524.G24	Gases
	Geochemistry see Z6033.G26
5524.G4	Germanium
5524.H4	Helium
5524.H9	Hydrocyanic acid
	Cf. Z5074.P4 Pests
5524.H94	Hydrogen
5524.I3	Indium
5524.I6	Iodine
5524.I65	Ion exchange
5524.I67	Ionic solutions
5524.I85	Isomerism
5524.L22	Lactams
5524.L29	Lanthanum
5524.L48	Levulinic acid
5524.L55	Liquid crystals
5524.L6	Lithium
	Macromolecules see Z5524.P7
5524.M15	Magnesium
5524.M2	Manganese
5524.M6	Molybdenum
5524.M7	Morphine
5524.N53	Nitrogen
5524.N55	Nitrosyl chloride
5524.N8	Nucleic acids
5524.O8	Organic chemistry

Z5051-7999

Chemistry
   Special topics, A-Z -- Continued

5524.O82	Organometallic chemistry
5524.O84	Oxidation-reduction
5524.O86	Oximes
5524.O87	Oxygen
5524.O9	Ozone
5524.P36	Periodic law
5524.P4	Permeability
5524.P5	Phase rule and equilibrium
5524.P54	Phenothiazine
	Cf. Z6664.H4 Helminthology
	Cf. Z6665.P45 Therapeutic use
5524.P56	Phosphorus
5524.P57	Photochemistry
5524.P6	Physical chemistry
5524.P66	Plutonium
5524.P68	Polarography
5524.P7	Polymers. Macromolecules
5524.P75	Porphin
5524.P83	Proteins
5524.Q35	Quantum chemistry
5524.R25	Radiation chemistry
5524.R27	Radioactivation analysis
5524.R3	Radiochemistry
5524.R4	Rare earths
5524.R5	Reaction rate
5524.R55	Rhenium
5524.R8	Ruthenium
5524.S35	Sampling
5524.S4	Selenium
5524.S5	Silicon
5524.S64	Solubility
5524.S75	Spectrum analysis
5524.S9	Strontium
5524.S93	Sulfur
5524.S95	Surface chemistry
5524.T2	Tannins
	Technical chemistry see Z7914.C4
5524.T36	Thallium
5524.T38	Thermal analysis
5524.T4	Thermochemistry
5524.T43	Thiazoles
5524.T5	Thorium
5524.T57	Tin
5524.T6	Titanium
5524.T67	Transition metals

	Chemistry
	Special topics, A-Z -- Continued
5524.T7	Tritium
5524.U7	Uranium
5524.V2	Vanadium
5524.W35	Water
5524.X4	Xenon
5524.Z5	Zein
5524.Z8	Zirconium
5541	Chess
	Circuses see Z7511+
	Civilization
	Cf. Z5111+ Anthropology
	Cf. Z6201+ History
	Cf. Z7164.T26 Technology and civilization
5579	General works
5579.15.A-Z	Special civilizations, A-Z
5579.15.E25	East and West
5579.15.H57	Hispanic
5579.2	Ancient
5579.5	Medieval
5579.6	Modern
5601	Coffee
5615	Collectors and collecting
	Cf. ML138.A+ Music manuscripts
	Cf. Z41.A2+ Autographs
	Cf. Z987+ Books
5630-5635	Communication. Mass media (Table Z4 modified)
	Cf. Z6514.S7 Speech, reading, etc.
	Cf. Z6940+ Periodicals, newspapers, etc.
	Cf. Z7164.T8+ Transportation and communication
	Cf. Z7204.S67 Social psychology, public opinion, etc.
	Cf. Z7221+ Radio
	Cf. Z7711+ Television
5633.A-Z	Special topics, A-Z
5633.A37	African Americans
5633.A39	Aged. Older people
5633.A53	Animals
5633.E35	Economic aspects
5633.H57	Hispanic Americans
5633.I67	Intercultural communication
5633.I68	International communication. International cooperation
	International cooperation see Z5633.I68
	Older people see Z5633.A39
5633.P79	Psychological aspects
	Cf. Z7204.C59 Interpersonal communication
5633.P82	Public opinion

Z5051-7999

	Communication. Mass media
	Special topics, A-Z -- Continued
5633.R45	Religious aspects
5633.S34	Science fiction
5633.T44	Technological innovations. Technology
	Technology see Z5633.T44
5633.V56	Violence
5633.V58	Visual communication
5633.W37	War
5633.W65	Women
	Computer science. Electronic data processing
5640.A1	Bibliography of bibliography
5640.A2	Theory, method, etc.
5640.A3-Z	General bibliography
5641	Periodicals. Societies
5642	Analog computers
	Digital computers
5642.2	General works
5642.3	Programming
	Programming languages
5642.4	General works
5642.5.A-Z	Individual languages, A-Z
5642.5.A25	ALGOL
5642.6.A-Z	Special computers. By name, A-Z
	e.g.
5642.6.G17	GIER (Computer)
5642.7	Computer software
5643.A-Z	Special topics, A-Z
5643.A28	Abstract data types
5643.B84	Bulletin boards
5643.C65	Computer security
5643.D36	Database management
5643.E956	Expert systems
5643.I57	Interactive computer systems
5643.M48	Microcomputers
5643.M5	Microprocessors
5643.M54	Minicomputers
5643.N37	Natural language processing
5643.N48	Networks, Computer
5643.O67	Optical data storage
	Security, Computer see Z5643.C65
5643.S55	Simulation, Computer
	Women and computers see Z7963.C67
5644	Catalogs
	Conservation of natural resources see Z7164.N3
5680	Cosmic physics
5691-5695	Costume (Table Z6 modified)

	Costume -- Continued
5693.A-Z	Special topics, A-Z
5693.A7	Armor and weapons
	Cf. Z6724.W4 Weapons systems
5693.B4	Beads
5693.C67	Corsets
5693.H4	Headgear
5701	Cotton
	Counseling see Z7204.A6
	Crafts see Z6151+
	Cremation see Z5994
	Criminology
	Cf. Z5118.C9 Crime in pre-literate societies
	Cf. Z7164.P76 Police
5703.A1	Bibliography of bibliographies
5703.A3-Z	General bibliography
5703.2	Bibliography of early works
5703.3	Periodicals. Societies
5703.4.A-Z	Special topics, A-Z
5703.4.A35	Aged and crime. Older people and crime. Older victims of crimes
5703.4.A75	Arson
5703.4.C36	Capital punishment
5703.4.C62	Commercial crimes
5703.4.C63	Computer crimes
5703.4.C65	Corrections
5703.4.C7	Crime prevention
5703.4.C72	Criminal anthropology
5703.4.C728	Criminal investigation
5703.4.C73	Criminal justice administration
5703.4.D48	Deviant behavior
5703.4.E38	Education of prisoners
5703.4.E46	Embezzlement
5703.4.E93	Ex-convicts
5703.4.F35	Family violence
5703.4.G35	Gangs
5703.4.G85	Gun control
5703.4.H35	Halfway houses
5703.4.H36	Handicapped and crime. People with disabilities and crime
	Cf. Z5703.4.M46 People with mental disabilities and crime
5703.4.H38	Hate crimes
5703.4.J33	Jails
5703.4.J87	Juvenile corrections
5703.4.J88	Juvenile delinquency
5703.4.K53	Kidnapping
5703.4.M33	Mafia

Z5051-7999

	Criminology
	Special topics, A-Z -- Continued
5703.4.M46	Mentally handicapped and crime. People with mental disabilities and crime
5703.4.M87	Murder
5703.4.O35	Offenses against the person
	Older people and crime see Z5703.4.A35
5703.4.O7	Organized crime
5703.4.P37	Parole
	People with disabilities and crime see Z5703.4.H36
	People with mental disabilities and crime see Z5703.4.M46
5703.4.P74	Prison furloughs
5703.4.P75	Prisons
5703.4.P76	Probation
5703.4.P8	Psychology
5703.4.R35	Rape
5703.4.R42	Recidivists
5703.4.R43	Rehabilitation of criminals
5703.4.R45	Reparation
5703.4.R87	Rural crimes
5703.4.S45	Sex crimes
5703.4.S5	Shoplifting
5703.4.S8	Statistics
	Terrorism see Z7164.T3
5703.4.V36	Vandalism
5703.4.W53	Wife abuse
5703.4.W66	Work release
5703.5.A-Z	By region or country, A-Z
5704	People with physical disabilities
	Cf. Z5943.H3 Architecture for people with disabilities
5705	Curiosities and wonders
	Dairying
5706.A1	General bibliography
5706.A5-Z	Special topics, A-Z
5706.B8	Butter
5706.C43	Cheese
5706.M6	Milk
5707	Catalogs
	Days. Holidays. Festivals. Birthdays
5710	General bibliography
5711.A-Z	Special topics, A-Z
5711.A8	Arbor day
5711.C37	Carnival
5711.C5	Christmas
5711.E2	Easter
5711.F6	Fourth of July
5711.H2	Halloween

	Days. Holidays. Festivals. Birthdays
	Special topics, A-Z -- Continued
5711.M3	May Day (Labor Day)
5711.M4	Memorial Day
5711.N48	New Year's Day
5711.T3	Thanksgiving Day
5721	Deaf-mutes
	Cf. Z6669.52.H43 Hearing aids
5725	Death
	Cf. Z5994 Funeral customs, disposal of the dead
	Cf. Z6675.T45 Terminal care
	Cf. Z7204.D4 Psychology
	Debating see Z7161.5
	Dentistry see Z6668+
	Dermatology see Z6670
5761	Devil
	Cf. Z6876+ Occult sciences
	Cf. Z7751+ Theology and religion
	Diaries see Z1201+; Z5301+
	Dictionaries see Z7004.D5
	Directories
5771	General
	By region or country
	United States
5771.2	General
5771.25.A-Z	By region or state, A-Z
5771.4.A-Z	Other regions or countries, A-Z
5772	Disasters
	Dolls see Z7893
	Domestic economy. Home economics
	Cf. Z5814.D6 Education
	Cf. Z7164.F7 Food supply
5775	General bibliography
5776.A-Z	Special topics, A-Z
5776.B15	Baking
5776.B4	Beverages
	Cf. Z6663.B48 Physiological effect
5776.C25	Candy
5776.C3	Canning and preserving
5776.C35	Cereals
5776.C4	Chemistry of goods
	Including food additives
	For toxicology of food additives see Z7891.F66
5776.C5	Chocolate. Cocoa
	Cf. Z5074.C25 Cacao
5776.C55	Clothing

Z5051-7999

	Domestic economy. Home economics
	Special topics, A-Z -- Continued
5776.C65	Consumer education
	Cf. Z7164.C92 Consumers. Consumer protection
5776.D4	Dehydrated food
	Disinfection see Z5776.S2; Z6673.1
	Ice cream, ices, etc. see Z6270
5776.F7	Food
	Food additives see Z5776.C4
	Food service see Z5986
	Fumigation see Z5776.S2
5776.G2	Gastronomy. Cookery
5776.H67	Housing management
5776.M4	Meat
5776.N8	Nutrition
5776.P8	Home economics as a profession
	Restaurants see Z5986
5776.S2	Sanitation (Household)
5776.S5	Servants
	Cf. Z7164.L1 Labor
5776.S63	Soybeans and soybean products
5776.S65	Spices
5776.V44	Vegetarianism
5776.Y4	Yeast
5777	Catalogs
5781-5785	Drama. Theater (Table Z5 modified)
	For national drama, see National bibliography, e. g. Z2001
	English drama; Z2161 French drama
	Bibliography of early works
	see Z5781.A2+
	Early
	By period
	Classical (Ancient) (General) see Z7018.D7
	Classical (Ancient) (Greek) see Z7023.D7
	Classical (Ancient) (Latin) see Z7028.D8
5782.A2	Medieval
	Cf. Z5784.M6 Miracle plays
5782.A3	Renaissance
	Cf. Z5784.J6 Jewish drama
5782.A4-Z	General bibliography
5784.A-Z	Special topics, A-Z
5784.A27	Acting
	African American drama see Z5784.B56
5784.A53	Amateur theater
5784.A73	Architecture
5784.B56	Black drama. African American drama
5784.C5	Children's plays

	Drama. Theater
	Special topics, A-Z -- Continued
5784.C58	College and school drama
5784.C6	Comedy and tragedy
	Dialogues see Z7156.R2
5784.F45	Feminism
5784.J5	Jesuit drama
5784.J6	Jewish drama
5784.L2	Labor plays
5784.L5	Little theater movement
5784.M37	Masks
5784.M6	Miracle and mystery plays
5784.M9	Motion pictures
	Including specific film genres
5784.M93	Music halls
	For architecture and construction see Z5943.T48
	Negro drama see Z5784.B56
5784.N6	Nō
5784.O6	Open-air theater
5784.P2	Pageants
5784.P3	Pantomimes. Shadow plays
5784.P33	Passion plays
5784.P52	Piarist drama
5784.P7	Production and direction
5784.P9	Puppet plays
	Radio plays see Z7223.P6
5784.R27	Realism
5784.R3	Religious drama
	School drama see Z5784.C58
5784.S78	Stage fighting
5784.S8	Stage setting and scenery
	Theater architecture and construction see Z5943.T48
5784.T7	Translations
	Tragedy see Z5784.C6
	Dueling see Z5906
	Dwellings see Z5943.D7
	Ecology see Z5322.E2; Z5354.E1
	Education
	Cf. Z5051+ Bibliography of the learned publications of academies, societies, universities
	Cf. Z5704 People with physical disabilities
	Cf. Z6724.E4 Military education
	Cf. Z7849 Religious education
	Cf. Z7963.E2 Education of women
5811	General bibliography
5813	Periodicals. Societies
5814.A-Z	Special topics, A-Z

Z5051-7999

Education
  Special topics, A-Z -- Continued
    Ability testing see Z5814.P8

5814.A19	Active learning
	Administration see Z5814.M26
5814.A24	Adult education
	African Americans see Z5814.B44
	Audio-visual instruction see Z5814.V8
5814.A85	Automation. Programmed instruction. Teaching machines. Computer-assisted instruction
5814.B255	Bilingual education
5814.B3	Biography, Collective
5814.B44	Blacks. African Americans
5814.B47	Boarding schools
5814.B5	Boards of education
5814.B6	Boys
	Business education see Z5814.C7
5814.C37	Career education
5814.C4	Centralization of schools
5814.C43	Certification of teachers
	Charter schools see Z5814.P66
5814.C5	Child study
5814.C52	Children with physical, mental, and social disabilities
5814.C57	Church and education
	Church colleges see Z5814.R34
	Church schools see Z5814.R34
5814.C6	Class size
	Colleges see Z5814.U7
5814.C67	Coeducation
5814.C7	Commercial education. Business education
5814.C73	Communication
5814.C74	Communist education
5814.C75	Communities and schools
5814.C76	Comparative education
5814.C77	Competency-based education
5814.C8	Compulsory education
	Computer-assisted instruction see Z5814.A85
5814.C812	Computer network resources
5814.C813	Constructivism
5814.C82	Correspondence schools and courses
5814.C83	Counseling
5814.C84	Creative thinking
5814.C85	Credits
	Critical pedagogy see Z5814.P55
5814.C88	Critical thinking
5814.C9	Curricula
5814.D4	School decoration

Education
Special topics, A-Z -- Continued

5814.D42	Departmental chairmen
5814.D47	Dictionaries
5814.D477	Differentiated teaching staffs
5814.D49	Discipline
5814.D5	Discrimination. Segregation. Integration
5814.D54	Distance education
5814.D6	Domestic economy
5814.D63	Domestic Education. Home schooling
5814.D7	Dropouts
5814.E15	Education and state. Educational policy
5814.E2	Educational anthropology
5814.E22	Educational change
5814.E23	Educational exchanges
	Educational policy see Z5814.E15
5814.E3	Educational sociology
5814.E34	Educational technology
	Educational tests and measurements see Z5814.P8
	Educational vouchers see Z5814.P66
5814.E55	Engineering education
5814.E68	Equalization of education
	Equipment see Z5814.F3
5814.E74	Ethnic schools
5814.E8	Evening schools
5814.E9	Examinations
5814.E93	Excursions, School
5814.E95	Extension teaching
5814.F3	School facilities, furniture, equipment, etc.
	Cf. Z5814.S4 School buildings
5814.F5	Finance
5814.F7	Food. Nutrition. School lunches
5814.F75	Free schools
5814.F8	Freedom of teaching
	Furniture see Z5814.F3
5814.G2	Gardens, School
5814.G5	Gifted children
5814.G8	Grading
5814.G84	Group work. Team learning
5814.H43	Health education. Patient education
5814.H5	Herbartianism
	High schools
5814.H55	General works
5814.H56	Junior high schools. Middle schools
	Higher education see Z5814.U7
5814.H57	History of education
	Home economics see Z5814.D6

Z5051-7999

Education
Special topics, A-Z -- Continued
Home schooling see Z5814.D63
Honor systems see Z5814.S65

5814.H85	Humanistic education
5814.H9	Hygiene, School
5814.I3	Illiteracy. Literacy
5814.I4	Immigrants' children
5814.I44	Industry and education
5814.I46	Instructional systems
	Intercultural education see Z5814.M86
5814.I5	International education
5814.I8	Islamic education
5814.J4	Jewish education
5814.J8	Junior colleges
	Junior high schools see Z5814.H56
5814.K5	Kindergarten
5814.L2	Laboratory schools
5814.L25	Lands, School
(5814.L4)	Law and legislation (School)
	see class K
5814.L45	Learning
5814.L492	Learning disabled
	Leisure (Education for) see Z7164.L53
5814.L6	Lighting, School
	Literacy see Z5814.I3
5814.M24	Mainstreaming
5814.M26	Management, School. School administration
5814.M29	Manual training. Woodworking
5814.M41	Medical inspection
	Mental tests see Z5814.P8
5814.M48	Mexican Americans
5814.M49	Migrant laborers' children
5814.M5	Minorities
5814.M6	Montessori method of education
5814.M7	Moral education. Character education
	Music see ML128.A+
5814.M8	Motion pictures in education
5814.M86	Multicultural education. Intercultural education
	Municipal junior colleges see Z5814.J8
5814.N37	National socialism and education
	Negroes see Z5814.B44
5814.N58	Nonformal education
5814.N6	Nongraded schools
5814.N97	Nursery schools
5814.O2	Object teaching
5814.O63	Open plan schools

Education
Special topics, A-Z -- Continued

5814.O85	Outdoor education
5814.P2	Parents' and teachers' associations
	Patient education see Z5814.H43
	Pensions see Z5814.S2
5814.P3	Perceptual-motor learning
	Personnel service see Z5814.C83
5814.P45	Planning
5814.P47	Play
5814.P55	Popular education. Critical pedagogy
5814.P6	Preschool children
5814.P65	Private schools
5814.P66	Privatization
	Including charter schools and educational vouchers
5814.P7	Problem method
5814.P72	Professional education
5814.P73	Professional ethics for teachers
	Programmed instruction see Z5814.A85
5814.P75	Project method
5814.P8	Psychology (Educational)
	Including ability testing, mental tests, educational tests and measurements, project method, etc.
	Cf. Z7204.A25 Psychology
5814.P9	Publicity
	Racial integration see Z5814.D5
5814.R2	Radio in education
5814.R3	Recreation centers. Community service
5814.R34	Religiously-affiliated educational institutions
5814.R4	Research
5814.R66	Romanies
5814.R9	Rural schools
5814.S2	Salaries. Pensions
5814.S35	Scholarships
5814.S4	School buildings
5814.S42	School safety
5814.S43	School social work
5814.S6	Secondary education
	Segregation see Z5814.D5
5814.S65	Self-government in education. Student participation. Honor systems
5814.S69	Simulated environment (Teaching method)
5814.S72	Social disabilities, People with
	Social studies see Z7161.A15
5814.S73	Special education
5814.S79	Student aid
	Student exchanges see Z5814.E23

Z5051-7999

	Education
	Special topics, A-Z -- Continued
5814.S86	Student political activity
5814.S88	Students
5814.S89	Students' societies. Extra-curricular activities
5814.S9	Study methods
5814.S95	Superintendents of schools
5814.S96	Surveys
	Teacher certification see Z5814.C43
	Teacher exchanges see Z5814.E23
5814.T3	Teachers. Teacher training
	Teaching machines see Z5814.A85
5814.T33	Teaching teams
	Team learning see Z5814.G84
5814.T4	Technical education. Vocational education. Industrial arts. Employee training
	Technology, Educational see Z5814.E34
5814.T45	Television in education. Telecommunication in education
5814.T5	Temperance instruction
5814.T7	Transportation of pupils
5814.U7	Universities and colleges. Higher education
	For individual institutions see Z5816.A+
	Cf. Z5814.J8 Junior colleges
	Cf. Z5814.M8 Motion pictures in education
5814.U8	Urban education
5814.V2	Vacation schools
5814.V4	Verbal learning
5814.V8	Visual instruction. Audiovisual instruction
	Vocational education see Z5814.T4
	Vouchers, Educational see Z5814.P66
5814.W32	War and schools
	Women see Z7963.E2
	Woodworking see Z5814.M29
5815.A-Z	By region or country, A-Z
	e.g.
5815.D44	Developing countries
(5815.U45)	Underdeveloped areas
	see Z5815.D44
5816.A-Z	By individual university or school, A-Z
5817	School books. Textbooks
	Cf. LB1028.7 Lists of materials for programmed instruction
5817.2	Teaching aids
5818.A-Z	Special disciplines and subjects, A-Z
5818.A5	Agriculture
5818.A7	Arithmetic. Number work
	Cf. Z5818.M3 Mathematics

	Education
	Special disciplines and subjects, A-Z -- Continued
5818.A8	Art. The arts (General)
5818.B4	Biology
5818.B84	Bulgarian language and literature
5818.C6	Classical languages and literatures
5818.C9	Czech language and literature
5818.D86	Dutch language and literature
5818.E3	Earth sciences
5818.E5	English language and literature
5818.F6	French language and literature
5818.G4	Geography
5818.G47	German language and literature
5818.H5	History
5818.I82	Italian language and literature
5818.L3	Language arts. Reading
5818.L35	Languages (Modern)
5818.L37	Latin language and literature
5818.M3	Mathematics
	Cf. Z5818.A7 Arithmetic
5818.M43	Medicine
	Including paramedical education
5818.N36	Natural history
	Number work see Z5818.A7
5818.N8	Nursing
	Paramedical education see Z5818.M43
5818.P6	Polish language and literature
5818.P75	Psychology
	Reading see Z5818.L3
5818.R8	Russian language and literature
5818.S3	Science
5818.S45	Serbo-Croatian language and literature
5818.S57	Slavic languages and literature
5818.S63	Spanish language and literature
5818.U47	Ukrainian language and literature
5819	Catalogs
	Electricity
	Cf. Z7141+ Physics
	Cf. Z7401+ Science
	Cf. Z7911+ Technology, useful arts, and applied science
5831	General bibliography
	Electric engineering (General)
5832.A1	Bibliography of bibliography
5832.A2-Z	General bibliography
5833	Periodicals. Societies
5834.A-Z	Special topics, A-Z
5834.A6	Apparatus and instruments

Z5051-7999

	Electricity
	Special topics, A-Z -- Continued
5834.B3	Electric batteries
5834.C2	Canal rays
5834.C5	Circuit breakers
5834.C55	Coils
5834.C6	Conductors
5834.C67	Electric contactors
5834.D37	Data processing
5834.D48	Dielectrics
5834.D55	Direct energy conversion
5834.D6	Discharges through gases, Electric
5834.D7	Driving, Electric
5834.D9	Electric generators. Dynamos
	Electric engineering see Z5832.A1+
5834.E56	Electromechanical devices
5834.E6	Electrostatics
5834.F4	Feedback
5834.F47	Ferroelectricity
5834.F8	Fuses
5834.G7	Grounding
5834.H3	Hall effect
5834.H5	Electric heating
5834.H55	High tension
5834.H6	Household appliances
	Hydro-electric power stations see Z5834.P7
5834.I6	Insulators and insulation
5834.I64	Interconnected electric utility systems
5834.L5	Lighting, Electric
5834.M2	Machinery, Electric
5834.M4	Measurements, Electric
5834.O6	Optics, Electron
5834.P65	Power distribution, Electric
5834.P7	Power plants, Electric. Hydroelectric power stations
5834.P73	Power systems, Electric
	Radio see Z7221+
	Radiography see Z5834.R7
5834.R25	Rectifiers
5834.R3	Electric relays
5834.R7	Röntgen rays. X-rays. Radiography
5834.R8	Rural electrification
5834.S3	Safety measures
5834.S4	Searchlights
5834.S49	Signal processing
	Signals and signaling see Z7234.S5
5834.S7	Stepping motors
5834.S8	Storage batteries

Electricity
  Special topics, A-Z -- Continued
5834.T4   Telecommunication
5834.T44   Telegraph
5834.T45   Telegraph, Wireless
                        Cf. Z7221+ Radio
5834.T47   Telemeter
5834.T48   Telephone
5834.T5   Thermionic converters
5834.T6   Thermoelectricity
                    Waterpower electric plants see Z5834.P7
5834.W4   Welding
                    X-rays see Z5834.R7
5835   Catalogs
                Electronic data processing see Z5640+
                Electronics
                    Cf. Z6724.E5 Military use of electronics
                  General bibliography
5836.A1   Bibliography of bibliography
5836.A2-Z   General bibliography
5837   Periodicals. Societies
5838.A-Z   Special topics, A-Z
5838.D5   Digital electronics
5838.H5   High-fidelity sound systems
5838.I5   Information display systems
5838.L3   Lasers
                        Cf. Z6675.L37 Lasers in medicine
5838.M25   Magnetic recording
5838.M3   Masers
5838.M34   Materials
5838.M5   Microelectronics
5838.M52   Microwaves
5838.O68   Optical storage devices
5838.P7   Printed circuits
5838.S34   Security systems
5838.S4   Semiconductors
5838.S65   Sound recording and reproducing
5838.S68   Speech processing systems
5838.T67   Transformers
5838.T7   Transistors
5839   Catalogs
(5841-5844)   Emblems
                    see Z1021.3
                Encyclopedias
5848   General
5849.A-Z   By language, A-Z

Z5051-7999

	Engineering
	Cf. Z5451+ Canals
	Cf. Z6736+ Mines and mining
	Cf. Z7231+ Railroads
	Cf. Z7911+ Useful arts
5851	General bibliography
5852	Periodicals. Societies
5853.A-Z	Special topics, A-Z
5853.A24	Acoustic emission
5853.A25	Acoustical engineering
5853.A3	Air conditioning
	Cf. Z5173.A5 Automobiles
5853.A8	Automatic control
	Bearings (Machinery) see Z5853.M2
5853.B6	Boilers
5853.B7	Breakwaters
5853.B8	Bridges
	Building see Z7914.B9
	Building materials see Z5853.M4
5853.C57	Coastal engineering
5853.C59	Cold weather conditions
5853.C593	Columns
	Cf. Z5943.C577 Architecture
5853.C6	Compressors
	Concrete see Z5853.M4
	Construction underground see Z5853.U53
5853.C67	Couplings
5853.D15	Dampness in buildings
5853.D16	Dams
5853.D45	Diamonds, Industrial
5853.D5	Diesel motors
5853.D74	Dredging
5853.E38	Elasticity
	Electric engineering see Z5832.A1+
5853.E39	Energy conservation
5853.E43	Engineering geology
5853.E45	Engineering mathematics
5853.E5	Engines
5853.E75	Estimates
5853.E8	Ethics
5853.F55	Finite element method
5853.F6	Fire prevention and extinction
5853.F62	Fireplaces
5853.F65	Floods and flood control
5853.F7	Fluid mechanics
5853.F75	Fluidic devices
5853.F76	Flywheels

Engineering
   Special topics, A-Z -- Continued

5853.G25	Gas and oil engines
5853.G3	Gas turbines
5853.G38	Geosynthetics
5853.G4	Geothermal engineering
5853.G57	Girders
5853.G7	Groins
5853.H2	Harbors
5853.H27	Heat engineering
5853.H29	Heat pipes
5853.H3	Heat pumps
5853.H4	Heating
	Highways see Z7295
5853.H9	Hydraulic engineering
5853.H95	Hydraulic turbines
5853.I77	Irrigation engineering
5853.J65	Joints
5853.L37	Lasers
5853.L6	Locks (Hydraulic engineering
5853.L9	Lubricants and lubrication
5853.M2	Machinery. Mechanical engineering. Machine-shop practice
	Cf. Z5853.P8 Power
5853.M25	Management
5853.M3	Marine engineering
5853.M35	Masonry
	Materials
5853.M38	General works
5853.M4	Building materials. Reinforced concrete
	Mechanical engineering see Z5853.M2
5853.M5	Measurement
	Metals. Metallurgy see Z6678+
5853.M6	Models
5853.N6	Nondestructive testing
	Nuclear engineering see Z5160+
5853.O6	Ocean engineering
5853.O65	Office buildings
5853.O7	Oil hydraulic machinery
5853.P47	Piling
5853.P5	Pipelines
5853.P55	Plumbing
	Pollution see Z5862+
5853.P8	Power
	Cf. Z5853.M2 Machinery, mechanical engineering
5853.P83	Power resources
	Cf. Z6675.E54 Energy development and health

Z5051-7999

Engineering
Special topics, A-Z -- Continued
| | |
5853.P84   Power transmission devices
                    Reclamation of land see Z5074.R4
5853.R4   Reservoirs
                    Roads see Z7295
5853.R58   Robotics
5853.R6   Rock mechanics
                        Cf. Z6033.R62 Rock fracture
5853.S22   Sanitary municipal engineering
                        Including sewage disposal, street cleaning, etc.
                        Cf. Z5862+ Pollution and pollution control
5853.S45   Servomechanisms
5853.S5   Shafting
5853.S53   Shells
5853.S54   Shop mechanics
5853.S56   Shore protection
                    Skyscrapers see Z5853.T35
5853.S6   Soil mechanics
5853.S62   Soil stabilization
5853.S63   Solar energy. Solar houses
5853.S67   Spillways
5853.S7   Springs (Mechanism)
5853.S8   Steam turbines
5853.S85   Strain gages
5853.S89   Surveying
5853.S94   System failures
5853.T35   Tall buildings
5853.T39   Terminals (Transportation)
5853.T4   Testing
5853.T6   Tools
                    Transportation
5853.T7   General works
                            Cf. Z5863.T7 Effect on environment
                            Cf. Z7164.T8+ Economics
5853.T72   Containerization
5853.T78   Trusses
5853.T8   Tubes
5853.U53   Underground construction
5853.V3   Vacuum technology
5853.V4   Ventilation
5853.V6   Vibration
5853.W4   Weirs
5853.W55   Windpower. Windmills
                    Women engineers see Z7963.E73
5854   Catalogs
5855.A-Z   By region or country, A-Z

	Engraving see Z5947+
5856-5860	Entomology (Table Z6 modified)
	Cf. Z5256 Bees
	Cf. Z6675.I6 Insects as carriers of disease
	Cf. Z7991+ Zoology
5858.A-Z	Special topics, A-Z
5858.A43	Alfalfa weevil
5858.A6	Ants
5858.A74	Aphids
5858.B37	Bark beetles
5858.B5	Black cutworm
5858.B64	Bombyliidae
5858.B68	Browntail moth
5858.B7	Bruchidae
5858.C39	Cercopidae
5858.C45	Chironomidae
5858.C65	Cockroaches
5858.C67	Codling moth
5858.C7	Coleoptera
5858.C73	Collembola
5858.D5	Diptera
5858.D8	Dragon flies
5858.D9	Drosophila
5858.E2	Economic entomology (General)
	Including insecticides, etc.
	For individual and groups of insect pests, see the individual or group, e. g. Z5858.G7 Green peach aphid
	Cf. Z5074.P4 Pests and diseases of plants
5858.E43	Elateridae
5858.E46	Empoasca fabae
5858.F45	Fleas
5858.F66	Food, feeding and feeds of insects
5858.G2	Gallflies
5858.G7	Green peach aphid
5858.G94	Gypsy moth
5858.H47	Heliothis zea
5858.H5	Hemiptera
5858.H6	Heteroptera
5858.H7	Homoptera
5858.H73	Horn fly
5858.H74	Housefly
5858.H9	Hymenoptera
(5858.I52)	Imbrasia belina
	see Z5858.M67
5858.L5	Lepidoptera
5858.L6	Lice
5858.L7	Locusts

Z5051-7999

Entomology
   Special topics, A-Z -- Continued

5858.L93	Lygus
5858.M44	Mediterranean fruit-fly
5858.M67	Mopane worm
5858.M7	Mosquitoes
5858.N4	Neuroptera
5858.N63	Noctuidae
5858.O8	Orthoptera
5858.P4	Pea aphid
(5858.P7)	Plant lice
	see Z5858.A74
5858.P78	Psylla
5858.S3	Scolytidae
5858.S6	Sound production
5858.S65	Sphecidae
5858.S66	Spodoptera
5858.S69	Spruce budworm
5858.S74	Stelidota
5858.S76	Stomoxys
5858.T4	Termites
5858.T47	Thrips
5858.W65	Wood borers

Environment (General and human). Human ecology
   Cf. Z5322.E2 Ecology (General)
   Cf. Z5322.P64 Pollution and the environment

5861	General bibliography
	Pollution and pollution control
5862	General works
5862.2.A-Z	Special types, A-Z
5862.2.A25	Acid mine drainage
5862.2.A26	Acid rain
5862.2.A35	Agricultural pollution
5862.2.A4	Air pollution
	Cf. Z6675.A33 Air pollution and health
5862.2.A53	Animal waste
5862.2.E8	Estuarine pollution
5862.2.F32	Factory and trade waste
5862.2.L4	Lead pollution
5862.2.M3	Marine pollution
5862.2.M4	Mercury pollution
5862.2.M44	Metal pollution
5862.2.N6	Noise pollution
5862.2.O5	Oil pollution
	Cf. Z5322.O4 Oil spills and wildlife
5862.2.R3	Radioactive pollution
5862.2.R45	Refuse and refuse disposal

	Environment (General and human). Human ecology
	Pollution and pollution control
	Special types, A-Z -- Continued
5862.2.S6	Soil pollution
5862.2.W3	Water pollution
5863.A-Z	Other special topics, A-Z
5863.A35	Agriculture
	Anthropogeography (Anthropology) see Z5118.A5
5863.C58	Civil engineering
5863.E54	Energy development
5863.E548	Environmental chemistry
5863.E55	Environmental education
5863.E57	Environmental engineering
5863.I56	Environmental impact analysis
5863.I57	Environmental impact statements
5863.L35	Landscape assessment
5863.M55	Mineral industries
5863.M65	Environmental monitoring
5863.P5	Pipelines
5863.P6	Environmental policy
5863.P7	Environmental protection
	Recycling see Z7914.R2
	Salvage see Z7914.R2
5863.S7	Strip mining
5863.T7	Transportation
5863.W6	Wood-using industries
	Erotic literature, facetiae, curiosa, etc.
	For national literatures see Z1201+ e.g. Z1624.E76, Argentina
	Cf. Z7961+ Woman
5865	General bibliography
5866.A-Z	Special topics, A-Z
5866.L4	Lesbianism
	Macaronic see PN1489
	Pasticcio see PN1475
5866.S3	Scatology
5867	Catalogs
	Esthetics see Z5069
5873	Ethics
	Cf. Z5814.P73 Professional ethics for teachers
	Cf. Z5853.E8 Engineering ethics
	Cf. Z6675.E8 Medical ethics
	Ethnology see Z5111+
5877	Etiquette
5883	Exhibitions
5885	Explosives

Z5051-7999

5896	Fables
	Cf. Z5981+ Folklore
	Cf. Z8018 Aesop
5906	Fencing and dueling
	Fiction
	Class here general and general special only
	For individual countries, see the National bibliography, e. g.
	Z1231.F4 American fiction
	Cf. Z5896 Fables
	Cf. Z5981+ Folklore
	Cf. Z6878.G5 Ghosts
5916	General bibliography
5917.A-Z	Special topics, A-Z
5917.A39	Adventure stories
5917.A7	Artists and authors in fiction
5917.C47	Christian fiction
	Christmas stories see Z5711.C5
5917.D5	Detective and mystery stories
5917.F3	Fantastic fiction
5917.G45	Ghost stories
5917.G66	Gothic revival
5917.H6	Historical fiction
5917.H65	Horror tales
	Imaginary voyages see Z6017.A1+
5917.J4	Jewish fiction
5917.L2	Labor and laboring class fiction
5917.L3	Legal novels
5917.M6	Moral and religious fiction
5917.M86	Musical fiction
5917.N83	Nuclear warfare
5917.O25	Occupations in fiction
5917.P3	Paperback editions
5917.P48	Photoplay editions
5917.P5	Picaresque literature
5917.S34	Schools in fiction
5917.S36	Science fiction
5917.S4	Sea stories
5917.S44	Sequels
5917.S45	Sequence novel
5917.S454	Sexual perversion in fiction
5917.S5	Short stories
5917.S69	Spy stories
5917.T7	Translations
5917.W33	War stories
5917.W6	Women authors
5918	Catalogs

	Fine arts (Visual arts). The arts (General)
	Cf. ML112.8+ Music
	Cf. Z5069 Aesthetics
	Cf. Z5131+ Archaeology
	Cf. Z6151+ Handicraft
	Cf. Z6514.A77 Literature
	Cf. Z6866+ Numismatics
5931	General bibliography
	By period
	Ancient
5932	General works
5932.3	Classical
	Medieval
5933	General works
5933.2	Early Christian
5933.3	Byzantine
5934	Renaissance. Reformation. 15th and 16th centuries
	Modern
5935	General works
5935.3	19th century
5935.5	20th century
5936.A-Z	Special aspects or movements, A-Z
5936.A76	Art deco
5936.A78	Artist-architect collaboration
5936.B38	Bauhaus
	Collaboration between artists and architects see Z5936.A78
5936.C8	Cubism
5936.D33	Dadaism
5936.E27	Earthworks (Art)
5936.E87	Experiments in art and technology
5936.E9	Expressionism
5936.F3	Fauvism
5936.F85	Futurism
5936.H57	Historiography
5936.M33	Mail art
5936.M34	Mannerism
5936.M63	Modernism
5936.N6	Art nouveau
5936.P47	Performance art
5936.P74	Psychoanalysis and the arts
5936.P82	Public art
5936.S65	Society and art
5936.S8	Surrealism
5936.S9	Symbolism
5937	Periodicals. Societies
5938	Biobibliography

Z5051-7999

Fine arts (Visual arts). The arts (General) -- Continued
By region or country see Z5961.A+

5939	Catalogs
5939.5	Forgeries
5940	Preservation of monuments. Conservation of artistic resources
(5940.3-.5)	Study and teaching
	see Z5818.A8
	Architecture
5941	General bibliography
	By period
	Medieval
5941.3	General works
5941.32	Byzantine
5941.34	Romanesque
5941.35	Gothic
	Modern
5941.353	General works
5941.36	Renaissance
	17th and 18th centuries
5941.37	General works
5941.38	Baroque
5941.39	Rococo
	19th century
5941.395	General works
5941.396	Art nouveau. Jugendstil
5941.4	Victorian
	20th century
5941.5	General works
5941.55	Deconstructivism
5941.6	Functionalism
5941.7	Postmodernism
5942	City planning, municipal improvement, etc.
	Cf. Z5943.D7 Domestic architecture
	Cf. Z7164.H8 Housing
	Cf. Z7164.U7 Urban renewal. Urbanization
5942.5.A-Z	Special aspects or movement, or architectural firms, A-Z
	Including special movements or firms identified with one country
5942.5.A35	Ahrends, Burton, and Koralek
5942.5.A72	Architects Collaborative, Inc.
5942.5.C45	Chicago Seven (Group of architects)
5942.5.C55	Classicism
5942.5.D38	Davis, Brody and Associates
5942.5.E83	Esherick, Homsey, Dodge, and Davis
5942.5.H38	Haus-Rucker-Co.
5942.5.H64	HOK, Inc.

Fine arts (Visual arts). The arts (General)
 Architecture
  Special aspects or movement, or architectural firms, A-Z --
   Continued

5942.5.M25	M. Roberto Arquitetos
5942.5.M57	Mitchell/Giurgola Associates Architects
5942.5.M63	Modern Architectural Research Group
5942.5.N54	Nikken Sekkei, Kabushiki Kaisha
5942.5.R67	Ross & Macdonald
5942.5.S48	Gruppo 7 (Group of architects)
5942.5.S57	SITE, Inc.
5942.5.S94	Superstudio (Group)
5942.5.T34	Taft Architects (Firm)
5942.5.T63	Tod Williams Billie Tsien and Associates
5942.5.W66	Woollen, Molzan, and Partners
5943.A-Z	Special topics, A-Z
5943.A22	Abbeys
5943.A34	Adobe houses
5943.A36	Aesthetics
5943.A37	African American architecture and architects
5943.A4	Aged and architecture. Older people and architecture
	Airports see Z5064.A28
5943.A48	Altars
5943.A63	Apartments. Apartment houses
5943.A66	Arcades
5943.A68	Architect-designed houses
5943.A69	Architects
	Architects, African American see Z5943.A37
	Architects, Women see Z7963.A73
5943.A693	Architects and community
5943.A7	Architectural acoustics
5943.A72	Architectural design
5943.A73	Architectural drawing
5943.A74	Architectural inscriptions
	Architectural models see Z5943.M63
5943.A75	Architectural practice
5943.A76	Architectural rendering
5943.A77	Art museums
	Including lighting
	Artist-architect collaboration see Z5936.A78
5943.A78	Artists' houses
5943.A79	Artists' studios
5943.A9	Auditoriums
5943.A93	Automobile factories
	Awards see Z5943.C595
5943.A96	Awnings. Canopies. Marquees
5943.B33	Bank buildings

Fine arts (Visual arts). The arts (General)
  Architecture
    Special topics, A-Z -- Continued

5943.B35	Barns
5943.B37	Bars, saloons, etc.
5943.B42	Beauty shops
5943.B56	Blocks (City planning)
5943.B73	Breweries. Distilleries. Wineries
	Cf. Z7914.B6 Brewing
5943.B83	Buddhist architecture
5943.B86	Bus terminals
	Canopies see Z5943.A96
5943.C34	Casinos
5943.C35	Castles
5943.C37	Cave architecture
5943.C45	Ceilings
	For painted ceilings see Z5948.M85
	Cf. Z7914.C35 Technology
5943.C47	Cemeteries
	Including sepulchral monuments
5943.C53	Children and architecture
	Christian architecture see Z5943.C56
5943.C56	Church architecture. Christian architecture. Cathedrals
5943.C563	City halls
5943.C564	City walls
5943.C57	Climate
	Including specific regions, e. g. Arctic regions
5943.C573	Clubhouses
	College buildings see Z5943.U5
5943.C574	Colonial architecture
5943.C575	Color
5943.C577	Columns
	Cf. Z5853.C593 Engineering
5943.C579	Commercial buildings
5943.C58	Communication in architectural design
5943.C583	Community centers
5943.C59	Company town architecture
5943.C595	Competitions. Awards
5943.C6	Conservation and restoration
5943.C62	Convention facilities
5943.C63	Cottages
5943.C635	Country homes
5943.C65	Courtyards
	Covered markets see Z5943.M38
5943.C75	Criticism
5943.D42	Decoration and ornament, Architectural
	Decorative plasterwork see Z5943.P53

Fine arts (Visual arts). The arts (General)
Architecture
Special topics, A-Z -- Continued
Department stores see Z5943.S77

5943.D48	Details, Architectural
5943.D53	Dictionaries
	Distilleries see Z5943.B73
5943.D68	Domes
5943.D7	Domestic architecture
5943.D74	Doors. Doorways
	Cf. Z7914.D66 Technology
5943.E4	Electronic data processing
5943.E45	Embassy buildings
5943.E5	Energy conservation
5943.E56	Entrance halls
5943.E58	Environmental aspects
5943.E95	Exhibition buildings
	Including buildings of special exhibitions
5943.F2	Facades
5943.F3	Farm buildings. Farmhouses
5943.F57	Fireplaces
	Fonts see Z5943.C56
5943.F67	Fountains
5943.F84	Funeral homes. Sepulchral chapels
5943.G35	Gargoyles
5943.G37	Gates. Gateways
5943.G43	Glass construction
5943.G76	Grotesque architecture
5943.G84	Guidebooks
5943.H27	Half-timbered houses
5943.H3	Handicapped, Architecture for. People with disabilities, Architecture for
	Including people with mental or physical disabilities
5943.H34	Harbors
5943.H56	Hindu architecture
5943.H58	Historic buildings
5943.H6	Historiography
5943.H67	Hotels
5943.H84	Human factors
5943.I53	Industrial architecture. Industrial buildings
5943.I56	Interior architecture
5943.I75	Ironwork, Architectural
5943.I84	Islamic architecture
	Cf. Z5943.M67 Mosques
5943.J48	Jewelry shops
5943.J64	Joint occupancy of buildings
5943.K56	Kitchens

Fine arts (Visual arts). The arts (General)
  Architecture
    Special topics, A-Z -- Continued

5943.L2	Laboratories
5943.L64	Lofts
5943.M36	Manors
5943.M37	Mantels
5943.M38	Markets. Covered markets
	Marquees see Z5943.A96
5943.M45	Memorials
	Including triumphal arches
5943.M57	Mirrors
5943.M63	Models, Architectural
5943.M64	Modular coordination (Architecture)
5943.M66	Monasteries
5943.M67	Mosques
	Motion picture theaters see Z5943.T48
5943.M87	Museum architecture
	Music halls see Z5943.T48
5943.N44	Neon lighting
5943.N48	New towns
5943.O35	Office buildings
	Older people and architecture see Z5943.A4
	Opera houses see Z5943.T48
5943.O7	Orangeries
5943.O73	Orders, Architectural
5943.O76	Orphanages
5943.P34	Palaces
5943.P45	Penthouses
	People with disabilities, Architecture for see Z5943.H3
	Photography, Architectural see Z7136.A73
5943.P53	Plasterwork, Decorative. Stucco
5943.P55	Plazas
5943.P65	Porches
	Including balconies and galleries
5943.P66	Post offices
5943.P7	Prefabricated buildings
5943.P74	Primitive architecture
5943.P75	Privacy
5943.P77	Psychological aspects
5943.P83	Public buildings
5943.R33	Radio stations. Television stations
5943.R36	Railroad stations
5943.R43	Recreation
5943.R45	Remodeling for other use
5943.R47	Research
5943.R49	Resort architecture

Fine arts (Visual arts). The arts (General)
Architecture
Special topics, A-Z -- Continued
Retail stores see Z5943.S77
5943.R68   Round buildings
5943.R72   Row houses
Saloons see Z5943.B37
Sepulchral chapels see Z5943.F84
Sepulchral monuments see Z5943.C47
5943.S55   Shopping malls. Shopping centers
5943.S57   Showrooms
Including showrooms for specific products
5943.S6   Sites
5943.S63   Skyscrapers
5943.S65   Society and architecture
5943.S653   Solar radiation
5943.S66   Space
5943.S7   Stables
5943.S72   Stadiums
5943.S74   Staircases
5943.S76   Stone buildings
5943.S77   Stores, Retail
Including department stores, supermarkets
Stucco see Z5943.P53
5943.S79   Study and teaching
5943.S88   Symbolism
5943.S9   Synagogue architecture
Taverns see Z5943.B37
Television stations see Z5943.R33
5943.T43   Terra-cotta
5943.T45   Terrace houses
5943.T46   Textile factories
5943.T48   Theaters
Including motion picture theaters, music halls, opera
houses, etc.
Tours see Z5943.G84
5943.T68   Towers
Including individual towers
5943.T73   Transportation buildings
5943.T75   Tropical architecture
Triumphal arches see Z5943.M45
5943.U5   University and college buildings
5943.U73   Urban renewal
5943.V32   Vacation homes
5943.V38   Vaults (Architecture)
5943.V47   Vernacular architecture
5943.V57   Visitors' centers

Z5051-7999

Fine arts (Visual arts). The arts (General)
Architecture
Special topics, A-Z -- Continued

5943.V62	Vocational guidance
	Walls, City see Z5943.C564
5943.W37	Warehouses
5943.W55	Windows. Window frames
	Wineries see Z5943.B73
	Women architects see Z7963.A73
5943.Y68	Youth and architecture
5944.A-Z	By region or country, A-Z
	For special movements identified with one country see Z5942.5.A+
5944.5	Societies
5945	Catalogs

Painting. Print media

5946	General bibliography

Print media. Engraving

5947.A3	General bibliography
5947.A5-Z	Special topics
	e. g.
5947.D3	Dance of death
5947.3.A-Z	By region or country, A-Z
5948.A-Z	Special topics in painting, A-Z
5948.A73	Architecture
5948.G45	Genre painting
	Illumination of books see Z5948.M6
5948.M3	Macchiaioli
5948.M6	Miniature painting. Illumination of books and manuscripts
5948.M85	Mural painting and decoration. Painted ceilings
	Painted ceilings see Z5948.M85
5948.P8	Portrait painting
5948.P9	Pre-Raphaelites
5948.W38	Watercolor painting
5949.A-Z	By region or country, A-Z
5950	Catalogs

Sculpture

5951	General bibliography
5953.A-Z	Special topics, A-Z
5953.D66	Doorways
	Including church doorways
5953.S37	Sculpture gardens
5953.S46	Sepulchral monuments
5954.A-Z	By region or country, A-Z
5955	Catalogs
5956.A-Z	Special topics (not otherwise provided for), A-Z

Fine arts (Visual arts). The arts (General)
Special topics (not otherwise provided for), A-Z -- Continued

5956.A47	African American art and artists. Black art and artists
	Cf. Z5943.A37 African American architecture and architects
5956.A5	Anatomy
	Antiques see Z5956.A68
	Architecture in art see Z5956.B84
5956.A66	Art auctions
5956.A68	Art industries. Antiques
	Artists, Women see Z7963.A75
5956.A69	Artists' books (Art form)
5956.A697	Arts and crafts movement
5956.A7	Arts management
	Black art and artists see Z5956.A47
	Book illustration see Z5956.I44
5956.B8	Buddhist art
5956.B84	Buildings in art
5956.C25	Calligraphy
5956.C3	Caricatures and cartoons
	Carpets see Z7914.T3
5956.C5	Christmas crib
5956.C55	Cities and towns in art
5956.C59	Collectors and collecting. Private collections
5956.C6	Comic books, strips, etc.
5956.C63	Conservation and restoration
5956.C7	Crucifixion. Crucifix
5956.D3	Decoration and ornament. Interior decoration
	Including works on the decoration and ornamentation of specific types of buildings, e. g. bank buildings, hotels, etc.
5956.D5	Design
5956.D65	Dollhouses
5956.D7	Drawing
	Embroidery see Z5956.L2
	Enamels and enameling see Z7914.E5
5956.E7	Erotic art. Erotica
5956.F34	Fantastic, The (Aesthetics)
	Fantastic fiction see Z5917.F3
5956.F44	Feminism
5956.F6	Folk art
	Forgeries see Z5939.5
	Furniture see Z5995+
5956.G5	Glass painting and staining
	Glassware see Z6046
	Gold and silversmiths' work see Z6055
5956.H64	Homosexuality

Z5051-7999

Fine arts (Visual arts). The arts (General)
Special topics (not otherwise provided for), A-Z -- Continued

5956.I44	Illustration of books
	Interior decoration see Z5956.D3
5956.I8	Islamic art
5956.J33	Jade
5956.J35	Japanese influences
5956.J4	Jewish art
5956.K5	Kitsch
5956.L2	Lace. Embroidery. Needlework, etc.
5956.L4	Lead work
5956.L45	Lettering
5956.M37	Marketing of the arts
5956.M5	Metalwork
5956.M6	Mosaics
	Needlework see Z5956.L2
5956.N37	Netsukes
5956.O85	Outsider art
5956.P4	Perspective
5956.P6	Postal cards
5956.P68	Primitive art
	Private collections see Z5956.C59
5956.P7	Proportion
5956.P74	Proverbs
	Silversmiths' work see Z6055
5956.S83	Stencilwork
	Tapestry see Z7914.T3
5956.T5	Tiles
	Ut picture poesis (Aesthetics) see Z5069
5956.V55	Visual perception
5956.W34	Wallpaper
5956.W45	West, The
	Women artists see Z7963.A75
5961.A-Z	By region or country, A-Z
5970	Fish culture. Aquaculture
	For culture of special organisms see Z5973.A+
5970.5	Fishery technology. Fishery processing
	For processing of special organisms see Z5973.A+
	Fishes see Z7996.F5
5971-5975	Fishing and fisheries. Angling (Table Z6 modified)
	Cf. Z7996.F5 Fishes
	Cf. Z8949 Walton, Izaak
	Cf. Z8949.22 Warburg, Aby
5973.A-Z	Special topics, A-Z
5973.A45	Algae culture
	Aquaculture see Z5970
5973.A7	Artificial reefs

	Fishing and fisheries. Angling
	Special topics, A-Z -- Continued
5973.B63	Black bass
5973.C7	Crabs
5973.E4	Electrofishing
	Fish culture see Z5970
5973.F49	Fish meal
5973.F5	Fish protein concentrate
5973.F54	Fish tagging
5973.F55	Fishery management
5973.F56	Fishery resources
5973.G73	Grayling
5973.M3	Marine algae
5973.M85	Muskellunge
5973.M87	Mussels
5973.O9	Oysters
5973.P3	Parasites
5973.S24	Salmon
5973.S45	Shellfish
5973.S5	Shrimp
	Tagging of fish see Z5973.F54; Z5973.F56
5973.T54	Tilapia
5973.T73	Trawling
5973.T9	Tuna fish
5973.W5	Whales
5979	Flagellants and flagellation
5980	Flags
	Floriculture see Z5996+
5981-5985	Folklore (Table Z6 modified)
	For works on specific peoples, see the geographic area in Z5984
	Cf. Z5865+ Erotic literature
	Cf. Z5896 Fables
	Cf. Z5916+ Fiction
	Cf. Z6374.F6 Jewish folklore
	Cf. Z6876+ Occult sciences
	Cf. Z7291 Riddles
5983.A-Z	Special topics, A-Z
5983.A6	Animals, Mythical
	Cf. Z7994.M77 Monsters (Zoology)
	Divining rod see Z6878.D6
5983.E43	Electronic data processing
5983.F17	Fairy tales
5983.L5	Folk literature
5983.M43	Folk medicine
	Cf. Z6665.H47 Herb therapy
5983.O72	Oral-formulaic analysis
5983.V36	Vampires

Z5051-7999

	Folklore
	Special topics, A-Z -- Continued
5983.W36	Water
5983.W65	Women
5986	Food service. Restaurants
	Cf. Z5185.F66 Food microbiology
	Cf. Z7914.F63 Food
5990	Forecasting
5991	Forestry
	Cf. Z5071+ Agriculture
	Cf. Z5074.A7 Agroforestry
	Cf. Z5322.F65 Forest ecology (General)
	Cf. Z5354.F75 Forest ecology (Botany)
	Cf. Z5356.T8 Trees and shrubs
5993	Freemasons
	Cf. Z6207.C55T3 Templars (Order of Chivalry)
5994	Funeral customs. Disposal of the bodies of the dead
	Including works on cremation, etc.
5994.6	Fur. Fur-bearing animals
	Including works on hunting, fur breeding, fur trade, etc.
	Furniture
5995	General bibliography
5995.3.A-Z	By region or country, A-Z
5995.5	Catalogs
	Gambling. Casino gaming see Z7164.G35
	Gardening. Horticulture. Floriculture. Landscape gardening and architecture
	Cf. Z5071+ Agriculture
	Cf. Z5351+ Botany
	Cf. Z5814.G2 School gardens
	Cf. Z6905 Parks
5996.A1	General bibliography
5996.A5-Z	Special plants, A-Z
5996.A6	Apricot
5996.A65	Aquatic plants
	Including water lilies, water gardens, garden pools
5996.A9	Avocado
5996.B35	Bambarra groundnut
5996.B37	Banana
5996.B4	Berries
5996.C36	Carrots
5996.C37	Cashew
5996.C5	Cherries
5996.C54	Chick-peas
5996.C6	Citrus fruits
5996.C7	Cranberries
5996.D72	Dracaena

Gardening. Horticulture. Floriculture. Landscape gardening and
architecture
Special plants, A-Z -- Continued

5996.F5	Figs
5996.F53	Filbert
5996.F55	Flowers
5996.F8	Fruit culture
5996.G37	Garlic
5996.G55	Gooseberries
5996.G6	Gourds
5996.G7	Grapes
	Including viticulture
5996.H37	Herbs
5996.H5	Houseplants
5996.M3	Macadamia nut
5996.N9	Nuts
5996.O5	Olives
5996.O58	Onions
5996.P38	Peach
5996.P4	Peas
5996.P55	Pineapple
5996.R5	Rhododendron
5996.R56	Rhubarb
5996.R7	Rose
5996.S55	Shiitake
5996.S8	Strawberries
5996.T66	Tomatoes
5996.T73	Trees
5996.T74	Trees in cities
5996.T76	Tropical fruit
5996.T8	Turf management. Turfgrasses
	Vegetable amaranths see Z5074.A816
5996.V4	Vegetables (General)
	Viticulture see Z5996.G7
5996.3.A-Z	Special topics, A-Z
5996.3.C65	Community gardening
	Cut flower industry see Z5996.3.O75
5996.3.D38	Data processing
5996.3.F56	Flower arrangement
5996.3.G37	Garden ornaments and furniture
5996.3.G73	Greenhouse culture and greenhouses
5996.3.I53	Industrial buildings
5996.3.O75	Ornamental plant industry. Cut flower industry
5996.3.R66	Roof gardening
5996.3.U73	Urban landscape architecture
5996.3.W37	Water conservation. Xeriscaping

Z5051-7999

	Gardening. Horticulture. Floriculture. Landscape gardening and architecture
	Special topics, A-Z -- Continued
5996.3.W38	Water in landscape architecture
	Cf. Z5996.A65 Water gardens
	Women in landscape architecture see Z7963.L3
	Xeriscaping see Z5996.3.W37
5996.5.A-Z	By region or country, A-Z
5997	Catalogs
5998	Gems
	Cf. Z6055 Gold and silversmiths' work
	Genealogy see Z5301+
6000	Geodesy
	Cf. Z6651+ Mathematics
	Geography and travels. Maps. Cartography
	Cf. Z1201+ Subdivision History and description under countries in National bibliography
	Cf. Z6201+ History
6001.A1	Bibliography of bibliography
6002	Bibliography of early works
6003	Periodicals. Societies
6004.A-Z	Special topics, A-Z
6004.A7	Arid regions
6004.B6	Biography
6004.C5	Cities and towns. Urban geography
6004.C6	Coasts
6004.C67	Cold regions
6004.C7	Commercial geography
6004.D36	Data processing
6004.D4	Deserts
6004.D5	Dictionaries. Gazetteers
6004.D76	Drumlins
6004.E8	Estuaries
6004.G4	Geographical perception
6004.G44	Geomorphology
6004.G46	Geothermal resources
6004.H9	Hydrology
	Cf. Z7935 Water supply. Ground water
6004.I2	Ice
6004.I85	Islands
6004.K3	Karst
6004.L5	Limnology
6004.M36	Mathematics
	Medical geography see Z6675.G44
6004.M57	Moraines
6004.M6	Mountains
6004.N3	Natural disasters

Geography and travels. Maps. Cartography
Special topics, A-Z -- Continued
Oceanography see Z6004.P6+
Physical geography
Including hydrography
Cf. Z6041+ Geophysics

6004.P5	General works
	Oceanography
	Cf. Z5853.O6 Ocean engineering
6004.P6	General works
6004.P62	Chemical oceanography
6004.P63	Continental shelf
6004.P66	Ocean currents
6004.P67	Ocean waves
6004.P68	Straits
6004.P7	Political geography
6004.R38	Remote sensing
6004.R4	Research
6004.R47	Rivers
6004.R55	Rural geography
	Scenic preservation see Z5940
6004.S7	Statistical methods
6004.S75	Storm surges
6004.S94	Swamps
6004.T6	Tourism
6004.T7	Tropics
6005.A-Z	Local. By region, physical feature, etc., A-Z
	For countries see Z1201+
6005.A45	Alps
6005.A5	Amazon River
6005.A55	Andes Mountains
6005.A57	Antarctica
6005.A73	Arctic regions
6005.A8	Atlantis
6005.B34	Baltic Sea
6005.C3	Carpathian Mountains
6005.C48	Chatham Rise
6005.H6	Himalaya Mountains
6005.K35	Karakoram Range
6005.P3	Pacific area
6005.P7	Polar regions
6005.U7	Ural Mountains
6009	Catalogs
	Voyages and travels
6011	General bibliography
6012	Bibliography of early works

Geography and travels. Maps. Cartography

Voyages and travels -- Continued

6014.A-Z	Special collections, A-Z
	e.g.
6014.B9	Bry, Theodor de
6014.C3	Carver, Jonathan
6014.H9	Hulsius, Levinus
6016.A-Z	Special, A-Z
	For topics by country see Z1201+
6016.H5	Hiking
6016.L6	Levant
6016.M7	Mountaineering
6016.P6	Pirates
6016.S55	Shipwrecks
6016.T7	Travel instructions
6016.T74	Treasure troves
	Imaginary voyages
6017.A1	General bibliography
6017.A3-Z	Special
6019	Catalogs
6020	Views
	Maps and cartography
6021	General bibliography
6022	Early printed maps
6026.A-Z	Special topics, A-Z
6026.A2	Aeronautical charts
	Astronomical charts, maps, etc. see Z5151.5
6026.B6	Botanical maps
6026.C56	City maps
6026.E3	Ecclesiastical maps
6026.E4	Electronic data processing
6026.E8	Ethnological maps
6026.G3	Geological maps
6026.H6	Historical and military maps
6026.H9	Hydrographic maps and nautical charts
	For maps and charts of individual places see Z6027.A+
6026.I7	Insurance maps
6026.I8	International world maps
	Including 1:1,000,000 and other smaller scale maps
6026.L57	Literary maps
6026.M3	Marketing maps
	Military maps see Z6026.H6
6026.P6	Population maps
6026.R3	Railroad maps
6026.R4	Relief models
6026.R6	Road maps

	Geography and travels. Maps. Cartography
	Maps and cartography
	Special topics, A-Z -- Continued
6026.S64	Soil maps
6026.T7	Treasure maps
6027.A-Z	By region or country, A-Z
	Subarrange each country (except Canada) by Table Z15
	Including hydrographic maps and nautical charts
	e. g.
6027.A2	Africa
6027.A5	America
6027.A9-.A92	Austria (Table Z15)
	Canada
6027.C21	General
6027.C22A-.C22Z	Local, A-Z
6028	Catalogs
6031-6035	Geology. Mineralogy. Paleontology (Table Z6 modified)
6033.A-Z	Special topics, A-Z
6033.A37	Algae
	Including stromatolites and systematic divisions of fossil algae
6033.A4	Alunite
6033.A44	Amber
6033.A62	Apatite
6033.A8	Astronautics in earth science
	Avalanches see Z6033.L3
6033.B3	Batholiths
6033.B4	Bauxite
6033.C28	Catastrophes
6033.C3	Caves. Speleology
6033.C6	Clay
6033.C7	Coal
6033.C74	Continental drift
6033.C88	Cryptoexplosion structures
6033.C9	Crystallography
6033.D5	Diamonds
6033.D55	Dinosaurs
	Earth temperature see Z6033.T35
6033.E1	Earthquakes. Volcanoes. Seismology
6033.E4	Economic geology
	Engineering geology see Z5853.E43
6033.F3	Faults (Geology)
6033.F4	Feldspar
6033.G26	Geochemistry
6033.G27	Geodynamics
6033.G3	Geological time
	Geophysics see Z6041+

Geology. Mineralogy. Paleontology
Special topics, A-Z -- Continued

6033.G5	Glaciers
6033.G8	Greensand
6033.I48	Insects (Fossil). Paleoentomology
6033.I5	Intrusions
6033.I8	Isostasy
6033.K3	Karst
6033.L3	Landslides. Avalanches
6033.L34	Lava
6033.L6	Loess
6033.M37	Magnetosphere
6033.M376	Mammoths
6033.M38	Manganese
6033.M4	Mass-wasting
6033.M5	Meteorites
6033.M6	Mineralogy
6033.M64	Models
6033.N45	Neogene
	Paleoentomology see Z6033.I48
6033.P19	Paleomagnetism
6033.P2	Paleontology. Paleobotany. Fossils
	Palynology see Z6033.P76
	Peat see Z6915
6033.P4	Petroleum
6033.P49	Petrology
6033.P55	Phosphates
6033.P7	Planation
6033.P713	Plate tectonics
6033.P72	Pleistocene
6033.P76	Pollen (Fossil). Palynology
6033.P8	Potash
6033.P83	Precious stones
6033.P85	Prospecting
6033.R3	Rare earth metals
6033.R4	Reefs
6033.R62	Rock fracture
6033.S4	Sediments
	Seismology see Z6033.E1
6033.S43	Selenium
	Speleology see Z6033.C3
6033.S75	Statistical methods
6033.S8	Stratigraphic geology
	Stromatolites see Z6033.A37
6033.S9	Submarine geology
6033.T35	Temperature, Earth
6033.T4	Terrestrial magnetism

	Geology. Mineralogy. Paleontology
	Special topics, A-Z -- Continued
6033.T6	Tin
6033.V3	Vanadium
6033.V45	Vertebrates (Fossil)
	Volcanoes see Z6033.E1
6033.Z46	Zeolites
6034.A-Z	By region or country, A-Z
	Subarrange each country (except the United States) by Table Z15
	e.g.
6034.C5-.C52	China (Table Z15)
6034.C95-.C952	Czechoslovakia (Table Z15)
6034.F79-.F792	France (Table Z15)
	United States
6034.U49	General works
6034.U5A-.U5Z	Local, A-Z
	e.g.
6034.U5A3	Alabama
6034.U5W9	Wyoming
6041-6045	Geophysics (Table Z6)
	For special topics see Z6033.A+
	Cf. Z6004.P5+ Physical geography
6046	Glass. Glassware
	Cf. Z6675.G55 Glass in medicine
	Cf. Z7911+ Useful arts and applied science
6055	Gold and silversmiths' work
	Cf. Z5956.M5 Metal work
	Cf. Z5998 Gems
6075	Graffiti
6081	Graphology
	Cf. Z40+ Writing
6121	Gymnastics. Physical education
	Cf. Z7511+ Sports
	Handicapped. People with disabilities
	Cf. Z5346.A2+ People with visual disabilities
	Cf. Z5704 People with physical disabilities
	Cf. Z6677+ People with mental disabilities
	Cf. Z7254 Rehabilitation
6122	General works
6123.A-Z	Special topics, A-Z
6123.S65	Sports
6151-6155	Handicraft (Table Z6 modified)
	Cf. Z5931+ Fine arts
	Cf. Z7911+ Technology
6153.A-Z	Special topics, A-Z
6153.A7	Artisans

Z5051-7999

	Handicraft
	Special topics, A-Z -- Continued
6153.B55	Blacksmithing
6153.E27	Easter eggs
	Including pysanky
6153.E42	Embroidery
	Furniture see Z5995+
6153.M56	Miniature craft
6153.M63	Models and modelmaking
6153.N43	Needlework
6153.P35	Paper work
	Pottery see Z7179
6153.Q54	Quilting
6153.T4	Textile crafts
6153.W65	Woodwork
	Heraldry see Z5301+
	History
	For comprehensive bibliographies of race-groups including language, literature, and history see Z7001+
	Cf. Z1201+ Subdivision History under countries in National bibliography
6201.A1	Bibliography of bibliography
6201.A2	Theory, method, etc.
6201.A21-Z	General bibliography
	By period
6202	Ancient
6203	Medieval
6204	Modern
6205	Periodicals. Societies
6207.A-Z	Special historical events, movements, etc., A-Z
6207.B9	Byzantine Empire and civilization
	Chivalry
6207.C5	General bibliography
6207.C53A-.C53Z	Orders. By country, A-Z
6207.C55A-.C55Z	By order, A-Z
	e. g.
6207.C55M3	Knights of Malta
6207.C55T3	Templars
6207.C55T35	Teutonic Knights
6207.C65	Classical civilization
	Cf. Z6207.G7 Greco-Roman civilization
6207.C87	Crimean War, 1853-1856
6207.C97	Crusades
	Cf. Z3005 Latin Orient
6207.D5	Displaced persons
	World War I
6207.E8	General and special bibliographies

	Information resources (General) see ZA3038
	Information science see Z666
	Internationalism see Z7164.I8
6331-6335	Iron and steel (Table Z6 modified)
	For Corrosion and anti-corrosives see Z6679.C7
	Cf. Z6678+ Metals, metallurgy
6333.A-Z	Special topics, A-Z
6333.A4	Agglomeration
6333.A8	Automation
6333.B5	Blast furnaces
6333.B7	Brittleness
6333.C3	Cast-iron
6333.E4	Electric furnaces
6333.E46	Energy conservation
6333.M47	Metallurgy
	Jews
	For Jewish education see Z5814.J4
	Cf. Z5917.J4 Jewish fiction
	Cf. Z5956.J4 Jewish art
	Cf. Z7070 Hebrew language and literature
	Cf. Z7963.J4 Jewish women
6366	General bibliography
6367	Periodicals. Societies
6368	Collected works (nonserial)
	Religion
6370	General bibliography
6371.A-Z	Special topics, A-Z
6371.C2	Cabala
6371.C6	Commandments
6371.D4	Dead Sea scrolls
6371.H3	Hasidism
6371.L5	Liturgy and ritual
6371.M5	Midrash
	Mysticism see Z6371.C2
6371.P7	Proselytes and proselytism
6371.S29	Sabbath
6371.S3	Sabbatical year
6371.S4	Sermons
6371.S9	Sukkoth
6371.T2	Talmud
6371.T6	Tosafot
6371.Z8	Zohar
	History
6372	General bibliography
6373.A-Z	By region or country, A-Z
6374.A-Z	Other special topics, A-Z
6374.A56	Antisemitism

	Jews
	Other special topics, A-Z -- Continued
6374.B5	Biography. Genealogy
	Books and reading see Z1039.J48
6374.F34	Family
6374.F6	Folklore
	Genealogy see Z6374.B5
6374.H6	Holocaust (1939-1945)
6374.L4	Law
	For bibliography on mishpat Ivri see KBM523.8
6374.S4	Sephardim
6374.S8	Statistics
6374.W5	Wit and humor
	Women see Z7963.J4
6374.Z5	Zionism
6375	Catalogs
	Landscape gardening see Z5996+
(6420.2)	Law
	see class K
	International law and relations
	Cf. Z6471+ League of Nations
	Cf. Z6481+ United Nations
	Cf. Z7164.I8 Internationalism
6461	General bibliography
6463	Periodicals. Societies
6464.A-Z	Special topics, A-Z
6464.A1	Collections
6464.A4	Aeronautics
6464.A45	Aggression
6464.A6	Aliens
6464.A7	Ambassadors
	Arbitration see Z6464.Z9
6464.B6	Blockade
6464.C6	Citizenship
6464.C74	Commissions of inquiry
6464.C75	Communication
6464.C77	Contraband of war
6464.C8	Criminal law
	Cf. Z6464.W33 War crimes
6464.D5	Diplomatic privileges and immunities
6464.D6	Disarmament
6464.E1	Eastern question
6464.E5	Enemy property
6464.E8	Extradition
6464.G56	Globalization
6464.I6	International organization
6464.I7	Intervention

Z5051-7999

International law and relations
Special topics, A-Z -- Continued
Law of the sea see KZA1002+
League of Nations see Z6471+
Maritime law

(6464.M2)	General works
	see K1150
(6464.M3)	Prizes
	see K7460.P7
6464.M5	Military occupation
6464.M6	Minorities
	Cf. Z7164.R4 Representation
6464.N4	Neutrality
6464.N62	Nonalignment
6464.N65	North Atlantic Treaty Organization
6464.P3	Paris, Declaration of
	Peace see Z6464.Z9
6464.P63	Police, International
6464.P8	Private international law
6464.P9	Psychology of international relations
6464.R3	Recognition
6464.R33	Regionalism (International organization)
6464.R4	Representatives, Diplomatic
	Cf. Z6464.A7 Ambassadors
6464.R59	Rivers, International
6464.S2	Sanctions
	Sea, Law of the see KZA1002+
6464.S62	Space law
6464.S73	State succession
6464.T47	Terrorism
6464.T8	Treaties
6464.T84	Trusteeships (International)
	United Nations see Z7911+
6464.W3	War (International law)
6464.W33	War crimes
6464.Z9	Peace, arbitration, etc.
	Including Permanent Court of International Justice at the Hague
6465.A-Z	Foreign relations. By region or country, A-Z
	e.g.
	Cf. Z1361.R4; Z1609.R4; Table Z1, subdivision 26.R4; etc., Relations (General) with foreign countries; Z7837 Diplomatic relations of the Roman Catholic Church
6465.A36	Africa
6465.B7	Brazil
6465.P2	Pan-Pacific
6465.U5	United States

	International law and relations -- Continued
	Catalogs
6466.A1-.Z8	General bibliography
6466.Z9	Sale catalogs
	League of Nations
6471	Serial publications
6472	Official lists
	General bibliography
6473	Comprehensive
6474	Minor
6475.A-Z	Special topics, A-Z
	e.g.
6475.C8	Covenant
6475.D5	Disarmament
6475.E3	Economic conditions
6475.H4	Health and hygiene
6475.I5	Intellectual cooperation
6476.A-Z	Relation to individual countries, A-Z
	Catalogs
6479.A1-.Z8	General
6479.Z9	Sale catalogs
6481-6485	United Nations (Table Z6)
	Leisure see Z7164.L53
6490	Letters
	Library science see Z666
	Literature
	For national literatures, see Z1201+
	Cf. Z5781+ Drama
	Cf. Z5916+ Fiction
	Cf. Z7001+ Philology
	Cf. Z7155+ Poetry
	Cf. Z7291 Riddles
6511	General bibliography
6513	Periodicals. Societies
6514.A-Z	Special subjects, A-Z
	Anecdotes see Z6514.W5
6514.A77	Art. The arts
6514.A85	Atheism
	Chapbooks see Z6514.P7
6514.C5A-.C5Z	Characters, themes, etc., A-Z
	Subarrange alphabetically by author
	e. g.
6514.C5F32-.C5F38	Faust
6514.C5J47-.C5J478	Jesus Christ
6514.C5J82-.C5J88	Juan, Don
6514.C5S42-.C5S48	Sex

Z5051-7999

Literature
Special subjects, A-Z
Characters, themes, etc., A-Z -- Continued

6514.C5W64- .C5W648	Women
6514.C55	Christian literature
6514.C7	Comparative literature

Class here works dealing with comparative literature
(General) or with three or more literatures
For bibliographies dealing with literatures of two
countries or regions, or emphasizing one literature
see Z1201+

6514.C97	Criticism
6514.E8	Essays
6514.F35	Fantastic literature
6514.F5	First editions
6514.F66	Food
6514.J48	Jewish literature
6514.L38	Law
6514.M43	Medicine
6514.N35	Names
6514.N8	Nursery rhymes
6514.P6	Philosophy. Theory, etc.
6514.P66	Plot summaries
6514.P68	Politics
6514.P7	Popular literature. Chapbooks
6514.P74	Prologues and epilogues
6514.P76	Proverbs in literature

For proverbs (General) see Z7191

6514.P78	Psychology

Reading see Z6514.S7

6514.R4	Religion
6514.S38	Satire
6514.S4	Sequels
6514.S6	Sociology
6514.S7	Speech. Reading, etc.
6514.S73	Sports
6514.S8	Style
6514.T7	Translations

Including translations of non-literary texts with no topical
focus

6514.U5	Underground literature

Utopian literature see Z7164.U8

6514.V56	Violence
6514.W5	Wit and humor. Anecdotes

By period

Literature

By period -- Continued

6515	Ancient
	Cf. Z7001+ Philology and linguistics
6517	Medieval
	Including general, especially vernacular. Latin medieval literature is included from the content of subject point of view rather than the language
	Modern
6519	General bibliography
6520.A-Z	Special topics, A-Z
6520.B36	Baroque literature
6520.C5	Children
6520.C66	Commonplace-books
6520.E4	Education
6520.G4	Gift books (Annuals, etc.). Keepsakes
6520.I5	Immigrants
6520.L32	Labor. Working class
6520.N44	Negritude
6520.R65	Romanticism
6520.R87	Russian Revolution, 1917-1921
6520.S6	Socialism
6520.S64	Spanish Civil War
6520.S9	Symbolism
6520.U53	Underground areas
6520.W37	War
	Women authors see Z7963.A8
6520.W67	World War II
	Working class see Z6520.L32
	Particular works (Anonymous)
	Including literary characters
	Cf. Z5896 Fables
	Cf. Z6617.A+ Manuscripts of particular works
	Cf. Z8001.A1+ Personal bibliography
6521.A-Z	Ancient and medieval, A-Z
6521.A53	Alexander, the Great
6521.A6	Amadis de Gaula
6521.A7	Arabian Nights
6521.A8	Ars moriendi
6521.A92	Aucassin et Nicolette
6521.B2	Barlaam and Joasaph
6521.C43	Charlemagne
6521.G38	Gawain and the Grene Knight
6521.G85	Guillaume d'Orange
6521.H75	Hsiano-ching
6521.H8	Huon de Bordeaux
6521.I2	I ching

Z5051-7999

	Literature
	Particular works (Anonymous)
	Ancient and medieval, A-Z -- Continued
6521.L9	Lucidarius
6521.M3	Mahabharata
6521.R6	Robin Hood
6521.R7	Chanson de Roland
6521.R73	Roman de Renart
6521.S4	Seven sages
6521.S55	Slovo o polku Igoreve
6521.T7	Tristan
6521.V53	Vie de saint Alexis
6521.W2	Wandering Jew
6523.A-Z	Modern, A-Z
	e.g.
	For fiction see Z5916+
6523.E38	Eikon basilike
6523.E5	Encyclopédie, ou Dictionnaire raisonné des sciences
6525	Catalogs
	Logic see Z7128.L7+
	Manuscripts
	Cf. CD921+ Archives and archival material
	Cf. Z105+ Paleography
6601.A1	Bibliography of bibliography
	Including lists of catalogs and manuscripts
6601.A3-Z	General bibliography
	Including catalogs
(6602)	General special
	see numbers for the specific topics
6603	Palm leaves
6604	Papyri
	Cf. Z6605.E35 Egyptian papyri
	Cf. Z6605.G7 Greek papyri
6605.A-Z	By language, or people, A-Z
	For catalogs of manuscript collections in particular
	languages held by individual libraries see Z6621.A+
6605.A39	Ahom
6605.A43	Akkadian
6605.A47	Albanian
6605.A5	Aleut
6605.A56	Anglo-Saxon
6605.A6	Arabic
6605.A66	Aramaic
6605.A7	Armenian
6605.A72	Armeno-Kipchak
6605.A75	Assamese
6605.A96	Azerbaijani

	Manuscripts
	By language, or people, A-Z -- Continued
6605.A97	Aztec
6605.B3	Batak
6605.B4	Bengali
6605.B87	Burmese
6605.C36	Catalan
6605.C5	Chinese
	Cingalese see Z6605.S45
6605.C7	Coptic
6605.D55	Dingal
6605.D9	Dutch
6605.E35	Egyptian
	Including papyri
6605.E5	English
	Including Middle English
6605.E8	Ethiopic
6605.F8	French
6605.G2	Gaelic
6605.G27	Georgian
6605.G3	German
6605.G5	Glagolitic
6605.G7	Greek
	Including papyri
6605.H4	Hebrew
6605.H5	Hindi
6605.H8	Hungarian
6605.I3	Icelandic and Old Norse
6605.I5	Indic
6605.I7	Irish
6605.I8	Italian
6605.J3	Japanese
6605.J37	Javanese
6605.K3	Kannada
6605.K8	Kurdish
6605.L25	Lao
6605.L3	Latin
6605.M28	Malay
6605.M29	Malay-Polynesian
6605.M3	Malayalam
6605.M33	Manchu
6605.M4	Marathi
6605.M6	Mexican
	Middle English see Z6605.E5
6605.M64	Moldavian
6605.M65	Mongolian
6605.M75	Moso

	Manuscripts
	By language, or people, A-Z -- Continued
	Nahuatl see Z6605.A97
6605.N67	Northern Thai
	Old English see Z6605.A56
	Oriental literature
6605.O7	General bibliography
6605.O75	Minor languages
	Including Indonesian, etc.
6605.O77	Oriya
6605.P26	Pali
6605.P3	Panjabi
6605.P4	Persian
6605.P8	Portuguese
6605.P9	Provençal
6605.P97	Pushto
6605.R8	Romanian
6605.S3	Sanskrit
6605.S33	Santali
	Scottish Gaelic see Z6605.G2
6605.S45	Sinhalese. Cingalese
	Slavic
6605.S49	General bibliography
6605.S5	Czech. Bohemian
6605.S55	Polish
6605.S6	Russian
	Minor Slavic languages
6605.S61	Bulgarian
6605.S62	Church Slavic
6605.S63	Croatian
	Lithuanian see Z6605.S69
	Ruthenian see Z6605.S675
6605.S65	Serbian
6605.S66	Slovakian
6605.S67	Slovenian
6605.S675	Ukrainian. Ruthenian
6605.S68	Wendic
6605.S69	Lithuanian
6605.S7	Spanish
6605.S84	Sundanese
6605.S85	Swahili
6605.S9	Syriac
6605.T3	Tamil
6605.T4	Tangut
6605.T45	Tatar
6605.T5	Tibetan
6605.T8	Turkish

	Manuscripts
	By language, or people, A-Z -- Continued
6605.U7	Urdu
6605.Y5	Yiddish
6611.A-Z	By subject, A-Z
	Including archival inventories on topics
	African Americans see Z6611.B63
6611.A33	Agriculture
6611.A37	Alchemy
6611.A67	Architecture
6611.A7	Art. The arts (General)
6611.A8	Astrology
6611.A85	Astronomy
6611.B52	Bible
6611.B58	Biochemistry
6611.B6	Biography. Memoirs. Diaries
6611.B62	Biology
6611.B63	Blacks. African Americans
6611.B64	Blind
6611.B66	Book industries and trade
6611.B7	Botany
6611.B74	Boxing
6611.C44	Celestines
6611.C54	Chemistry
6611.C56	Children's literature
6611.C57	Christian saints
6611.C58	Church architecture
6611.C59	Church history
	For general inventories of particular church archives not
	devoted to a specific subject, see CD
6611.C62	Cistercians
6611.C64	Colonies
	Communism see Z6611.S64
	Diaries see Z6611.B6
6611.D6	Dominicans
6611.E5	Engineering
6611.F55	Fish and fisheries
6611.F57	Folklore
6611.F6	Forests and forestry
6611.F73	Franciscans
6611.F8	Freemasons
6611.F83	Friends, Society of
6611.G43	Genealogy
6611.G45	Geography
6611.G46	German Americans
6611.G84	Guilds
6611.H47	Heraldry

Manuscripts
    By subject, A-Z -- Continued

6611.H49	Hinduism
6611.H5	History

        For manuscripts on the history of specific regions or
          countries see Z1201+

6611.H75	Huguenots
6611.H8	Humanists
6611.H95	Hymns
6611.I84	Islam. Islamic civilization
6611.J3	Jainism
6611.J46	Jesuits
6611.J48	Jews and Judaism
6611.K65	Koran. Qur'ān
6611.L56	Lingayats
6611.L7	Literature and philology
6611.L76	Liturgy
	Maritime history see Z6611.N38
6611.M38	Mass media
6611.M4	Mathematics
6611.M5	Medicine
	Memoirs see Z6611.B6
6611.M6	Military science
6611.M64	Mines and mining
6611.M65	Missions
6611.M74	Monasticism. Religious orders
6611.M77	Mormons and Mormonism
	Music see ML135
6611.N37	Natural history
6611.N38	Navigation. Maritime history
	Negroes see Z6611.B63
6611.O44	Olympics
6611.O76	Orthodox Eastern Church
6611.P48	Pharmacy. Pharmacology
6611.P5	Philosophy
6611.P53	Photography
6611.P57	Physics
6611.P59	Physiology
6611.P74	Presbyterian Church
6611.P78	Psychology
6611.P83	Public health
	Quakers see Z6611.F83
	Qur'ān see Z6611.K65
6611.R3	Railroads
	Religion see Z6611.T3
	Religious orders see Z6611.M74
6611.R63	Rocketry

	Manuscripts
	By subject, A-Z -- Continued
6611.S26	Saint Thomas Christians
6611.S35	Sanskrit philology
6611.S4	Science
6611.S47	Sermons
6611.S56	Sikhism
6611.S64	Socialism. Communism
6611.S67	Spelling reform
6611.S72	Statistics
	Suffrage, Women's see Z6611.W6
6611.S84	Sufism
6611.T24	Temperance
6611.T28	Theater
6611.T3	Theology and religion
6611.T72	Trade unions
6611.V48	Veterinary medicine
6611.W34	Waldenses
6611.W48	Whaling
6611.W6	Women
	Including suffrage, etc.
6611.Z54	Zionism
6611.Z65	Zoology
6616.A3-Z	Manuscripts of individual authors, A-Z
	Class here lists of private papers and records of any individual unless devoted to a single subject, in which case classify by subject in Z6611.A+
	For autographs see Z42.5.A+
6617.A-Z	Manuscripts of individual anonymous works, A-Z
	e.g.
	Bible see Z7771.M3
6617.R4	Reynard the Fox
6620.A-Z	By region or country, A-Z
	e.g.
6620.I8	Italy
6620.I8B6	Bluhme's Iter italicum

Manuscripts -- Continued

6621.A-Z   Catalogs of manuscript collections in specific libraries. By name of library, A-Z

Under each library (unless otherwise provided for):

.x	*General catalogs*
.x2A-.x2Z	*Special collections. By name, A-Z*
.x3A-.x3Z	*Manuscripts in special languages. By language, A-Z*
.x4A-.x4Z	*Monographs (nonofficial). By author, A-Z*

Including university, museum, and other institutional libraries open to the public

For special topics in individual libraries see Z6611.A+

British Museum

6621.B84   General catalogs

Private collections now in the British Museum

6621.B85C8   Cottonian collection

6621.B85H3   Harleian collection

6621.B86S24   Samaritan manuscripts

6621.B86S7   Spanish manuscripts

6621.B87M3   Maps

6621.B87R7   Romances

6621.B88   Monographs (nonofficial)

New York. Public Library

6621.N56   General catalogs

6621.N563   Emmet collection

6621.N57   Medieval manuscripts

6623.A-Z   Private collections. By owner, A-Z

For family archives, see CD

6625   Sale catalogs

For sale catalogs of illuminated manuscripts with plates see ND2899.5

Maps and cartography see Z6021+

Mass media see Z5630+

6651-6655   Mathematics (Table Z5 modified)

Cf. Z5151+ Astronomy

Cf. Z5853.E45 Engineering mathematics

Cf. Z6000 Geodesy

Cf. Z7144.W4 Weights and measures

6654.A-Z   Special topics, A-Z

6654.A5   Algebra

6654.A7   Arithmetic

6654.B47   Bernoulli numbers

6654.C2   Calculus

6654.C6   Coding theory

6654.C65   Combinatorial analysis

Computer science see Z5640+

Mathematics
Special topics, A-Z -- Continued

6654.C67	Combinatorial enumeration problems
6654.C68	Control theory
6654.C69	Counting
6654.C9	Curves (Plane)
6654.D45	Differential equations
6654.D5	Diophantine analysis
6654.E4	Elasticity
6654.E8	Estimation theory
6654.E9	Experimental design
6654.F5	Finite groups
6654.F85	Functional analysis
6654.F87	Functional equations
6654.F9	Functions
6654.G3	Game theory
6654.G4	Geometry
6654.G65	Goodness-of-fit tests
6654.G8	Graph
6654.G88	Groups (Theory of)
6654.I58	Interpolation
6654.K5	Kinematics
6654.L5	Least squares
6654.L83	Logarithms
6654.M26	Mathematical logic
6654.M28	Mathematical optimization
6654.M3	Mathematical recreations
6654.M33	Mathematical statistics
6654.M36	Matrices
6654.M76	Multigrid methods
6654.M78	Multiple and paired comparisons
6654.M8	Multivariate analysis
6654.N6	Nomography
6654.N67	Nonparametric statistics
6654.N8	Numerical analysis
6654.N84	Numerical integration
6654.O73	Order statistics
6654.P7	Probabilities
6654.P75	Programming (Linear, etc.)
6654.Q19	Quasiconformal mappings
6654.Q2	Quaternions
6654.R36	Ranking and selection
6654.R45	Regression analysis
6654.R5	Rings (Algebra)
	Selection see Z6654.R36
6654.S27	Semirings
6654.S3	Series

Mathematics

Special topics, A-Z -- Continued

6654.S47	Set theory
6654.S8	Statistical decision
6654.S83	Statistical hypothesis testing
6654.S86	Stochastic processes
	Study and teaching see Z5818.M3
6654.T3	Tables
6654.T6	Topology
6654.T7	Triangle
6654.U54	Univalent functions
6654.V5	Vibration
6654.W38	Wavelets
	Women see Z7963.M42

Medicine

For works on rehabilitation see Z7254

Cf. Z5180+ Bacteriology. Microbiology

Cf. Z5704 People with physical disabilities

6658.A1	Bibliography of bibliography
6658.A3-Z	General bibliography
6659	Bibliography of early works
6659.5	History of medical bibliography
6660	Periodicals. Societies
6660.3	Directories
6660.4	Information centers
6660.5	Biography

History of medicine

6660.8	General bibliography
6660.85	Paleopathology
6661.A-Z	By region or country, A-Z

Anatomy and physiology

6662	General bibliography
6663.A-Z	Special topics, A-Z
6663.A3	Aging
6663.A33	Alcohol

Cf. Z6665.7.A43 Alcoholism

6663.A36	Alpha rhythms
6663.A4	Altitude (Physiological effect)
6663.A44	Amines
6663.B48	Beverages (Physiological effect)
6663.B54	Biomechanics

Blood. Blood plasma

6663.B6	General bibliography
6663.B65	Blood pressure

Cf. Z6664.H9 Hypertension

6663.B68	Body fluids
6663.B7	Bones

Medicine
Anatomy and physiology
Special topics, A-Z -- Continued

6663.B8	Brain
6663.C34	Caffeine (Physiological effect)
6663.C36	Cannabis. Marijuana (Physiological effect)
6663.C63	Cocaine (Physiological effect)
	Death see Z5725
6663.D45	Deformities
6663.E44	Electricity (Physiological effect)
6663.E46	ELF electromagnetic fields (Physiological effect)
6663.E56	Endocrinology
	Cf. Z6664.E57 Endocrine diseases
6663.E9	Exercise (Physiological effect)
6663.E95	Eye movements
6663.F3	Fat
6663.F34	Fatigue
6663.F53	Fish oils (Physiological effect)
6663.F56	Fluorescent lighting (Physiological effect)
6663.G34	Gait. Walking
	Generative organs see Z6663.R4
6663.H4	Hearing
6663.H43	Heat
6663.H9	Hyaluronidase
6663.I4	Immunology
	Cf. Z6665.V3 Vaccination
6663.L54	Light (Physiological effect)
6663.L56	Lipids
6663.L58	Lithium
6663.L8	Lymphatics
	Marijuana see Z6663.C36
6663.M58	Metabolism
6663.M62	Microwaves (Physiological effect)
6663.M86	Muscles
	Cf. Z6663.V36 Vascular smooth muscle
6663.N48	Neural conduction
6663.N49	Neurochemistry
6663.N498	Neurolinguistics
6663.N5	Neurology
6663.N52	Neuropeptides
6663.N54	Neurophysiology
6663.N85	Nucleotides
6663.N9	Nutrition
	Cf. Z6671.2.N87 Nutritional aspects of pregnancy
	Cf. Z6671.52.N86 Pediatrics
6663.P4	Perspiration
6663.P44	Pesticides (Physiological effect)

Z5051-7999

Medicine
  Anatomy and physiology
    Special topics, A-Z -- Continued

6663.P57	Phosphorus
6663.P7	Potassium
6663.P75	Prostaglandins
6663.P8	Psychophysiology
6663.R4	Reproduction. Reproductive system. Generative organs
6663.R46	Respiration
6663.R53	Ribonucleic acid
6663.R86	Running (Physiology)
	Cf. Z7514.R85 Running as a sport
6663.S3	Saliva
6663.S4	Selenium (Physiological effect)
6663.S44	Sephadex
6663.S46	Skin
6663.S5	Sleep
6663.S57	Smell
6663.S58	Snoring
6663.S8	Steroids
6663.S83	Stress
	Cf. Z6675.S75 Stress management
6663.T36	Taste
6663.T5	Tissue culture
6663.U48	Ultraviolet radiation (Physiological effect)
6663.V36	Vascular smooth muscle
6663.V8	Vitamins
	Walking see Z6663.G34
6663.Z5	Zinc
6664.A-Z	Internal medicine. Diseases and manifestations, A-Z
6664.A1	General bibliography
6664.A27	Acquired immune deficiency syndrome
	AIDS see Z6664.A27
6664.A44	Allergy
6664.A6	Anthrax
6664.A7	Appendicitis
6664.A74	Arthritis
6664.A77	Asbestosis
6664.A79	Atherosclerosis
6664.A8	Asthma
6664.B27	Balkan nephropathy
6664.B3	Beri-beri
6664.B5	Blood diseases
6664.B7	Bone diseases
6664.B77	Burkitt's lymphoma
	Burns and scalds see Z6667.B8
6664.C2	Cancer

Medicine
   Internal medicine. Diseases and manifestations, A-Z --
      Continued

6664.C25	Carpal tunnel syndrome
6664.C44	Cerebrovascular disease
6664.C46	Chagas' disease
6664.C5	Chilblains
6664.C54	Cholera
6664.C6	Cold disorders
6664.C63	Communicable diseases
6664.C9	Cystic fibrosis
6664.D4	Dengue
6664.D5	Diabetes
6664.D53	Diarrhea
6664.D55	Digestive organ diseases
6664.D59	Diphtheria
6664.E55	Encephalitis
6664.E57	Endocrine diseases
6664.E6	Epilepsy
6664.F4	Fever
6664.G26	Gallbladder diseases
6664.G3	Gangrene
6664.G4	Genito-urinary diseases
6664.G7	Glands
	Cf. Z6664.E57 Endocrine diseases
6664.G75	Goiter
6664.H27	Headache
6664.H3	Heart diseases
6664.H4	Helminthology
6664.H42	Hemorrhagic fever
6664.H43	Hemorrhoids
6664.H45	Hepatitis
6664.H48	Herpesvirus diseases
6664.H7	Hookworm disease
6664.H9	Hypertension
6664.I28	Iatrogenic diseases
6664.I44	Impotence
6664.I47	Incontinence
	Infectious diseases see Z6664.C63
6664.I5	Influenza
6664.J34	Jakob-Creutzfeldt disease
6664.K5	Kidney diseases
6664.K8	Kuru
6664.L38	Legionnaires' disease
6664.L4	Leishmaniasis
6664.L6	Leprosy
6664.L63	Leptospirosis

Medicine
  Internal medicine. Diseases and manifestations, A-Z --
    Continued
6664.L9   Lungs (Dust diseases)
6664.M3   Malaria
6664.M35   Marfan syndrome
                        Mouth diseases see Z6668+
6664.M85   Multiple sclerosis
6664.M87   Muscular dystrophy
6664.M9   Mycotic diseases
6664.N5   Nervous system diseases
                            Cf. Z6665.5 Psychosomatic medicine
                            Cf. Z6665.6+ Psychiatry. Psychopathology
                            Cf. Z6667.N4 Neurosurgery
                            Cf. Z6671.52.N48 Pediatric neurology
                            Cf. Z6677+ Mental retardation
                            Cf. Z7892.B44 Behavioral toxicology
6664.O34   Obesity
6664.O5   Onchocerciasis
6664.P24   Pain
6664.P27   Pancreas diseases
6664.P3   Paralysis
6664.P33   Paraplegia
6664.P35   Parasitic diseases
6664.P36   Parkinsonism
                        Pathological psychology see Z6664.N5
6664.P5   Plague
                        Pneumonokonioses see Z6664.L9
6664.P8   Poliomyelitis
6664.P87   Prostate diseases
                        Psychopathology see Z6664.N5
6664.R3   Rabies
6664.R5   Rheumatism and rheumatic fever
6664.S3   Sarcoidosis
6664.S33   Schistosomiasis
6664.S48   Sexual disorders
                        Shock see Z6667.S4
6664.S53   Sickle cell anemia
                        Silicosis see Z6664.L9
                        Skin diseases see Z6670
6664.S75   Staphylococcal infections
6664.S8   Stomach diseases
                        Stomatology see Z6668+
6664.T45   Thrombosis
6664.T5   Tickborne diseases
6664.T57   Tourette syndrome
6664.T6   Toxoplasmosis

	Medicine
	Internal medicine. Diseases and manifestations, A-Z -- Continued
6664.T8	Trypanosomiasis
6664.T84	Tsutsugamushi disease
6664.T9	Tuberculosis
6664.T93	Tumors
6664.T95	Typhoid fever
6664.U5	Undulant fever
6664.U8	Urology
6664.V45	Venereal diseases
6664.V55	Virus diseases
6664.Y3	Yaws
6664.Y4	Yellow fever
6664.Z66	Zoonoses
6664.15	Transportation medicine
6664.2	Automotive medicine
6664.3	Aviation medicine
6664.33	Circumpolar medicine
6664.34	Emergency medicine. Critical care. Intensive care. First aid
6664.35	Space medicine
6664.4	Submarine medicine
6664.6	Sports medicine
6664.7	Tropical medicine
6664.75	Pathology
	Diagnosis
6664.8.A1	General
6664.8.A3-Z	Special topics, A-Z
6664.8.B74	Breath tests
6664.8.D4	Electroencephalography
6664.8.D47	Dermatoglyphics
6664.8.D5	Diagnostic errors
6664.8.H44	Hemagglutination tests
6664.8.L3	Laboratory diagnosis
6664.8.N83	Nuclear magnetic resonance
6664.8.P64	Polymerase chain reaction
6664.8.T66	Tomography
6664.8.U48	Ultrasonic diagnosis
6664.8.U74	Urinalysis
6664.8.V57	Visual evoked response
	Therapeutics and materia medica
	For toxicologic aspects see Z7891.D7
6665.A1	General bibliography
6665.A3-Z	Special topics, A-Z
6665.A4	Acetaminophen
6665.A45	Acupuncture
6665.A55	Antibiotics

Z5051-7999

Medicine
Therapeutics and materia medica
Special topics, A-Z -- Continued

6665.A57	Antidepressants
6665.A62	Antioxidants
6665.A67	Aromatic plants. Aromatherapy
	Including essences and essential oils
6665.A7	Aspirin
6665.A8	Aureomycin
6665.B55	Blood transfusion
6665.C4	Cephalosporin
6665.C5	Chemotherapy
6665.C8	Curare
6665.D53	Diet therapy
6665.D56	Dimethyl sulfoxide
6665.E43	Eleuterococcus
	Essences and essential oils see Z6665.A67
6665.G3	Ganglionic blocking agents
6665.G34	Garlic
6665.G65	Gold. Gold compounds
	Gold compounds see Z6665.G65
6665.H34	Hallucinogenic drugs
6665.H47	Herbs
	Cf. Z5354.M42 Medical botany
	Cf. Z5983.M43 Folk medicine
6665.H54	High-fiber diet
6665.H6	Hormones
6665.L29	Lanolin
6665.L57	Lithium
6665.L9	Lysergic acid diethylamide
6665.M37	Massage
6665.M52	Mifepristone
6665.M55	Minoxidil
6665.M7	Morphine
	Cf. Z5524.M7 Morphine (Chemistry)
	Music therapy see ML128.M77
6665.O2	Occupational therapy
6665.O9	Oxygen (Therapeutic use)
6665.P3	Parenteral therapy
6665.P4	Penicillin
6665.P45	Phenothiazine
6665.P46	Phenytoin
	Physical therapy see Z6665.25
6665.P49	Physiological therapeutics
6665.P94	Pyromen
6665.R2	Radium. Radiotherapy
6665.R3	Rauwolfia

	Medicine
	Therapeutics and materia medica
	Special topics, A-Z -- Continued
6665.R37	Reducing diets
6665.R4	Resuscitation
6665.S4	Self-medication
6665.S5	Shock therapy
6665.S56	Side effects of drugs
6665.S7	Streptomycin
6665.S9	Sulfur drugs
6665.T47	Terramycin
6665.T73	Tranquilizing drugs
6665.U7	Urecholine chloride
6665.V3	Vaccination
6665.V34	Valproic acid
6665.W5	Wine
6665.Z7	Zinc peroxide
6665.25	Physical medicine. Physical therapy
6665.3	Family medicine
6665.5	Psychosomatic medicine
	Psychiatry. Psychopathology
6665.6	General bibliography
6665.7.A-Z	Special topics, A-Z
6665.7.A33	Aging
6665.7.A43	Alcoholism
	Cf. Z6663.A33 Physiological effect of alcohol
6665.7.A45	Alzheimer's disease
6665.7.A53	Animal models of mental illness
6665.7.A55	Anorexia nervosa
	Appetite disorders see Z6665.7.E28
6665.7.B43	Behavior therapy
6665.7.C45	Child molesting
	Cf. Z6671.52.S48 Sexually abused children
6665.7.C55	Clinical psychology
6665.7.C65	Cognitive therapy
6665.7.D44	Dementia
6665.7.D46	Depression
6665.7.D52	Diagnosis
6665.7.D57	Dissociative disorders
6665.7.E28	Eating disorders
6665.7.E64	Epidemiology
6665.7.F35	Family psychotherapy
6665.7.F42	Fear
6665.7.F45	Feminist therapy
6665.7.G44	Gender identity disorders
6665.7.G76	Group psychotherapy
6665.7.L65	Logotherapy

Z5051-7999

	Medicine
	Psychiatry. Psychopathology
	Special topics, A-Z -- Continued
6665.7.P47	Personality disorders
6665.7.P66	Post-traumatic stress disorder
6665.7.P76	Psychiatric nursing
6665.7.P78	Psychiatric rating scales
	Psychopharmacology see Z6675.P79
6665.7.P79	Psychotherapy
6665.7.R45	Remotivation therapy
6665.7.S35	Schizophrenia
6665.7.S92	Substance abuse
6665.7.T7	Transactional analysis
	Surgery
6666	General bibliography
6667.A-Z	Special topics, A-Z
6667.A6	Anesthesiology
	Including specific anesthetics
6667.A67	Antiseptics
6667.A75	Artificial organs
	Including specific apparatus
	Artificial pacemaker (Heart) see Z6667.P32
6667.B32	Backache
	Blood-vessel surgery. Blood-vessel injuries see Z6667.V35
6667.B67	Brain injuries
6667.B8	Burns and scalds
6667.C35	Cardiopulmonary bypass
6667.C57	Circumcision
	Cf. Z5118.C57 Anthropology
	Facial injuries see Z6667.H4
	Finger surgery. Finger injuries see Z6667.H35
6667.F7	Fractures
6667.H35	Hand surgery. Hand injuries
	Including finger surgery and injuries
6667.H37	Harelip
6667.H4	Head and neck injuries. Facial injuries
6667.H45	Heart injuries
6667.J38	Jaw surgery
	Knee injuries see Z6667.K64
6667.K64	Knee surgery. Knee injuries
	Leg injuries see Z6667.L44
6667.L44	Leg surgery. Leg injuries
6667.L6	Lithotomy
6667.M53	Microsurgery
	Neck injuries see Z6667.H4
6667.N39	Nerve injuries

	Medicine
	Surgery
	Special topics, A-Z -- Continued
6667.N4	Neurosurgery
	Orthopedia see Z6667.O8
6667.O8	Orthopedic surgery. Orthopedia
6667.O86	Overuse injuries
6667.P32	Pacemaker, Artificial (Heart)
6667.P5	Plastic surgery
6667.S36	Scoliosis
6667.S4	Shock
	Skin injuries see Z6667.S55
6667.S55	Skin surgery. Skin injuries
6667.S65	Spinal cord injuries
	Spine injuries see Z6667.S66
6667.S66	Spine surgery. Spine injuries
	Including specific vertebrae
6667.S7	Sterilization (Birth control)
6667.T7	Transplantation
6667.V35	Vascular surgery. Vascular injuries
6667.V37	Vasectomy
6667.W6	Wounds
	Dentistry. Stomatology
6668	General works
6668.2.A-Z	Special topics, A-Z
6668.2.A57	Antiseptics
6668.2.D45	Dental care
6668.2.F55	Fillings
	Fluoridation of water see Z6668.2.W37
6668.2.M35	Malocclusion
6668.2.P83	Public health dentistry
6668.2.W37	Water fluoridation
6669	Ophthalmology
	Otorhinolaryngology
6669.5	General works
6669.52.A-Z	Special topics, A-Z
6669.52.H43	Hearing aids
6669.52.O85	Otitis media
6670	Dermatology
	Gynecology and obstetrics
6671	General bibliography
6671.2.A-Z	Special topics, A-Z
6671.2.A2	Abortion
	Birth injuries see Z6671.52.B57
6671.2.B73	Breast diseases. Mammography
6671.2.C66	Complications of pregnancy
6671.2.D53	Diabetes in pregnancy

Z5051-7999

	Medicine
	Gynecology and obstetrics
	Special topics, A-Z -- Continued
6671.2.D78	Drug effects on fetus
6671.2.F46	Fetal alcohol syndrome
6671.2.F48	Fetal monitoring
	Including heart rate monitoring
6671.2.G45	Generative organ diseases
6671.2.H84	Human reproductive technology
6671.2.L32	Labor
	Mammography see Z6671.2.B73
6671.2.M37	Maternal health services
6671.2.M46	Menopause
6671.2.M47	Menstruation disorders
6671.2.N37	Narcotics and pregnancy
	Including effects on fetus
6671.2.N87	Nutritional aspects of pregnancy
6671.2.O33	Occupational health in pregnancy
6671.2.P42	Pelvic inflammatory disease
6671.2.P44	Perinatology
6671.2.P73	Pregnancy
	Pregnancy and narcotics see Z6671.2.N37
6671.2.P75	Premenstrual syndrome
6671.2.R47	Reproductive health
6671.2.R48	Rhythm method of birth control
	Smoking and pregnancy see Z6671.2.T63
6671.2.T63	Tobacco effects on fetus. Smoking and pregnancy
6671.2.V5	Virus diseases in pregnancy
	Pediatrics
	Cf. Z6667.C57 Circumcision
	Cf. Z6667.O8 orthopedic surgery
	Cf. Z6673.3 Infant mortality
6671.5	General bibliography
6671.52.A-Z	Special topics, A-Z
6671.52.B57	Birth injuries
6671.52.B73	Brain damage
	Including minimal brain dysfunction
6671.52.C37	Cardiology
6671.52.D97	Dyslexia
6671.52.G76	Growth and development
6671.52.H67	Hospitals
6671.52.L43	Learning disorders
6671.52.M35	Malnutrition
	Mental health see Z6671.52.P78
	Minimal brain dysfunction see Z6671.52.B73
6671.52.N48	Neurology
6671.52.N86	Nutrition

	Medicine
	Pediatrics
	Special topics, A-Z -- Continued
6671.52.P45	Phenylketonuria
6671.52.P55	Play therapy
6671.52.P78	Psychiatry. Mental health
6671.52.S48	Sexually abused children
	Cf. Z6665.7.C45 Child molesting
6671.52.T47	Terminally ill children
6671.55	Geriatrics
6671.7	Medical radiology
6672	State medicine
6672.A1	General bibliography
6672.B5	Health boards, councils, etc.
	Hygiene see Z6673+
6672.J9	Jurisprudence, Medical
6672.M6	Military and naval medicine
	Cf. Z6675.N65 Medical aspects of nuclear warfare
6672.P38	Paternity testing
6672.Q34	Quality control
	Hygiene. Public health
	Cf. Z6668.2.P83 Public health dentistry
6673	General bibliography
6673.1	Disinfection and disinfectants
	Disposal of the dead see Z5994
6673.3	Infants
	Including hygiene, mortality, etc.
6673.35	Older people
6673.4	Health planning. Health services administration
	Including medical policy
6673.5	Health status indicators. Health surveys
6673.6.A-Z	By region or country, A-Z
6674	Veterinary
6675.A-Z	Other, A-Z
6675.A33	Air pollution and health
6675.A42	Alternative medicine
6675.A43	Ambulance services
6675.A54	Animals as carriers of disease. Zoonoses
6675.A57	Anthroposophical therapy
	Apparatus see Z6675.I7
6675.A72	Arabic medicine
6675.A74	Arthropod vectors
6675.A8	Atomic medicine
6675.A94	Ayurvedic medicine
	Baths. Mineral waters
6675.B32	General bibliography
6675.B33A-.B33Z	By place, A-Z

Z5051-7999

                                    Medicine
                                      Other, A-Z -- Continued
6675.B5   Bibliotherapy
                                        Biomedical engineering see Z6675.I7
6675.B53   Blacks and health
                                        Botany, Medical see Z5354.M42
                                        Charities see Z7164.C43
6675.C5   Chiropody
6675.C55   Chiropractic
6675.C62   Climatology, Medical
6675.C64   Clothing
                                        Collective bargaining see Z6675.T83
6675.C648   Communication in medicine
6675.C65   Coronary care units
6675.D44   Decision making
                                        Disaster medicine see Z6675.E45
6675.D74   Drinking water contamination
6675.D78   Drug withdrawal symptoms
6675.E2   Medical economics (General)
                                            Including health insurance, medical care of employees, etc.
                                        Education, Health see Z5814.H43
                                        Education, Medical see Z5818.M43
                                        Education, Patient see Z5814.H43
6675.E4   Electronic data processing. Medical informatics
6675.E45   Emergency medicine. Disaster medicine
                                            Including emergency medical services
6675.E54   Energy development and health
6675.E58   Environmental health
6675.E6   Epidemiology
6675.E8   Ethics, Medical
6675.E95   Euthanasia
                                        Folk medicine see Z5983.M43
6675.G44   Geography, Medical
6675.G55   Glass in medicine
6675.G7   Group medical practice
                                        Health education see Z5814.H43
                                        Health facilities see Z6675.H75
6675.H4   Health maintenance organizations
6675.H43   Health resorts
                                        Herbal medicine see Z6665.H47
6675.H68   Holistic medicine
6675.H69   Home care services
6675.H7   Homeopathy
6675.H73   Homosexual men and women, and health
6675.H75   Hospitals and health facilities
                                            Cf. Z6671.52.H67 Pediatrics
6675.H77   Housing and health

Medicine
    Other, A-Z -- Continued

6675.H82	Human experimentation in medicine
6675.H9	Hypnotism
6675.I5	Industrial medicine. Industrial hygiene
	Cf. Z6671.2.O33 Occupational health in pregnancy
	Cf. Z7892.I53 Industrial toxicology
6675.I6	Insects as carriers of disease
	Including specific insects
6675.I7	Instruments and apparatus. Biomedical engineering.
	Medical electronics
6675.L37	Lasers in medicine
6675.L65	Long-term care of the sick
	Cf. Z6675.N85 Nursing homes
	Medical education see Z5818.M43
	Medical electronics see Z6675.I7
6675.M4	Medical genetics
	Cf. Z5322.H8 Human genetics
	Medical informatics see Z6675.E4
6675.M43	Medical offices
6675.M44	Medical technology
6675.M45	Medical wastes
	Medicine, Oriental see Z6675.O74
6675.M64	Milk
6675.M68	Minorities and health
6675.N37	Naturopathy
6675.N5	Noise
6675.N6	Nosology. Nomenclature
	Nuclear warfare see Z6675.A8
6675.N65	Nuclear warfare
6675.N67	Nurse-physician joint practice
	Nursing
	Cf. Z5818.N8 Nursing education
	Cf. Z6665.7.P76 Psychiatric nursing
	Cf. Z7164.C43 Medical charities
6675.N7	General bibliography
6675.N8A1-.N8A49	General bibliography
6675.N8A5-.N8Z	By region or country, A-Z
	Red Cross
6675.N85	Nursing homes
6675.O74	Oriental medicine
	Paramedical education see Z5818.M43
	Patient education see Z5814.H43
	Patient-physician relations see Z6675.P58
6675.P4	Personnel
6675.P5	Pharmacy. Pharmacology
	Physician-nurse joint practice see Z6675.N67

Medicine
Other, A-Z -- Continued

6675.P58	Physician-patient relations
6675.P582	Physicians
6675.P585	Plastics in medicine
6675.P59	Poor and health. Poverty and health
	Cf. Z7164.C43 Medical charities
6675.P7	Preventive medicine
	Primitive medicine. Medical anthropology see Z5118.M4
6675.P78	Psychology and medicine
6675.P79	Psychopharmacology. Psychotropic drugs
6675.R39	Regional medical programs
6675.R4	Rehabilitation
	Religion see Z7830.5
6675.R9	Rural medicine
6675.S53	Social medicine
6675.S54	Specialties. Medical specialists
6675.S55	Speech
	Cf. Z6514.S7 oral reading, public speaking, etc.
6675.S75	Stress management
6675.T45	Terminal care
	Therapeutic systems see Z6675.A42
6675.T55	Tibetan medicine
	Toxicology see Z7890+
6675.T83	Trade unions in health facilities
	Including collective bargaining
6675.U47	Ultrasonics in medicine
	Cf. Z6664.8.U48 Ultrasonic diagnosis
6675.V53	Video display terminals and health
	Women and health see Z7963.H42
	Women in medicine. Women physicians see Z7963.M43
6675.W67	World health
	Zoonoses see Z6675.A54
	Catalogs
6676	General
6676.Z9	Sale catalogs

Mental retardation. People with mental disabilities
    Cf. Z5703.4.M46 People with mental disabilities and crime
    Cf. Z5814.C52 Children with physical and mental
        disabilities
    Cf. Z5943.H3 Architecture for people with disabilities
    Cf. Z6664.N5 Nervous system. Pathological psychology

6677	General works
6677.2.A-Z	Special topics, A-Z
6677.2.C66	Communications. Language
6677.2.D68	Down syndrome
	Language see Z6677.2.C66

	Meteorology
	Special topics, A-Z -- Continued
6683.A7	Astronautics
6683.A8	Atmosphere, Upper
6683.A83	Atmospheric circulation
	Atmospheric radioactivity see Z5158
6683.C45	Charts
6683.C5	Climatology
	Cf. Z6675.C62 Climatology, Medical
6683.C6	Clouds
6683.C64	Condensation
6683.D37	Data processing
6683.D46	Dendroclimatology
6683.D7	Droughts
	Electronic data processing see Z6683.D37
6683.E9	Evaporation
6683.F75	Frost
6683.G46	Global warming
6683.G74	Greenhouse effect, Atmospheric
6683.H8	Humidity
6683.I5	Instruments (Meteorological)
6683.I6	Ionosphere
6683.L5	Lightning
6683.L8	Lunar influences
	Meteorological satellites see Z6683.A7
6683.P7	Precipitation
6683.R3	Radio meteorology
6683.S4	Sea breeze
6683.S7	Snow
6683.S8	Storms
	Including cyclones, hurricanes, tornadoes, etc.
6683.T8	Turbulence
6683.W35	Weather control and rainmaking
6683.W4	Weather forecasting
6683.W5	Winds
6684.A-Z	Local, A-Z
	For works on special topics in specific places, see the topic
	Microbiology see Z5180+
	Microscopy
	Cf. Z5180+ Bacteriology
	Cf. Z5320+ Biology
	Cf. Z7401+ Science
6704	General bibliography
6705.A-Z	Special topics, A-Z
6706	Catalogs

6721-6726	Military science (Table Z4 modified)
	Cf. Z5693.A7 Arms and armor
	Cf. Z5704 People with physical disabilities
6724.A-Z	Special topics, A-Z
6724.A25	Aeronautics (Military)
6724.A3	Air defenses. Blackouts
6724.A38	Air warfare
6724.A4	Airborne troops
6724.A6	Amphibious warfare
6724.A73	Arms control verification. Nuclear/atomic arms control verification
6724.A75	Arms race
6724.A8	Artillery
6724.A9	Atomic warfare. Nuclear warfare
	Cf. Z5322.N83 Nuclear warfare and the environment. Nuclear winter
	Cf. Z6675.N65 Medical aspects
6724.B6	Biography
6724.B63	Biological warfare
6724.B7	Bounties (Military)
6724.C18	Camouflage (Military science)
6724.C185	Camps
6724.C2	Cavalry
6724.C48	Chaplaincy
6724.C5	Chemical warfare
6724.C58	Civil action
6724.C6	Civilian defense
6724.C62	Communications
6724.C63	Compulsory service
6724.D43	Deception
	Defenses of individual countries or areas see Z1201+
6724.D47	Dependents (Military)
6724.D5	Dictionaries
6724.E4	Education (Military)
	Education (Nonmilitary) see Z6724.N64
6724.E5	Electronics
6724.E7	Engineering
	Enlistment see Z6724.R4
6724.E75	Environmental aspects of war
	Espionage see Z6724.I7
6724.F56	Flags, standards, etc.
6724.F67	Fortification
6724.G2	Gas warfare
6724.G7	Guerrilla warfare
6724.G8	Guided missiles
6724.H6	History (Military)
6724.I5	Industrial mobilization

Z5051-7999

Military science
  Special topics, A-Z -- Continued

6724.I55	Infantry
6724.I7	Intelligence. Espionage
6724.J8	Jungle warfare
	Law
	see class K
6724.L4	Leadership (Military)
6724.M26	Management
6724.M3	Manpower
6724.M4	Mechanization (Military)
6724.M67	Mountain warfare
6724.M9	Munitions
	Cf. Z6724.O8 Ordnance
6724.N37	National security
6724.N62	Noncommissioned officers
6724.N64	Nonmilitary education of soldiers
	Nuclear arms control verification see Z6724.A73
	Nuclear warfare see Z6724.A9
6724.O8	Ordnance
6724.P53	Planning (Military)
	Primitive warfare see Z5118.W3
6724.P57	Protective clothing
6724.P6	Psychological warfare
6724.P65	Psychology (Military)
6724.R2	Railroads (Military)
6724.R4	Recruiting, enlistment, etc.
6724.R48	Research (Military)
6724.S5	Shooting (Military)
6724.S6	Sociology (Military)
6724.S64	Space warfare
6724.S66	Special forces
	Standards (Flags) see Z6724.F56
6724.S8	Strategy
6724.S9	Supplies
6724.T3	Tactics
6724.T73	Transportation
6724.U5	Uniforms
6724.V34	Vehicles (Military)
	Verification of arms control see Z6724.A73
6724.V4	Veterans
	Including retraining, rehabilitation, employment, etc.
6724.W4	Weapons systems
	Cf. Z5693.A7 Weapons (Costume arms and armor)
	Women soldiers see Z7963.S55

Mineralogy see Z6033.M6

6736-6740	Mines and mining (Table Z6 modified)
	Cf. Z5851+ Engineering
	Cf. Z6678+ Metals. Metallurgy
	Cf. Z7911+ Technology
6738.A-Z	Special topics, A-Z
6738.A48	Aggregates (Mineral)
6738.A6	Apatite
6738.B6	Boring and blasting
6738.B84	Building stones
6738.C6	Coal mines and mining
6738.C66	Copper and copper mining
6738.D7	Drainage
6738.D8	Dusts
6738.E4	Electronic data processing
6738.G7	Gold and gold mining
6738.H9	Hydraulic mining
6738.I75	Iron ore
6738.L4	Lead and lead mining
6738.L5	Lignite
6738.M5	Mica
6738.M54	Mine filling
6738.M55	Mine maps
6738.N53	Nickel and nickel mining
6738.O75	Ore deposits
	Petroleum see Z6972
6738.P47	Phosphate mines and mining
6738.P7	Prospecting
6738.Q37	Quarries and quarrying
6738.R3	Radioactive substances
6738.S3	Safety measures
6738.S7	Strip mining
6738.S76	Subsidences
6738.S8	Surveying
6738.T7	Transportation
6738.U7	Uranium ores
6738.V35	Valuation
	Miniature painting see Z5948.M6
	Motor vehicles see Z5170+
	Museums see Z5051+
	Music see ML112.8+
6824	Names
	For works on geographical names of individual countries,
	cities, etc. see Z1201+
6827	Nature
	Cf. Z7401+ Natural history
6831-6836	Naval science (Table Z4 modified)
6834.A-Z	Special topics, A-Z

Z5051-7999

Naval science
 Special topics, A-Z -- Continued
6834.A4	Aeronautics
6834.A5	Anchors
6834.A7	Atomic ships
6834.B37	Battleships. Battle cruisers
6834.B6	Biography
6834.C5	Civil engineering
6834.E4	Engineering psychology. Human engineering
6834.H5	History
	Human engineering see Z6834.E4
6834.H8	Hydrofoil boats
	Hygiene, Naval see Z6834.M4
6834.M4	Medicine, Naval. Naval hygiene
6834.M8	Museums
6834.S5	Ships. Shipbuilding. Naval architecture
	Cf. Z6834.A7 Atomic ships
6834.S54	Signals and signaling
6834.S9	Submarine warfare
6834.T3	Tactics
6834.T35	Tankers
6834.T7	Torpedoes

Navigation
 Cf. Z6026.H9 Hydrographic maps and charts
6837	General bibliography
6838	Bibliography of early works
6839.A-Z	Special topics, A-Z
6839.A38	Aids to navigation
6839.C3	Cargo handling
6839.H57	History
6839.H92	Hydrographic surveying
6839.I25	Ice navigation
6839.I6	Inland navigation
6839.L7	Lighthouses
6839.R8	Rule of the road
6839.S2	Safety measures
	Wrecks see Z6016.S55
6839.Y2	Yachts
6840	Catalogs
6841.A-Z	Local, A-Z

Newspapers see Z6940+
Nonbook materials
 Class here bibliographies of nonbook materials
 For bibliographies of works about nonbook materials, see
  Z688.N6 Z692 Z695.66 Z697.N64 etc.
6850	General bibliographies
6851	Catalogs of libraries. Union lists

	Nonbook materials -- Continued
	By place
	United States
6852	General works
6853.A-Z	By region or state, A-Z
6853.5.A-Z	By city, A-Z
6854.A-Z	Other regions or countries, A-Z
	Nuclear engineering see Z5160+
6866-6870	Numismatics (Table Z6)
	Cf. Z7421 Seals
6876-6880	Occultism (Table Z6 modified)
	Cf. Z5524.A35 Alchemy
	Cf. Z8658 Paracelsus
6878.A-Z	Special topics, A-Z
6878.A54	Animal magnetism
6878.A88	Astrology
6878.C7	Conjuring
6878.D6	Divining rod
6878.E9	Exorcism
6878.G5	Ghosts
6878.M3	Magic
6878.M9	Mysticism
	Cf. Z6371.C2 Cabala
	Cf. Z7128.M9 Philosophy
	Cf. Z7819 Theology
6878.P8	Psychical research. Parapsychology
6878.R7	Rosicrucians
6878.S8	Spiritualism
6878.S85	Superstition
6878.T4	Theosophy
6878.W4	Werewolves. Lycanthropy
6878.W8	Witchcraft
	Ocean engineering see Z5853.O6
	Oceanography see Z6004.P6+
	Ornithology see Z5331+
	Painting (Fine arts) see Z5946+
	Paleontology see Z6031+
6895	Pamphlets
6900	Parasitology
6905	Parks
	Cf. Z1251.A2 National parks (U.S.)
	Cf. Z7405.M35 Marine parks and reserves
	Cf. Z7511+ Recreation. Amusement parks
6915	Peat
	People with disabilities see Z6122+

Z5051-7999

6935	Performing arts
	Cf. ML112.8+ Music
	Cf. Z5781+ Theater
	Periodicals, newspapers, and other serials
6940	Journalism
6940.5	Theory, method, etc.
6941	General bibliography
	Including directories of periodicals and newspapers
6944.A-Z	Special topics, A-Z
	Class here periodicals not otherwise provided for under subjects
	African American newspapers see Z6944.N39
6944.A6	Amateur journals
	Black newspapers see Z6944.N39
6944.C38	Catalan newspapers
6944.C5	Children's periodicals
6944.C64	Community newspapers
	Employees' magazines see Z7164.L1
6944.E6	Ephemeral periodicals
6944.E8	Ethnic press
6944.F67	Foreign news
6944.G68	Government and the press
	House organs see Z7164.C81
6944.I58	Investigative reporting
6944.L5	Little magazines
6944.N39	Negro (African American, Black) newspapers
6944.N44	Newsletters
6944.P84	Pulitzer Prizes
6944.R44	Regional periodicals
6944.S3	Scholarly periodicals
6944.S45	Sensationalism
6944.S6	Socialist press
6944.S8	Student periodicals (College and school)
6944.T7	Translations
6944.U5	Underground press
6944.W6	Women's periodicals
6944.Y68	Youths' periodicals
	Catalogs of libraries. Union lists
6945.A2	Abbreviations of titles
6945.A3-Z	General
6946	Booksellers' catalogs
	By region or country
	America
6947	General
	United States
6951	General bibliography
6952.A-Z	By region or state, A-Z

Periodicals, newspapers, and other serials
By region or country
America
United States -- Continued

6953.A-Z	By city, A-Z
6953.5.A-Z	Ethnic press. Foreign language press, A-Z
6953.5.A1	General bibliography
6953.5.B7	Bohemian. Czech
6953.5.C45	Chinese
6953.5.F8	French
6953.5.G3	German
6953.5.H4	Hebrew
6953.5.I8	Italian
6953.5.N7	Norwegian
6953.5.P7	Polish
	Ruthenian see Z6953.5.U37
6953.5.S3	Scandinavian
6953.5.S4	Serbo-Croatian
6953.5.S62	Slavic
6953.5.S66	Spanish
6953.5.S9	Swedish
6953.5.S92	Swiss
6953.5.U37	Ukrainian. Ruthenian
6953.5.V53	Vietnamese
6953.5.Y5	Yiddish
6953.8	Latin America (General)
6954.A-Z	Other American countries, A-Z
	Europe
6955	General bibliography
6955.Z9	Catalogs and lists
6956.A-Z	By region or country, A-Z
	Asia
6957	General bibliography
6957.Z9	Catalogs and lists
6958.A-Z	By region or country, A-Z
	Arab countries
6958.5	General bibliography
6958.5.Z9	Catalogs and lists
	Africa
6959	General bibliography
6959.Z9	Catalogs and lists
6960.A-Z	By region or country, A-Z
	Australia and Oceania
6961	General bibliography
6961.Z9	Catalogs and lists
6962.A-Z	By region or country, A-Z
	Arctic regions

Periodicals, newspapers, and other serials
By region or country
Arctic regions -- Continued

6963	General bibliography
6963.Z9	Catalogs and lists
6964.A-Z	By region or country, A-Z
6967	Developing countries
6972	Petroleum
6980	Pets

Philology and linguistics
Class here general bibliography, groups of languages such as Germanic, Romance, etc., and bibliographies of African, Australian, Oceanian, Oriental, and American Indian languages
Class here also lists of imprints in groups of languages such as Germanic, Romance, etc., and in African, Australian, Oceanian, Oriental, and American Indian languages
For French, German, etc., see the national bibliography, subdivision 15, Table Z1; subdivision 7, Table Z2; subdivision 3, Table Z3

7001	General bibliography
7002	Bibliography of early works
7003	Periodicals. Societies
7004.A-Z	Special topics, A-Z
7004.A33	Abbreviations
7004.A45	Alphabet
7004.A52	Analogy
7004.A58	Anthropological linguistics
7004.A6	Applied linguistics
7004.B5	Bilingualism
7004.C36	Case
7004.C45	Children's language. Language acquisition
7004.C53	Clitics
	Communication, Oral see Z7004.S68
7004.C6	Contrastive linguistics
7004.D48	Dialectology
7004.D5	Dictionaries
	Including bibliographies covering several subject areas
7004.D53	Diglossia
7004.D57	Discourse analysis
7004.F63	Focus
7004.G3	Geographies (Linguistic)
7004.G7	Grammar
7004.H57	History of linguistics
7004.I56	Intonation
	Language acquisition see Z7004.C45
7004.L3	Language data processing

Philology and linguistics
  Special topics, A-Z -- Continued

7004.L33	Language planning
7004.L332	Language policy
7004.L34	Languages in contact
7004.L48	Lexicography
7004.L54	Linguistic minorities
7004.L63	Logic
7004.M3	Mathematical linguistics
7004.M4	Metaphor
7004.M67	Morphology
	Names. Onomastics see Z6824
7004.N44	Negatives
7004.O75	Origin of language
7004.O8	Orthography
7004.P37	Particles
7004.P5	Phonology
7004.P73	Pragmatics
7004.P74	Prepositions
7004.P8	Psychology of languages
7004.R5	Rhetoric
7004.S4	Semantics
7004.S43	Semiotics
7004.S6	Slang and cant
7004.S65	Sociolinguistics
7004.S68	Speech. Oral communication
	Cf. Z6514.S7 Oral reading, public speaking, etc.
	Cf. Z6675.S55 Speech pathology
7004.S72	Statistical methods
	Study and teaching see Z5818.C6; Z5818.L35
7004.S78	Style
7004.S94	Syntax
7004.T47	Terminology
7004.T7	Translating, Machine
7004.T72	Translating and interpreting
7004.T73	Transliteration
7004.V8	Vocabulary
7004.W6	Word
7004.W69	Writing systems. Written communication
	Cf. Z40+ Writing
	Written communication see Z7004.W69
	Catalogs
7005	General
7005.Z9	Sale catalogs
	Modern European languages (General)
7006	General bibliography
	Catalogs

Z5051-7999

	Philology and linguistics
	Modern European languages (General)
	Catalogs -- Continued
7007	General
7007.Z9	Sales catalogs
7009.A-Z	Isolated languages, A-Z
7009.B3	Basque
7009.M3	Macedonian
	Celtic
7011	General bibliography
7012.A-Z	Special topics, A-Z
7012.B74	Breton
7012.I73	Irish
7012.W44	Welsh
	Classical languages and literatures
7016	General bibliography
7018.A-Z	Special topics, A-Z
7018.D7	Drama
7018.E63	Epic poetry
7018.F5	First editions
7018.I5	Inscriptions
7018.T7A-.T7Z	Translations. By language, A-Z
	Catalogs
7019	General
7019.Z9	Sale catalogs
7021-7025	Greek (Table Z6 modified)
7023.A-Z	Special topics, A-Z
7023.B5	Biblical Greek
7023.D5	Dictionaries
7023.D7	Drama
7023.H6	History
7023.I5	Inscriptions
7023.P63	Poetry
7026-7030	Latin (Table Z6 modified)
7028.A-Z	Special topics, A-Z
7028.C44	Celtic authors
7028.D6	Dictionaries
7028.D8	Drama
7028.E88	Etymology
7028.I5	Inscriptions
7028.L47	Lexicology
7028.M47	Metrics and rhythmics
7028.P64	Poetry
7028.P75	Pronunciation
	Rhythmics see Z7028.M47
7028.S4	Scholia
7031-7035	Romance (Table Z6 modified)

	Philology and linguistics
	Romance -- Continued
7031	General bibliography
7032	Periodicals
7033.A-Z	Special topics, A-Z
7033.C37	Catalan
7033.F75	Friulian
7033.G35	Galician
7033.J48	Jews
7033.L3	Ladino
7033.O25	Occitan. Langue d'oc. Modern Provençal
7033.P5	Phonology
7033.P8	Provençal
7033.R7	Raeto-Romance
7033.T7	Translations
7036-7040	Germanic (Table Z6 modified)
7038.A-Z	Special topics, A-Z
7038.F75	Frisian
7038.T7	Translations
7038.V4	Versification
7038.W6	Word formation
7038.Y53	Yiddish
	Slavic
7041.A1	Bibliography of bibliography
7041.A2	Theory, method, etc.
7041.A3-Z	General bibliography
7042	Bibliography of early works
7043	Periodicals. Societies. Congresses
7044.A-Z	Special topics, A-Z
7044.C4	Church Slavic
7044.E37	Eastern Slavic
7044.F64	Folk songs
7044.G7	Grammar, Comparative
7044.I5	Inscriptions
7044.L3	Letters
7044.P6	Polabian
7044.W4	Wendic
	Catalogs
7044.5	General
7044.5.Z9	Sale catalogs
	Baltic
7044.6.A1-.A5	General
7044.6.A6-Z	Special, A-Z
(7044.6.L3)	Latvian
	see Z2535
(7044.6.L4)	Lithuanian
	see Z2537

Z5051-7999

	Philology and linguistics -- Continued
	Uralic. Finno-Ugric
7045.A1-.A5	General
7045.A6-Z	Special, A-Z
	Estonian see Z2533
	Finnish see Z2520
7045.K64	Komi
7045.U4	Udmurt
	Oriental
7046	General bibliography
7047.A-Z	Special topics, A-Z
	e. g.
7047.D7	Drama
7047.T7	Translations
7048	Periodicals. Societies. Collections
7049.A-Z	Groups of languages, A-Z
7049.A85	Austroasiatic
7049.A9	Austronesian
7049.C3	Caucasian
7049.D35	Dardic
7049.D7	Dravidian
7049.I3	Indic. Indo-Aryan
7049.I53	Indo-Iranian
7049.I8	Iranian
7049.M3	Malayan
7049.M6	Mon-Khmer
7049.P45	Philippine
7049.S5	Semitic
7049.S58	Sino-Tibetan
7049.T87	Turkic
7049.U5	Ural-Altaic
	Catalogs
7050	General
7050.Z9	Sale catalogs
	Individual languages
7052	Arabic
7053	Aramaic. Chaldean. Mandaean, etc.
	Cf. Z7049.S5 Semitic
	Cf. Z7070 Hebrew
	Cf. Z7094 Syriac
7054	Armenian
7055	Assyriology
7057	Bengali
7059	Chinese
7061	Coptic
7064	Egyptian. Egyptology
7066	Ethiopic

Philology and linguistics
Oriental
Individual languages -- Continued

7068	Gujarati
7070	Hebrew
	Cf. Z7038.Y53 Yiddish
7071	Hindi
7071.5	Indonesian
7072	Japanese
7073	Kannada
7074	Korean
7077	Malagasy
7078	Malay
7079	Malayalam
7080	Manchu
7082	Marathi
7083	Mongolian
7083.2	Nepali
7083.5	Oriya
7083.8	Pakistani
7084	Panjabi
7085	Persian
7090	Sanskrit. Pali. Prakrit. Vedic
(7091)	Saurashtri
	see Z7068
7094	Syriac
	Cf. Z7053 Aramaic, Chaldaic, Mandaean, etc.
7094.2	Tamil
7094.5	Telugu
7094.8	Thai
7095	Tibetan
7096	Turkish
7098	Ugaritic
7099	Urdu
7101.A-Z	Other languages, A-Z
7101.A39	Adygei
7101.A94	Azerbaijani
7101.B37	Bashkir
7101.C42	Cebuano
7101.C53	Chagatai
7101.C56	Chuvash
7101.I3	Iloko
7101.K34	Kalmyk
7101.K57	Kirghiz
7101.K7	Konkani
7101.L54	Limbu
7101.M32	Magahi

Z5051-7999

	Philology and linguistics
	Australia. Oceania
	Individual languages, A-Z -- Continued
7112.R37	Rarotongan
7112.S25	Samoan
7112.T33	Tahitian
7112.V35	Vanuatu
	American Indian
7116	General bibliography
	North America
7118	General bibliography
7119	Individual languages, A-Z
7119.A4	Algonquian
7119.A9	Athapascan
7119.C4	Cherokee
7119.C6	Chinookan
7119.E7	Eskimo
7119.I7	Iroquoian
7119.M7	Mohawk
7119.M9	Muskhogean
7119.N3	Navajo
7119.S1	Salishan
7119.S55	Siksika
7119.S6	Siouan
7119.W2	Wakashan
	Mexico and Central America. Latin America
7120	General bibliography
7121.A-Z	Individual languages, A-Z
(7121.A95)	Aztec
	see Z7121.N34
7121.M2	Mayan
7121.N34	Nahuatl. Aztec
	South America
7122.A3	General bibliography
7122.A4-Z	Individual languages or language families, A-Z
7122.A6	Araucanian
7122.A9	Aymara
7122.G9	Guarani
7122.K4	Kechua
7122.P34	Panoan
7122.S3	Saliva
7122.T9	Tupi
7122.5	Developing countries
7123	Artificial languages. Universal language
	Including Esperanto, Volapuk, etc.
7124	Mixed languages
	Including Creole, Pidgin English, etc.

Z5051-7999

7125-7130	Philosophy (Table Z4 modified)
	see also individual philosophers, e. g. Z8044, Aristotle; Z8460, Kant
	Cf. Z5069 Aesthetics
	Cf. Z5873 Ethics
	Cf. Z7201+ Psychology
	Cf. Z7751+ Theology and religion
7128.A-Z	Special topics, A-Z
7128.A53	Ancient philosophy
7128.B93	Buddhist philosophy
7128.C55	Children and philosophy
7128.C65	Confucian philosophy
7128.D48	Dialectic
7128.D5	Dialectical materialism
7128.E55	Enlightenment
7128.E6	Epiphanism
7128.E87	Events
7128.E9	Existentialism
7128.F2	Fate and fatalism
7128.H47	Hermeneutics
7128.H55	Hindu philosophy
7128.H9	Humanism
7128.I53	Indic philosophy
7128.I57	Islamic philosophy
	Logic
7128.L7	General bibliography
7128.L72	Buddhist logic
7128.M3	Man
7128.M46	Methodology
7128.M66	Monism
7128.M9	Mysticism
	Cf. Z6371.C2 Cabala
	Cf. Z6878.M9 Occultism
	Cf. Z7819 Theology
7128.N93	Nyaya
7128.P47	Personalism
7128.P5	Phenomenology
7128.P6	Positivism
7128.P8	Pragmatism
7128.P83	Pre-Socratic philosophers
7128.P88	Process philosophy
7128.R4	Realism
7128.R44	Reference
7128.S25	Sankhya
7128.S3	Scholasticism
7128.S7	Structuralism
	Thomism, Thomists see Z7128.S3; Z8870

Z5051-7999

	Physics
	Special topics, A-Z -- Continued
7144.E45	Emission
	Including special types of emission, e. g., ion emission
7144.F4	Ferroelectricity
7144.F45	Fluid dynamics
7144.F5	Fluorescence
7144.F6	Force and energy
	Geophysics see Z6041+
7144.G9	Gyroscope
7144.H4	Heat
7144.H5	High pressure
7144.H55	History
7144.H6	Holography
7144.H9	Hydrodynamics
7144.I5	Instruments
7144.I8	Isotopes
7144.L6	Low temperatures
7144.M3	Magnetism. Nuclear magnetism
7144.M4	Mechanics
	Metric system see Z7144.W4
7144.M6	Mössbauer effect
7144.N77	Nuclear counters
	Nuclear magnetism see Z7144.M3
7144.N8	Nuclear physics
	Including elementary particles
7144.O6	Optics
7144.P3	Particle accelerators
7144.P4	Pendulum
7144.P5	Plasma (Ionized gases)
7144.P6	Polywater
7144.P9	Pyroelectricity. Piezoelectricity
7144.Q3	Quantum theory
7144.R17	Radiation
7144.R2	Radioactivity
	Cf. Z5158 Atmospheric radioactivity
	Cf. Z7221+ Radio
7144.R3	Radiocarbon dating
7144.R4	Relativity
7144.R45	Rheology
7144.S58	Solids. Thin films
7144.S6	Sound
7144.S7	Spectrum
7144.S76	Statistical physics
7144.S8	Superconductors
7144.S94	Synchrocyclotrons
7144.T41	Thermodynamics

Physics

Special topics, A-Z -- Continued

7144.T43	Thermoluminescence
	Thin films see Z7144.S58
7144.U53	Underwater acoustics
7144.V25	Vacuum
7144.V3	Vapor pressure
7144.W2	Waves
7144.W4	Weights and measures. Metric system

Physiology see Z6662+

Playgrounds see Z7164.C5

Poetry

For national poetry, see national bibliography, e. g. Z1231.P7
American poetry; Z2014.P7 English poetry

Cf. Z5069 Aesthetics

Cf. Z6511+ Literature

7155	General bibliography
7156.A-Z	Special topics, A-Z
7156.A1	Anthologies
7156.C64	Concrete poetry
7156.E6	Epic poetry
7156.H3	Haiku
7156.P7	Popular poetry, ballads, etc.
7156.R2	Recitations
	Including prose monologues, dialogues, etc.
7156.S6	Sonnets
7156.V6	Versification
7156.W37	War
7157	Catalogs

Political and social sciences

Cf. Z5118.C9 Criminal anthropology

Cf. Z7231+ Railroads

Cf. Z7551+ Statistics

Cf. Z7721 Temperance

Cf. Z7961+ Women

7161.A1	Bibliography of bibliography
7161.A15	General special
7161.A2	Theory, method, etc.
7161.A22-Z	General bibliography
7161.5	Debate manuals
	Including outlines and references on public questions
	For outlines with arguments in extenso, see the subject, e. g.
	for Pearson's Inter-collegiate debates, see H35
	For treatises on debate see PN4181
7162	Bibliography of early works
7163	Periodicals. Societies
7164.A-Z	Special topics, A-Z

Z5051-7999

Political and social sciences
Special topics, A-Z -- Continued

7164.A17	Accidents and accident insurance
	Accounting see Z7164.C81
7164.A2	Administration, Public
7164.A23	Adoption
	Advertising see Z7164.C81
7164.A26	Affirmative action programs
7164.A3	Agricultural colonies
7164.A4	Alien (Foreign) workers
	Americanization see Z1361.A51
7164.A52	Anarchism
	Animal rights see Z7164.C45
	Animal welfare see Z7164.C45
7164.A85	Associations, institutions, etc.
	Banking see Z7164.F5
7164.B35	Barter
7164.B5	Birth control
7164.B6	Boards of trade
	Business see Z7164.C81
7164.B91	Business cycles
7164.B92	Business intelligence. Trade secrets
7164.B95	Buying. Purchasing. Procurement
7164.C11	Cabinet system
7164.C18	Capital investments
	Casino gaming see Z7164.G35
7164.C2	Caste
7164.C36	Chain stores
	Charities. Public welfare. Social service
7164.C4	General
7164.C43	Medical charities
7164.C45	Animal welfare. Animal rights
7164.C5	Children. Child welfare

Including care and hygiene, foster homes, playgrounds, etc.
Cf. Z6673.3 Infant mortality

	Church and state see Z7776.72
7164.C57	Citizenship
	Civil rights see Z7164.L6
7164.C6	Civil service
7164.C64	Clothing trade
7164.C66	Cloture
7164.C68	Collective farms
7164.C69	Collective settlements. Communal settlements
7164.C7	Colonies

For colonies of individual countries see Z1201+
For agricultural colonies see Z7164.A3
Cf. Z7164.N4 New states

Political and social sciences
Special topics, A-Z -- Continued
Commerce
7164.C8   General bibliography
7164.C81   Business
Including administration, organization, advertising, etc.
7164.C83   Commodity exchanges
Communal settlements see Z7164.C69
Communism see Z7164.S67+
7164.C84   Community centers
7164.C842   Community development. Rural development
Competition see Z7164.O7
Conservation see Z7164.N3
7164.C9   Consular service
7164.C92   Consumers. Consumer protection
7164.C93   Cooperation
Corporations see Z7164.T87
7164.C94   Corruption in politics
7164.C95   Cost of living
7164.C97   Country life
7164.C98   Coups d'état
Crime and criminals see Z5703+
Crises see Z7164.B91
7164.C99   Customs administration
7164.D2   Democracy
7164.D3   Demography
Developing countries see Z7164.U5
7164.D53   Dictionaries. Encyclopedias
Divorce see Z7164.M2
Drug abuse see Z7164.N17
7164.E12   Econometrics
7164.E13   Economic development projects
7164.E14   Economic forecasting
7164.E15   Economic policy
7164.E17   Economic relations, International
7164.E2   Economics
Economics, Primitive, see Z5118.E25
Elections, see Z7164.R4
Electoral college, see Z7164.R4
7164.E4   Elite
Emigration see Z7164.I3
7164.E55   Employees' representation in management
7164.E57   Employers' associations
Encyclopedias see Z7164.D53
7164.E6   Energy policy
7164.E68   Enterprise zones
Environmental policy, see Z5863.P6

Z5051-7999

Political and social sciences
Special topics, A-Z -- Continued
Ethnicity and ethnic groups (General), see Z5118.E84

7164.E9	Eugenics
	Cf. Z7164.D3 Demography
	Family see Z7164.M2
	Fascism see Z2000.7
7164.F4	Federal government. Federalism
7164.F5	Finance. Money. Banking. Investments
	Cf. Z7164.C18 Capital investments
	Cf. Z7164.P9555 Public finance
	Finance, Personal see Z7164.T4
7164.F6	Floods
7164.F64	Focus groups
7164.F7	Food supply
	Foreign workers see Z7164.A4
7164.F8	Fringe benefits. Non-wage payments
7164.F85	Fruit industry
7164.G35	Gambling. Casino gaming
	Gay and lesbian studies see Z7164.H74
7164.G45	Genocide
	Geography, Political see Z6004.P7
	Gild socialism see Z7164.S675
7164.G59	Government ownership. Privatization
7164.G6	Government property
7164.G7	Government publications
	For publications of an individual country see Z1201+
	Cf. ZA5049+ Government information resources in general
7164.G8	Grain trade
7164.G82	Grandparents
7164.G83	Group insurance
	Guild socialism see Z7164.S675
7164.H54	High technology industries
7164.H7	Home labor
	Cf. Z7164.L1 labor
7164.H72	Homeless persons. Tramps. Vagabonds
7164.H74	Homosexuality. Lesbianism. Gay and lesbian studies
7164.H77	Hours of labor
7164.H8	Housing
	Cf. Z6675.H77 Housing and health
	Human rights see Z7164.L6
7164.H85	Human settlements
7164.I25	Illegitimacy
7164.I3	Immigration. Emigration
7164.I34	Imperialism
7164.I37	Income

Political and social sciences
Special topics, A-Z -- Continued

7164.I39	Individualism
	Industrial hygiene see Z6675.I5
	Industrial management see Z7164.O7
7164.I42	Industrial promotion
7164.I43	Industrial security measures
7164.I45	Industrial sociology
	Industry and state see Z7164.S84
7164.I5	Initiative and referendum
7164.I6	Institution building
	Institutions see Z7164.A85
7164.I7	Insurance

Cf. Z7164.A17 Accident insurance
Cf. Z7164.G83 Group insurance
Cf. Z7164.S6635 Social security
Cf. Z7164.U56 Unemployment insurance
Cf. Z7164.W67 Workers' compensation

7164.I78	Interest
7164.I786	Internal security
7164.I79	International business enterprises. Multinational corporations
	International economic relations see Z7164.E17
7164.I8	Internationalism

Cf. Z6461+ International law
Cf. Z6471+ League of Nations

Investments see Z7164.F5

7164.L1	Labor

Cf. Z7164.A4 Foreign workers
Cf. Z7164.C93 Cooperation
Cf. Z7164.H7 Home labor
Cf. Z7164.T7 Trade unions (Labor unions)
Cf. Z7164.U56 Unemployment
Cf. Z7164.W67 Workers' compensation

7164.L3	Land
7164.L38	Leadership
	League of Nations see Z6471+
7164.L49	Legal aid
7164.L53	Leisure
	Lesbianism see Z7164.H74
7164.L6	Liberty

Including civil rights, human rights, individual rights, etc.
Cf. Z1019+ Condemned and prohibited books

7164.L7	Lobbying
7164.L8	Local (Municipal) government

Cf. Z5942 City planning, municipal improvement, etc.
Cf. Z7164.P97 Public works

Z5051-7999

Political and social sciences
Special topics, A-Z -- Continued

7164.L9	Location of industries
	Management see Z7164.O7
7164.M15	Mandates
7164.M18	Marketing
7164.M2	Marriage. Family. Divorce
	Cf. Z5703.4.W53 Wife abuse
7164.M3	Materials management
7164.M45	Meat industry and trade
7164.M49	Men
7164.M67	Monarchy
	Money see Z7164.F5
	Multinational corporations see Z7164.I79
7164.N17	Narcotics. Drug abuse
	Cf. Z6671.2.N37 Narcotics and pregnancy
	National planning see Z7164.O7
7164.N2	Nationalism
7164.N3	Natural resources. Conservation
	Cf. Z7164.W2 Water rights, waterways
7164.N4	New states
7164.N6	Non-governmental organizations
7164.N64	Nonprofit organizations
7164.O4	Old age
	Cf. Z6663.A3 Aging (Physiology)
	Older people see Z7164.O4
7164.O7	Organization of production. Industrial management
	Including general theory of management
	Cf. Z7164.C81 Business
	Cf. Z7914.A2+ Industrial engineering
	Panics see Z7164.B91
7164.P18	Parliamentary practice
7164.P19	Passive resistance to government
7164.P2	Patriotism
7164.P3	Peace Corps
7164.P4	Pensions
	Personnel management see Z7164.C81
	Philanthropy see Z7164.C4+
7164.P76	Police
	Political geography see Z6004.P7
7164.P79	Political participation
7164.P8	Political parties
7164.P83	Political socialization
	Population see Z7164.D3
7164.P84	Pornography
7164.P85	Postal, telegraphy, and telephone service
7164.P94	Prices

                        Political and social sciences
                          Special topics, A-Z -- Continued
                            Primaries see Z7164.R4
                            Prisons see Z5118.C9
                            Privatization see Z7164.G59
                            Propaganda see Z7204.S67
                            Proportional representation see Z7164.R4
7164.P95   Prostitution
                            Public administration see Z7164.A2
7164.P9555   Public finance
7164.P956   Public opinion
7164.P957   Public relations
7164.P96   Public utilities
                            Public welfare see Z7164.C4+
7164.P97   Public works
                            Purchasing, procurement see Z7164.B95
7164.Q34   Quality of life
7164.R12   Race problems
                            Radio see Z7221+
7164.R15   Raw materials
7164.R2   Recall
7164.R3   Reconstruction
                                Class here works on economic and social reconstruction
                                For reconstruction after World War I see Z6207.E81
                                For reconstruction after World War II see Z6207.W81
                            Refugee relief see Z7164.R32
7164.R32   Refugees. Refugee relief
7164.R33   Regional, state, and national planning
                                Cf. Z7164.E15 Economic policy
7164.R34   Regionalism
                            Religion and sociology see Z7831
                            Religion and state see Z7776.72
7164.R38   Reports
                                Including preparation, etc.
7164.R4   Representation
                                Including ballots, elections, electoral college, primaries,
                                    proportional representation, etc.
7164.R45   Retail trade
7164.R5   Retirement
7164.R54   Revolutions
                            Rights, Human see Z7164.L6
                            Rural development see Z7164.C842
                            Rural sociology see Z7164.S688
7164.S3   Sabotage
7164.S33   Scouts and scouting
7164.S36   Secret societies
7164.S37   Securities

Z5051-7999

Political and social sciences
Special topics, A-Z -- Continued

7164.S38	Self-help groups
	Cf. Z7204.S44 Psychology
7164.S39	Service industries
7164.S42	Sex
	Cf. Z7204.S48 Psychology
7164.S46	Sexual harassment
7164.S55	Shipping. Ship subsidies
7164.S6	Slavery (General)
	Class local with local history
7164.S63	Social action
7164.S64	Social classes
7164.S66	Social conditions and problems
7164.S662	Social networks
7164.S663	Social prediction
	Social psychology see Z7204.S67
7164.S6635	Social security
	Social service see Z7164.C4+
7164.S665	Social settlements
7164.S667	Social surveys
	Socialism. Communism
7164.S67	General bibliography
7164.S675	Guild socialism
7164.S677	Socialist competition
7164.S678	Socialization
	Sociology
7164.S68	General bibliography
7164.S685	Christian sociology
7164.S686	Islamic sociology
7164.S688	Sociology, Rural
	Sociology and religion see Z7831
7164.S76	Sound recording industry
	Standardization of production (Economic aspects) see Z7164.O7
7164.S84	State and business
	State and church see Z7776.72
	State planning see Z7164.O7
	Student political activity see Z5814.S86
7164.S9	Substance abuse
7164.S92	Success
7164.S98	Syndicalism
7164.T2	Tariff
7164.T23	Taxation
	Cf. Z5074.T38 Agriculture
7164.T26	Technology and civilization

	Political and social sciences
	Special topics, A-Z -- Continued
7164.T28	Telecommunication
	Cf. Z5834.T4 Electricity
	Telegraph and telephone service see Z7164.P85
7164.T3	Terrorism
7164.T4	Thrift
7164.T55	Time allocation surveys
	Trade secrets see Z7164.B92
7164.T7	Trade unions. Labor unions. Guilds
	Including collective bargaining, etc.
	Cf. Z6675.T83 Health facilities
	Trades see Z7164.C81
	Tramps see Z7164.H72
	Transportation and communication
	Cf. Z5074.E3 Agricultural economics
	Cf. Z5451+ Canals
	Cf. Z5853.H2 Harbors
	Cf. Z5853.T7+ Engineering
	Cf. Z5863.T7 Effect of environment
	Cf. Z6724.R2 Military railroads
	Cf. Z7164.C8+ Commerce
	Cf. Z7164.P85 Postal, telegraphy, and telephone
	service
	Cf. Z7164.S55 Shipping
	Cf. Z7164.T81 Street and highway traffic
	Cf. Z7164.U72 Urban transportation
	Cf. Z7164.W2 Waterways
	Cf. Z7221+ Radio
	Cf. Z7231+ Railroads
7164.T8	General bibliography
7164.T81	Street and highway traffic. Traffic accidents
7164.T87	Trusts. Corporations
7164.U5	Underdeveloped areas. Developing countries
7164.U56	Unemployment. Unemployed. Unemployment insurance,
	etc.
7164.U58	Unmarried mothers
	Urban anthropology see Z5118.U72
7164.U7	Urban renewal. Urbanization
	Cf. Z5942 City planning
7164.U72	Urban transportation
7164.U8	Utopias
	Vagabonds see Z7164.H72
7164.V3	Valuation
7164.V55	Violence
7164.V6	Vocational guidance. Occupations
7164.V65	Voluntarism

Z5051-7999

	Political and social sciences
	Special topics, A-Z -- Continued
7164.W1	Wages
	Cf. Z7164.F8 Fringe benefits
7164.W16	Warehouses
7164.W2	Water rights. Waterways
	Cf. Z5074.I7 Irrigation
	Cf. Z5451+ Canals
	Cf. Z6004.P5+ Physical geography
	Cf. Z7164.C8+ Commerce
7164.W4	Wealth
	Women in politics see Z7963.P64
7164.W67	Workers' compensation
7164.Y8	Youth. Youth movement
7165.A-Z	By region or country, A-Z
	Subarrange each country by Table Z15
	For developing countries see Z7164.U5
7166	Catalogs
7166.Z9	Sales catalogs
	Pollution see Z5862+
7179	Pottery. Ceramics
	Cf. Z5118.P67 Anthropology
	Cf. Z7914.C6 Clay
	Printing see Z117
7191	Proverbs
7201-7205	Psychology (Table Z5 modified)
	Cf. Z5814.P8 Educational psychology
	Cf. Z6464.P9 Psychology of international relations
	Cf. Z6664.N5 Nervous system
	Cf. Z6665.6+ Psychiatry. Psychopathology
	Cf. Z6876+ Occultism
	Cf. Z7125+ Philosophy
7204.A-Z	Special topics, A-Z
7204.A25	Ability testing
	Cf. Z5814.P8 Psychology (Educational)
7204.A28	Adjustment
7204.A3	Adolescence
7204.A38	Aggressiveness
7204.A42	Aging
7204.A5	Alienation
7204.A55	Anxiety
7204.A6	Applied psychology. Counseling
	Cf. Z5814.C83 Educational counseling
7204.A78	Assertiveness
7204.A8	Attitude. Attitude change
7204.B45	Behavior modification
7204.B56	Biofeedback training

	Psychology
	Special topics, A-Z -- Continued
7204.P452	Performance
7204.P46	Personality
	Including personality tests
7204.P47	Phrenology
	Physiological psychology see Z6663.P8
7204.P54	Political psychology
7204.P67	Problem solving
	Psychical research see Z6878.P8
	Psychiatry see Z6665.6+
7204.P79	Psychoacoustics
7204.P8	Psychoanalysis
7204.P85	Psychological tests
	Cf. Z7204.P46 Personality tests
7204.P88	Psychometrics
	Psychopharmacology see Z6675.P79
	Psychophysiology see Z6663.P8
7204.R35	Reaction time
7204.R4	Religious psychology. Psychology and religion
7204.R57	Risk-taking
7204.R6	Rorschach test
7204.S42	Self-actualization
7204.S43	Self-disclosure
7204.S44	Self-help techniques
	Cf. Z7164.S38 Social sciences
7204.S45	Separation
7204.S48	Sex
	Cf. Z7164.S42 Social sciences
7204.S65	Social interaction
7204.S67	Social psychology
7204.S76	Space perception. Space
7204.S78	Stress
7204.S83	Subconsciousness
7204.S9	Symbolism
7204.S94	Szondi test
7204.T5	Thought
7204.T53	Time perception. Time
7204.V5	Vigilance
7204.V55	Visual perception
7215	Radar
7221-7225	Radio (Table Z6 modified)
7223.A-Z	Special topics, A-Z
7223.P6	Plays
7223.P74	Programs
7223.S3	Scripts
7223.S5	Single-sideband radio

	Radio
	Special topics, A-Z -- Continued
7223.S67	Spread spectrum communications
7223.W2	Waves, Radio
7231-7236	Railroads (Table Z4 modified)
	Cf. Z5851+ Engineering
	Cf. Z6724.R2 Military railroads
	Cf. Z7161+ Political and social sciences
	Cf. Z7164.T8+ Transportation
7234.A-Z	Special topics, A-Z
7234.A17	Accounts, bookkeeping, etc.
7234.A9	Automation
7234.B7	Brakes
7234.B8	Buildings and structures
7234.C3	Cars
7234.C75	Consolidation
7234.C8	Crews
7234.C82	Crossings
7234.E5	Eight-hour movement
7234.E55	Electrification. Electric equipment
7234.E57	Electronic equipment
7234.E6	Engineering
7234.F2	Fares
7234.F5	Finance
7234.F7	Freight
7234.H53	High speed ground transportation
7234.I6	Interoceanic
7234.L5	Lighting
7234.L6	Locomotives
7234.M27	Maintenance and repair
7234.M3	Management
7234.M7	Motorcars (Railway)
7234.P3	Passenger traffic
7234.R2	Rails
7234.R3	Rates
7234.S17	Safety measures
7234.S2	Salaries, pensions, etc.
7234.S5	Signals and signaling
7234.S7	State control. Government ownership
7234.S74	Stations
7234.S8	Street railroads
7234.S9	Subways
7234.T5	Ties
7234.T85	Tunnels
7234.V2	Valuation
7234.Y3	Yards
	Recitations see Z7156.R2

Z5051-7999

	Recreation see Z7511+
	Reference books see Z1035.1
7254	Rehabilitation
	Cf. Z6122+ People with mental disabilities
	Cf. Z6675.R4 Medical rehabilitation
	Cf. Z7925 Vocational rehabilitation
	Religion see Z7751+
	Research (Scientific) see Z7405.R4
	Research (Technology) see Z7914.R5
	Restaurants see Z5986
7291	Riddles
7295	Roads. Highways
	Rubber see Z6297
7335	Salt
	Science. Natural history
	Cf. Z5151+ Astronomy
	Cf. Z5320+ Biology
	Cf. Z5351+ Botany
	Cf. Z5521+ Chemistry
	Cf. Z6000 Geodesy
	Cf. Z6031+ Geology, mineralogy, paleontology
	Cf. Z6651+ Mathematics
	Cf. Z6662+ Anatomy and physiology (Medicine)
	Cf. Z6704+ Microscopy
	Cf. Z6827 Nature
	Cf. Z7141+ Physics
	Cf. Z7844.5 Science and religion
	Cf. Z7911+ Applied science, technology
	Cf. Z7991+ Zoology
7401	General bibliography
7402	Bibliography of early works
7403	Periodicals. Societies
7404	Biobibliography
7405.A-Z	Special topics, A-Z
7405.A6	Apparatus and instruments. Instrumentation
7405.A7	Artificial intelligence
7405.A8	Atlases
7405.B5	Bionics
7405.C6	Communication in science
7405.C64	Coral reefs. Coral reef conservation
7405.C9	Cybernetics
	Cycles see Z7405.P66
7405.D37	Data processing
7405.D5	Dictionaries. Encyclopedias
7405.D55	Directories
	Encyclopedias see Z7405.D5
7405.E9	Expeditions

Science. Natural history

Special topics, A-Z -- Continued

7405.F73	Fraud in science
	Habitat conservation see Z7405.N38
7405.H6	History
	Indicators, Science see Z7405.S36
	Industry and science see Z7405.S34
	Instruments, instrumentation see Z7405.A6
7405.L3	Laboratories
7405.M35	Marine parks and reserves
	Cf. Z6905 Parks
7405.M4	Methodology
7405.N38	Nature conservation. Habitat conservation
	Cf. Z7164.N3 Conservation of natural resources
	Operations research see Z7671+
7405.P66	Periodicity. Cycles
7405.P7	Personnel. Scientists
7405.P74	Philosophy
7405.P8	Public policy
7405.R4	Research
7405.S34	Science and industry
7405.S36	Science indicators
7405.S45	Self-organizing systems
7405.S6	Social aspects
	State and science see Z7405.P8
7405.S94	System theory
	Cf. Z7671+ System analysis
7405.T3	Tables
7405.T38	Technical editing
7405.T4	Technical writing
7405.W47	Wetland conservation
7405.W48	Wetlands
	Including marshes, swamps, moors, bogs, riparian areas, etc.
7405.W54	Wilderness areas
7407.A-Z	Science. By region or country, A-Z
7408.A-Z	Natural history. By region or country, A-Z
7409	Catalogs
	Sculpture see Z5951+
7421	Seals. Sigillography
	Cf. Z6866+ Numismatics
	Ship subsidies see Z7164.S55
	Shipbuilding see Z6834.S5
	Social sciences see Z7161+
	Societies see Z5051+

7511-7516	Sports. Amusements. Recreation (Table Z4 modified)
	Cf. Z5170+ Automobiles and automobiling
	Cf. Z5349.S65 Sports for the blind
	Cf. Z5481 Cards and card playing
	Cf. Z5541 Chess
	Cf. Z5814.P47 Educational play
	Cf. Z5814.R3 Recreation centers
	Cf. Z5906 Fencing and dueling
	Cf. Z5971+ Fishing
	Cf. Z6121 Gymnastics, physical education
	Cf. Z6123.S65 Sports for people with disabilities
	Cf. Z6240 Horsemanship
	Cf. Z6905 Parks
	Cf. Z7631 Swimming
	Cf. Z7893 Toys
	Cf. Z7963.S6 Women in sports
7514.A-Z	Special topics, A-Z
	African Americans see Z7514.B43
7514.A58	Amusement parks
7514.A7	Archery
	Athletics see Z6121
7514.B3	Baseball
7514.B34	Basketball
7514.B43	Blacks. African Americans
7514.B6	Boats and boating
7514.B7	Boxing
7514.B9	Bull fights
7514.C2	Camping. Outdoor life
7514.C3	Canoeing
	Caving see Z6033.C3
7514.C5	Checkers
	Chess see Z5541
7514.C6	Circuses
7514.C7	Cricket
7514.C73	Croquet
7514.C9	Cycling
7514.D18	Dance notation
7514.D2	Dancing
7514.D44	Deer hunting
	Ethical aspects see Z7514.M66
7514.F2	Falconry
	Fishing see Z5971+
7514.F7	Football
7514.F75	Forests, Recreation in
7514.G6	Golf
	Handball, Team see Z7514.T25
7514.H73	Hockey. Ice hockey

Sports. Amusements. Recreation
Special topics, A-Z -- Continued

7514.H8	Horse racing
7514.H9	Hunting
7514.I53	Indoor games
7514.M37	Martial arts
7514.M66	Moral and ethical aspects
7514.M68	Motorsports
	Mountaineering see Z6016.M7
7514.N8	Nudism
7514.O5	Olympic games
7514.O8	Outdoor recreation
	Playgrounds see Z7164.C5
7514.P65	Political aspects. Sports and state
7514.P79	Psychological aspects
7514.R32	Racket games
7514.R58	Rivers, Recreational use of
7514.R63	Rock climbing
7514.R85	Running
	Cf. Z6663.R86 Physiology of running
7514.S2	Sailing
7514.S6	Skating
7514.S65	Skiing
7514.S7	Soccer
7514.S72	Social aspects
	Spelunking see Z6033.C3
7514.S75	Sports facilities
	Including gymnasiums, stadiums, etc.
	Swimming see Z7631
7514.T25	Team handball
7514.T3	Tennis
	Toys see Z7893
7514.T8	Track athletics
7514.V64	Volleyball
7514.W56	Wilderness, Recreational use of
7514.W73	Wrestling
7536	Stammering
7551-7555	Statistics (Table Z6 modified)
	Cf. Z7161+ Political and social sciences
7553.A-Z	Special topics, A-Z
	Agriculture see Z5074.S76
7553.C3	Census
7553.C7	Commerce
7553.E2	Economics
7553.L2	Labor
	Mathematical statistics see Z6654.M33
7553.M43	Medicine

	Sugar
7609	General bibliography
7610.A-Z	Special topics, A-Z
7610.M7	Molasses
7610.S8	Sugarcane
7615	Suicide
	Surgery see Z6666+
7631	Swimming
7660	Symbolism
	Class here general works only
	For symbolism in special subjects, see the subject
7671-7675	System analysis. Systems engineering. Operations research (Table Z6)
	Tea see Z5074.T4
	Technology see Z7911+
7711-7715	Television (Table Z6 modified)
7713.A-Z	Special topics, A-Z
7713.S47	Series
7721	Temperance
	Including alcoholism, liquor problem, prohibition, etc.
	Cf. Z6663.A33 Physiological effect of alcohol
	Cf. Z6665.7.A43 Alcoholism as a disease
	Theology and religion
	Cf. Z5761 Devil
	Cf. Z6366+ Jews
	Cf. Z6876+ Occultism
	Cf. Z7125+ Philosophy
7751	General bibliography
	Including comparative religion
7753	Periodicals. Directories. Yearbooks
7755	Catalogs
7757.A-Z	By region or country, A-Z
7759	Children's literature. Juvenile literature
7761	Aged and religion. Older people and religion
7763	Angels
7765	Atheism. Free thought. Skepticism
	Bible
7770	General bibliography
7771.A-Z	Versions, A-Z
7771.A4	African Bibles
7771.A5	American Bibles
7771.D86	Dutch Bibles
7771.E5	English Bibles
7771.F8	French Bibles
7771.G3	German Bibles
7771.I3	Illustrated Bibles. Hieroglyphic Bibles
7771.I4	Indian Bibles

	Theology and religion
	Bible
	Versions, A-Z -- Continued
7771.I53	Indic Bibles
7771.L2	Latin Bibles
7771.M3	Manuscripts
7771.O3	Oceanic (Polynesian, etc.) Bibles
7771.P7	Polish Bibles
7771.S7	Spanish Bibles
7771.S9	Swedish Bibles
7771.T58	Thumb Bibles
7771.W4	Welsh Bibles
7771.5.A-Z	Special topics, A-Z
7771.5.B52	Bible stories
7771.5.E84	Ethics
	Parts
	Old Testament
7772.A1	General bibliography
	Groups of Old Testament books
7772.B2	Five Scrolls
7772.B25	Former Prophets
7772.B3	Hagiographa
7772.B35	Heptateuch
7772.B4	Hexateuch
7772.B45	Historical Books
7772.B5	Minor Prophets
7772.B55	Pentateuch
7772.B6	Poetical Books
7772.B65	Prophets
7772.B7	Prophets (Nevi'im)
	Individual Old Testament books (alphabetically)
7772.C1	Amos
7772.C2	Chronicles 1 and 2
7772.C3	Daniel
7772.C42	Ezra
7772.C82	Hosea
7772.D37	Jeremiah
7772.D38	Kings 1 and 2
(7772.E1)	Psalms
	see Z7772.I1
7772.H1	Nahum
7772.I1	Psalms
(7772.J1)	Prophets
	see Z7772.B65
7772.J2	Ruth
7772.K1	Apocryphal books
	New Testament

Z5051-7999

Theology and religion -- Continued

7798	Glossolalia
7799	History (Theology)
7799.2	Holy Shroud
7799.3	Holy Spirit
	Cf. Z7798 Glossolalia
7799.8	Human ecology
7800	Hymnology
7803	Imitatio Christi
7805	Inquisition
7806	Jesus Christ
	Cf. Z6514.C5J47+ Literature
7808	Laity
7809	Liberation theology
7813	Liturgy. Prayer books
	For Roman Catholic liturgy see Z7838.L7
	For Russian and other Orthodox Eastern churches see Z7842.L5
7815	Martyrs
7815.5	Mass media in religion
7815.7	Meditation
7816	Miracles
	Cf. Z5784.M6 Miracle plays
7817	Missions
	Including general, and Protestant
	For Roman Catholic missions see Z7838.M6
	Monasticism see Z7839+
7819	Mysticism (Theology)
	Cf. Z6878.M9 Occultism
	Cf. Z7128.M9 Philosophy
	Older people and religion see Z7761
7820	Pastoral theology
7820.5	Pentecostolism
7821	Philosophy of religion
7825	Pilgrimages
7825.4	Practical theology
7825.5	Prayer
7826	Preaching
	Cf. Z7847 Sermons
7827	Prophecy (Old Testament)
	Psychology (Religious) see Z7204.R4
7830	Reformation and Counter-Reformation
	Cf. Z8141.5 Calvin
	Cf. Z8429 Hus
	Cf. Z8528 Luther
	Cf. Z8999 Zwingli
7830.5	Religion and medicine

Z5051-7999

	Theology and religion -- Continued
7831	Religion and sociology
7831.5	Religion and technology
	Religions (non-Christian)
7833	General bibliography. General special bibliography
	Including primitive religions, sex worship, phallicism, etc.
	For comparative religion see Z7751+
7834.A-Z	By region or country, A-Z
	e.g.
7834.A3	African religions
7835.A-Z	Special, A-Z
7835.A5	Anthroposophy
	Cf. Z6675.A57 Anthroposophical therapy
7835.B2	Bahai Faith
7835.B5	Black Muslims
7835.B64	Bon. Bonpo
7835.B8	Brahmanism. Hinduism
	Buddhism see Z7860+
	Church of Scientology see Z7835.S35
7835.C6	Confucianism
7835.C86	Cults
	Dianetics see Z7835.S35
7835.D7	Druidism
7835.I14	I AM Religious Activity
	Islam see Z7835.M6
7835.J2	Jainism
	Judaism see Z6370+
7835.K64	Konkokyo
	Mandaeism see Z7845.M3
7835.M54	Millennialism
7835.M6	Mohammedanism. Islam
7835.N48	New Age movement
7835.N55	Nimbarka (Sect)
7835.S25	Sami (European people)
7835.S35	Scientology. Church of Scientology. Dianetics
7835.S43	Shamanism
	Shinto
7835.S5	General bibliography
7835.S58	Tenri
7835.S64	Sikhism
7835.T2	Taoism
7835.V34	Vaishnavism
7835.V4	Vedanta
7835.Z8	Zoroastrianism. Mazdeism. Mithraism. Parseeism
7836	Mythology
7836.5	Restorationism
7836.7	Revivals

Theology and religion -- Continued
Roman Catholic Church

7837	General bibliography
7837.5	Periodicals. Societies
7837.7.A-Z	By region or country, A-Z
7838.A-Z	Special topics, A-Z
7838.A6	Apologetics
7838.B95	Byzantine rite
7838.C3	Catechisms and creeds
7838.C45	Chaldean rite
7838.C65	Communism
7838.C7	Concilia
7838.C73	Converts
7838.D6	Documents. Bulls
7838.E5	Encyclicals (Papal)
7838.E6	Episcopacy
7838.H6	Books of Hours
	Immaculate Conception see Z8552
7838.I54	Initiation rites. Rite of Christian initiation of adults
7838.L34	Laity
7838.L7	Liturgy and ritual (Breviary, Missal)
7838.M35	Maronite rite. Maronites
	Maronites see Z7838.M35
7838.M6	Missions
7838.P53	Papacy. Popes
7838.P54	Peace
	Popes see Z7838.P53
	Rite of Christian initiation of adults see Z7838.I54
7838.R7	Rosary
7838.S3	Sacred Heart, Devotion to the
7838.S63	Sociology. Social problems
	Vatican City see Z2373
7838.Y6	Young Christian Workers
	Religious orders. Monasticism
7839	General bibliography
7839.5.A-Z	By region or country, A-Z
7840.A-Z	Special, A-Z
7840.A9	Augustinians
7840.B2	Barnabites
7840.B25	Basilians
7840.B28	Beguines
7840.B3	Benedictines
7840.B74	Brothers of Our Lady of Mercy
7840.B76	Brothers of the Common Life
7840.C15	Camaldolites
7840.C17	Capuchin nuns
7840.C18	Capuchins

Theology and religion
Roman Catholic Church
Religious orders. Monasticism
Special, A-Z -- Continued

7840.C2	Carmelites
7840.C3	Carthusians
7840.C5	Cistercians
7840.D7	Dominicans
7840.F4	Felician Sisters
7840.F8	Franciscans
7840.F82	Frères de l'instruction chrétienne
7840.J5	Jesuits
7840.L3	Lazarists. Vincentians. Congregation of the Mission
7840.M3	Marianists
7840.M34	Maryknoll Sisters of St. Dominic
7840.M4	Mercedarians
7840.O2	Oblates of Mary Immaculate
7840.O7	Oratorians
7840.P38	Pauline Fathers (Order of St. Paul the First Hermit)
7840.P53	Piarists
7840.P9	Premonstrants
7840.R2	Recollets
7840.R3	Redemptorists
7840.S34	Salesians
7840.S4	Servites
7840.S55	Sisters of the Holy Family of Nazareth
7840.S63	Society of Mary Reparatrix
7840.S9	Sulpicians
7840.T5	Theatines
7840.T8	Trinitarians
7840.V53	Viatorians
7841.A-Z	Sects, schools, etc., A-Z
7841.J3	Jansenists
7841.O4	Old Catholics
7841.P36	Polish National Catholic Church of America
	Thomists (Scholasticism) see Z7128.S3
	Thomists (Saint Thomas Aquinas) see Z8870

Russian and other Orthodox Eastern churches
For individual non-Russian bodies see Z7845.A+

7842.A3	General bibliography
7842.A35	Periodicals. Societies
7842.A4-Z	Special topics, A-Z
7842.A5	Aesthetics
7842.E48	Education
7842.L5	Liturgy
7842.M66	Monasteries
7842.R2	Raskolniks

Theology and religion -- Continued

7843	Sabbath
	Sacraments
7843.4	General bibliography
7843.5.A-Z	By sacrament, A-Z
7843.5.B3	Baptism
7844	Saints
7844.5	Science and religion
7845.A-Z	Sects, churches, movements, heresies (Christian), A-Z

Prefer classification under special topics, e. g. Z7843.5.B3
Baptism

7845.A35	Adventists
7845.A4	Anabaptists

Cf. Z7845.M4 Mennonites

7845.A5	Anglican Church
7845.A8	Arminians
7845.B2	Baptists
7845.C45	Children of God
7845.C48	Christian and Missionary Alliance
7845.C5	Christian Science
7845.C52	Church of Ireland
7845.C53	Church of Jesus Christ (Bickertonites)
7845.C7	Congregational churches
7845.C73	Coptic Church
7845.D6	Disciples of Christ
7845.D62	Dissenters
7845.D8	Dukhobors
7845.E3	Eastern churches

Cf. Z7842.A3+ Russian and other Orthodox Eastern
churches

Ethiopian Orthodox Church see Z7845.Y32

7845.F8	Friends, Society of. Quakers
7845.G6	Gnosticism
7845.H6	Holiness Church
7845.H8	Huguenots

For Huguenots as an ethnic group in the United States
see Z1361.H83

7845.H85	Hussites

Cf. Z7845.M7 Moravians

7845.H86	Hutterites
7845.I35	Iglesia Christiana Evangelica
7845.J45	Jehovah's Witnesses
7845.L9	Lutheran Church
7845.M3	Madaeans
7845.M34	Manichaeism
7845.M4	Mennonites

Cf. Z7845.A4 Anabaptists

Z5051-7999

	Theology and religion
	Sects, churches, movements, heresies (Christian), A-Z --
	Continued
7845.M5	Methodist Church
7845.M7	Moravians
7845.M8	Mormons
7845.N4	Nestorians
	New Jerusalem Church see Z7845.S9
	Nonconformists see Z7845.D62
	Orthodox Eastern Church see Z7842.A3+
7845.O77	Orthodoxos Ekklēsia tēs Hellados
7845.O83	Oxford movement
7845.P4	Pentecostal churches
7845.P45	Pietism
7845.P5	Plymouth Brethren
7845.P9	Presbyterian Church
7845.P93	Protestant churches
7845.R37	Rastafarians
7845.R4	Reformed churches
7845.R45	Remonstrants
7845.R6	Rogerenes
	Roman Catholic Church see Z7837+
	Russian Church see Z7842.A3+
7845.S24	Salvation Army
7845.S35	Seventh-Day Adventists
7845.S5	Shakers
7845.S86	Suomen Ortodoksinen Kirkko
7845.S9	Swedenborgians. New Jerusalem Church
7845.U35	Ukraïns'ka pravoslavna t͡serkva
7845.U45	Unification Church
7845.U5	Unitarian
	Unitas fratrum see Z7845.M7
	United Brethren see Z7845.M7
7845.U65	United Church of Christ
7845.W2	Waldenses
7845.Y32	Ya' Ityoṗyā 'ortodoks tawāḥedo béta kerestiyān
7845.1	Christian unity
7847	Sermons
	Cf. Z7826 Preaching
	Sociology and religion see Z7831
7847.5	Spiritual healing
7848	Study and teaching. Theological seminaries
7849	Sunday schools. Religious education in secular schools
7850	Theodicy
7851	Tracts and religious reading
7851.5	Trinity
7852	Votive offerings

Theology and religion -- Continued
7853   War and religion
                       Women and religion see Z7963.R45
7854   Work
7855.A-Z   Individual works. By author or title, A-Z
                           e. g.
7855.S7   Speculum humanae salvationis
                               Cf. Z241.S74 Speculum (the block book)
                       Buddhism
                           Cf. Z5956.B8 Buddhist art
7860   General bibliography
7860.3   Periodicals. Societies. Yearbooks
7861.A-Z   By region or country, A-Z
                       Tripiṭaka. Canonical literature
7862   General works
                           Versions
                               Including bibliographies of single piṭakas, e. g. Tibetan
                                   version of Kanjur
7862.2   Pāli version
7862.3   Chinese version
7862.4   Tibetan version
                           By piṭaka
                               Class individual commentaries with the original text
                           Sūtrapiṭaka
7862.7.A2   General works
7862.7.A3-Z   Individual. By title, A-Z
                           Vinayapiṭaka
7862.8.A2   General works
7862.8.A3-Z   Individual. By title, A-Z
                           Abhidharmapiṭaka
7862.9.A2   General works
7862.9.A3-Z   Individual. By title, A-Z
7863.A-Z   Other individual works. By author or title, A-Z
                       Special modifications, schools, sects, etc.
7864.A2   General works
7864.A3-Z   Individual, A-Z
(7864.B65)   Bonpo (Sect)
                                   see Z7835.B64
7864.J5   Ji (Sect)
7864.J6   Jōdoshū
7864.L35   Lamaism
7864.N53   Nicheren (Sect)
7864.P87   Pure Land Buddhism
7864.R56   Ritsu (Sect)
7864.R64   Rñiṅ-ma-pa (Sect)
7864.S27   Sa-skya-pa (Sect)
7864.S5   Shin (Sect)

Z5051-7999

	Theology and religion
	Buddhism
	Special modifications, schools, sects, etc.
	Individual, A-Z -- Continued
7864.S53	Shingon (Sect)
7864.S65	Sōtōshū
7864.T3	Tachikawa School
7864.T35	Tantric Buddhism
7864.T45	Tendai
7864.Y64	Yogācāra (Buddhism)
7864.Z4	Zen Buddhism
7865.A-Z	Special topics (Doctrinal and non-doctrinal), A-Z
7865.C67	Cosmology, Buddhist
	Philosophy, Buddhist see Z7128.B93
7865.5	Catalogs
7876	Time and timekeepers
	Cf. Z7204.T53 Time perception
	Tin soldiers see Z7893
7882	Tobacco. Smoking
	Cf. Z6671.2.T63 Tobacco effects on fetus
	Toxicology
7890	General bibliography
7891.A-Z	Special poisons, A-Z
7891.A82	Asbestos
7891.C36	Cannabis. Marijuana
7891.C45	Chlorine
7891.D56	Dioxins
7891.D7	Drugs
7891.F5	Fluorine
7891.F66	Food additives
7891.I57	Insecticides
7891.L4	Lead
	Marijuana see Z7891.C36
7891.M4	Mercury
7891.M47	Minerals
7891.P47	Pesticides
7891.R3	Radioactive substances
7891.S64	Solvents
7891.T7	Tritium
7891.U73	Uranium
7891.V45	Venom
7891.V55	Vinyl chloride
7892.A-Z	Special topics, A-Z
7892.B44	Behavioral toxicology
7892.I53	Industrial toxicology
7893	Toys
	Travels see Z6011+

	Universities see Z5051+
7911-7916	Useful arts and applied science. Technology (Table Z4 modified)
	For bibliographies on the manufacture, use, etc. of individual chemicals see Z5524.A+
	Cf. Z5071+ Agriculture
	Cf. Z5521+ Chemistry
	Cf. Z5831+ Electricity
	Cf. Z5836+ Electronics
	Cf. Z5851+ Engineering
	Cf. Z5941+ Architecture
	Cf. Z5971+ Fishing and fisheries
	Cf. Z6046 Glass
	Cf. Z6055 Gold and silver smithing
	Cf. Z6151+ Handicraft
	Cf. Z6331+ Iron and steel
	Cf. Z6678+ Metals and metallurgy
	Cf. Z6736+ Mines and mining
	Cf. Z7179 Pottery. Ceramics
	Cf. Z7231+ Railroads
	Cf. Z7401+ Science
	Cf. Z7609+ Sugar
	Cf. Z7951 Wine
7914.A-Z	Special topics, A-Z
	Industrial efficiency. Industrial engineering
7914.A2	General bibliography
7914.A22	Standardization
7914.A3	Adhesives
7914.A5	Alcohol
7914.A64	Appropriate technology
	Artisans see Z6153.A7
7914.A7	Asbestos
7914.A8	Asphalt
	Assessment, Technology see Z7914.T25
7914.B3	Bagasse
7914.B32	Biomolecules
7914.B33	Biotechnology
	Blacksmithing see Z6153.B55
7914.B37	Blueprints and blueprinting
7914.B4	Boots and shoes
7914.B5	Brazing
7914.B6	Brewing
	Cf. Z5943.B73 Breweries
7914.B8	Brickmaking
7914.B9	Building
	Cf. Z7914.H6 House construction
7914.B93	Burglary protection

Useful arts and applied science. Technology
Special topics, A-Z -- Continued

7914.B94	Buttons
7914.C25	Carbon fibers
7914.C3	Carbonization
7914.C32	Carriages and carts
7914.C33	Casting
7914.C35	Ceilings
	Cf. Z5943.C45 Architecture
7914.C37	Charcoal
7914.C4	Chemical engineering. Technical chemistry
7914.C5	Chimneys
7914.C6	Clay
7914.C64	Cleaning compounds
7914.C75	Computer graphics
7914.C8	Cooling towers
7914.C84	Cosmetics
	Cryogenics see Z7914.L75
7914.C87	Cutain walls
7914.C9	Cutlery
7914.D43	Decks
	Diamonds, Industrial see Z5853.D45
7914.D45	Dictionaries
7914.D5	Dies (Metal working)
7914.D66	Doors
	Cf. Z5943.D74 Architecture
7914.D8	Drying
7914.D85	Dust removal
7914.D87	Dwellings
7914.D9	Dyes and dyeing. Coloring matter
7914.E36	Electrochemical cutting
7914.E37	Electrophoretic deposition
7914.E4	Electroplating
7914.E45	Elevators. Escalators
7914.E5	Enameling
	Escalators see Z7914.E45
7914.E93	Exterior walls
7914.F25	Facility management
7914.F3	Factory layout
7914.F55	Floors and flooring
7914.F63	Food
	Cf. Z5185.F66 Food microbiology
	Cf. Z5986 Food service
	Forecasting, Technological see Z7914.T245
7914.F65	Forging
7914.F7	Foundry work

Useful arts and applied science. Technology
Special topics, A-Z -- Continued

7914.F8	Fuel
	Cf. Z6915 Peat
7914.G2	Gas
7914.G7	Grain milling
7914.G74	Grinding and polishing
7914.G9	Gypsum
	Heating see Z5853.H4
7914.H45	High temperatures
7914.H5	History
7914.H6	House construction
7914.H9	Hydrogenation
	Ice-cream industry see Z6270
	India-rubber industry see Z6297
7914.I48	Industrial archaeology
7914.I5	Industrial design
	Industrial safety see Z7914.S17
7914.I53	Industrial tours
7914.I55	Information services
	Innovations, Technological see Z7914.T247
7914.I57	Interior walls. Partitions
7914.I8	Isotopes
7914.J4	Jet cutting
	Keys see Z7914.L72
7914.L15	Lac
7914.L2	Lampblack
7914.L25	Laundry
7914.L27	Leather industry
7914.L3	Lighting
7914.L5	Lignite
7914.L6	Lime
7914.L7	Loading and unloading
	Location of industries see Z7164.L9
7914.L72	Locks and keys
7914.L75	Low temperature engineering
	Cf. Z7914.R33 Refrigeration and refrigerating machinery
7914.L8	Lumber
7914.M25	Machinery in industry
7914.M27	Management information systems
7914.M3	Manufacturers
7914.M32	Manufacturing processes
7914.M34	Materials handling
7914.M38	Mead
7914.M4	Mechanical drawing
7914.M5	Metalwork

Z5051-7999

Useful arts and applied science. Technology
Special topics, A-Z -- Continued

7914.M6	Mills and mill work
7914.M65	Mixing
	Noise control see Z5862.2.N6
7914.N83	Nuclear bomb shelter construction
7914.O23	Office buildings
7914.O28	Oil shales
7914.O3	Oils and fats. Waxes
7914.O6	Optical brighteners
7914.P13	Packaging
7914.P15	Painting (Industrial)
7914.P17	Paneling
7914.P2	Papermaking
	Partitions see Z7914.I57
7914.P3	Patents
7914.P33	Pattern making
	Peat see Z6915
7914.P5	Pigments
	Pipelines see Z5863.P5
7914.P7	Plastic materials
	Cf. Z5074.P665 Plastics in agriculture
	Cf. Z6675.P585 Plastics in medicine
	Polishing see Z7914.G74
7914.P75	Printing ink
7914.P78	Production engineering
7914.P8	Protective coatings
7914.Q3	Quality control
	Radio see Z7221+
7914.R2	Recycling. Salvage
7914.R3	Refractory materials
7914.R33	Refrigeration and refrigerating machinery
	Cf. Z6270 Ice cream, ices, etc.
7914.R5	Research (Industrial)
7914.R6	Risk communication
	Robotics see Z5853.R58
7914.R7	Roofs
	Rubber industry see Z6297
7914.S17	Safety. Safety engineering
	Salvage see Z7914.R2
7914.S2	Sand
7914.S6	Silk
7914.S66	Soap
7914.S663	Social aspects
7914.S68	Soluble glass. Water glass
	Soundproofing see Z5862.2.N6
7914.S73	Space frame structures

Useful arts and applied science. Technology
Special topics, A-Z -- Continued

7914.S79	Stairs
	Standardization see Z7914.A22
7914.S8	Starch
7914.S96	Syrups
7914.T22	Technical translating
	Technical writing see Z7405.T4
7914.T245	Technological forecasting
7914.T247	Technological innovations
	Technology and civilization see Z7164.T26
7914.T249	Technology and state
7914.T25	Technology assessment
7914.T256	Technology transfer
7914.T27	Temporary structures
7914.T28	Terminology
7914.T3	Textile industry
	Including fabrics, carpets, rugs, tapestry
	Cf. Z7971+ Wool
	Transfer, Technology see Z7914.T256
7914.T74	Tree houses
7914.T78	Turning
7914.T8	Turpentine
7914.U4	Ultrasonic waves
	Cf. Z6675.U47 Ultrasonics in medicine
7914.V3	Value engineering
7914.V32	Vapor plating
7914.W34	Walls
7914.W37	Waste products
7914.W38	Waterproofing
7914.W4	Welding
	Cf. Z5834.W4 Electric welding
	Cf. Z6679.W4 Welded joints
7914.W67	Windows
7914.W7	Wire
7914.W8	Wood
	Cf. Z5354.W64 Botany
	Cf. Z6153.W65 Craft woodwork
7914.W84	Work environment
	Veterinary medicine see Z6674
	Visual disabilities, People with see Z5346.A2+
7925	Vocational rehabilitation
	Voyages and travels see Z6011+

Z5051-7999

7935	Water supply. Ground water
	Cf. Z5074.W3 Water in agriculture
	Cf. Z5185.W37 Water microbiology
	Cf. Z5853.H9 Hydraulic engineering
	Cf. Z5862.2.W3 Water pollution
	Cf. Z6668.2.W37 Water fluoridation (Dentistry)
	Waterways (Hydraulic engineering) see Z5853.H9
	Waterways (Transportation and communication) see Z7164.T8+
	Waterways (Water rights) see Z7164.W2
	Whaling see Z5973.W5
7951	Wine and wine making
	Cf. Z5996.G7 Grapes and viticulture
7961-7965	Women (Table Z6 modified)
	see also Women as authors, a subdivision under countries in National bibliography, e. g. Z2350.5 Italian women as authors
	Cf. Z5111+ Anthropology and ethnology
	Cf. Z5865+ Erotic literature
	Cf. Z7161+ Political and social sciences
7963.A-Z	Special topics, A-Z
7963.A3	Women in aeronautics
7963.A4	Aged women. Older women
7963.A73	Women in architecture. Women architects
7963.A75	Women artists (General)
7963.A8	Women authors (General)
	Cf. Z5917.W6 Women authors
7963.B6	Biography
7963.C58	Women and city planning
7963.C65	Comfort women
7963.C67	Computers and women
7963.E18	Economics and women. Women in development
7963.E2	Education of women
7963.E7	Employment of women
	Including works on women in agriculture, industry, etc., and maternity insurance, night work, etc.
7963.E73	Women engineers
7963.F44	Feminism
	Women in folklore see Z5983.W65
7963.H42	Women and health
7963.J4	Jewish women
7963.L3	Women in landscape architecture. Women landscape architects
	Women in literature see Z6514.C5W64+
7963.M42	Women and mathematics
7963.M43	Women in medicine. Women physicians
7963.M67	Mothers
	Older women see Z7963.A4

	Women
	Special topics, A-Z -- Continued
7963.P64	Women in politics
7963.R45	Women and religion
7963.S3	Women in science
7963.S55	Women soldiers. Women and war
7963.S6	Women in sports
7963.S9	Suffrage. Women's rights
7963.T43	Women and technology
	Wonders and curiosities see Z5705
7971-7965	Wool (Table Z6)
	Zoology
	Cf. Z5856+ Entomology
7991	General bibliography
7992	Bibliography of early works
7993	Periodicals. Societies
7994.A-Z	General, A-Z
7994.A5	Anatomy and physiology. Comparative anatomy
7994.A56	Animals and civilization. Human-animal relationships
7994.A67	Aquariums, Public
7994.A68	Aquatic invertebrates
7994.E7	Embryology
	Endangered species see Z7994.W5
7994.F56	Flight
	Fur-bearing animals see Z5994.6
7994.G3	Game and game birds
7994.G33	Game protection
7994.H3	Habitations
	Human-animal relationships see Z7994.A56
7994.I34	Identification
7994.I4	Immobilization
7994.L3	Laboratory animals
	Cf. Z5074.L24 Laboratory animal culture
	Livestock see Z5074.L7
7994.M33	Marine fauna
7994.M77	Monsters
	Cf. Z5983.A6 Mythical animals
7994.M8	Morphology
7994.P3	Pathology and abnormalities of invertebrates
	For vertebrate pathology see Z6674
	Cf. Z5858.E2 Economic entomology
	Pets see Z6980
7994.P6	Populations
	Poultry see Z5074.P8
	Public aquariums see Z7994.A67
7994.S65	Soil fauna
7994.T2	Taxidermy

Z5051-7999

Zoology
   General, A-Z -- Continued
7994.W5	Wildlife conservation. Endangered species
7994.W55	Wildlife management
7994.W57	Wildlife reintroduction
7994.W58	Wildlife rescue
7994.Z65	Zoo animals
7994.Z66	Zoological gardens
7996.A-Z	Taxonomic groups and special animals, A-Z
7996.A1	General. Nomenclature
7996.A42	American bison
7996.A45	Amphibians
7996.A47	Annelida
7996.A57	Apes
7996.A59	Arabian oryx
7996.A6	Arachnida
7996.A74	Arthropoda
7996.A8	Ascidians
7996.A95	Axolotls
	Batrachia see Z7996.A45
7996.B37	Bats
7996.B43	Bears
7996.B44	Beavers
	Bees see Z5256
7996.B54	Bighorn sheep
	Birds see Z5331+
7996.B58	Black-footed ferret
7996.B6	Black-tailed prarie dog
7996.B65	Bonobo
7996.B73	Brachiopoda
7996.B77	Brown tree snake
7996.C25	Callitrichidae
7996.C27	Canidae
7996.C28	Caribou
	Cats see Z5491
	Cattle see Z5074.C33
7996.C34	Cebidae
7996.C38	Cercopithecidae
7996.C4	Cetacea
7996.C45	Chimpanzees
7996.C6	Coelenterata
7996.C73	Crayfish
7996.C74	Crocodilia
7996.C95	Crustacea
	Decapoda see Z7996.C95
(7996.D55)	Dinoflagellida
	see Z5356.D56

Zoology
   Taxonomic groups and special animals, A-Z -- Continued

7996.D64	Dogs
7996.D645	Dolphins
7996.D65	Donkeys
7996.E35	Echinodermata
7996.E43	Elk
7996.E65	Epitoniidae
7996.E89	Euphausiacea
7996.E893	European mink
7996.E95	European polecat
7996.F5	Fishes

         Cf. Z5970 Fish culture. Aquaculture
         Cf. Z5971+ Fishing and fisheries. Angling

7996.F72	Foraminifera
7996.G2	Gastropoda
7996.G53	Giant panda
7996.G57	Giraffe
7996.G65	Goldfish
7996.G67	Gorilla
7996.H47	Herpestidae
7996.H64	Holothurians
	Horses see Z6240
7996.I4	Infusoria
	Insects see Z5856+
7996.I47	Invertebrates
7996.J35	Japanese macaque
7996.K62	Koala
7996.K65	Komodo dragon
7996.L43	Leadbeater's possum
7996.L64	Loggerhead turtle
7996.M23	Macaques
7996.M3	Mammals
7996.M53	Mice
7996.M7	Mollusks
7996.M74	Monkeys
	Monsters see Z7994.M77
7996.M87	Muskox
7996.M95	Myriapoda
7996.N4	Nematoda
7996.N43	Nephropidae
7996.N67	Northern fur seal
7996.O33	Okapi
7996.O74	Orangutan
7996.O77	Oryx
7996.O88	Ostracoda
7996.P37	Parasitiformes

Z5051-7999

	Zoology
	Taxonomic groups and special animals, A-Z -- Continued
	Pigeons see Z5074.P6
7996.P5	Pinnipedia
7996.P54	Platypus
7996.P6	Polyzoa
7996.P8	Porifera
7996.P85	Primates
7996.P89	Prosimians
7996.P9	Protozoa
7996.R33	Raccoons
7996.R37	Reindeer
7996.R4	Reptiles
7996.R45	Rhinoceros
7996.R6	Rodentia
7996.S27	Sasquatch
7996.S36	Scorpions
7996.S57	Sirenia
7996.S64	Snakes
7996.S66	Snow leopard
7996.S69	Squirrels
7996.S85	Sticklebacks
7996.S87	Strombus
7996.S88	Sturgeons
	Tunicata see Z7996.A8
7996.V4	Vertebrates
7996.W76	Wolves
7996.W92	Worms
7996.Z43	Zebras
	Zebus see Z5074.Z4
(7997.A-Z)	Special animals, etc., A-Z
	see Z7996
7998.A-Z	Local, A-Z
7999	Catalogs

	Personal bibliography
8001.A1	Bibliography
	A
8003	Aakjaer, Jeppe
8003.2	Aalto, Alvar
8003.23	Adam, Sergiu
8003.26	Anaya, R.A.
8003.3	Angström, A.K.
8003.4	Aarestrup, Emil
8003.47	Abascal y Sousa, J.F.
8003.5	Abbagnano, Nicola
8003.6	Abbasov, A. (Alik)
8003.7	Abbot, George, abp. of Canterbury
8004	Abbott, Jacob
8004.45	'Abd al-Laṭīf, Shah
8004.47	'Abd al-Qādir ibn Muḥyī al-Dīn, Amir
8004.49	Abdullaev, G.B.
8004.52	'Abdullāh, Sayyid, 1906-1986
8004.75	Abe, Kōbō
8005.5	Abercrombie, Lascelles
8005.6	Åberg, Alf
8005.7	Äbīlqasymov, B.
8005.8	Abraham a Sancta Clara, Father
8006.5	Abramov, A.M.
8006.8	Abramov, Fedor
8006.9	Abramov, Kuźma
8007.2	Abramov, N.M.
8007.3	Abramowitz, S.J.
8008	Abreu, J.C. de
8008.5	Abreu Gómez, Ermilo
8009	Abū al-'Alā', al-Ma'arrī
8009.2	Abū al-Faẓl Maybudī, Rashīd al-Dīn, fl. 1126
8009.3	Abū Hayyān al-Tawḥīdī, 'Alī ibn Muhammad
8009.4	Abū Qurrah, Thāwdhūrus
8009.5	Abū Tammām, Ḥabīb ibn Aws al-Ṭā'ā
8010	Abutalybov, M.G.
8012	Acevedo Diaz, Eduardo
8012.6	Achebe, Chinua
8013	Acheson, E.G.
8013.2	Achleitner, H.K.
8013.3	Achterberg, Gerrit
8013.4	Ackermann, Kurt
8013.6	Acosta Saignes, Miguel
8013.8	Acton, H.M.M.
8014	Acton, J.E.E.D.A., baron
8014.6	Adam, Robert
8015	Adam de la Halle

Z8001-8999

A -- Continued

8015.2	Adamic, Louis
8015.24	Adamov, Arthur
8015.26	Adamovich, Georgiĭ
8015.28	Adams, F.W.L.
8015.3	Adams, Henry
8015.6	Adams, John
8015.7	Adams, John Q.
8015.75	Adams, Joseph Q.
8015.78	Adams, R.G.
8015.8	Adams, W.T.
8015.85	Addams, Jane
8015.87	Addison, Joseph
8016.3	Ade, George
8016.4	Adhin, Jan Hansdew
8016.5	Adler, Dankmar
8016.6	Adler, Max
	Adrianova-Peretts, Varvara Pavlova see Z8672.88
8017	Ady, Endre
8017.3	Aelfric, Abbot of Enysham
8017.5	Aeschylus
8017.6	Aescoly, A.S.
8018	Aesop
8019	Afanas'ev, A.Z.
8019.2	Afanas'ev, IŪriĭ N.
8019.22	Ăfăndĭev, Ămin
8019.23	Ăfăndĭev, Iĺias
8019.26	Ăfăndiyev, A. A. (Ayaz Adil oğlu)
8019.3	Afferden, Pieter van
8019.4	al-afghānī, Jamāl al-Dīn
8019.5	Afonin, L.N.
8019.56	Agabeįli, A.A.
8019.6	Agârbiceanu, Ion
8019.66	Agashina, M.K.
8019.7	Agassiz, Louis
8019.8	Ağayev, Telman Mämmädäli oğlu, 1935-
8019.9	Aggrey, J.E.K.
8020	Agnello, Giuseppe
8020.11	Agnese, Battista
8020.12	Agnon, S.J.
8020.122	Agoncillo, T.A.
8020.124	Agrest, Diana
8020.126	Agricola, Georg
8020.13	Agricola, M.O., bp.
8020.14	Agricola, Rodolphus
8020.15	Aguayo, A.M.
8020.153	Aguilera Malta, Demetrio

A -- Continued

8020.155	Aguirre, Mirta
8020.17	Ahlberg, Alf
8020.173	Aḥmad, Salīm
8020.176	Ahund-zâde, F.A.
8020.18	Aĭdarov, Gh.
8020.185	Aĭgi, Gennadiĭ, 1934-
8020.19	Aiken, Conrad
8020.193	Ain, Gregory
8020.195	Aini, Sadriddin
8020.2	Ainsworth, W.H.
8020.24	Aĭtmatov, Chingiz
8020.3	Akenside, Mark
8020.32	Akhmatova, A.A.
8020.33	Akhmetov, Z.A.
8020.34	Akilandam, P.V.
8020.35	Akimov, G.V.
8020.4	Aksakov, S.T.
8020.45	Akutagawa, Ryūnosuke
	Alain see Z8162.13
8020.9	Alardus Amstelredamus
8020.95	Alas, Leopoldo
8021.17	Albee, Edward
8021.2	Alberdi, J.B.
8021.35	Albert, José
8021.37	Alberti, L.B.
8021.4	Albertus Magnus, Saint, bp. of Ratisbon
8021.5	Albini, Franco
8021.6	Albizu Campos, Pedro
8022	Albrecht, Paul
8022.5	Albright, W.F.
8023	Alciati, Andrea
8024	Alcoforado, Marianna
8024.8	Alcott, L.M.
8025.3	Alcuin
8025.4	Aldington, Richard
8025.45	Aldiss, B.W.
8025.49	Aldrich, Robert
8025.5	Aldrich, T.B.
8025.52	Alecsandri, Vasile
8025.524	Alekperov, U. K.
8025.526	Aleksandrov, Zdravko
8025.53	Alekseev, M.P.
8025.54	Alekseev, V.M.
8025.55	Alekseev, Veniamin Vasilévich
8025.6	Alexander, Lloyd
8025.65	Alexander the Great

Z8001-8999

A -- Continued

8025.653	Alexander III, emperor of Russia
8025.8	Alexandre de Villedieu
8026	Alexius I Comnenus, emperor of the East
8026.2	Alexy, Janko
8026.6	Alfieri, Vittorio
8026.63	Alfonso X, el Sabio
8027	Alfred the Great, king of England
8027.15	Alger, Horatio
8027.16	Algren, Nelson
8027.17	Alî, 1541-1599 or 1600
8027.2	Ali, Sabahattin
8027.24	'Alī ibn Abī Ṭālib, Caliph, 660(ca)-661
8027.25	Ali Kusci
8027.3	'Alī Shīr, Mīr, called al-Nawāī
8027.4	Aliev, G.A.
8027.414	Aliev, M.M.
8027.417	Aliev, Rustam M.
8027.42	Aliev, V.S.
8027.43	Alimzhanov, Anuar
8027.436	Äliyev, Seyfäddin Väli oğlu, 1930-
8027.44	Alizade, A.A.
8027.447	Allacci, Leone
8027.45	Allard, H.A.
8027.6	Allen, F.L.
8027.7	Allen, H.T.
8028	Allen, J.A.
8028.5	Allingham, William
8028.57	Allon, Yigal
8028.6	Allwood, M.S.
8028.65	Almada Negreiros, José de
8028.79	Almeida, J.A. de
8028.793	Almeida, M.A.
8028.8	Almeida Garrett, J.B. da Silva Leitao de
8028.817	Alonso, Amado
8028.82	Alonso, Damaso
8029.2	Alt, Robert
8029.4	Altamira y Crevea, Rafael
8029.5	Altamirano, I.M.
8029.8	Altheim, Franz
8029.85	Althin, T.K.V.
8030.1	Alvares de Azevedo, M.A.
8030.7	Alvares Pereira, Nuno
8030.8	Alvaro, Corrado
8031	Alzate y Ramírez, J.A.
8031.2	Amado, Jorge
8031.24	Ambartsumīān, S.A.

A -- Continued

8031.25	Ambartsumi̇̄an, V.A.
8031.3	Ameln, Henrik
8031.8	Ames, J.S.
8032	Ames, Nathaniel
8032.2	Ameuille, Pierre
8032.3	Amichai, Yehuda
8032.5	Amiel, Michel
8032.515	ʿĀmilī, Bahāʾ al-Dīn Muḥammad ibn Ḥusayn, 1547-1621
8032.517	Amīn, Aḥmad
8032.518	Amirkhanov, R. U. (Ravilʹ Usmanovich)
8032.52	Amis, Kingsley
8032.53	Ammannati, Bartolomeo
8032.54	Amonov, Rajab
8032.57	Amshewitz, J.H.
8032.62	Amtmanis-Brieditis, Alfreds
8033	Amunátegui, M.L.
8033.4	Amunátegui y Solar, Domingo
8033.5	Amur-Sanan, A.M.
8033.6	Amyraut, Moïse
8034.2	Anand, M.R.
8034.4	Anastās Mārī, al-kirmilī
8034.5	Anchev, Angel
8034.7	Anchipolovskiĭ, Z.
8035	Ancona, Alessandro d'
8035.25	Ancsel, Éva
8035.28	Anders, Władysław, 1892-1970
8035.3	Andersen, H.C.
8035.35	Anderson, Alexander, 1775-1870
8035.38	Anderson, F.I.
8035.42	Anderson, I.W. (Perkins)
8035.5	Anderson, Maxwell
8035.55	Anderson, Poul
8035.6	Anderson, Sherwood
8035.67	Andersson, Ingemar
8035.69	Ando, Tadao
	Andrada e Silva, J.B. de see Z8819.13
8035.7	Andrade, C.D. de
8035.9	Andrade, Manuel Correia de
8036	André, John
8036.2	Andreev, Ĭordan
8036.4	Andreevskii, I.E.
8036.45	Andrews, C.C.
8036.452	Andrews, John
8036.4525	Andreyev, Leonoid
8036.453	Andrianov, K.A.
8036.455	Andrić, Ivo

Z8001-8999

A -- Continued

8036.48	Angell, J.R.
8036.485	Angelov, Stefan
8036.495	Angliss, Sir W.C.
8036.6	Anis, M.B.A.
8036.72	Anjos, Augusto dos
8036.74	Annadurai, C.N.
8037.3	Annunzio, Gabriele d'
8037.4	Anouilh, Jean
8037.6	Anreith, Anton
8037.65	Anselm, Saint, Archbishop of Canterbury
8037.7	Anspach, Eduard
8037.8	Antić, Miroslav, 1932-
8037.82	Antonicelli, Franco
8037.85	Antonio, prior of Crato
8038	Antonio da Padova, Saint
8038.1	Antonio das Chagas, Father
8038.2	Antōniou, D.I.
8038.3	Antonych, Bohdan-Ihor
8038.5	Anuchin, D.N.
8038.8	Anuman Rajadhon, Phrayā
8039	Anville, J.B.B. d'
8039.4	Apanovych, O.M.
8039.5	Aparicio, Francisco de
8040	Apianus, Petrus
8040.2	Apine, I.
8040.4	Apollinaire, Guillaume
8040.5	Appaya Dikshita, Pattamadai
8040.6	Appelfeld, Aron
8040.8	al-'Aqqād, 'Abbās Mahmud
8040.87	Aquarone, Alberto
8040.9	Aquinaldo y Famy, Emilio
8041.2	Aragon, Louis
8041.3	Arai, A.T.
8041.4	Arak's
8041.6	Arana Goiri, Sobino de
8041.7	Aranha, J.P. da. Graca
8041.73	Aráoz Anzoátegui, Raúl
8041.75	Arasly, H.M.
8041.8	Araujo Porto-Alegre, Manuel de, barão de Santo Angelo
8042	Arber, Edward
8042.6	Arbois de Jubainville, Henry d'
8042.66	Arbuthnot, M.H.
8042.667	Arbuzov, Aleksandr E.
8042.67	Arbuzov, Alekse' N.
8042.676	Arbuzov, B.A.
	Arc, Jeanne d', Saint see Z8451

A -- Continued

8042.69	Archila, Ricardo
8042.695	Arciniegas, Germán
8042.7	Arctowski, Henryk
8042.75	Ardizzone, Edward
8042.8	Arellano, J.E.
8042.82	Arendt, Hannah
8042.825	Arezzo, Bartyra, 1924-
8042.83	Arghezi, Tudor
8042.87	Arias, Abelardo
8042.9	Arif, Mamed
8042.96	Arima, Yoriyasu
8043	Ariosto, Lodovico
8043.7	Arisi, Ferdinando
8044	Aristotle (Aristoteles)
8044.22	Arlegui, José
8044.25	Armas Chitty, J.A. de
8044.33	Armitage, Merle
8044.37	Armsby, H.P.
8044.39	Armstrong, H.E.
8044.393	Armstrong, H.W.
8044.4	Armstrong, John
8044.415	Arnaldus, de Villanova
8044.418	Arnaud, François-Thomas-Marie de Baculard d'
8044.42	Arnaud, G.-J.
8044.425	Arnaudov, Mikhail
8044.43	Arndt, E.M.
8044.47	Arnim, L.A., freiherr von
8044.49	Arnold, Benedict
8044.5	Arnold, Matthew
8044.6	Arnold, Thomas
8044.7	Arnolfo, di Cambio, 13th cent.
8044.9	Aron, Willy
8044.915	Arp, Jean
8044.92	Arrabal, Fernando
8044.94	Arráiz, Antonio
8044.96	Arrieta, R.A.
8044.97	Arsenych, P.I.
8044.99	Artaud, Antonin
8045	Arthur, King
8045.03	Arthur, C.A.
8045.1	Artigas, J.G.
8045.12	Artis, W.E.
8045.124	Artmane, Vija
8045.13	Artobolevskiĭ, I.I.
8045.14	Art͡sikhovskiĭ, A.V.
8045.15	Artsybashev, M. (Mikhail)

A -- Continued

8045.157	Arumuga Navalar
8045.16	Arup, O.N.
8045.17	Arze, J.A.
8045.19	Asatur, Zapēl
8045.2	Asbjørnsen, P.C.
8045.27	Ascham, Roger
8045.29	Asenov, Dragomir
8045.36	Äsgärov, Şahlar
8045.44	Ashbery, John
8045.5	Ashe, W.W.
8045.57	Ashkenazi, Tovia
8045.59	Asimov, Isaac
8045.62	Aslanov, Azi Akhadovich
8045.63	Asplund, E.G.
8045.65	Asratīān, E.A.
8045.7	Assas, Louis, chevalier d'
8045.72	Astaf'ev, V.P.
8045.74	Astaurov, B.L.
8045.8	Asturias, M.A.
8046.5	Atatürk, Kamâl
8046.6	Atl, Dr.
8046.94	Atroshchenko, V.I.
8046.947	Atwood, M.E.
8046.95	Atwood, W.W.
8047.5	Aubigné, T.A. d'
8047.53	Auchincloss, Louis
8047.55	Auden, W.H.
8047.57	Audet, F.J.
8047.62	Auezov, M.O.
8047.68	Augier, Angel I., 1910-
8047.7	Augustinus, Aurelius, Saint, bp. of Hippo
8047.75	Aulén, G.E.H., bp
8047.77	Aulenti, Gae
8047.8	Aurelius, Marcus
8047.85	Aurobindo, Sri
8048	Austen, Jane
8048.4	Austin, Henry
8048.5	Austin, Mary (Hunter)
8048.6	Avagyan, Ēduard, 1927-
8048.72	Avdyshev, A.I.
8048.73	Aveline, Claude
8048.74	Avempace
8048.75	Averint͡sev, Sergeĭ Sergeevich
8048.77	Avicenna
8049	Avogadro, Amedeo
8049.4	Avrech, Isaiah

A -- Continued

8049.6	Axters, S.G.
8049.8	Axvlediani, Giorgi
8050.2	Ayala, Francisco
8050.4	Aymonino, Carlo
8050.5	Azād, Abūlkalām
8050.6	Azadovskiĭ, M.K. (Mark Konstantinovich)
8050.7	Azevedo, Ario L.
8051	Azevedo, Arthur
8051.15	Azikiwe, Nnamdi
8051.23	Azorín
8051.3	Azuela, Mariano

B

8052	Babaev, A.G.
8053	Babeuf, F.N.
8053.2	Babīāk, P.H.
8053.24	Babić, Sava, 1934-
8053.3	Babinets, A.E.
8053.4	Babinger, F.C.H.
8053.45	Babini, Jose
8053.47	Babits, Mihály
8053.5	Babko, A.K.
8053.6	Babych, V.S.
8053.7	Bacchelli, Riccardo
8053.9	Bach, A.N.
8054.4	Bachelard, Gaston
8054.5	Bacheller, Irving
8055	Bacher, Wilhelm
8056	Bachmann, Ingeborg
8057	Bachofen, J.J.
8061	Backer, Augustin de
8061.18	Bacon, E.N.
8061.7	Bacon, Henry
8062	Bacon, Roger
8062.2	Bacovia, George
8062.3	Badía Margarit, A.M.
8062.4	Baeck, Leo
8062.5	Baekeland, L.H.
8062.7	Bager, Einar
8062.8	Baggesen, Jens
8062.85	Bagrīt̃skiĭ, É.G.
8062.9	Bahdanovich, M.A.
8062.92	Bahrānī, Maytham ibn 'Alī, d. 1280?
8062.93	Bahrdt, K.F.
8063	Bahrīanyī, Ivan
8063.16	Bailey, A.G.
8063.2	Bailey, J.E.

B -- Continued

8063.23	Bailey, J.W.
8063.5	Bailey, Phinehas
8065	Baillairgé, C.P.F.
8065.5	Bain, Alexander
8065.53	Bain, Andrew Geddes
8065.56	Bainov, P.M.
8065.58	Bainton, R.H.
8066	Baird, S.F.
8066.3	Baĭzaqov, Isa
8066.5	Bajcsy-Zsilinszky, Endre
8068	Bakalov, Georgi
8068.49	Baker, R.S.
8068.5	Baker, R.T.
8068.52	Bakhtin, M.M.
8068.53	Bakikhanov, Abbas-Kuli
8068.54	Bakken, H.S.
8068.568	Bakunin, A.V.
8068.57	Bakunin, M.A.
8068.59	Balabanov, V.F.
8068.6	Balandin, A.A.
8068.62	Balassi, Bálint
8068.64	Balázs, Béla
8068.67	Balcescu, Nicolae
8068.69	Baldessari, Luciano
8068.696	Balducci, Ernesto, 1922-1992
8068.7	Baldung, Hans, called Grien
8068.74	Baldwin, James
8068.76	Balevski, Angel
8068.78	Balfour, Arthur
8068.85	Ball, Hugo
8068.9	Ballantyne, R.M.
8068.94	Ballard, J.G.
8069	Balmes, J.L.
8069.11	Bal'mont, Konstantin Dmitrievich, 1867-1942
8069.12	Balogh, Gyula
8069.13	Balthasar, H.U. von
8069.2	Balzac, Honoré de
8069.22	Balzac, J.L.G. sieur de
8069.225	Balzano, Vincenzo
8069.25	Ban, Imre
8069.27	Bancroft, W.D.
8069.28	Bandeira, Manuel
8069.29	Banfi, Antonio
8069.3	Banham, Reyner
8069.313	Bankovskis, Juris
8069.316	Baptista, Mantuanus, 1448-1516

B -- Continued

8069.32	Bar, K.L. von
8069.47	Baradin, Bazar Baradievich, 1878-1937
8069.53	Baranov, P.A.
8069.54	Baranyó, Sándor
8069.55	Barash, Asher
8069.57	Barata, A.F.
8069.6	Baratz, Joseph
8069.7	Barbeau, C.M.
8069.75	Barbi, Michele, 1867-1941
8069.8	Barbizet, Jacques
8070	Barbo, Ludovico
8070.2	Barbosa, Ruy
8070.4	Barbusse, Henri
8071	Barclay, John
8071.2	Bardili, C.G.
8071.3	Bárdosi Németh, János
8071.5	Baretti, G.M.A.
8073	Baring, Hon. Maurice
8073.3	Barlach, Ernst
8073.6	Barlow, H.C.
8073.7	Barlow, R.H.
8074	Barnard, Henry
8074.2	Barnard, K.H.
8074.26	Barnes, Djuna
8074.27	Barnes, E.L.
8074.3	Barnikal, Ernst
8074.4	Barnum, P.T.
8074.5	Baroja y Nessi, Pío
8074.8	Barragań, Luis
8075	Barrell, Joseph
8075.6	Barres, Maurice
8075.8	Barreto de Menezes, Tobias
8076	Barrie, Sir J.M.
8076.13	Barriga, V.M.
8076.2	Barros Arana, Diego
8076.3	Barsov, E.V.
8076.5	Bartels, Adolf
8076.7	Barth, John
8076.72	Barth, Karl
8076.73	Bartha, Tibor
8076.76	Barthelme, Donald
8076.77	Barthes, Roland
8076.9	Bartol'd, V.V.
8076.93	Bartolini, Luigi, 1892-1963
8076.95	Bartucz, L.
8076.96	Basanga, B.

Z8001-8999

B -- Continued

8077	Basava
8077.4	Bashkirov, A.N.
8077.5	Basso, Lelio
8077.6	Bastias, Kōstēs
8077.8	Bataille, Georges
8077.85	Batalha, Graciete Nogueira
8077.9	Bates, H.E.
8078.4	Batllori, Miguel
8078.7	Battaglia, Felice
8078.8	Battalova, Sh. B.
8079	Battin, J.J.
8079.12	Battiss, W.W.
8079.126	Battistessa, Angel José
8079.2	Battisti, Carlo
8079.3	Baudelaire, C.P.
8080	Baum, L.F.
8080.3	Bavli, Hillel
8080.4	Baxter, J.K.
8080.5	Baxter, Richard
8081	Bayle, Pierre
8081.21	Baynes, N.H.
8081.22	Bayram, Muḥammad ibn Muṣṭafá
8081.5	Bazhov, P.P.
8081.7	Bazin, Hervé
8081.75	Bazorkin, Idris
8081.8	Bazovský, M.A.
8082	Beaconsfield, Benjamin Disraeli, 1st earl of
8083	Beaglehole, J.C.
8085	Beaumarchais, P.A.C. de
8085.5	Beaumont, Charles
8085.6	Beaumont, Ernest
8086	Beaumont and Fletcher
8086.03	Beauvoir, Simone de
8086.05	Beazley, Sir J.D.
8086.1	Bebel, August
8086.25	Beccaria, G.B.
8086.3	Becher, J.R.
8086.33	Bechstein, Lugwig
8086.35	Beck, Mihály
8086.37	Beckett, Samuel
8086.4	Beckford, William
8086.43	Bécquer, G.A.
8086.45	Beda Venerabilis
8086.48	Bednyi, Dem'ian
8086.49	Beebe, C.W.
8086.5	Beecher, C.E.

B -- Continued

8086.57	Beekman, Vladimir
8086.65	Beer, Johann
8086.68	Beerbohm, Sir Max
8086.72	Beguin, Albert
8086.74	Behan, Brendan
8086.75	Behn, Aphra
8086.76	Behrens, Peter
8086.78	Beke, Manó
8086.79	Békefi, Antal
8086.8	Bekker, Balthasar
8086.82	Bél, Mátyás
8086.825	Belaīa, G. A. (Galina Andreevna), 1931-
8086.84	Bel'chikov, N.F.
8086.85	Belevtsev, IA. N.
8086.86	Belgrano, Manuel
8086.87	Belinskii, V.G.
8086.88	Bell, Clive
8086.93	Bellamy, Edward
8087	Belli, G.G.
8087.6	Bello, Andrés
8087.7	Belloc, Hilaire
8087.8	Bellow, Saul
8087.83	Belluschi, Pietro
8087.835	Beloborodov, V.K.
8087.86	Belousov, Vladimir
8087.867	Belov, Sergeĭ Vladimirovich
8087.87	Belov, Vasilĭ
8088	Beltrami, Luca
8088.3	Beltrán Guerrero, Luis
8088.4	Beltran y Rozpide, Ricardo
8088.5	Beltrani, G.B.
8088.6	Bem, A.L.
8088.8	Ben-Gurion, David
8088.84	Ben-Jacob, Abraham
8088.9	Ben-Zvi, Itzhak
8089.1	Benavides, Alonso de
8089.12	Benchley, Robert
8089.13	Bendefy, László
8089.15	Benedictus, Saint, abbot of Monte Cassino
8089.2	Beneš, Edvard
8089.24	Benes-Trebizsky, Vaclav
8089.244	Benitez, H.Z.
8089.246	Benjamin, Asher
8089.25	Benjamin, Laszlo
8089.255	Benjamin, Walter
8089.26	Benn, Gottfried

B -- Continued

8089.3	Bennett, Arnold
8089.34	Bennett, H.S.
8089.37	Bense, Max
8089.4	Bentham, George
8089.43	Bentham, Jeremy
8089.5	Bentley, Richard
8089.55	Bényi László
8089.57	Benz, Ernst
8089.6	Béranger, P.J. de
8089.618	Béraud, Henri
8089.62	Berdīāev, N.A.
8089.624	Berdichevsky, M.J.
8089.625	Berdinskikh, V. A. (Viktor A.)
8089.627	Berdyev, T.B.
8089.63	Berendsohn, W.A.
8089.65	Berenson, Bernhard
8089.75	Beresteyn, E.A. van, jonkheer
8089.752	Berezovskii, F.A.
8089.753	Berg, Gosta
8089.76	Berge, Wendell
8089.79	Bergman, S.H.
8089.8	Bergman, T.O.
8089.9	Bergson, H.L.
8089.93	Bering, V.J.
8089.95	Beristain de Souza, J.M.
8089.96	Beritashvili, I.S.
8090	Berkeley, George, bp. of Cloyne
8090.17	Berkopec, Oton
8090.19	Berkouwer, G.C.
8090.2	Berkov, P.N.
8090.28	Berlin, Leonid
8090.3	Berliner, Abraham
8090.33	Berliner, Rudolph
8090.5	Bernadotte, House of
8090.8	Bernanos, Georges
8091	Bernard de Clairvaux, Saint
8091.13	Bernard, Jean
8091.14	Bernardus, de Lutzenburgo
8091.15	Bernardus Guidonis, bp.
8091.21	Bernays, E.L.
8091.35	Béroalde de Verville
8091.4	Beroes, Pedro
8091.42	Berrigan, Daniel
8091.424	Berrigan, Ted
8091.43	Berryman, John
8091.435	Bērsons, Ilgonis

B -- Continued

8091.44	Bertani, Agostino
8091.5	Bertuch, F.J.
8091.55	Berzelius, J.J., friherre
8091.56	Bērziņš, Ludis
8091.6	Besant, Annie (Wood)
8091.7	Beshkov, Līuben
8091.8	Besold, Christoph
8092	Bessel, F.W.
8092.15	Besson, Louis
8092.2	Bestuzhev-Riumin, K.N.
8092.25	Betancourt, Rómulo
8092.3	Betekhtin, A.G.
8092.33	Bethlen Gábor, Prince of Transylvania
8092.34	Betjeman, Sir John
8092.4	Bevk, France
8092.45	Bevzenko, S.P.
8092.5	Bewick, John and Thomas
8092.7	Beyer, W.L.
8092.73	Beyer, W.R.
8092.8	Beyle, M.H. ("Stendhal")
8093	Bèze, Théodore de
8093.2	Bezymenskii, A. (Aleksandr)
8093.24	Bezzina, Joseph, 1950-
8093.3	Bialik, H.N.
8093.5	Bianciardi, Luciano
8094	Biedma, J.J.
8094.27	Bierbaum, O.J.
8094.3	Bierce, Ambrose
8094.6	Biggers, Earl Derr
8094.7	Bihalji-Merin, Oto
8095	Bilderdijk, Willem
8095.6	Billeskov Jansen, F.J.
8096	Billings, Hammatt
8097	Bilokin', Serhīĭ
8097.5	Binni, Walter
8098	Bir Singh, Bhai
8098.5	Birgitta, Saint, of Sweden
8098.6	Birkerts, Gunnar
8098.7	al-Biruni
8098.9	Bishop, Elizabeth
8099.5	al-Bishrī, 'Abd al-'Azīz ibn Salīm
8100	Bismarck, Otto, furst von
8100.9	Bitsadze, A.V.
8101	Bittard, Michel
8101.8	Bitzius, Albert
8101.95	Bjørneboe, Jens

Z8001-8999

B -- Continued

8102	Bjørnson, Bjørnstjerne
8102.05	Bjurstrm̃, Carl Gustaf
8102.1	Blackmore, R.D.
8102.2	Blackstone, Sir William
8102.23	Blackwood, Algernon
8102.4	Blättner, Fritz
8102.6	Blage, Lucian
8102.8	Blagoev, Dimitұr
8102.83	Blagoeva, Vela
8102.85	Blais, M.C.
8102.9	Blake, L.J.
8102.95	Blake, Peter
8103	Blake, William
8103.2	Blake, William P.
8103.27	Blakey, R.G.
8103.38	Blanco, A.E.
8103.4	Blanco, Eduardo
8103.42	Blanco-Fombona, Rufino
8103.6	Blasco Ibáñez, Vicente
8103.66	Blaumanis, Rūdolfs
8103.7	Blaĭek, Oldřich
8103.74	Blaẑhkevych, Ivanna
8104.5	Bleek, W.H.I.
8105	Bleeker, Pieter
8105.15	Bleicken, Jochen
8105.2	Bleksley, Arthur
8105.25	Blicher, S.S.
8105.3	Blinkena, A. (Aina)
8105.36	Blīukher, V.K.
8105.38	Blīumina, I.M.
8105.4	Blixen, Karen
8105.54	Bloch, Ernst
8105.55	Bloch, Robert
8105.56	Bloesch, Donald G., 1928-
8105.57	Blok, A.A.
8105.58	Blomfield, R.T.
8105.59	Blondel, Maurice
8105.63	Bloodgood, J.C.
8105.76	Blumgarten, Solomon
8105.77	Blunck, H.F.
8105.78	Blunden, E.C.
8105.79	Blunt, Anthony
8105.793	Bly, Robert
8105.798	Bobbio, Norberto
8105.8	Bobchev, S.S.
8105.85	Bobrov, V. V. (Vladimir Vasilevich)

B -- Continued

8105.86	Bobrowski, Johannes
8106	Boccaccio, Giovanni
8106.13	Boccalini, Traiano
8106.15	Bocher, Maxine
8106.16	Bock, Alfred
8106.17	Bockwitz, N.H.
8106.19	Bocquet, Leon
8106.2	Bode, B.H.
8106.214	Bode, Wilhelm von
8106.22	Bodin, Jean, 1530-1596
8106.226	Bodini, Vittorio
8106.23	Bodkin, Thomas
8106.26	Bodtcher, L.A.
8106.263	Bofill, Ricardo
8106.264	Bofill i Mates, Jaume
8106.267	Bognár, Rezsö
8106.269	Bohm, Gottfried
8106.27	Böhme, Jakob
8106.274	Böhme, Rudolf
8106.28	Böll, Heinrich
8106.283	Boelter, L.M.K.
8106.286	Böök, Fredrik
8106.29	Boerhaave, Herman
8106.296	Boesen, Gudmund
8106.3	Boethius
8106.37	Bogan, Louise
8106.4	Bogatskiĭ, A.V.
8106.42	Bogdanov, A. (Aleksandr)
8106.45	Bogoars, Waldemar
8106.47	Bogucka, Maria
8106.5	Boiardo, M.M.
8106.7	Boĭko, IUrii
8106.8	Boiko, Maksym
8107	Boileau-Despréaux, Nicolas
8107.27	Boisier, Sergio
8107.3	Boissard, J.J.
8107.33	Boissier, Edmond
8107.35	Boissier, Gaston
8107.357	Bokov, Viktor
8107.36	Bokros, László
8107.37	Boles, D.D.
8107.38	Bolivar, Simon
8107.4	Bolkay, S.J.L.
8107.42	Bolkhovitinov, N.N. (Nikolaĭ Nikolaevich)
8107.43	Bolt, R.A.
8107.45	Bolton, H.C.

Z8001-8999

B -- Continued

8107.5	Bolton, Samuel
8107.85	Bolza, Oskar
8107.87	Bolzano, Bernard
8107.9	Bonaparte, C.J.
8108	Bonaparte, L.L.
8108.2	Bonaparte, R.N.
8108.29	Bonaparte family
8108.32	Bonaventura, Saint
8108.35	Bonch-Bruevich, V.D.
8108.4	Bonestell, Chesley
8108.5	Bongs, Rolf
8108.7	Bonhoeffer, Dietrich
8108.81	Bonney, W.H. (Billy the Kid)
8108.814	Bonomelli, Geremia
8108.815	Bonomi, Ivanoe, 1873-1951
8108.82	Boon, L.P.
8109	Boone, Daniel
8109.16	Boorstin, D.J.
8109.2	Boos, Roman
8109.23	Borchardt, Rudolf
8109.25	Borden, Lizzie
8109.27	Bordiga, Amadeo
8109.29	Bordiūgov, G. A. (Gennadiĭ Arkadévich)
8109.33	Boreman, Thomas
8109.34	Boreskov, G.K.
8109.35	Borgen, Johan
8109.36	Borges, J.L.
8109.37	Borgoña, Juan de
8109.375	Bori, Imre
8109.38	Borlaug, N.E.
8109.384	Börner, Holger
8109.386	Borowitz, E.B.
8109.39	Borromini, Francesco
8109.4	Borrow, G.H.
8109.5	Boruta, Kazys
8109.67	Boscán Almogaver, Juan
8109.678	Bosch, Hieronymus
8109.68	Bosch Vinelli, J.B.
8109.69	Bosco, Giovanni
8109.695	Boscovich, Ruggero Giuseppe, 1711-1787
8109.7	Bose, W.B.L.
8109.8	Bosl, Karl
8109.9	Bosman, H.C.
8109.93	Bosnyák, István
8110	Bossuet, J.B., bp. of Meaux
8110.2	Boswell, James

B -- Continued

8110.3	Botero, Giovanni
8110.33	Botev, Khristo
8110.34	Botha, Louis
8110.35	Boti y Barreiro, R.E.
8110.36	Botta, Mario
8110.368	Bottasso, Enzo
8110.37	Boturini Benaducci, Lorenzo
8110.38	Bouchet, Alvin
8110.4	Bouhey, Jean
8110.43	Boulainvilliers, Henri, comte de
8110.435	Boulanger, Georges-Ernest-Jean-Marie
8110.44	Boulton, Alfredo
8110.45	Boumpoulidēs, P.K.
8110.48	Bouraoui, Hédi André
8110.5	Bourdaloue, Louis
8110.7	Bourgin, Georges
8111	Bourquelot, Felix
8111.4	Bowen, Elizabeth
8111.47	Bowering, George
8111.5	Bowers, Edgar
8111.6	Bowles, P.F.
8111.7	Boxer, C.R.
8111.8	Boyd, J.P.
8111.82	Boyd, Martin
8111.92	Boyle, Kay
8112	Boyle, Hon. Robert
8112.2	Bozhkov, Atanas
8113	Brackenridge, H.H.
8113.3	Bradbury, Ray
8113.5	Bradford, Gamaliel
8113.54	Bradley, F.H.
8113.6	Bradstreet, Annie
8113.74	Bragaglia, A.C.
8113.8	Braginskiĭ, I.S.
8114	Brahinsky, M.L.
8114.4	Brañas, César
8114.46	Branca, Vittore
8114.5	Brande, W.T.
8114.7	Brandner, Gary
8115	Brandsen, Federico de
8115.44	Brandstaetter, Roman
8115.5	Brandt, Willy
8115.6	Brandt Corstius, J.C.
8115.64	Brant, Sebastian
8115.66	Braque, Georges
8115.68	Bratanov, Georgi, 1944-

B -- Continued

8115.7	Brătescu-Voineşti, I.A.
8115.8	Brathwaite, Edward
8115.85	Braude, L.ĨŪ.
8115.9	Brautigan, Richard
8116	Bravo Villasante, Carmen
8116.5	Brecht, Bertolt
8116.7	Bredel, Willi
8117	Bredero, G.A.
8117.23	Breithaupt, F.A.
8117.26	Brendan, Saint, the Voyager
8117.3	Brennan, C.J.
8117.32	Brenner, J.H.
8117.4	Brent, C.H., bp.
8117.45	Brentano, C.M.
8117.47	Brentano, F.C.
8117.5	Brentano, Lujo
8117.6	Brenz, Johann
8118.44	Bretnor, Reginald
8118.46	Breton, André
8118.49	Breton, Nicholas
8118.5	Breton, Raymond
8118.7	Breuer, Marcel
8118.76	Breymayer, Reinhard
8118.8	Brezhnev, D.D.
8118.82	Brezhnev, L.I.
8118.84	Březina, Otokar
8118.97	Briceño-Iragorry, Mario
8119	Briceno Perozo, Mario
8119.2	Bridges, R.S.
8119.7	Brigham, A.P.
8119.8	Brigham, G.B.
8119.83	Brinkmann, R.D.
8120	Brinton, D.G.
8120.25	Brito Figueroa, Federico
8120.3	Brĩūsov, V.ĨA.
8121.66	Broby-Johansen, Rudolf
8121.7	Brocard, H.P.J.B.
8121.72	Brock, Peter
8121.75	Brod, Max
8121.77	Brodskii, I.I.
8121.78	Brodsky, Joseph
8121.8	Brøndum-Nielsen, Johanne
8121.84	Brofferio, Angelo
8121.86	Brohult, S.F.A.
8121.93	Bronnem, Arnolt
8121.98	Brontë, Emily

B -- Continued

8122	Brontë family
8122.6	Brooke, Rupert
8122.7	Brooks, C.T.
8122.72	Brooks, Cleanth
8122.73	Brooks, Van Wyck
8122.77	Broomé, Bertil
8123	Brosse, M.I.
8123.5	Brougham and Vaux, H.P. Brougham, baron
8123.55	Brown, A.T.
8123.58	Brown, C.F.
8123.585	Brown, C.B.
8123.6	Brown, G.M.
8123.63	Brown, Guillermo
8123.8	Brown, John, 1715-1766
8124	Brown, John, 1800-1859
8124.12	Brown, T.E.
8124.14	Brown, W.W.
8124.15	Browne, J.R.
8124.18	Browne, Sir Thomas
8124.4	Browning, Elizabeth (Barrett)
8124.5	Browning, Robert
8124.6	Brownson, O.A.
8124.7	Brownstone, E.A.M.
8124.85	Brugmans, Hajo
8124.93	Brun, André
8124.95	Brunat, Maud
8124.97	Brune, Johande
8124.98	Brunelleschi, Filippo
8125	Brunet, Jacques-Charles, 1780-1867
8126	Brunetiere, Ferdinand
8126.14	Bruni, Leonardo
8126.2	Brunner, Emil
8126.4	Brunner, Otto
8126.5	Bruno, Giordana
8127	Bryant, W.C.
8127.25	Bryce, James Bryce, viscount
8127.27	Brzezinski, Z.K.
8127.4	Buber, Martin
8127.55	Bubnys, Algimantas, 1937-
8127.7	Buchan, John
8128	Buchanan, George
8128.45	Buc'hoz, P.J.
8128.5	Buchvarov, Stefan
8129.4	Bucke, R.M.
8129.45	Buckinx, Pieter G. (Pieter Geert), 1903-
8129.5	Buckland, William

Z8001-8999

B -- Continued

8129.53	Buckley, William F.
8129.58	Budagov, B.A.
8129.6	Budagov, R.A.
8129.65	Budevska, Adriana
8129.67	Budrys, Algis
8129.7	Büchner, Georg
8129.8	Buero Vallejo, Antonio
8129.9	Buganov, V.I. (Viktor Ivanovich
8130	Bugenhagen, Johann
8130.2	Bugge, A.R.
8130.3	Bukharin, N.I.
8130.4	Bukowski, Charles
8130.44	Bulfinch, Charles
8130.45	Bulgakov, M.A.
8130.46	Bulgakov, S.N.
8130.5	Bull, Francis
8130.55	Bullen, H.L.
8130.57	Bullinger, Heinrich
8130.6	Bulst, Walther
8130.63	Bultmann, Rudolf, 1884-1976
8130.64	Buńiadov, Teĭmur
8130.65	Buniiatov, Z.M.
8130.67	Bunin, I.A.
8130.7	Bunshaft, Gordon
8130.8	Bunting, Basil
8131	Bunyan, John
	Buonarroti, M.A. see Z8572
8131.65	Burchfield, Charles
8131.7	Burckhardt, C.J.
8132	Burdenko, N.N.
8132.18	Burganov, A. Kh. (Agdas Khusainovich)
8132.2	Burgess, Anthony
8132.3	Burgess, T.W.
8132.5	Burgos, Julia de
8133.23	Burke, Edmund
8134	Burney, Fanny
8134.3	Burnham, D.H.
8135	Burns, Robert
8136	Burr, Aaron
8136.15	Burroughs, E.R.
8136.17	Burroughs, W.S.
8136.18	Burstall, Tim
8136.2	Burton, Sir R.F.
8136.3	Burton, Robert
8136.5	Bury, J.B.
8136.6	Buschbell, K.G.W.

B -- Continued

8136.7	Bushiazzo, M.J.
8136.8	Bushnell, Horace
8137	Bustamante, C.M. de
8137.3	Butanaev, V. IA.
8137.4	Butler, H.C.
8137.6	Butler, N.M.
8137.8	Butler, Samuel
8138	Butterworth, James
8138.5	Buysse, Cyriel
8138.7	Bychkov, A.F.
8138.8	Bykovs'kyĭ, Lev
8138.86	Bynner, E.L.
8138.87	Bynner, Witter
8138.88	Byrne, Bonifacio
8138.89	Byrne, Donn
8139	Byron, G.G.N. Byron, 6th baron
8139.3	Byvanck, W.G.C.

C

8139.6	Çabej, Eqrem
8139.7	Cabell, J.B.
8139.9	Cable, G.W.
8140	Cabot, John and Sebastian
8140.117	Cabral, Paulino António, 1719-1789
8140.12	Cabral, Pedro Alvares, d. 1520?
8140.13	Cabrol, Christian
8140.14	Cackowski, Zdzisław
8140.15	Cadillac, Antoine de la Mothe
8140.153	Cádiz, D.J. de
8140.17	Cady, Harrison
8140.2	Cagliostro, Alessandro, conte di (Giuseppe Balsamo)
8140.3	Cahan, Abraham
8140.4	Cajori, Florian
8140.45	Calamis, 5th century B.C.
8140.46	Calatrava, Santiago
8140.5	Calderón de la Barca, Pedro
8140.55	Caldwell, Charles
8140.62	Calhoun, J.C. (John Caldwell)
8140.63	Cälilov, Qurban Nizamäddin oğlu
8140.64	Călinescu, George
8140.68	Calkins, G.N.
8140.7	Calkins, W.W.
8140.72	Callimachea
8140.73	Callister, C.W.
8140.75	Callmer, Christian
8141	Calvert, G.H.
8141.3	Calvert, Jean

Z8001-8999

C -- Continued

8141.5	Calvin, Jean
8141.6	Calvino, Italo
8141.8	Cambronne, P.J.E., baron de
8141.85	Cameron, John
8142	Camões, Luiz de
8142.3	Camón Aznar, José
8142.35	Campana, Augusto
8142.4	Campana, Dino
8142.5	Campanella, Tommaso
8142.85	Campbell, Roy
8142.9	Campbell, W.W.
8143.5	Campos Ferreira Lima, Henrique de
	Camps, Juan Comas see Z8188
8143.8	Camus, Albert
8143.84	Camus, J.P., bp.
8144.2	Cancellieri, F.G.
8144.5	Cândido, Antônio, 1918-
8144.6	Candolle, A.L.P.P. de
8144.614	Canetti, Elias
8144.616	Canilleros, M.M. de San Pedro, conde de
8144.62	Cankar, Ivan
8144.64	Canth, Ulrika Vilhelmina (Johnson)
8144.67	Canto, Ernesto do
8144.68	Canudo, Ricciotto
8145	Capart, Jean
8145.13	Čapek, Karel
8145.15	Čapek, Karel Matěj
8145.16	Capetillo, Luisa
8145.165	Capo, H.B.C.
8145.17	Capote, Truman
8145.175	Capra, Frank
8145.177	Caproni, Giorgio
8145.18	Capuana, Luigi
8145.185	Caragiale, I.L.
8145.187	Caramella, Santino
8145.188	Caramuel Lobkowitz, Juan, 1606-1682
8145.193	Card, O.S.
8145.194	Cardoso, Jorge
8145.195	Cardoso, Lúcio
8145.3	Čarek, Jan
8145.4	Caretti, Lanfranco
8145.5	Carey, R.N.
8145.8	Carleton, William
8145.85	Carli, Enzo
8146	Carlo Alberto, King of Sardinia
8146.2	Carlquist, Gunnar

C -- Continued

8146.5	Carlson, A.J.
8147	Carlyle, Thomas
8148	Carman, Bliss
8148.3	Carmiggelt, Simon
8148.6	Caro, Joseph
8148.8	Carpenter, Edward
8148.9	Carpenter, F.A.
8149	Carpenter, W.B.
8149.3	Carpentier, Alejo
8149.6	Carrasquilla, Tomás
8149.7	Carrera, J.M.
8149.8	Carreras y Candi, Francisco
8149.85	Carrere, J.M.
8149.9	Carrión, Benjamín
8150	Carroll, Charles
8150.15	Carson, H.L.
8150.155	Carvalho, Rómulo de
8150.6	Carvalho e Vasconcellos, E.J. de
8150.7	Carver, G.W.
8150.8	Cary, Joyce
8150.9	Casa, Giovanni della, Abp.
8151	Casanova, Giacomo, 1725-1798
8153	Casas, Bartolomé de las, bp. of Chiapa
8153.3	Casavis, J.N.
8153.35	Cascudo, Luís da Camara
8153.4	Casement, Sir Roger
8153.43	Caspari, Gertrud
8153.45	Cassirer, Ernst
8154.5	Castellanos, Alfredo
8154.8	Castello Branco, Camillo
8154.84	Casteret, Norbert
8154.87	Castex, M.R.
8155	Castiglione, Baldassare, conte
8155.24	Castro, Cipriano, Pres. Venezuela
8155.27	Castro, Eugenio de
8155.3	Castro Alves, Antonio de
8155.45	Catarina de San Juan
8155.5	Catarina de Siena, Saint
8155.53	Caterina de' Ricci, Saint
8155.55	Catherine II, empress of Russia
8155.65	Cather, W.S.
8155.7	Catilina, L.S.
8156	Catlin, George
8156.2	Cato, Marcus Porcius, 234-149 B.C.
8156.3	Cattaneo, Carlo
8156.4	Catullus, C.V.

C -- Continued

8156.8	Cavafy, Constantine
8156.9	Čavčavaże, Ilia
8157	Cavour, E.B., conte di
8157.15	Caxias, L.A. de Lima e Silva, duque de
8157.2	Cazi, Josip
8157.28	Cecchi, Emilio
8157.3	Čech, Svatopluk
8157.45	Cela, C.J.
8157.46	Celan, Paul
8157.47	Celine, Louis-Ferdinand
8157.48	Celliers, J.F.E.
8157.5	Cellini, Benvenuto
8157.55	Celms, Teodors
8157.6	Cendrars, Blaise
8157.66	Čepytė, Julija, 1942-
8157.76	Cerbulėnas, Klemensas
8157.85	Čermák, Rudolf
8157.87	Černý, Adolf
8158	Cervantes Saavedra, Miguel de
8158.3	Césaire, Aimé
8158.33	Cesar, Jaroslav
8158.34	Céspedes, C.M. de
8158.36	Cetto, Max
8158.37	Cevdet, M. (Mehmed), 1883-1935
8158.4	Chabanenko, V.A.
8158.48	Chacón y Calvo, J.M.
8158.54	Chadwick, Nora (Kershaw)
8158.543	Chagall, Marc
8158.544	Chagas, Carlos
8158.545	Chagin, G. N.
8158.546	Chaitanya
8158.55	Chalmers, Thomas
8158.82	Chamberlain, B.H.
8158.827	Chamberlain, Joseph
8158.83	Chamberlain, Joshua Lawrence
8158.84	Chamberlain, Samuel
8159	Chamisso, Adelbert von
8159.13	Champollion, J.F.
8159.15	Chandler, Raymond
8159.16	Chandrasekhar, S. (Sripati)
8159.17	Chang, Chi-yun
8159.2	Channing, Edward
8159.25	Chanthaburinarunat
8159.33	Chaplin, Charles
8159.38	Chapman, F.M.
8159.4	Chapman, George

C -- Continued

8159.43	Chapman, H.H.
8159.45	Chapman, John
8159.46	Chaptal de Chanteloup, J.A.C., comte
8159.48	Char, Rene
8159.5	Charavay, Étienne
8159.8	Charbonnier, Andre
8159.9	Charēs, Petros
8160	Charlemagne
8161.4	Charles, d'Orleans
8161.5	Charles I, King of Great Britain
8161.6	Charles II, King of Great Britain
8161.69	Charney, Samuel
8161.73	Charrière, Isabelle de
8161.8	Charteris, Leslie
8162	Chartier, Alain
8162.13	Chartier, Émile
8162.3	Chateaubriand, F.A.R., vicomte, de
8162.5	Chateillon, Sébastien
8162.7	Chatelain, J.B.F.E. de
8162.8	Chater, Elizabeth
8162.9	Chatterji, Saratchandra
8163	Chatterton, Thomas
8163.5	Chatzēiōannou, K.P.
8163.7	Chatzēmichaēl, Theophilos
8163.8	Chatzēs, Dēmētrēs
8164	Chaucer
8164.4	Chauncy, Charles
8164.88	Chavez, Angelico
8164.9	Chavez, C.E.
8165	Cheever, H.T.
8165.2	Cheever, John
8165.26	Cheguillaume, Jean
8165.3	Cheikho, Louis
8165.4	Chekhov, A.P.
8165.45	Chekhov, Michael
8165.5	Chelčický, Petr.
8165.53	Ch'en, Chien-min
8165.55	Ch'en, Yin'k'o
8165.58	Ch'en, Yüan
8165.59	Cheney, W.M.
8165.6	Chénier, A.M.
8165.74	Cheremshyna, Marko, pseud.
8165.75	Cherkashin, Pavel, 1972-
8165.76	Chernyĭ, Sasha, pseud.
8165.78	Chernyshev, F.N.
8165.8	Chernyshevskij, N.G.

Z8001-8999

C -- Continued

8165.85	Cherskiĭ, N.V.
8166	Chervenkov, Vŭlko
8166.2	Chesnutt, C.W.
8166.4	Chesterfield, P.D.S., 4th earl of
8166.5	Chesterton, G.K.
8166.8	Cheval, Ferdinand
8166.9	Chevalier, Jean-Claude
8167	Chevreul, M.E.
8167.15	Ch'i, Piao-chia
8167.2	Chiang, Kai-shek
8167.22	Chiarini, Giuseppe
8167.24	Chibisov, K.V.
8167.26	Chibotaru, S.S.
8167.27	Chicherin, A. V. (Alekseĭ Vladimirovich)
8167.3	Childers, Erskine
8167.34	Chilingirov, Stilīān
8167.36	Chimot, Edouard
8167.4	Chiocchetti, Emilio
8167.413	Chiovini, Ferenc
8167.42	Chippendale, Thomas
8167.44	Chirpanliev, Stefan
8167.45	Chirvinskiĭ, P.N.
8167.47	Chisholm, Shirley
8167.5	Chiyo-ni
8168.17	Cholmondeley, Mary
8168.18	Chomsky, Noam
8168.19	Chopin, Kate
8168.2	Chou, Shu-jên
8168.4	Chou, Yang
8169.1	Chrestien de Troyes
8169.22	Christensen, Povl
8169.23	Christensen, V.P.
8169.3	Christiaens, J.L.
8169.32	Christianopoulos, Dinos
8169.34	Chrysanthēs, Kypros
8169.35	Chrysostomus, Joannes, Saint, patriarch of
8169.37	Ch't'ch'yan, Geghuni, 1929-
8169.38	Ch'ü, Ch'iu-pai
8169.383	Chubinashvili, G.N.
8169.384	Chudomir
8169.386	Chukovskiĭ, Korneĭ Ivanovich
8169.395	Church, T.D.
8169.4	Churchill, Charles
8169.45	Churchill, Sir, W.L.S.
8169.46	Churchill, Winston
8169.5	Churchyard, Thomas

C -- Continued

8169.6	Chyžhevs'kyĭ, Dmytro
8169.7	Cialdi, Alessandro
8169.76	Ciardi, John
8169.765	Ciavarella, Angelo
8170	Cicero, Marcus Tullius
8170.13	Cicognini, Giacinto Andrea, 1606-ca. 1650
8170.14	Cieco, Francesco
8170.2	Cienfuegos, Camilo
8170.6	Č'ik'obava, Arnold, 1898-
8171	Čiurlionis, M.K.
8172	Clare, John
8172.3	Clare, of Assisi, Saint
8172.5	Clarendon, E.H.
8172.7	Claretie, Jules
8173	Claretta, Gaudenzio
8173.6	Clark, Badger
8173.8	Clark, G.R.
8173.9	Clark, Kenneth Bancroft
8174	Clark, Kenneth McKenzie, Baron Clark
8174.6	Clarke, A.C.
8174.7	Clarke, Austin
8175	Clarke, F.W.
8175.2	Clarke, J.M.
8175.24	Clarke, M.A.H.
8175.4	Claudel, Paul
8175.5	Claussen, Sophus
8175.6	Clavijero, F.J.
8175.8	Clay, Grady
8176	Clemens, S.L. ("Mark Twain")
8176.2	Clement, Hal
8176.3	Clénard, Nicolas
8176.45	Cleveland, Grover
8176.5	Cleveland, John
8176.55	Clinton, Bill
8176.6	Clotet, Lluis
8176.7	Clough, A.H.
8176.9	Cnattingius, B.J.
8177	Cobbett, William
8177.2	Cobden, Richard
8177.3	Coblentz, Stanton Arthur
8177.4	Coblentz, W.W.
8178	Cochet, J.B.D.
8178.2	Cockerell, T.D.A.
8178.3	Cockrell, M.F.
8178.6	Cocteau, Jean
8178.7	Codman, Ogden

C -- Continued

8178.8	Cody, H.A. (Hiram Alfred)
8179.2	Coelho, J.G.G.
8179.5	Coelho de Senna, Nelson
8179.7	Coelho Netto, Henrique
8179.8	Coetzee, J.M.
8180.16	Cohen, Albert
8180.2	Cohen, M.R.
8180.5	Cohn, William
8180.6	Cohon, S.S.
8181.9	Cole, G.W.
8181.95	Coleman, J.W.
8181.97	Colenso, J.W.
8182	Coleridge, S.T.
8182.3	Colette
8182.7	Colhoun, E.R.
8183	Colin, Élie
8183.4	Colín, Mario
8184	Collier, J.P.
8184.17	Collijn, I.G.A.
8184.18	Collingwood, R.G.
8184.2	Collins, A.F.
8184.3	Collins, Charles
8184.4	Collins, H.O.
8184.45	Collins, J.C.
8184.53	Collins, S.D.
8184.6	Collins, Wilkie
8184.7	Collins, William
8184.85	Collitz, Klara (Hechtenberg)
8184.88	Collodi, Carlo
8184.94	Colombo, J.R.
8184.98	Colombo, Michele, 1747-1838
8185.2	Colonna, Egidio
8185.3	Colonna, Francesco
8185.5	Č'oloqašvilli, Solomon
8185.7	Colter, M.E.J.
8187	Columbus
8188	Comas, Juan
8188.8	Comenius, J.A.
8188.9	Cominos, Antony
8189.5	Comstock, G.C.
8189.52	Comte, Auguste
8189.59	Conant, J.B.
8189.6	Congreve, William
8189.64	Connally, T.T.
8189.66	Connor, Ralph, 1860-1937
8189.68	Conrad, Frank

C -- Continued

8189.7	Conrad, Joseph
8189.75	Conrad, von Soest
8189.8	Constant de Rebecque, H.B.
8189.84	Contini, Gianfrance
8189.9	Conway, H.M.
8190.7	Conwell, R.H.
8190.85	Conybeare, F.C.
8190.88	Cook Sir A.R.
8191	Cook, James
8191.15	Cook, Peter
8191.2	Cooke, J.E.
8191.4	Coolen, Antoon
8191.45	Coolidge, Calvin
8191.5	Coomaraswamy, A.K.
8191.7	Cooper, J.F.
8191.75	Cooper, Peter
8192	Cope, E.D.
8192.3	Copeau, Jacques
8192.5	Copernicus, Nicolaus
8192.6	Cópić, Branko
8192.8	Coppard, A.E.
8193.5	Corazzini, Francesco
8193.7	Cordeiro, Luciano
8193.8	Cordier, Henri
8193.85	Corey, Herbert
8194	Corneille, Pierre
8194.2	Cornford, Frances
8194.5	Cornu, Maxime
8194.93	Correa Luna, Carlos
8195	Correggio, A.A., known as
8195.12	Corretjer, J.A.
8195.13	Corrozet, Gilles
8195.2	Corso, Gregory
8195.25	Corsten Severin
8195.3	Cortés, Hernando
8195.35	Cortesao, Jaime
8195.38	Corvalán L., Luis
8195.42	Coșbuc, George
8195.43	Coser, L.A.
8195.45	Costa, Amoroso, 1885-1928
8195.48	Costa y Martínez, Joaquín
8195.52	Costanzi, Giulio
8195.56	Coster, C.T.H. de
8196	Cotton, Charles
8196.3	Coulson, C.A.
8196.4	Coulter, J.M.

Z8001-8999

C -- Continued

8196.47	Couperus, Louis
8196.48	Courtois, J.E.
8196.5	Cousins, J.H.
8196.6	Coward, Noel
8196.6	Coward, Noel
8196.7	Cowley, Abraham
8196.8	Cowley, Malcolm
8196.88	Cowper, William
8196.9	Cozzens, J.G.
8197.17	Crabbe, George
8197.2	Craig, E.G.
8197.4	Cram, R.A.
8197.5	Cramer, C.E.
8197.8	Cramer, K.G.
8198	Cranach, Lucas
8198.05	Crane, D.A.
8198.1	Crane, Hart
8198.17	Crane, R.S.
8198.2	Crane, Stephen
8198.3	Crane, T.F.
8198.4	Crane, Walter
8198.8	Cranmer, Thomas, abp. of Canterbury
8198.84	Crashaw, Richard
8198.9	Creeley, Robert
8199	Creighton, Mandell
8199.4	Crew, Henry
8199.5	Crews, Harry
8199.54	Crichton Smith, Iain
8199.6	Croce, Benedetto
8199.613	Croce, G.C.
8199.62	Crocioni, Giovanni
8199.63	Crockett, Davy
8199.65	Croisille, Marc
8199.7	Croll, James
8199.9	Crompton, Richmal
8200	Cromwell, Oliver
8200.4	Cronin, A.J.
8200.7	Crook, A.R.
8201.7	Crosse, J.C.H.
8201.77	Crowe, Sylvia
8201.8	Crowley, Aleister
8201.9	Crowne, John
8202.4	Crumb, R.
8202.5	Crunden, F.M.
8202.7	Crusafont Pairó, Miguel
8202.8	Cruz, Ramōn de la

C -- Continued

8203	Cruz Cano y Olmedilla, R.F. de la
8203.15	Cséby, Géza
8203.2	Csokonai Vitéz, Mihály
8203.27	Csoóri, S.
8203.3	Csorba, Győző
8203.4	Csuka, Zoltán
8204	Cuervo, R.J.
8204.5	Culberton, W.S.
8204.58	Cumberland, George
8204.63	Cummings, E.E.
8204.64	Cummings, Ray
8204.7	Cunha, Euclydes da.
8204.8	Cunningham, J.V.
8204.9	Cuoco, Vincenzo
8205.5	Curel, François, vicomte de
8206.5	Curtis, H.D.
8206.52	Curtius, E.R.
8206.53	Curtius, Ludwig
8206.55	Curtius Rufus, Quintus
8206.58	Curzon, G.N.
8206.67	Cushing, H.W.
8206.7	Custer, G.A.
8207.3	Cuvier, Georges
8207.8	Cvijíc, Jovan
8207.9	Cvirka, Petras
8208.2	Cyrano de Bergerac, Savinien
8208.4	Cyrillus, Saint, of Thessalonica
8208.45	Czapski, Józef, 1896-1993
8208.5	Czernik, Stanislaw
8208.54	Czóbel, Bela

D

8208.57	Da gun' Rvhe Myhā"
8208.6	Dabrowski, Maria
8209.5	Dagerman, S.H.
8209.7	Dahinden, Justus
8210	Dahlberg, Edward
8210.3	Dahlström, Svante
8211.8	Dakin, J.H.
8211.9	Daley, Victor J.
8211.95	Dalin, M.A. (Mark Aleksandrovich)
8212	Dall, W.H.
8212.7	Dalton, John
8212.75	Damião, frei, 1898-
8212.8	Damdinsuren, TSėdėm
8213	Dạmirchizadạ, Ạ.M. oghlu
8213.4	Damrong, Rajanubhab

Z8001-8999

D -- Continued

8213.8	Dan, Kazuo
8213.98	Dana, H.J.
8214	Dana, J.C.
8214.5	Danchev, Georgi
8214.69	Dānī, Uthmān ibn Sa īd
8214.75	Daniel, Samuel
8214.85	Danilov, S.P.
8214.92	Dann, Jack
8215	Dante Alighieri
8216	Darío, Rubén
8216.8	Dart, R.A.
8217	Darwin, Charles
8217.3	Daskalov, S. TS.
8217.5	Dassonville, G.A.
8218	Dati, Gregorio
8218.2	Daudet, Alphonse
8218.212	Daujotytė, Viktorija
8218.213	Daukša, Mikalojus
8218.214	Daukšas, Vitas, 1935-
8218.215	Dausset, Jean
8218.218	Dauthendey, Max
8218.22	Dávalos, J.C.
8218.225	D'Avenant, William, Sir
8218.227	Davenport, Guy
8218.23	Davičǒ, Oskar
8218.25	David, Saint
8218.26	David, the Invincible
8218.28	Davidov, Angel
8218.3	Davidson, George
8218.4	Davidson, John
8218.5	Davidson, Julius R.
8218.6	Davidsson, Åke
8218.7	Davie, Donald
8218.8	Davies, W.H.
8219	Dávila Garibi, J.I.P.
8219.2	Davis, A.J.
8219.3	Davis, J.J.
8219.34	Davis, M.
8219.4	Davis, R.H.
8219.5	Davis, W.M.
8219.7	Davy, Sir Humphrey
8219.75	Dawson, Fielding
8219.78	Day, A.G.
8219.785	Day, Clarence
8219.79	Day, Dorothy
8219.8	Day-Lewis, Cecil

D -- Continued

8219.83	Dayānanda Sarasvatī, Swami
8219.85	Dazai, Osamu
8219.92	De Sanetis, Francesco
8219.95	De Ville, Winston
8220	Dean, Bashford
8220.5	Dean, J.W.
8220.53	Debelīānov, Dimcho
8220.54	Debenedetti, Giacomo
8220.56	Deborin, A.M.
8220.59	De Bow, J.D.B.
8220.63	Debrot, Cola
8220.65	Debry, Gérard
8220.68	Decreus, Juliette
8220.7	Decroly, Ovide
8220.8	Décsy, Gyula
8220.9	Dee, John
8221	Defoe, Daniel
8221.2	De Gasperi, Alcide
8221.24	Deguy, Michel
8221.27	Deilmann, Harald
8221.3	Deinard, Ephraim
8221.47	Dekker, E.D.
8221.5	Dekker, Thomas
8221.7	Dekkers, Eligius
8222	Delabarre-Duparcq, N.E.
8223.1	De La Mare, W.J.
8223.2	Delany, S.R.
8223.4	Delchev, Gotse
8223.8	De Leon, Daniel
8224	Delepierre, J.O.
8224.55	Delgado, Rafael
8224.6	Delhave, Philippe
8224.65	Delibes, Miquel
8224.7	Deligne, G.F.
8224.75	Delimarskiĭ, IU. K.
8225	Delisle, L.V.
8225.15	Dell, Floyd
8225.2	Dellenbach, Pierre
8225.4	Del Mar, Alexander
8225.42	Delteil, Joseph
8225.43	De Luca, Giuseppe
8225.44	Demaría, Giovanni
8225.45	De-María, Isidoro
8225.53	Deneke, Otto
8225.6	Denk Petr, pseud.
8225.68	Dennis, C.J.

D -- Continued

8225.76	Dent, Lester
8225.8	Denton, Daniel
8226	De Quincey, Thomas
8226.5	Derby, O.A.
8226.55	Derevīanko, A.P.
8226.7	Derleth, A.W.
8226.8	Dermanis, Vilis
8226.85	Derrida, Jacques
8226.9	Derzhavin, N.S.
8226.95	Derzhavin, Vladimir
8227.3	Desai, M.R.
8227.7	Descartes, Rene
8227.78	Desio Ardito
8227.79	Despierres, Gabriel
8227.793	Dessì, Giuseppe, 1909-1977
8227.795	Destouches, L.F.
8227.81	Deustua, A.O.
8227.82	Deutsch, Gotthard
8227.92	De Voto, B.A.
8227.925	Dévai
8227.93	DeVries, Peter
8227.95	Dewar, Sir James
8228	Dewey, John
8228.5	Dexter, Timothy
8228.7	Dézsi, Lajos
8228.9	Diaghilev, Serge, 1872-1929
8229	Dias, A.G.
8229.4	Díaz de Escovar, Narcisco
8229.5	Diaz del Castillo, Bernal
8229.6	Diaz Mirón, Salvador
8229.64	Díaz Rodríquez, Manuel
8229.65	Diaz Sanchez, Ramon
8229.7	Dibdin, T.F.
8229.87	Dick, P.G.
8229.9	Dick, P.K.
8230	Dickens, Charles
8230.2	Dickey, James
8230.3	Dickins, Bruce
8230.5	Dickinson, Emily
8230.7	Dickinson, J.M.
8230.8	Dickson, G.R.
8230.9	Diderot, Denis
8230.94	Didion, Joan
8231	Diego, Eliseo
8231.2	Diem, Carl
8231.25	Diercke, Carl

D -- Continued

8231.3	Dieudonné, J.A.
8231.5	Digby, Sir Kenelm
8231.75	Dilas Milovan
8231.77	Dilov, Liuben
8231.8	Dilthey, Wilhelm
8231.83	Dima, Alexandru
8231.85	Dimitrie Cantemir, Voivode of Moldavia
8231.9	Dimitrov, Georgi
8231.93	Dimitrov, Mikhail
8231.95	Dimitrov, Stefan
8231.96	Dimitrov, Vladimir
8231.97	Dimitrov-Rudar, Petur
8231.972	Dimitŭr, Khadzhi
8231.974	Dimov, Dimitŭr
8231.976	Dimov, G.K.
8231.978	Dinaburskiĭ, V.D.
8231.98	Dinekov, P.N.
8232	Dionne, N.E.
8232.5	Disch, T.M.
8232.6	Disertori, Benvenuto
8232.75	Disney, Walt
	Disraeli, Benjamin 1st earl of Beaconfield see Z8082
8232.87	Dixon, Jeremy
8232.92	Djojohadikusumo, Sumitro
8232.94	Dniestrański, Stanislaus
8232.95	Dniprovs'kyĭ, Ivan
8233	Dobie, J.F.
8233.5	Dobrokhotov, N.N.
8233.6	Dobroli͡ubov, N.A.
8233.84	Dobrovic, Petar
8233.87	Dobrovský, Josef
8234	Dobson, Austin
8234.2	Dock, George
8234.4	Doctorow, E.L.
8234.6	Dodd, C.H.
8234.8	Dodgson, C.L. ("Lewis Carroll")
8235.2	Döblin, Alfred
8235.3	Dölger, Franz
8235.4	Dörpfeld, F.W.
8235.5	Dogel, V.A.
8235.6	Dōgen
8235.8	Dolenko, G.N.
8235.9	Dombay, János, 1900-1961
8235.94	Dominik, Hans, 1872-1945
8236	Donatello i.e. Donato di Niccolo di Betto Bardi
8236.2	Donazzan, Michel

Z8001-8999

D -- Continued

8236.25	Donchev, D.M.
8236.3	Donelaitis, Khristijonas
8236.4	Donev, D.P.
8236.6	Doni, A.F.
8236.7	Donish, Aḣmadi
8237	Donne, John
8237.3	Dontsov, Dmytro
8237.4	Doolittle, Hilda
8237.8	Doré, Gustave
8237.82	Doria, Gino
8237.83	Dorman, Menahem
8237.84	Dorn, Edward
8237.86	Doroshenko, Dmytro
8237.87	Doroshenko, V.V.
8237.875	Dorozhkin, N.A.
8237.88	Dosoftei, metropolitan of Moldavia
8237.89	Dos Passos, John
8237.895	Dossi, Carlo
8237.896	Dostál, Vladimír
8237.9	Dostoyevsky, Fyodor
8238	Douët d'Arcq, L.C.
8238.43	Douglas, Lady Eleanor (Touchet)
8238.5	Douglas, Norman
8238.8	Douglas, S.A.
8238.85	Douglass, Frederick
8238.86	Dovz̄ḣenko, O.P.
8238.9	Downing, A.J.
8238.92	Doxiades, K.A.
8240	Doyle, Sir A.C.
8240.3	Dózsa, György
8240.5	Dozy, R.P.A.
8241.13	Drabble, Margaret
8241.15	Dragan, Mykhaĭlo
8241.2	Dragoĭcheva, TSola
8241.4	Drayton, Michael
8241.7	Dreiser, Theodore
8241.85	Drewermann, Eugen
8242	Dreyfus, Alfred
8242.5	Driesch, H.A.E.
8242.6	Drinkwater, John
8242.75	Drīzulis, A.
8242.78	Dron, I. V. (Ivan Vasil'evich)
8242.8	Drosinēs, G. (Geōrgios)
8243	Droste-Hülshoff, A.E. freiin von
8243.5	Drută, Ion, 1928-
8243.85	Dryden, H.L.

D -- Continued

8244	Dryden, John
8244.4	Du Bartas, Guillaume de Salluste, seigneur
8244.5	Duane, William
8244.55	Du Bellay, Joachim
8244.56	Dubecq, M.E.
8244.6	Dublin, L.I.
8244.7	Dubnov, S.M.
8244.9	Du Bois, W.E.B.
8245	Dubosc, Georges
8245.22	Dubrovin, Evgeniĭ
8245.24	Duburs, Gunārs
8245.3	Duchêne-Marullaz, Pierre
8245.32	Duchess, 1855?-1897
8245.35	Duclos, Jaques
8245.4	Duda, H.W.
8245.6	Dudek, Louis
	Dudevant, Mme. see Z8781.4
8245.65	Dudko, Ivan Petrovych
8245.7	Dudok, W.M.
8246	Dürer, Albrecht
8246.2	Dürrenmatt Friedrich
8246.5	Dufour, Léon
8246.6	Dugdale, Sir William
8246.65	Dugonics, András
8246.7	Duhamel, Georges
8246.78	Dulac, Edmund
8246.83	Dulichenko, A. D.
8246.85	Dulles, J.F.
8246.87	Dul'skiĭ, Petr
8247	Dumas, Alexandre, 1802-1870
8247.1	Dumas, Alexandre, 1824-1895
8247.2	Dumas, J.B.A.
8247.25	Dumézil, Georges
8247.3	Dumont, Martial
8247.35	Dunaevskiĭ, V.A.
8247.38	Dunant, J.H.
8247.39	Dunántúl
8247.4	Dunbar, P.L.
8247.47	Duncan, R.E.
8247.5	Duncker, G.A.
8247.6	Dunlap, William
8248	Dunn, Gano
8248.4	Duns, Joannes, Scotus
8248.42	Dunsany, Edward John Moreton Drax Plunkett, Baron
8249	Dupetit-Thomas, L.M.A.A.
8249.4	Du Plessis, I.D.

Z8001-8999

D -- Continued

8249.7	Dupree, Louis
8250.54	Durrell, Lawrence
8250.56	Durrieu, Paul comte
8250.6	Dushkov, Atanas
8250.8	Dutčak, J.I.
8251.3	Du Toit, J.D.
8251.4	Duun, Olav
8251.5	Duval, Alexandre
	Duval, P.A.M. see Z8517.8
8251.55	Dvali, Rap'iel
8251.6	Dvořák, Vilém
8252.9	Dzhabaev, Dzhambul
8252.93	Dzhafarov, M.D.
8252.94	Dzhagarov, Georgi
8252.948	Dzhambinov, IAroslav Saĭkovich, 1922-1995
8252.95	Dzhanuzakov, T. (Telʹkhozha)
8252.96	Dzhumaliev, G. (Georgi)
8253	Dziatrzko, Karl
8253.6	Dzi͡uba, Viktor Ilarionovych, 1936-
8253.7	Dzʹoban, O. O.

E

8253.8	Eames, Charles
8253.84	Eastlake, William
8253.87	Eberhart, Richard
8253.9	Eberlein, H.D.
8254	Eca de Queiroz J.M. de
8254.4	Echeverría, Estéban
8254.46	Eckbo, Garrett
8254.47	Eckhart, Meister
8254.48	Eckstein, Ernst
8254.5	Eckstrom, F.H.
8254.6	Eco, Umberto
8254.7	Edelstadt, David
8254.74	Eden, Anthony
8254.83	Edfelt, Johannes
8255	Edgeworth, Maria
8255.2	Edison, T.A.
8255.25	Édokov, V.I.
8255.3	Edschmid, Kasimir
8255.4	Edward, Georg
8255.5	Edwards, Jonathan
8256	Eekhoud, Georges
8256.2	Efendiev, G. Kh.
8256.25	Efremov, Oleg
8256.3	Egana, Juan
8256.8	Egle, W.H.

E -- Continued

8257.3	Eichendorff, J.K.B., freiherr von
8257.4	Eidemanis, Roberts
8257.5	Eielsen, Elling
8257.55	Eiermann, Egon
8257.6	Eigner, Larry
8258.2	Einaudi, Luigi
8258.46	Einstein, Albert
8258.47	Eisenhower, D.D.
8258.48	Eisenman, Peter
8258.5	Ekelund, E.R.S.
8258.6	Ekwall, Eilert
8258.65	Elbogen, Ismar
8258.66	Elchin
8258.665	Elepov, B.S.
8258.67	Eliade, Mircea
8258.68	Elias Levita
8258.69	Elijah ben Solomon, gaon of Vilna
8258.8	Elin Pelin, pseud.
8259	Eliot, George, pseud
8260	Eliot, John
8260.5	Eliot, T.S.
8262	Elizabeth, queen of Romania
8262.3	Elizarova, Anna Il'inichna Ul'ianova
8262.4	Elkin, Stanley, 1930-1995
8262.5	Elling, Christian
8262.55	Elliot, J.M.
8262.57	Elliott, Ebenezer
8262.6	Elliott, Mary (Belson)
8262.7	Ellison, Harlan
8263.3	Ellul, Jacques
8263.4	Ellwood, Craig
8263.5	Ellwood, Thomas
8264.5	Elskamp, Max
8264.7	Eluard, Paul
8264.8	Elvestad, Sven
8264.9	Emanuel', N.M.
8264.95	Emeneau, M. B. (Murray Barnson), 1904-2005
8265	Emerson, R.W.
8265.25	Eminescu, Mihail
8265.3	Emiot, Israel
8265.4	Emmanuel, Pierre
8265.5	Emmet, Robert
8265.56	Empeirikos, Andreas
8265.6	Empson, William
8265.76	Endzelīns, Jānis
8265.8	Engels, Friedrich

Z8001-8999

E -- Continued

8265.85	Engström, Albert
8265.9	Enikolopīan, N.S.
8265.95	Enno, Ernst
8266.2	Ensor, James, baron
8266.4	Entin, Joel
8266.6	Eötvös, Károly
8267	Epictetus
8268	Erasmus, Desiderius
8268.5	Erben, K.J.
8268.58	Erchmann, Emile
8268.6	Ercilla y Zúñiga, Alonso de
8268.65	Eremenko, V.N.
8268.75	Erickson, Arthur
8268.8	Ericsson, John
8268.85	Erigena, J.S.
8268.9	Erist'avi, Giorgi
8269	Erixon, S.E.
8269.8	Ermengem, Frederick, van
8270.4	Erné, Nino
8270.8	Ernst, Adolph
8270.9	Ernst, Alfred
8270.95	Ertel', Aleksandr Ivanovich
8271	Escragnolle Tavnay, Affonso de
8272	Esenin, S.A.
8272.4	Esherick, Joseph
8272.44	Eshleman, Clayton
8272.65	Espinosa Pólit, Aurelio
8272.68	Espronceda, José de
8273	Estanove, Suzanne
8273.2	Estelrich, J. L. (Juan Luis), 1857-1923
8273.4	Estreicher, K.J.T.
8273.46	Ethelred, Saint
8273.47	Etherege, George, Sir
8273.49	Etō, Shinkichi, 1923-
8274	Ettinger, Solomon
8274.5	Ettner, J.C.
8275	Euclid
8278	Euler, Leonhard
8278.5	Evans, L.H.
8278.6	Evans, U.R.
8278.65	Evans, W.C.
8278.7	Evans-Pritchard, E.E.
8279	Evelyn, John
8279.3	Everson, William
8279.4	Ewald, Gustaf
8279.55	Ewart, J.C.

	E -- Continued
8279.8	Eyck, Aldo van
8280	Eyerman, John
8280.7	Ezerietis
	F
8281	Fabergé, P.C.
8281.4	Fabian, Gyula, 1884-1955
8281.7	Fàbregas, Xavier
8282.4	Fabricius von Hilden, Wilhelm
8282.45	Fabricius-Kovács, Ferenc
8282.5	Fabricius family
8282.7	Fábry, Zoltán
8282.8	Fackler, St. Michael
8283	Fadeev, A.A.
8283.4	Fafard, Eugène
8283.5	Faguet, Émile
8283.6	Faidatti, Bernard
8283.65	Fairburn, A.R.D.
8283.7	Fairchild, H.L.
8283.73	Faisal, King of Saudi Arabia
8283.74	Fajnzylber, Fernando
8283.76	Falkberget, Johan
8283.78	Fallada, Hans
8283.8	Faller Clément
8283.82	Faludi, Ferenc
8283.84	Fang, I-chih
8283.86	Fanon, Frantz
8283.88	Fantin, Mario, 1921-
8284.15	Fārābī
8284.2	Faraday, Michael
8284.25	Farāhī, Ḥamīduddīn
8284.37	Farisse, Jacques
8284.39	Farjeon, Eleanor
8284.4	Farkas, Julius
8284.6	Faron, Bolesław
8285.8	Farquhar, F.P.
8285.9	Farquhar, George
8286.3	Farragut, D.G.
8286.7	Farrell, J.T.
8286.8	Farrukh, Umar
8286.9	Fathy, Hassan
8286.93	Fāṭimah, d. 632 or 3
8286.95	Fatma Aliye, 1862-1936?
8287	Faucher de Saint Maurice, N.H.E.
8288	Faulkner, William
8288.7	Faure-Fremiet, Emmanuel

Z8001-8999

F -- Continued

8288.78	Fayḍ al-Kāshī, Muḥammad ibn Murtaḍá. 1598 or 9-1680 or 81
8288.8	Fazekas, Magdolna
8289.6	Febres Cordero, Tulio
8290	Febvre, Lucien
8290.2	Fechner, G.T.
8290.3	Federn, Paul
8290.36	Fedorov, A. M. (Aleksandr Mitrofanovich), 1868-1949
8290.38	Fedorov, F.I.
8290.4	Fedorov, G.A.
8290.42	Fedorov, Ivan, ca. 1510-1583
8290.45	Feffer, Itzik
8290.5	Feigin, S.I.
8290.7	Feijóo y Montenegro, B.J.
8290.8	Feitsma, Anthonia
8290.87	Felder, F.M.
8290.9	Feledy, Gyula
8291.5	Felix, E.R.
8291.6	Fellini, Federico
8292	Fénelon, François de Salignan de La mothe-, abp.
8292.2	Fenoglio, Beppe
8292.3	Fényes, Adolf
8292.5	Ferguson, James
8292.54	Ferguson, M.J.
8292.66	Fergusson, Harvey
8292.7	Fergusson, Robert
8292.8	Ferko, Milan
8292.9	Ferlinghetti, Lawrence
8293	Fermat, Pierre de
8293.27	Fernandes, Valentim
8293.275	Fernandes Thomaz, Manuel
8293.3	Fernandes de Castro, J.A.
8293.316	Fernández, Lucas, 1474-1542
8293.32	Fernández Saldaña, J.M.
8293.33	Fernando V, el Católico, king of Spain
8293.34	Ferrari, Antonio de
8293.342	Ferriss, Hugh
8293.344	Ferron, Jacques
8293.347	Ferrua, Antonio
8293.35	Fersman, A.E.
8293.36	Fessenden, Reginald Aubrey
8293.37	Fett, Harry
8293.39	Feuchtwanger, Lion
8293.5	Fewkes, J.W.
8293.54	Fichte, Hubert
8293.56	Fichte, J.G.

F -- Continued

8293.57	Ficino, Marsilio
8293.62	Fiedler, Arkady
8293.63	Field, Henry
8293.72	Fielding, Henry
8294.8	Fiesole, Giovanni da, called Fra Angelico
8294.93	Figgis, Darrell
8295.15	Figueiredo, Fidelino
8295.2	Figueiredo, Manuel de
8295.27	Figueres Ferrer, Jose
8295.3	Figueroa, A.A.
8295.45	Figuli, Margita
8295.8	Filgueira Valverde, Jose
8295.84	Filin, F.P.
8295.9	Fillmore, Millard
8296	Fillon, Benjamin
8296.4	Filopanti, Quirico
8296.8	Findley, Timothy
8297	Fink, Albert
8297.3	Fink, Eugen
8297.4	Finkelstein, Louis
8297.7	Finsch, Otto
8298	Firbank, A.A.R.
8298.5	Firdawsi
8298.9	Firth, Sir C.H.
8299.5	Fischer, Heinrich
8299.59	Fischer von Erlach, J.B.
8299.62	Fisenko. G.L.
8299.65	Fish, G.S.
8299.68	Fisher, Fred (Frederick)
8299.7	Fisher, Irving
8299.9	Fisher, Vardis
8300	Fisher, W.L.
8300.3	Fishman, J.L.
8300.4	Fiske, Minnie Maddern (Davey)
8301	Fitzgerald, Edward
8301.2	Fitzgerald, F.S.K.
8301.4	Fitzgerald, R.D.
8301.6	Fiumi, Lionello
8302	Flagg, Edmind
8302.3	Flagg, Ernest
8302.4	Flaiano, Ennio
8302.6	Flam, Leopold
8303	Flaubert, Gustave
8303.2	Flaxman, John
8303.5	Fleischback, Ernst
8303.6	Fleischner, Lugwig

Z8001-8999

F -- Continued

8303.7	Fleming, Ian
8304	Fletcher, John
8304.13	Fletcher, John Gould
8304.2	Fleure, H.J.
8304.3	Fleury, Jules
8304.45	Floch, H.A.
8304.47	Florenskiĭ, P. A. (Pavel Aleksandrovich), 1882-1937
8304.48	Flores Galindo, Alberto
8304.5	Flower, Sir William
8304.75	Foch, Ferdinand
8304.76	Focillon, Henri
8304.78	Fockema, Andreae, S.J.
8304.792	Fodor, Jozsef
8304.8	Förstemann, E.W.
8304.9	Förstemann family
8304.95	Foerster, Max
8305	Fogazzaro, Antonio
8305.22	Fogelström, Per Anders, 1917-
8305.24	Folengo, Teofilo
8305.26	Folmanis, Zanis
8305.28	Fombeure, Maurice
8305.29	Fønhus, Mikkjel
8305.296	Fonseca Filho, Olympio da, b. 1895
8305.3	Fontane, Theodor
8305.5	Fontenelle, Bernard Le Bovier de
8305.6	Fonvizin, D.I.
8306	Foote, A.R.
8307.2	Foppens, J.F.
8307.6	Forbes, Esther
8307.8	Force, Peter
8308	Forchheimer, Frederick
8308.3	Ford, F.M.
8308.34	Ford, Gerald
8308.45	Ford, Jesse H
8308.5	Ford, John
8309	Forel, A.H.
8309.2	Foreman, Grant
8309.24	Forman, Miloš
8309.26	Formsma, W.J.
8309.3	Forster, E.M.
8309.35	Forster, Georg
8309.4	Forsyth, P.T.
8309.6	Fortune, Mary
8310	Foscolo, Ugo
8310.41	Fosdick, C.A.
8310.43	Foster, Norman

F -- Continued

8310.45	Foster, Sir William
8310.46	Foster, William Z
8310.62	Fothergill, Jessie
8310.8	Foucault, Michel
8311	Foulché-Delbosc, Raymond
8311.2	Fourier, J.B.J., baron
8312	Fournier, Edouard
8312.15	Fourrier, Andre
8312.155	Fourrier, Paul
8312.157	Fowler, O.S.
8312.158	Fowles, John
8312.159	Fox, C.J.
8312.2	Fox, George
8312.22	Fox, H.M.
8312.3	Fracastoro, Girolamo
8312.5	France, Anatole
8312.7	Francesco d'Assisi, Saint
8312.75	Francisco de Vitoria
8312.8	Francisco Xavier, Saint
8312.85	Franck, Hans
8312.86	Franck, Sebastian
8312.87	Francke, A.H.
8312.88	Franckenberg, Abraham von
8312.91	Francois de Sales, Saint, bp. of Geneva
8312.94	Franěk, Otakar
8312.97	Frank, Herman
8312.98	Frank, Leonhard
8312.983	Frank, Robert
8313	Franklin, Benjamin
8313.3	Franko, Ivan
8313.5	Frantsev, I.P.
8313.55	Frantsev, V.A.
8313.6	Frantsevich, I.N.
8313.7	Franz Ferdinand, archduke of Austria
8314	Fraser, C.L.
8314.3	Frazer, Sir J.G.
8314.4	Fréchette, L.H.
8314.42	Frederic, Harold
8314.43	Frederick William, I, King of Prussia, 1688-1740
8314.44	Freehof, S.B.
8314.45	Freeman, D.S.
8314.47	Freeman, R. Austin
8314.515	Freiligrath, F.
8314.53	Freimane, Lidija
8314.6	Freire, L.J.J.
8315	Freneau, Philip

F -- Continued

8315.3	Frenssen, Gustav
8315.4	Freud, Anna
8315.5	Freud, Sigmund
8315.6	Frey, F.H.
8315.7	Freyer, Hans
8315.74	Freyre, Gilberto
8315.8	Frich, Ø.R.
8315.9	Friedberg, M.P.
8316.2	Friederichs, H.F.
8316.4	Friedlaender, Israel
8316.5	Friedman, D.A.
8316.7	Friedman, Philip
8317	Friedrich II, der Grosse, king of Prussia
8317.15	Friel, Brian
8317.2	Fries, J.F.
8317.3	Friis, Aage
8317.4	Frisch, Max
8317.45	Frischlin, Nicodemus, 1547-1590
8317.5	Froebel, F.W.A.
8317.58	Fröding, Gustaf
8317.65	Froissart, Jean
8317.67	Frolova, I.I.
8317.7	Fromentin, Eugene
8317.775	Frost, John
8317.78	Frost, Robert
8317.787	Froude, J.A.
8317.792	Frug, S.G.
8317.8	Fruin, R.J.
8317.817	Frumkin, R.M.
8317.82	Frunze, M.V.
8317.827	Fry, R.E.
8317.829	Frycz Modrzewski, Andrzej
8317.83	Frye, Northrop
8317.84	Fučík, Julius
8317.86	Fühmann, Franz
8317.87	Fuente Benavides, Rafael de la
8317.88	Fürst, Ludvik
8317.92	Fugard, Athol
8317.93	Fuji, Masaharu
8317.94	Fujii, Hiromi
8317.95	Fukada, Kyūya
8318	Fukuzawa, Yukichi
8318.25	Fuller, H.B.
8318.26	Fuller, Margaret
8318.27	Fuller, R.B.
8318.28	Fuller, Roy

F -- Continued

8318.3	Fumagalli, Giuseppe
8318.4	Funes, Gregorio
8318.5	Fúrlong Cárdiff, Guillermo
8318.53	Furmanov, D.A.
8318.57	Furness, Frank
8318.6	Furnivall, F.J.
8318.63	Furphy, Joseph
8318.65	Furtenbach, Joseph
8318.655	Furuland, Lars
8319	Fustel de Coulanges, N.D.
8319.4	Fuzulî, Mehmet

G

8319.6	Gabaldon Marquez, Joaquin
8319.7	Gabe, Dora
8319.76	Gabrielyan, Gurgen
8319.8	Gacon, Francois
8319.87	Gadamer, H.G.
8319.9	Gadda, C.E.
8320	Gaddesden, John of
8320.13	Gadgil, G.G.
8320.14	Gadkari, R.G.
8320.17	Gadzhiev, S.N. (Salekh Novruzovich)
8320.2	Gafurov, B.G.
8320.3	Gagarin, IU. A.
8320.4	Gaïdaenko, Ivan
8320.48	Gál, István
8320.5	Galanis, D.E.
8320.6	Galczynski, K.I.
8320.7	Galiani, Ferdinando
8321	Galilei, Galileo
8321.18	Galindo y Villa, Jesus
8321.32	Gallardo, B.J.
8321.38	Gallé, Emile
8321.4	Gallegos, Rómulo
8321.43	Gallun, R.Z.
8321.45	Galsworthy, John
8321.6	Gálvez, Manuel
8322	Gama, Vasco de
8322.2	Gamber, Klaus
8322.3	Gamburt͡sev, G.A.
8322.6	Gandhi, I.N.
8322.7	Gandhi, M.K.
8322.8	Gandhi, Rajiv
8322.9	Ganiev, M.K.
8322.94	Ganivet, Angel
8323.4	Garai, Gabor

Z8001-8999

G -- Continued

8323.43	Garboli, Cesare
8323.45	Garcia, Rodolpho, 1873-1949
8323.47	García Bacca, J.D.
8323.5	García Icazbalceta, Joaquín
8323.6	García Lorca, Federico
8323.63	García Márquez, Gabriel
8323.633	García Martín, José Luis, 1952-
8323.64	García Moreno Gabriel, Pres. Ecuador
8324	Gardiner, S.R.
8324.13	Gardner, Edmund Garratt
8324.15	Gardner, Erle Stanley
8324.17	Gardner, J.C.
8324.18	Garfield, J.A.
8324.2	Garibaldi, Giuseppe
8324.3	Garin, Eugenio
8324.32	Garipova, F.G.
8324.34	Garland, Hamlin
8324.36	Garnier, Charles
8324.4	Garrett, George
	Garrett, J.B. de Silva Leitão de Almeida see Z8028.8
8324.45	Garrick, David
8324.48	Garufi, C.A.
8324.49	Garvey, Marcus
8324.495	Garzoni, Tomaso, 1549?-1589
8324.52	Gascoigne, George
8324.6	Gaskell, E.C. (Stevenson)
8324.7	Gaskell, William
8325.5	Gassendi, Pierre
8326	Gastaldo, Jacopo
8326.12	Gaster, Moses
8326.2	Gasymzada, F.S. Oghlu
8326.6	Gatto, Alfonso
8327.8	Gaudí y Cornet, Antonio
8328	Gaudin, M.A.A.
8328.3	Gauguin, Paul
8328.5	Gaulle, Charles de
8328.7	Gauss, K.F.
8329	Gautier, Théophile
8329.5	Gavidia, F.A.
8330	Gay, John
8330.2	Gayer, Gyula
8330.3	Gazdanov, Gaito
8330.6	Gebauer, Jan
8330.8	Gebhardt, Peter von
8330.83	Gębik, Władysław
8330.85	Gecse, Árpád

G -- Continued

8331	Geddes, James
8331.2	Geddes, N.B.
8331.3	Geddes, Sir Patrick
8331.33	Gedeōn, M.I.
8331.35	Géfin, Gy.
8331.38	Gehry, F.O.
8331.4	Geijer, Agnes
8332.8	Gelsted, Otto
8332.9	Gemelli, Agostino
8333	Genala, Francesco
8333.3	Genée, Rudolf
8333.6	Genet, John
8333.64	Genghis Khan, 1162-1227
8333.8	Genlis, Stéphanie Félicité, comtesse de
8334	Gennep, Arnold van
8336	George, Henry
8336.2	George, S.A.
8336.5	Gérard de Nerval, Gérard Labrunie, known as
8336.53	Gerasimov, I.P
8336.535	Gerchunoff, Alberto
8336.537	Gerd, Kuzebaĭ
8336.54	Gerlach, Walther
8336.544	Gerlo, Aloïs
8336.546	Gernez, D. (Désiré), 1834-1910
8336.55	Gerson, Joannes
8336.6	Geyl, Pieter
8336.65	Gezelle, Guido
8336.7	Gfeller, Simon
8336.8	Ghalib
8336.82	Ghallāb, 'Abd al-Karīm
8336.88	Ghazaryan, Ṛafik
8339.2	al-Ghazzāĭī
8339.4	Ghelderode, Michel de
8339.45	Gherardo, da Cremona
8339.7	Ghica, Ion
8340.3	Ghisleri, Arcangelo
8340.6	Ghose, Aurobindo
8341	Gibbings, Robert
8341.3	Gibbon, Edward
8341.4	Gibbs, James
8341.5	Gibson, W.B.
8341.6	Gide, A.P.G.
8341.7	Gideonse, H.D.
8341.8	Gierow, K.R.
8341.88	Gilbert, Cass
8341.9	Gilbert, Sir W.S.

G -- Continued

8341.93	Giliarov, M.S.
8341.95	Giliazhev, Khakim
8342.2	Gill, Eric
8342.23	Gill, Irving
8342.25	Gill, Stanley
8342.35	Gilliams, Maurice
8342.4	Gilliéron, J.L.
8342.415	Gilman, C.P.
8342.42	Gilson, Étienne
8342.427	Gimbutas, M.A.
8342.43	Giménez Caballero, Ernesto
8342.436	Gindev, P.A.
8342.44	Giner de los Rios, Francisco
8342.5	Ginsberg, Allen
8342.52	Ginsburg, S.M.
8342.57	Ginzberg, Louis
8342.577	Ginzburg, Natalia
8342.58	Ginzburg, V.L.
8342.6	Gioberti, Vincenzo
8343	Giordani, Pietro
8343.2	Girotto, Alexandre, 1902-1996
8343.3	Giotto di Bondone
8343.47	Gippius, Z.N.
8343.5	Gipson, L.H.
8344	Girard, Charles
8344.17	Girard, J.B.
8344.18	Girard, René, 1923-
8344.7	Giraudoux, Jean
8344.75	Girdenis, Aleksas
8345.4	Giroud, Paul
8346	Gissing, G.R.
8346.2	Gistel, Johannes von Nepomuk Franz Xaver
8346.6	Giuzelev, Vasil
8346.7	Gjerstad, Einar
8346.8	Gjorgjević, Bartholomaeus
8346.9	Gladkov, F.V.
8347	Gladstone, W.E.
8347.2	Glasenapp, Helmuth von
8347.3	Glasser, J.A.
8347.5	Glasgow, Ellen Anderson Gholson
8347.55	Glassbrenner, Adolf
8348	Glendowner, Owen
8348.3	Glinka, M.I.
8348.34	Glissant, Edouard
8348.45	Glover, D.J.M.
8348.5	Głowacki, Aleksander

G -- Continued

8348.8	Gluek, Nelson
8348.9	Glushko, V.V.
8349.4	Gobetti, Piero
8349.46	Gode, Haralds
8349.48	Gode, P.K.
8349.5	Godefroy, Maximilian
8349.55	Godoy, Alcayaga, Lucila
8349.6	Godwin, William
8349.64	Goens, R.M. van
8349.7	Gökalp, Ziya
8349.85	Goes, Damiao de
8350	Goeth, J.W. von
8350.2	Goetz, Hermann
8350.3	Goeverneur, J.J.A.
8350.5	Goff, Bruce
8350.7	Gogebašvili, Iakob, 1840-1912
8351	Gogh, Vincent van
8351.7	Gogol', N.V.
	Góis, Damiao de see Z8349.85
8351.74	Goitein, S.D.F.
8351.75	Gokak, V.K.
8351.753	Gołąb, Kazimierz
8351.755	Gol'danskiĭ, V.I.
8351.76	Goldberg, Leah
8351.78	Goldfaden, Abraham
8351.79	Golding, William
8351.8	Golding-Bird, C.H.
8352	Goldoni, Carlo
8353	Goldsmith, Oliver
8353.3	Goldstein, Kurt
	Goldszmit, Henryk see Z8467.434
8353.5	Goldziher, Ignác
8353.535	Goll, Yvan, 1891-1950
8353.55	Gollwitzer, Helmut
8353.6	Golovnītskiĭ, L.N.
8353.75	Gómara, F.L. de
8353.78	Gombrowicz, Witold
	Gomes Coelho, J.G. see Z8179.2
8353.96	Gómez, Máximo
8353.98	Gómez Carrillo, Enrique
8354	Gómez de Avellaneda y Arteaga, Gertrudis
8354.196	Gompers, Samuel
8354.3	Goncharov, I.A.
8354.8	Góngora y Argote, Luis de
8355.15	Gonzaga, T.A.
8355.2	González Alcorta, Leandro

Z8001-8999

G -- Continued

8355.25	González de Mendoza, Juan, bp.
8355.3	González del Valle y Ramírez, Francisco
8355.32	González Ortega, Jesús
8355.34	Gonzalo Maeso, David
8355.37	Goodhue, B.G.
8355.4	Goodman, Herman
8355.43	Goodman, K.S.
8355.5	Goodman, Paul
8355.7	Goodwin, A.J.H.
8355.8	Goossenaaerts, J.
8355.86	Gorban', N. V.
8355.87	Gorchakovskiĭ, P.L.
8355.88	Gordeĭchev, Vladimir
8355.9	Gordimer, Nadine
8356	Gordon, Aaron D.
8356.13	Gordon, Adam Lindsay
8356.15	Gordon, Armistead C.
8356.6	Gordon, Thomas
8357	Gordon family
8357.5	Goris, J.A.
8357.6	Goriūshkin, L.M.
8357.8	Gorky, Maksim
8357.9	Gorlov, D.V.
8357.97	Gornung, Mikhail Borisovich
8358	Gorostiza, M.E. de
8359	Gosse, Philip
8359.2	Gosse, Philip H.
8359.225	Gössmann, Wilhelm
8359.23	Goswāmī, Hemacandra
8359.3	Goto, Katsuichi
8359.36	Gotsche, Otto
8359.4	Gottfried von Strassburg
8359.5	Gottwald, Klement, Pres. Czechoslovak Republic
8361	Gould, G.M.
8362	Gould, John
8362.3	Gourmont, Remy de
8362.32	Goutelle, Alain
8362.324	Gouveia, Delmiro, 1863-1917
8362.326	Gover, Robert
8362.33	Govinda Simha, 10th guru of the Sikhs
8362.335	Govrin, Nurith
8362.34	Gowans, Alan
8362.35	Gower, John
8362.4	Goya y Lucientes, F.J. de
8362.45	Goyen, William
8362.5	Gozzi, Carlo, conte

G -- Continued

8364	Grabar', I.É.
8364.2	Grabbe, C.D.
8364.23	Grace, Daddy
8364.25	Gracq, Julien
8364.3	Gradmann, Robert
8364.45	Gradnik, Alojz
8364.47	Graf, O.M.
8364.48	Graftio, G.O.
8365	Graham, R.B.C.
8365.4	Gramsci, Antonio
8365.45	Grand, Sarah, pseud.
8365.5	Grandmaison, Charles
8365.55	Granin, Daniil Aleksandrovich
8365.6	Granlund, J.E.L.
8365.7	Granovskii, T.N.
8366.4	Grases, Pedro
8366.48	Grass, Gunter
8366.5	Grassi, Carmelo
8366.52	Grassi, Giorgio
8366.75	Grau, Reinhold
8366.8	Grauls, Jan
8367.3	Graux, Pierre
8367.4	Graves, Michael
8367.5	Graves, Robert
8368.4	Gray, Eileen
8368.9	Gray, Thomas
8368.93	Grecu, Mihai
8368.95	Greeley, A.M.
8368.975	Green, Edward B.
8368.98	Green, Julien
8368.985	Greenaway, Kate
8368.986	Greenberg, U.Z.
8368.987	Greene, Graham
8368.988	Greene, Robert
	Greene and Greene see Z8368.987
8368.9885	Greenidge, C.W.W.
8369	Greenlaw, E.A.
8369.08	Gregor, Joseph
8369.09	Gregor-Tajovský, Joseph
8369.1	Gregorio, Antonio de, marchese
8369.16	Gregorius, Saint, Bp, of Nyssa
8369.19	Gregorius I, the Great, Saint, pope
8369.195	Gregorová, Hana
8369.2	Gregory, J.W.
8369.23	Gregory, Lady
	Greif, Martin see Z8315.6

G -- Continued

8369.25	Grenón, Pedro
8369.253	Grenville, George
8369.255	Grenville, W.W.G., Baron
8369.26	Greve, Karl
8369.2613	Greve, Ludwig
8369.262	Grew, Nehemiah
8369.263	Grey, Sir George
8369.2633	Grey, Zane
8369.2636	Gribaudi, Pietro
8369.264	Griboedov, A.S.
8369.2642	Grickat, Irena
8369.2643	Gridnev, V.N.
8369.2645	Grieco, Agrippino
8369.2646	Grierson, John
8369.2647	Grieve, C.M.
8369.2649	Griffin, W.B.
8369.265	Griffith, Arthur
8369.2654	Griffith, D.W.
8369.2675	Grigor'eva, M.V. (Margarita Vasil'evna)
8369.268	Grigorovich, V.I.
8369.2687	Grillparzer, Franz
8369.269	Grimal, Pierre
8369.27	Grimm, J.L.K.
8369.293	Grimmelshausen, H.J.C. von
8369.295	Grin, A. (Aleksandr)
8369.3	Gringoire, Pedro
8369.33	Grisebach, E.R.A.
8369.335	Grit͡skevich, A.P.
8369.34	Groen van Prinsterer, Guillaume
8369.345	Gronbech, V.P.
8369.35	Grondal, B.S.
8369.37	Grönloh, B.S.
8369.4	Groote, Gerard
8369.43	Gropius, Walter
8369.5	Grosart, A.B.
8369.55	Grosididier, Jean
8369.74	Gross, Bernhard, 1905-
8369.75	Gross, Otto
8369.77	Gross, Villem
8369.8	Grosseteste, Robert, bp. of Lincoln
8369.85	Grossman, M.S.
8369.9	Grot, I͡A. K.
8370	Grotius, Hugo
8370.2	Groulx, L.A.
8370.5	Groussac, Paul
8370.75	Gruelle, Johnny

G -- Continued

8370.8	Gruen, Victor
8370.9	Gruev, Ĭoakim
8370.95	Grunberg, Arnon
8371	Grunewald, Mathias
8371.5	Gruntvig, N.F.S.
8371.7	Grunwald, Kurt
8373.1	Guadagnoli, Antonio
8373.25	Guasti, Cesare
8373.3	Gubkin, I.M.
8373.316	Gudelis, Vytautas
8373.32	Gudovshchikova, I.V.
8373.34	Guénon, René
8373.4	Güntekin, R.N.
8373.43	Günther, J.C.
8373.5	Güernsey, R.S.
8373.63	Guerra Junqueiro, A.M.
8373.8	Guerrazzi, F.D.
8373.9	Guevara, Antonio de, Bp.
8373.94	Guevara, Ernesto
8374.1	Guicciardini, Francesco
8374.2	Guichot y Parodi, Joaquin
8374.4	Guidetti, Giuseppe
8374.6	Guilelmus Parisiensis
8374.64	Guilhem, André
8374.647	Guillard, J.M.
8374.6478	Guillaume, de Lorris
8374.648	Guillaume, Gustave
8374.649	Guillemin, Henri
8374.65	Guillén, Nicolas
8374.67	Guillot, Rene
8374.7	Guimarães, Luiz
8374.73	Guimard, Hector
8375	Guizot family
8375.2	Guliam, Gafur
8375.3	Gulik, R.H. von
8375.36	Gullans, C.B.
8375.4	Gullberg, H.R.
8375.41	Gullón, Ricardo, 1908-
8375.43	Gŭlŭbov, Ivan
8375.45	Gulyás, Mihály
8375.47	Gumilev, L.N.
8375.48	Gumilev, N. (Nikolaj)
8375.5	Gumplowicz, Ludwig
8375.53	Gundel, H.G.
8375.54	Gundolf, Friedrich
8375.55	Gunn, J.E.

Z8001-8999

G -- Continued

8375.555	Gunn, N.M.
8375.56	Gunn, Thom
8375.57	Gurdjieff, G.I.
8375.58	Guseĭnov, A.I.
8375.6	Guseĭnov, D.IU
8375.614	Guseĭnov, D.M.
8375.62	Guseĭnov, Geĭdar
8375.65	Gusev, V.E. (Viktor Evgen'evich)
8375.67	Gushchin, N.I.
8375.7	Gusinde, Martin
8375.8	Guthrie, T.A.
8375.87	Gutmann, Joseph
8375.9	Guttari, Tobias
8375.93	Gutyrīa, V.S.
8375.935	Gutzkow, Karl
8375.94	Gwathmey, Charles
8375.947	Gyllenstens, Lars
8375.95	Gÿore, Pál
8375.97	G'yu-thog Yon-tan-mgon-po

H

8376.2	Haarhoff, T.J.
8376.24	Haas, Richard
8376.25	Haas, Willy
8376.26	Haavelmo, Trygve
8376.27	Habermas, Jürgen
8376.3	Hackett, H.B.
8376.4	Hackländer, F.W.
8376.5	Ḥafiz, 14th cent.
(8376.8)	Hällsjö, K.E.
	see Z8383.15
8377	Hagedorn, Friedrich von
8377.5	Haggard, Sir H.R.
8378.2	Ḣajÿiev, Magsud
8378.37	Hake, J.A. von der
8378.4	Haken, Josef
8378.415	Hakhverdyan, Levon
8378.42	Ḥakīm, Tawfīq
8378.44	Halas, František
8378.45	Halbertsma, J.H.
8378.55	Haldas, Georges
8378.6	Hale, G.E.
8378.8	Haliburton, T.C.
8379	Hall, Asaph
8380	Hall, G.S.
8382	Haller Albrecht von
8382.3	Halley, Edmond

H -- Continued

8383	Halliwell-Phillipps, J.O.
8383.15	Hällsjö, Karl Edward, 1866-1950
8383.2	Hallstein, Walter
8383.3	Halpern, M.L.
8383.4	Halprin, Lawrence
8383.5	Ham, Thomas
8383.6	Hamberg, Axel
8383.8	Hamelin, L.E.
8384	Hamilton, Alexander
8384.2	Hamilton, Charles
8384.3	Hamilton, Edith
8384.77	Hamilton, Sir William
8384.8	Hamilton, Sir William Rowan
8384.9	Hammersten, Olof
8385	Hammett, Dashiell
8385.13	Hammond, Beeby, and Babka
8385.2	Hamsun, Knut
8385.24	Hamzah, Amir, Tengku
8385.29	Hanabusa, Yoshimoto
8385.3	Haney, J.P.
8385.4	Hankiss, János
8385.5	Hanks, H.G.
8385.64	Hansberry, Lorraine
8385.67	Hansen, H.P.
8385.685	Hansen, Thorkild
8385.7	Hansjakob, Heinrich
8385.8	Hanus, Ladislav
8385.9	Hara, Hiroshi
8385.93	Hara Takashi
8385.96	Haraszty, Árpád
8385.97	Harbaugh, Henry
8386.2	Harding, W.G.
8386.3	Hardouin-Mansart, Jules
8386.4	Hardy, Hugh
8386.5	Hardy, Thomas
8386.55	Harig, Ludwig
8386.58	Harkavi, Zvi
8386.6	Harkavy, Alexander
8386.8	Harms, Bernhard
8387	Harnack, Adolf von
8387.3	Harriman, F.J.
8387.4	Harriot, Thomas
8387.6	Harris, H.H.
8387.7	Harris, J.C.
8387.8	Harris, T.L.
8387.9	Harrison, Harry

Z8001-8999

H -- Continued

8387.92	Harrison, Jim, 1937-
8387.93	Harrison, Michael
8387.94	Harrison, Peter
8387.95	Harrison, Tony
8387.97	Harrison, W.H.
8388	Harrisse, Henry
8388.3	Harrisson, Tom
8388.42	Harry, J.E.
8388.65	Harte, Bret
8388.66	Harth-Terré, Emilio
8388.75	Hartman, Bruno
8388.8	Hartmann, Richard
8388.86	Hartmann von Aue
8389	Hartzenbusch, J.E.
8389.5	Haruyama, Yukio
8389.7	Harvey, William
8389.75	Ḥasan ibn ʻAlī, d. ca. 669
8389.78	Hasdeu, B.P.
8389.79	Hasegawa, Nyozekan
8389.8	Hašek, Jaroslav
8390	Haskins, C.H.
8390.47	Hastings, Thomas
8390.5	Hastings, Warren
8390.8	Hasumi, Yasushi
8390.9	Hasund, S.M.
8391.4	Hauglid, Roar
8391.7	Hauptmann, G.J.R.
8392	Havet, J.P.E.
8392.3	Havránek, Bohuslav
8392.5	Hawkes, John
8392.9	Hawthorne, Julian
8393	Hawthorne, Nathaniel
8393.13	Hayama, Yoshiki
8393.135	Ḥaydar Mīrzā, 1499 or 1500-1551
8393.14	Haym, R. (Rudolf)
8393.15	Haynes, Lemuel
8393.17	Haywood, Elizabeth Fowler
8393.2	Hazard, Paul
8393.3	Hazaz, Haim
8393.4	Hazlitt, William
8393.5	Head, Bessie
8393.6	Heaney, Seamus
8393.7	Hearn, Lafcadio
8393.8	Heath-Stubbs, J.F.A.
8394.2	Hebbel, Friedrich
8394.37	Heber, Gustav

H -- Continued

8394.39	Heckscher, E.F.
8394.395	Hedenius, Ingemar
8394.397	Hedenvind-Eriksson, Gustav
8394.4	Hedin, S.G.
8394.47	Heeger, V.E.
8394.49	Heer, Friedrich
8394.5	Heever, C.M. van den
8394.6	Hegel, G.W.F.
8394.9	Heiberg, J.L.
8394.95	Heidegger, Martin
8394.965	Heidenstam, Verner von
8394.98	Heilfurth, Gerhard
8395	Heine, Heinrich
8395.3	Heinemann, G.W.
8395.4	Heinesen, William
8395.5	Heinrich von Langenstein
8395.513	Heisenberg, Werner
8395.514	Heissenbüttel, Helmut
8395.516	Helgason, Jon
8395.518	Heliade-Radulescu, Ion
8395.519	Heller, Joseph
8395.52	Hellman, Lillian
8395.53	Hellström, Gustav
8395.58	Hellwig, Johann
8396.3	Hemingway, Ernest
8396.5	Hémon, Louis
8397	Hennepin, Louis
8397.125	Henning, Friedrich-Wilhelm
8397.13	Henning, Herzeleide
8397.15	Henrique, o Navegador, Infante of Portugal
8397.2	Henry, the minstrel
8397.4	Henry, Joseph
8397.42	Henscheid, Eckhard
8397.47	Henty, G.A.
8397.85	Heraclitus, of Ephesus
8398	Herbart, J.F.
8398.2	Herberg, Will
8398.27	Herbert, Frank
8398.3	Herbert, George
8398.4	Herbert, H.W.
8398.45	Herczeg, Ferenc
8398.5	Herder, J.G. von
8398.55	Herdman, Sir W.A.
8398.58	Heredia, J.M.
8398.6	Hergesheimer, Joseph
8398.65	Herling-Grudziński, Gustaw

Z8001-8999

H -- Continued

8398.67	Herman, L.M.
8398.675	Herman, Otto
8398.68	Hermans, W.F.
8398.683	Hermlin, Stephan
8398.69	Hernández, Felisberto
8398.7	Hernández, José
8398.74	Hernández i Sanahuja, Bonaventura, 1810-1891
8398.8	Herodotus
8398.9	Herrera, Alfonso L.
8398.93	Herrera, L.A. de
8399	Herrera y Tordesillas, Antoniode
8400	Herrick, Robert
8400.2	Herrlinger, Robert
8400.3	Hersey, J.R.
8400.7	Hertzen, A.I.
8400.73	Hertzog, J.B.M.
8400.95	Hess, J.C.
8401	Hess, Moses
8401.3	Hesse, Herman
8401.4	Heuschele, Otto
8401.42	Hewer, H.R.
8401.5	Hewett, E.L.
8402	Hewlett, M.H.
8402.3	Heyen, William
8402.4	Heyer, Georgette
8402.5	Heym, Stefan, 1913-2001
8402.54	Heyne, Christian Gottlob
8402.6	Heynicke, Kurt
8402.7	Heyse, P.J.L. von
8402.9	Heywood, John
8403	Heywood, Thomas
8405	Hicks, Granville
8405.2	Hidāyat, Ṣādiq, 1903-1951
8405.4	Hierro, José
8405.6	Higashionna, Kanjun
8406	Higginson, T.W.
8406.5	Hildeaardis, Saint
8406.52	Hildesheimer, Esriel
8406.53	Hildesheimer, Wolfgang
8406.56	Hillebrecht, Rudolf
8406.6	Hiller, Kurt
8406.65	Hillerman, Troy
8406.7	Hillers, Solomons
8406.8	Himes, C.B.
8407	Hindenburg, Paul von
8407.2	Hino, Ashihei, pseud.

H -- Continued

8407.3	Hinrichs, G.D.
8407.35	Hinton of Bankside, Christopher Hinton, Baron
8407.4	Hippocrates
8407.5	Hirabayashi, Taiko
8407.55	Hiranuma, Kiichirō
8407.6	Hirata, Atsutane
8407.7	Hirsch, Emanuel
8407.8	Hirsch, Helmut
8407.9	Hirsch, Samson Raphael
8408	Hirsch, Samuel
8408.3	Hirschfeld, Magnus
8408.8	Hitchcock, Alfred
8409	Hitchcock, C.H.
8409.2	Hitchcock, H.R.
8409.6	Hitler, Adolf
8409.82	Hjärne, H.G.
8409.84	Hjelmqvist, Bengt
8409.87	Hnatiuk, Volodymyr
8409.89	Hô, Chí Minh
8409.9	Hobbes, Thomas
8409.92	Hoca Celebi
8409.93	Hocart, A.M.
8409.935	Hocĕvar, Joze
8409.94	Hoch, Edward D.
8409.95	Hocking, W.E.
8410	Hodge, F.W.
8410.2	Hodgetts, Craig
8410.3	Hodgson, Margaret Livingston
8410.4	Hodgson, Ralph
8410.53	Höffner, Joseph
8410.56	Höger, J.A.
8410.57	Hölderlin, Friedrich
8410.6	Hoene-Wroński, J.M.
8410.63	Hoernlé, Agnes Winifred (Tucker)
8410.64	Hoey, F.C.
8410.7	Hoff, J.H. van't
8410.8	Hoff, K.E.A. von
8410.88	Hoffman, Daniel
8410.9	Hoffman, F.L.
8411	Hoffmann, E.T.A.
8411.5	Hoffmann von Fallersleben, A.H.
8411.8	Hofmannsthal, H.H., edler von
8411.85	Hofrén, Manne
8411.9	Hofstein, David
8412	Hogarth, William
8413	Holas, Bohumil

Z8001-8999

H -- Continued

8413.7	Holbach, P.H.T., baron d'
8414	Holbein, Hans, the younger
8414.2	Holberg, Ludvig, baron
8414.25	Holcroft, Thomas
8414.266	Holland, Philemon
8414.27	Hollander, W.G.H. von
8414.28	Hollar, Vaclar
8414.284	Hollein, Hans
8414.29	Holmberg, Arne
8414.3	Holmes, O.W.
8414.5	Holmes, W.H.
8414.54	Holmqvist, Wilhelm
8414.55	Holobuts'kyĭ, V. O. (Volodymyr Oleksiĭovych), 1903-1993
8414.58	Holst, Wilhelm
8414.6	Holtby, Winifred
8414.7	Holyoake, G.J.
8414.8	Holzbach, Antonín
8414.83	Homer, Winslow
8414.84	Homerús
8414.845	Honchar, Oles'
8414.85	Honecker, Erich
8414.87	Hood, R.M.
8414.93	Hooft, P.C.
8414.935	Hooghe, Romein de
8414.938	Hook, Sidney
8414.94	Hooke, Robert
8414.95	Hooker, Richard
8414.97	Hoover, H.C.
8415.4	Hope, A.D.
8415.6	Hopkins, G.M.
8415.8	Hora, Josef
8416	Horace (Quintus Horatius Flaccus)
8416.4	Horák, Jiří
8416.5	Horbach, Anna-Halīa
8416.6	Hordīīenko, Havrylo
8416.7	Horgan, Paul
8416.8	Horkheimer, Max
8417	Horn, G.H.
8417.15	Hornborg, Eirik
8417.2	Horne, R.H.
8417.4	Horowitz, David
8417.6	Horta, Victor Baron
8417.7	Hørup, V.L.B.
8417.8	Horvat, Andela
8418	Hosseus, C.C.
8418.3	Hostos y Bonilla, E.M. de

H -- Continued

8418.5	Hough, F.B.
8418.57	Householder, F.W. (Fred Walter)
8418.6	Houseman, A.E.
8418.66	Housman, Laurence
8418.8	Houssaye, Henry
8419	Houzeau, J.C.
8419.48	Howard, John
8419.5	Howard, R.E.
8420	Howe, M.A.
8420.17	Howell, A.H.
8420.2	Howell, James
8420.25	Howells, W.D.
8420.27	Hoxha, Enver
8420.43	Hrabák, Josef
8420.44	Hrabovets'kyĭ, V.V.
8420.45	Hrabovs'kyĭ, P.A.
8420.5	Hrdlička, Aleš
8420.525	Hrebinka, ĪEvhen Pavlovych, 1812-1848
8420.54	Hrozný, Bedřich
8420.56	Hrushevs'kyĭ, Mykhaïlo
8420.567	Hryharovich, ĪA. D. (ĪAdviha Daminikaŭna)
8420.57	Hrynchyk, M.M.
8420.575	Hrynchyshyn, Dmytro Hryhoriĭovych
8420.6	Hu. Shih
8420.65	Hubbard, Elbert
8420.66	Hubbard, F.M.
8420.67	Hubbard, William
8420.7	Huberinus, Caspar
8420.8	Hublard, Émile
8420.9	Huch, Ricarda Octavia, 1864-1947
8421	Hudson, Henry
8422	Hudson, W.H.
8423	Huet, G.B.
8423.3	Hughes, Langston
8423.4	Hughes, Lewis
8423.43	Hughes, Ted
8423.45	Hughes, Thomas
8423.5	Hugi, F.J.
8423.7	Hugo of Saint Victor
8424	Hugo, V.M. comte
8424.5	Hugolin, père
8426	Hulbert, A.B.
8427	Humboldt, Alexander, freiherr vonn
8427.3	Hume, David
8427.31	Hume, E.E.
8427.6	Humphrey, H.A.

Z8001-8999

H -- Continued

8427.8	Ḥunayn ibn Isḥāq al-'Ibāī
8428.2	Hunt, Leigh
8428.26	Hunt, R.M.
8428.3	Hunter, John
8428.6	Hurban Vajanský, Svetozár
8428.63	Hurd, Richard
8428.66	Hurston, Z.N.
8428.7	Hurz̄hiĭ, I.O.
8429	Hus, Jan
8429.13	Husain, Zakir, 1897-1969
8429.15	Ḥusayn, Ṣaddām
8429.16	Ḥusayn ibn 'Alī, d. 680
8429.165	Ḥusaynī Dilījānī, 'Abd al-Hādī, 17th cent.
8429.17	Huseĭnzoda, Sh.
8429.2	Husén, Torsten
8429.25	Hushchak, Ivan
8429.3	Husylstyi, K.H.
8429.4	Husserl, Edmund
8429.48	Hutchinson, R.C. (Ray Coryton)
8429.5	Hutchinson, Thomas
8429.7	Huĭsalo, ĬEvhen
8430	Hutten, Ulrich von
8430.12	Hutton, Edward
8430.18	Huussen, A. H.
8430.2	Huxley, A.L.
8430.3	Huxley, Elspeth
8430.5	Huxley, T.H.
8430.53	Huxtable, A.L.
8430.55	Huysmans, J.K.
8430.58	Hybeš, Josef
8430.593	Hyde, Douglas
8430.7	Hyma, Albert

I

8430.9	ĬAblochkov, P.N.
8430.92	ĬAchevskii, A.A.
8430.9217	ĬAkhimovich, V.L.
8430.922	ĬAkir, I.E.
8430.923	ĬAkovlev, N.N.
8430.925	ĬAkubov, A.A. ogly
8430.9255	ĬAkushko, Ol'ga Filippovna
8430.92553	ĬAkymovych, B.Z. (Bohdan Z)
8430.9256	ĬAnin, V.L. (Valentin Lavrent'evich)
8430.9257	ĬAnkov, Nikolaĭ
8430.926	Ianovici, Virgil
8430.9262	ĬAnovskiĭ, N.N.
8430.92624	ĬAnovs'kyĭ, ĬUriĭ

I -- Continued

8430.9263	︠IA︡nshin, A.L.
8430.9266	︠IA︡rt︠s︡eva, V.N.
8430.927	︠IA︡tsimirskii, A.I.
8430.9274	︠IA︡t︠s︡imirskiĭ, K.B.
8430.9278	︠IA︡vornyt︠s︡'kyĭ, D. I. (Dmytro Ivanovych), 1855-1940
8430.928	︠IA︡vorov, P.K.
8430.92816	︠IA︡zykov, N.M.
8430.9282	Ibargüengoitia, Jorge
8430.93	Ibn al-Jawzī, Abū al-Faraj'Abd al-Rahmān ibn 'Alī
8430.933	Ibn al-Muṭahhar al-Ḥillī, al-Ḥasan ibn Yūsuf
8430.935	Ibn Bāz, 'Abd al-'Azīz ibn 'Abd Allāh
8430.94	Ibn Gabirol
8430.947	Ibn Kammūnah, Sa'd ibn Manṣūr, 13th cent.
8430.95	Ibn Khaldūn
8430.97	Ibn Sa'ūd, king of Saudi Arabia
8430.98	Ibn Taymīyah, Ahmad ibn 'Abd al-Ḥalīm
8430.99	Ibragimov, G.G.
8430.995	Ibrahimov, Mirză
8431	Ibsen, Henrik
8431.4	Ibuse, Masuji
8431.7	Idel, Moshe
8432	Ienaga, Saburō
8433	Ievinš, Alfréds
8433.2	Ignatīĭ, Saint, Bishop of Caucasus and Chernomore, 1807-1867
8433.3	Iha, Fuyú
8433.4	Ihara, Saikaku
8433.6	Ilaṅkōvaṭikal
8433.7	Il'in, Mark Aleksandrovich
8433.72	Ilʹnyt︠s︡kyĭ, Mykola Mykolaĭovych, 1934-
8433.8	Imahori, Seiji
8433.83	Imangulieva, A. N. (Aida Nasirovna)
8433.9	Immermann, K.L.
8434	Imshenet︠s︡kiĭ, A.A.
8435	Inan, Abdülkadir
8435.3	Inchbald, Elizabeth (Simpson)
8436	Inez de Castro
8436.6	Ing, Dean
8437	Ingalls, J.M.
8437.5	Inge, William
8437.7	Ingemann, B.S.
8438	Ingersoll, R.G.
8438.5	Inman, S.G.
8438.74	Innocentius XI, pope
8438.774	Inoue, Enryo
8438.776	Inoue, Kaoru

Z8001-8999

I -- Continued

8438.778	Inoue, Mitsusada
8438.782	Ionesco, Eugene
8438.7823	Ionescu, Nae, 1890-1940
8438.783	Iordan, Iorgu
8438.7833	Ĭordanov, Daki
8438.784	Iorga, Nicolae
8438.8	Iovkov, Iordan
8438.92	Ipatieff, V.N.
8438.97	Iqbal, Sir Muhammad
8439.3	Irchan, Myroslav, pseud.
8439.5	Irmscher, Johannes
8439.7	Irving, Washington
8439.8	Iryŏn
8439.9	Isaacs, Jorge
8439.925	Isachenkova, Anna Ivanovna, 1946-
8439.93	Isaev, S.
8439.97	Isahakian, Avetik'
8439.975	Isaǐevich, ĪAroslav
8439.98	Isakov, S.G.
8440	Isakovskiĭ, M.V.
8441	Isherwood, Christopher
8441.14	Ishikawa, Takuboku
8441.16	Ishkhanyan, R.A. (Rafayel Avetisi)
8441.2	Iskander, Fazil'
8441.3	Islam
8441.6	Ismail, Tun
8441.8	Isozaki, Arata
8441.9	Israel Meir, ha-Kohen
8442	Istvan, Saint, king of Hungary
8442.4	Italiaander, Rolf
8442.5	Itō, Toyoo
8442.57	ĪUkin, Vladimir ĪAkovlevich, 1920-
8442.6	ĪUrkevich, I.D.
8442.61	ĪUrovskikh, Vasiliĭ Ivanovich
8442.62	ĪUshkin, N.P.
8442.625	Ivanov, I.G.
8442.63	Ivanov, Konstantin
8442.65	Ivanov, V.I.
8442.68	Ivanova, Margarita Grigorévna
8442.685	Ivanović, Radomir V.
8442.7	Iwakura, Tomomi
8442.8	Iwaszkiewicz, Jarosław
8442.9	'Iyāḍ ibn Mūsá

J

8442.94	Jabès, Edmond
8443	Jackson, Andrew

J -- Continued

8443.3	Jackson, J.B. (John Brinckerhoff)
8443.4	Jackson, Laura (Riding)
8443.5	Jackson, Shirley
8443.53	Jackson, William Henry, 1843-1942
8443.6	Jacob, Max
8443.7	Jacob of Serug
8443.8	Jacobi, F.H.
8444	Jacobi, M.H. von
8444.22	Jacobs, W.W.
8444.23	Jacobsen, H.N.
8444.24	Jacobsen, Jens P.
8444.25	Jacobsen, Josephine
8444.4	Jacobson, Dan
8444.8	Jacobson, W.H.A.
8444.87	Jaeger, Frank
8444.93	Jaffe, Leib
8444.94	Jahn, Freidrich Ludwig
8444.95	Jahn, H.H.
8444.958	Jahukyan, G.B. (Gevorg Beglari)
8444.96	Jaisohn, Philip
8444.98	Jakobson, C.R.
8445.1	Jakobson, Roman
8445.2	Jakšić, Dura
8445.3	Jalal, Mir
8445.5	Jalal al-Din Runi, Mawlana
8445.8	Jalil, Musa
8445.9	Jalil, Rahim
8446.4	'Jam-dbyaṅs-bźad-pa Ṅag-dbaṅ-brtson-'grus
8446.5	Jamalzadah, M.A.
8446.7	James, C.L.R. (Cyril Lionel Robert), 1901-
8447	James, Henry
8447.4	James, M.R.
8447.47	James, Will
8447.5	James, William
8448	Jāmī
8448.5	Janasia, Simon
8448.7	Janelize, Alek'sandre
8448.9	Janickis, Jonas
8449	Janin, J.G.
8449.4	Janonis, Julius
8449.417	Janoušek, Antonín
8449.42	Janovsky, S.J.
8449.43	Jansons, Edgars
8449.434	Janssen, Horst, 1929-1995
8449.436	Jansson, Jan-Magnus, 1922-
8449.44	Jansson, Tove

Z8001-8999

J -- Continued

8449.45	Janulaitis, Augustinas
8449.72	Jarc, Miran, 1900-1942
8449.75	Jarnés, Benjamín
8450.1	Jarrell, Randall
8450.12	Jarring, Gunnar
8450.14	Järv, Harry
8450.17	Jaspers, Karl
8450.2	Jastrow, Morris
8450.4	Jaunsudrabinš, Jānis
8450.5	Javaxišvili, Ivanne
8450.7	Javid, Hùseĭn
8451	Jeanne d'Arc, Saint
8451.13	Jeanneret-Gris, C.É.
8451.2	Jebavý, Václav
8451.4	Jefferies, Richard
8451.5	Jeffers, Robinson
8452	Jefferson, Thomas
8452.6	Jeffreys, M.D.W.
8452.75	Jeleński, Konstanty A. (Konstanty Aleksander), 1922-1987
8452.8	Jenner, Edward
8453	Jennings, O.E.
8453.5	Jensen, J.V.
8453.56	Jensen, M.K.D.
8454.5	Jespersen, Otto
8455	Jesus Christ
8455.27	Jewitt, S.O.
8455.273	Jewsbury, Geraldine Endsor
8455.275	Jeżowska-Trzebiatowska, Bogusława
8455.28	Jhering, Rudolph von
8455.29	Jilemnický, Peter
8455.3	Jillson, W.R.
8455.313	Jiménez, J.R.
8455.314	Jinnah, Fatimah, 1894-1967
8455.315	Jinnah, M.A.
8455.3154	Jinzai, Kiyoshi
8455.316	Jippensha, Ikku
8455.32	Jirásek, Alois
8455.323	Jiricna, Eva
8455.327	Jñānadeva, fl. 1290
8455.33	Joachim, of Fiore
	Joan of Arc, Saint see Z8451
8455.335	Jo'gyī
8455.34	Jørgensen, Aage
8455.35	Jørgensen, Ellen
8455.37	Jørgensen, Severin
8455.4	Jørn, A.O.

J -- Continued

8455.5	Johann Sigismund, elector of Brandenburg
8455.55	John, Alois
8455.554	John Paul II, Pope
8455.56	Johnsen, O.A.
8455.567	Johnson, Andrew
8455.57	Johnson, Charles
8455.58	Johnson, Charles S
8455.6	Johnson, E. Pauline, 1861-1913
8455.65	Johnson, J.W.
8455.68	Johnson, L.B.
8455.72	Johnson, P.C.
8455.73	Johnson, R.L.
8455.79	Johnson, Samuel, 1696-1772
8455.8	Johnson, Samuel, 1709-1784
8455.87	Johnson, T.B.
8455.88	Johnson, Uwe
8456	Johnston, Arthur
8456.22	Johnston, F.B.
8456.23	Johnston, H.H.
8456.3	Johnston, R.M.
8456.36	Johnston-Lavis, H.J.
8456.48	Jókai, Mór
8456.5	Jolobe, J.J.R.
8456.55	Jonckheere, Karel
8456.555	Jones, D.M.
8456.556	Jones, E.F.
8456.557	Jones, Inigo
8456.56	Jones, James
8456.563	Jones, John H.C.
8456.57	Jones, LeRoi
8456.585	Jones, L.R.
8456.587	Jones, R.M.
8456.589	Jones, T.G.
8456.591	Jones, Sir William
8456.6	Jonson, Ben
8457.15	Jordan, D.S.
8457.17	Jorgaqi, Nasho V.
8457.2	Joris, David
8457.3	Jorn, Asger
8457.4	José I, king of Portugal
8457.44	Joseph, Mother
8457.45	Joseph, Saint
8457.5	Josephson, Ragnar
8457.53	Josephus, Flavius
8457.6	Joubert, Joseph
8457.65	Jouhandeau, Marcel

Z8001-8999

J -- Continued

8457.8	Jovanović, V.M.
8458	Jovellanos, G.M. de
8458.1	Joyce, James
8458.13	József, Attila
8458.14	Jrbashyan, Ē.M.
8458.15	Juan de la Cruz, Saint
8458.17	Juan Manuel, Infante of Castile
8458.2	Juana Inés de la Cruz, sor.
8458.23	Juárez, B.P., Pres. Mexico
8458.4	Junger, Ernst
8458.47	Juhász, Ferenc
8458.5	Juhász, Géza
8458.68	Julin, Charles
8458.75	Jung, C.G.
8458.8	Jung-Stilling, J.H.
8458.83	Jünger, Friedrich Georg
8458.86	Junghuhn, F.W.
8459	Junius, pseud.
	Junqueira Freire, L.J. see Z8314.6
8459.14	Juodka, Benediktas, 1943-
8459.18	Jurginis, Juozas
8459.25	Jusselin, Maurice
8459.253	Just, Cart

K

8459.256	Kabaj, Mieczysław
8459.257	Kabakchiev, K.S.
8459.258	Kabdebó, Tamás
8459.26	Kablukov, I.A.
8459.27	Kafarov, V.V.
8459.28	Kafka, Franz
8459.2812	Kagarov, Evgeniĭ
8459.2813	Kagawa, Toyohiko
8459.2815	Kageyama, Masaharu
8459.282	Kahana, Mozes
8459.283	Kahn, Albert
8459.284	Kahn, L.I.
8459.2844	Kaĭdarov, Abdu-Ali Tuganbaevich
8459.2847	Kaiko, Takeshi
8459.2849	Kaiser, Friedrich
8459.285	Kaiser, J.B.
8459.2854	Kaiser, Joachim, 1928-
8459.286	Kalchev, Kamen
8459.287	Kalesnik S.V. (Stanislav Vikent'evich)
8459.29	Kalidasa
8459.295	Kaljo, D.
8459.3	Kalm, Pehr

K -- Continued

8459.32	Kalma, J.J.
8459.33	Kálmáncsehi, Domokos, bp.
8459.4	Kalvos, Andreas
8459.46	Kamalā Hampanā
8459.5	Kamenev, L.B.
8459.52	Kamenskiĭ, G.N.
8459.53	Kamentśeva, E. I. (Elena Ivanovna)
8459.55	Kamiński, I.J.
8459.57	Kammerer, Hans
8459.59	Kampar
8459.66	Kan, S.B.
8459.7	Kanazawa, Harutomo
8459.74	Kaneko, Mitsuharu
8459.75	K'ang, Yu'wen
8459.78	Kano, Aminu
8459.8	Kanō, Jigorō
8460	Kant, Immanuel
8460.2	Kaplan, M.M.
8460.24	Kapustinskii, A.F.
8460.243	Karacaoğlan
8460.244	Karácsonyi, János
8460.246	Karadžić, V.S.
8460.247	Karag'ozov, Vasil
8460.2475	Karakis, Ĭosyp I͡Uliĭovych
8460.248	Karaliĭchev, Angel
8460.25	Karamzin, N.M.
8460.2515	Karandikar, G.V.
8460.252	Karanth, K.S.
8460.253	Karantōnēs, Antreas
8460.256	Karapents', Hakob
8460.26	Karaslavov, Georgi
8460.262	Karaslavov, S.K.
8460.2634	Karataev, Mukhamedzhan
8460.264	Karavelov, Li͡uben
8460.265	Kardelj, Edvard
8460.267	Kardos, Pál
8460.27	Kargin, V.A.
8460.275	Karimov, I.A., 1938-
8460.28	Karkhu, Ė.G.
8460.3	Karklinš, Romans
8460.4	Karl V, emperor of Germany
8460.7	Karl, Ludwig
8460.77	Karlfeldt, E.A.
8460.79	Karpenko, H.V.
	Karpenko-Karyĭ, I. 1845-1907 see Z8882.97
8460.83	Karpinskiĭ, A.P.

Z8001-8999

K -- Continued

8460.832	Karryev, Aga
8460.8326	Karvăs, Peter
8460.833	Kasack, Wolfgang
8460.834	Kaschnitz, M.L.
8460.835	Kashkaĭ, Mir-Ali
8460.836	Kasian, Sargis
8460.837	Kasiīan, V.I.
8460.8375	Kasperavičius, Petras
8460.838	Kasprowicz, Jan
8460.84	Kastriotes, Georgios, called Scanderbeg, prince of Epirus
8460.85	Katō, Shigeshi
8460.855	Katona, Jozsef
8460.86	Katsarov, G.I.
8460.868	Kaurismöki
8460.87	Kautsky, Karl
8460.875	Kavanagh, Patrick
8460.8753	Kaveĭskiĭ, R.E. (Rostislav Evgen'evich)
8460.876	Kaviraj, G.N.
8460.878	Kawabata, Yasunari
8460.88	Kawakami, Hajime
8460.89	Kawatake, Mokuami, 1816-1893
8460.93	Kaygusuz, Abdal
8460.943	Kazanecki, Wiesław
8460.945	Kazanskiĭ, B.A.
8460.95	Kazantzakes, Nikos
8460.96	Kazarin, V.P. (Vladimir Pavlovich)
8460.98	Keats, E.J.
8461	Keats, John
8461.5	Keidel, G.C.
8461.68	Kekilev, Aman
8461.75	Kekule von Stradonitz, Stephan
8462	Keller, Gottfried
8462.32	Kellogg, Elijah
8462.5	Kelly, Edward
8462.52	Kelly, Walt
8462.53	Kelsen, Hans
8462.6	Kemp, Pierre
8462.64	Kempowski, Walter
8462.67	Kendall, Henry
8462.7	Keñgesbaev, I.K.
8462.75	Kennan, G.F.
8462.8	Kennedy, J.F.
8462.83	Kenner, Hugh
8462.85	Kent, Rockwell
8462.9	Kenyon, J.S.
8463	Kepler, Johann

K -- Continued

8463.1	Ker, W.P.
8463.115	Kerekesh, I.I.
8463.12	Keres, Harold
8463.15	Kerim, Usin
8463.2	Kern, Hendrik
8463.4	Kerouac, John
8463.44	Kerschensteiner, G.M.A.
8463.45	Kertész, Imre, 1929-
8463.47	Ketkar, Shridhar Venkatesh
8463.5	Ketskhoveli, N.N.
8463.6	Ketteler, Wilhelm Emmanuel, Freiherr von, 1811-1877
8463.7	Keyes, C.R.
8463.75	Kéz, Andor
8463.755	Khach'eryan, L. G. (Levon Gevorgi)
8463.76	Khachikyan, L.S.
8463.77	Khălăfov, Abuzar
8463.78	Kharchev, Veselin
8463.8	Kharitonov, L.N.
8463.83	Khatibi, Abdelkebir
8463.85	Khayr Allāh, 'Adnān
8463.9	Khetagurov, K.L.
8463.92	Kholodnyĭ, Mykola
8463.93	Kholodnyĭ, Petro Ivanovych
8463.934	Khomeini, Ruhollah
8463.937	Khorunzhyĭ, ĪŪriĭ, 1937-
8463.97	Khristov, Kiril
8463.975	Khropko, P.P.
8463.98	Khrushchev, N.S.
8464.1	Khrushchov, K.D.
8464.2	Khusainov, G.B.
8464.23	Khydyrov, M.N.
8464.25	Kierkegaard, S.A.
8464.27	Kikuchi, Hiroshi
8464.28	Kikutake, Kiyonori
8464.285	Kilian, Saint
8464.3	Kim, Il-song
8464.32	al-Kindi
8464.33	Kindler, Arie
8464.34	King, Basil
8464.35	King, Charles
8464.38	King, Henry, Bp. of Chichester
8464.4	King, Judson
8464.44	King, M.L.
8464.5	King, William
8464.56	Kingdom-Ward, Francis
8464.6	Kingo, Thomas

Z8001-8999

K -- Continued

8464.7	Kingsley, Charles
8464.9	Kinnell, Galway
8464.94	Kinomiya, Yasuhiko
8464.97	Kinzhalov, R.V.
8465	Kipling, Rudyard
8465.06	Kipnis, Levin
8465.1	Kippenberg, Anton
8465.32	Kirby, David
8465.33	Kircher, Athanasius
8465.37	Kirk, Russell
8465.38	Kirkconnell, Watson
8465.4	Kirkman, Francis
8465.43	Kirkov, Georgi
8465.45	Kirov, S.M.
8465.455	Kirpicheva, Iraida
8465.46	Kirstein, Lincoln
8465.48	Kiselev, A.V.
8465.5	Kishimoto, Ken'ichi
8465.57	Kiss, Árpád
8465.6	Kiss, Lajos
8465.7	Kittredge, G.L.
8465.74	Kivi, Aleksis
8465.76	Kizildağli, Edip
8465.8	Kjellberg, S.T.
8465.816	Kjetsaa, Geir
8465.85	Klafki, Wolfgang
8466.45	Klausner, Joseph
8466.5	Kleihues, J.P.
8466.55	Klein, A.M.
8466.6	Kleist, Heinrich von
8466.63	Klemke, Werner
8466.65	Klesch, Daniel
8466.7	Klinefelter, Walter
8466.72	Klingberg, Göte
8466.75	Klokov, ĨŪ. A.
8466.8	Klopstock, F.G.
8466.9	Klugh, A.B.
8467	Knapp, Charles
8467.12	Knigge, Adolf, Freiherr von
8467.13	Knipovich, N.M.
8467.15	Knudsen, H.A.H.
8467.153	Knuriants, I.L.
8467.155	Kobayashi, Hideo
8467.156	Kobayashi, Yoshiharu
8467.158	Kobrin, V.B.
8467.16	Kobylĩāns'ka, Ol'ha

K -- Continued

8467.167	Koch, Carl
8467.17	Kochanowski, Jan
8467.1712	Kochetkov, N. K.
8467.17125	Kochur, Hryhoriĭ
8467.1713	Kocsis, László
8467.1715	Kodolányi, Janos
8467.1718	Kodukhov, V.I.
8467.172	Koefoed, H.A.
8467.173	Köhler, Walther
8467.175	Köppen, P.I.
8467.177	Köprülü, M.F.
8467.1773	Kösemihal, N.S.
8467.1774	Koestler, Arthur
8467.1775	Kogălniceanu, Mihail
8467.1777	Kogltin, Dava, 1922-
8467.18	Kohler, E.P.
8467.19	Kohler, Josef
8467.2	Kohler, Kaufmann
8467.22	Kohler, M.J.
8467.337	Koht, Halvdan
8467.34	Kohut, Alexander
8467.35	Kohut, G.A.
8467.353	Kohut, Heinz
8467.36	Koidula, Lydia
8467.364	Kojo, Viljo
8467.365	Kokona, Vedat
8467.367	Kolakowski, Leszek
8467.37	Kolarov, V.P.
8467.373	Kolberg, Oskar
8467.375	Kolesnikov, Aleksandr
8467.38	Kollár, Jan
8467.382	Kolmaš, Josef
8467.384	Kolotyrkin, IA.M.
8467.39	Kolsrud, Oluf
8467.394	Koltès, Bernard-Marie
8467.396	Kolʹt͡sov, A.V.
8467.3968	Kondratovich, R. IA
8467.397	Koneski, Blaze
8467.3974	Konjović, Milan
8467.398	Kononov, A.N.
8467.4	Konopnicka, Maria
8467.415	Konrad, Nikolaĭ
8467.42	Konstantinov, Aleko
8467.422	Kontrimavichus, Vitautas Leonovich
8467.423	Koolhaas, Rem
8467.4236	Kopnin, P.V.

Z8001-8999

K -- Continued

8467.426	Korablinov, V.A.
8467.43	Koraēs, Adamantios
8467.432	Kořalka, Jiřī
8467.434	Korczak, Janusz
8467.435	Koren, Hanns
8467.44	Korolenko, V.G.
8467.45	Korolev, F.A.
8467.453	Koroleva, Natalena, 1888-1966
8467.46	Korsakas, Kostas
8467.465	Korshak, V.V.
8467.47	Korzhinskiĭ, D.S.
8467.49	Kós, Károly
8467.5	Kościuszko. T.A.B.
8467.52	Koščo, Jozef
8467.523	Kosinski, J.N.
8467.53	Kosmas ho Aitōlos, Saint
8467.54	Kossuth, Barbara
8467.55	Kossuth, Lajos
8467.56	Kostevich, M.M.
8467.563	Kostić, Dušan
8467.564	Kostomarov, N.I.
8467.5645	Kostyrīā, Ivan
8467.565	Kosygin, I.A.
8467.57	Kotlīārevs'ryĭ, Ivan
8467.58	Kotsiubyns'kyĭ, Mykhailo
8467.583	Kott, Jan
8467.587	Kovachevski, I.K.
8467.588	Kovács, Imre
8467.5884	Kovalćhenko, Ivan Dmitrievich
8467.59	Kovalevsky, Pierre
8467.6	Kovalivs'kyĭ, A.P.
8467.62	Koyré, A.
8467.624	Kozhinov, Vadim Valerianovich
8467.63	Kožík, František
8467.64	Kracauer, Siegfried
8467.65	Krachkovskii, I. IU
8467.66	Kraft, Robert, 1869-1916
8467.67	Kral, Frano
8467.672	Kramařík, Jaroslav
8467.68	Kranjec, Miško
8467.69	Kranz, Gisbert
8467.7	Kranzmayer, Eberhard
8467.72	Krastins, Janis
8467.724	Kraszewski, J.I.
8467.725	Kratochvíl, Jaroslav
8467.726	Kraulinīā, E.K.

K -- Continued

8467.727	Kraulinš, Kārlis
8467.73	Kraus, Carl von
8467.733	Kraus, Hans-Joachim
8467.735	Kraus, Karl
8467.755	Kravchuk, M. (Mykhaĭlo)
8467.77	Khălăfov Abuzar
8467.79	Kreĭn, M. G.
8467.795	Krejčí, Dobroslav
8467.7957	Krejčí, Jan
8467.796	Krejčí, Karel
8467.79615	Kressel, Getzel
8467.79617	Kretzenbacher, Leopold
8467.7962	Kreutzwald, F.R.
8467.7965	Krieck, Ernst
8467.7966	Krier, Léon
8467.7967	Krier, Rob
8467.797	Krige, Uys
8467.799	Krikščiūnas, Jonas
8467.7994	Krisciunas, Jonas
8467.7995	Krishnamurti, Jiddu
8467.79957	Kristeller, Paul Oskar, 1905-
8467.7996	Kristensen, Tom
8467.7997	Kristeva, Julia
8467.7998	Krleza, Miroslav
8467.8	Kroeber, A.L.
8467.814	Krogmann, Willy
8467.815	Krohg, Chris
8467.816	Kroĭchik, L. E. (Lev Efremovich)
8467.817	Kroll, Lucien
8467.82	Krolow, Karl
8467.83	Kropotkin, P.A., Kniaz
8467.834	Kross, Jean
8467.84	Kruczkowski, Leon
8467.845	Krúdy, Gyula
8467.847	Krul, J.H.
8467.848	Krupin, V.N.
8467.85	Kruss, James
8467.87	Krupskaia, N.K.
8467.875	Krushel'nyt͡s'ka, L.I.
8467.88	Krutch, J.W.
8467.89	Kruus, Hans
8467.895	Krvavych D.P., 1926-
8467.9	Krylov, A.N.
8467.913	Krylov, I.A.
8467.92	Krymov, I͡U.S.
8467.923	Krym'kyĭ, A. I͡U

Z8001-8999

	K -- Continued
8467.93	Krzhizhanovskiĭ, G.M.
8467.934	Krzyzaniak, Lech
8467.938	Ku, Yen-wu
8467.939	Kuan, Chung
8467.94	Kubiiovych, Volodymyr
8467.95	Kubilius, Jonas
8467.956	Kubin, Alfred
8467.96	Kubka, František
8467.965	Kucherov, E. V.
8467.97	Kuchĭĭak, Pavel
8467.972	Kudaba, Č.
8467.975	Kudirka, Vincas, 1858-1899
8467.98	Kudri͡avt͡sev, A.E.
8467.982	Kudri͡avt͡sev, V.N.
8467.985	Kufaev, M.N.
8468	Kühn, C.H.
8468.12	Kuindzhi, A.I.
8468.13	Kükelhaus, Hugo
8468.15	Küzig, Johannes
8468.2	Küttner, C.G.
8468.3	Kulakovskiĭ, I͡Ulĭan
8468.4	al-Kulaynī, Muhammad ibn Ya'qūb
8468.45	Kuliev, S.M.
8468.47	Kulizade, K.N.
8468.475	Kul′man, Elisaveta
8468.48	Kul'skiĭ, Leonid Adol'povich
8468.49	Kun, Béla
8468.5	Kunanbaev, Abaĭ
8468.52	Kundera, Milan
8468.522	Kunert, Günter
8468.53	Kunitz, Heinrich
8468.54	Kunnert, Heinrich
8468.55	Kunz, G.F.
8468.554	Kunze, Erich
8468.56	Kuo, Mo-jo
8468.576	Kupchyns′kyĭ, O. A.
8468.58	Kupiainen, Unto
8468.59	Kupka, František
8468.595	Kuprii͡anov, I.T.
8468.6	Kuprin, A.I.
8468.611	Kurahashi, Yumiko, 1935-2005
8468.612	Kuramata, Shirō
8468.613	Kurata, Satoru
8468.615	Kurokawa, Kisho
8468.616	Kurokawa, Noriaki
8468.67	Kurtz, Paul

K -- Continued

8468.68	Kurz, Josef
8468.7	Kurzweil, Baruch
8468.73	Kushch, O.P.
8468.75	Kusy, Ivan
8468.78	Kut͡sarov, Stefan
8468.796	Kutumba Rao
8468.8	Kutuzov, M.I., svetleĭshiĭ kni͡az'Smolenskiĭ
8468.85	Kutz, Kazimierz
8468.9	Kuusberg, Paul
8469	Kuyper, Abraham
8469.114	Kuypers, Julien
8469.117	Kuzeev, Rustem
8469.12	Kuznet͡sov, E.V.
8469.135	Kuznet͡sov, Valeriĭ Alekseevich, 1906-
8469.19	Kyd, Thomas
8469.25	Kyrylīūk, ĪE. P.

L

8469.27	L.E.L. (Letitia Elizabeth Landon), 1802-1838
8469.3	La Boétie, Estienne de
8469.34	La Harpe, Jean François de
8469.347	La Pira, Giorgio
8469.35	Labra y Cadrana, R.M. de
8469.355	Labiş, Nicolae
8469.36	Labrouste, Henri
	Labrunie de Nerval, Gérard see Z8336.5
8469.37	La Bruyère, Jean de
8469.38	Labutis, Vitas
8469.39	Lacan, Jacques
8469.42	Lācis, Vilis
8469.44	Lack, D.L.
8469.45	Laclos, P.A.F. Choderlos de
8469.46	Lacombe, Albert
8469.65	Lacunza, Manuel
8469.73	Ladrière, Jean
8469.8	Laestadius, L.I.
8470.1	La Fayette, M.M. (Pioche de La Vergne), Comtesse de
8470.5	La Follette, R.M.
8470.6	La Fontaine, Jean de
8470.82	Lafayette, M.J.P.Y.R.G. du Motier, marquis de
8470.84	Lafever, Minard
8470.85	Lafferty, R.A.
8470.86	Lafontaine, A.H.J.
8470.92	Lagercrantz, Sture
8470.93	Lagergren, C.G.
8470.96	Lagerkvist, P.F.
8471.1	Lagerlöf, S.O.L.

Z8001-8999

L -- Continued

8471.3	Lagrange, J.L., comte
8471.4	Laguerre, Enrique A.
8471.5	Lahontan, L.A. de Lom d'Arce, baron de
8471.8	Laicens, Linards
8472	Laínez, Diego
8472.6	Lakó, György
8472.8	Lalana Saha
8473.5	La Marche Olivier de
8473.8	Lamartine, A.M.L. de
8473.9	Lamas, Andrés
8473.93	Lamas, Maria
8474	Lamb, Charles and Mary
8474.4	Lambeck, Peter
8474.45	Lambert, Franz
8474.5	Lambert, J.H.
8475	Lamennais, H.F.R. de
8476	Lamotte, Étienne
8476.5	L'Amour, Louis
8477.6	Lancaster, Clay
8477.7	Lancaster, Osbert, Sir
8478	Lancetti, Vincenzo
8479	Land, E.S.
8479.5	Landacre, Paul
8480	Landaeta Rosales, Manuel
8480.3	Landau, Jacob M.
8481.15	Landívar, Rafael
	Landon, Letitia Elizabeth see Z8469.27
8481.3	Landor, W.S.
8481.37	Landsbergis, Vytautas
8481.4	Lane, H.H.
8481.7	Lang, Andrew
8481.8	Lang, J.D.
8482	Langenhoven, C.J.
	Langenstein, Heinrich von see Z8395.5
8482.3	Langgässer, Elisabeth
8482.4	Langland, William
8482.5	Langley, S.P.
8482.6	Langlois, Ernest
8482.7	Langmuir, Irving
8482.8	Langren, M.F. van
8482.85	Langsdorff, G.H., freiherr von
8483.2	Lanier, Sidney
8483.22	Lanoye, Tom
8483.24	Lao, She
8483.26	Lao-tzu
8483.3	Laoust, Henri

L -- Continued

8483.5	Lapérouse, J.F. de Galaup, comte de
8483.6	Lapidus, Morris
8483.64	Lapomarda, Vincent A.
8483.65	Lapouge, Georges Vacher de
8483.67	Lappo, D.D. (Dimitriĭ Danilovich)
8483.7	Laprade, W.T.
8483.8	Laqueur, Walter
8483.9	La Ramée, Pierre de
8483.93	Lardner, R.W.
8483.98	Larkin, Philip
8483.99	La Roche, Sophie von
8484	La Rochefoucauld, François, duc de
8484.52	Larsen, Thøger
8484.546	Larsson, Carl, 1853-1919
8484.55	Larsson, Hans
8484.558	Larsson, Hugo
8484.85	La Salle, R.C.
8485	La Sicotière, Léon de
8485.5	Lasdun, Denys
8485.6	Lasker-Schüler, Else
8485.8	Lasunskiĭ, O.G.
8485.9	Laswell, H.D.
8485.98	László, Péter
8485.99	László, Vajthó
8487	Lateur, Frank
8487.3	Latham, Ian
8488.3	Latrobe, B.H.
8488.4	Lauffer, Pierre
8488.5	Laugier, J.F.
8488.54	Laurel, J.P.
8488.55	Laurent, M.H.
8488.6	Laurier, Sir Wilfrid
8488.65	Lauring, Palle
8488.67	Lautner, John
8488.7	La Varende, Jean de
8488.8	Lavendel, E.E. (Egon Edgarovich)
8488.9	La Villemarqué, T.H., vicomte de
8488.95	Lavin, Mary
8489	Lavoisier, A.L.
8489.2	Lavrenev, Boris
8489.5	Law, John
8489.6	Lawes, J.B.
8490.5	Lawrence, D.H.
8491	Lawrence, G.N.
8491.5	Lawrence, T.E.
8491.9	Lawrence family

Z8001-8999

L -- Continued

8492	Lawson, H.A.H.
8492.4	Layton, Irving
8492.47	Lazarev, A.I.
8492.5	Lazarev, P.P.
8492.514	Lazarevskiĭ, A.M.
8492.52	Lazarīan, V.A.
8492.56	Lazo, S.G.
8492.7	Le Fanu, J.S.
8493	Lea, Isaac
8493.3	Lea, M.C.
8494	Leacock, S.B.
8494.14	Leal, Ildefonso
8494.16	Leal, Luis
8494.18	Leander, Sigfrid
8494.19	Leary, T.F.
8494.2	Leavis, F.R.
8494.27	Lebedev, A.A.
8494.28	Lebedev, D.V.
8494.29	Lebedev, P.F.
8494.3	Lebedev, P.N.
8494.7	Le Cacheux, P.C.N.M.J.
8494.8	Leclercq, Jean
8495	Leconte, J.L.
8495.2	Leconte de Lisle, C.M.R.
	Le Corbusier see Z8451.13
8495.4	Lee, R.E.
8495.42	Lee, S.P.
8495.45	Leech, John
8495.46	Leemann-Van Elck, Paul
8495.47	Leeuw, Gerardus van der
8495.48	Lefebvre, Georges
8495.49	Lefebvre, Henri
8495.5	Leffmann, Henry
8495.7	Le Gallienne, Richard
8495.74	Leger, A.S.
8495.8	Legros, Michel
8495.85	Leguia, J.G.
8495.88	Le Guin, U.K.
8495.93	Lehmann, Alfred
8495.95	Lehmann, Karl
8496	Lehrs, Max
8496.16	Leĭbenzon, L.S.
8496.18	Leibniz, G.W. freiherr von
8496.2	Leichhardt, Ludwig
8496.3	Leidy, Joseph
8496.45	Leipoldt, C.L.

	L -- Continued
8496.47	Leiris, Michel
8496.48	Leite, Serafim
8496.5	Leite de Vasconcellos Pereira de Mello, Jose
8496.8	Leith, C.K.
8496.9	Leivick, Halper
8497	Le jolis, A.P.
8498	Leland, C.G.
8498.5	Lelewel, Joachim
8498.84	Lemaire de Belges, Jean
8499	Lemoine, Sir J.M.
8499.5	Lemonnier, Camille
8500	Lenau, Nicolaus
8500.6	L'Enfant, P.C.
8500.8	Lenin, V.I.
8501	Lennep, Jakob van
8501.3	Lenski, Lois
8501.5	León, Hermano
8501.6	León, L.P. de
8501.65	León, Luis de
8501.8	León, Nicolás
8502	Leonardo da Vinci
8502.3	Leoni, G.D.
8502.5	Leonov, L.M.
8502.55	Leonov, V.P. (Valeriĭ Pavlovich)
8502.8	Leopardi, Giacomo, conte
8502.85	Lepik, Kalju
8502.87	Leppik, E.E.
8502.9	Leprince, Andre
8502.95	Lermontov, M.IU
8502.96	Lernet-Holenia, Alexander
8502.97	Leroux, Etienne
8503	Le Sage, A.R.
8503.2	Lesage, Pierre
8503.3	Leser, Paul
8503.4	Leshchuk, ÎEvheniïa
8503.5	Leskov, N.S.
8503.7	Lesnea, George
8503.8	Lessing, Doris May
8504	Lessing, G.E.
8504.2	Leti, Gregorio
8504.24	LeVaillant, Francois
8504.3	Le Vavasseur, Gustave
8504.315	Lévay József
8504.32	Levchev, Līubomir
8504.33	Leverhulme, W.H.L., Viscount
8504.34	Le Verrier, Urbain

L -- Continued

8504.342	Levertov, Denise
8504.343	Levi, Ezio
8504.347	Levi della Vida, Giorgio
8504.35	Levi-Strauss, Claude
8504.352	Levin, I.D.
8504.353	Levin, Meyer
8504.354	Levinas, Emmanuel
8504.355	Levison, Wilhelm
8504.356	Levitin, Mikhail (Mikhail Zakharovich)
8504.357	Levski, V.I.
8504.364	Lewandowski, Herbert
8504.37	Lewis, C.S.
8504.38	Lewis, Sinclair
8504.385	Lewis, William
8504.39	Lewis, Wyndham
8504.4	Leyden, John
8504.412	Lezama Lima, José
8504.413	Li, Chin-hsi
8504.414	Li, Kuo-ting
8504.416	Li, Shih-chen
8504.42	Li, Ta-chao
8504.427	Liang, Chì-chào
8504.429	Līāpunov, A.A.
8504.43	Līāpunov, A.M.
8504.436	Līātskiĭ, E.A.
8504.438	Libeskind, Daniel
8504.44	Lichtenberg, G.C.
8504.45	Lichtveld, Lou
8504.452	Lichtwark, Alfred
8504.46	Liddel, Duncan
8504.5	Lie, Sophus
8504.52	Liebig, Justus, freiherr von
8504.54	Liebknecht, K.P.A.F.
8504.56	Lieh-tzŭ
	Līēskov, N.S. see Z8503.5
8504.6	Lièvre, A.F.
8504.65	Ligne, Charles Joseph, prince de
8504.7	Likhachev, D.S.
8504.72	Likhachev, N.P.
8504.74	Lilje, Hanns
8504.75	Liljegren, S.B.
8504.8	Lill, Georg
8504.84	Lima, Jorge de
8504.86	Lima Barreto
8504.9	Linck, Wenzeslaus
8505	Lincoln, Abraham

L -- Continued

8505.5	Lindberg, S.G.
8505.53	Lindberger, Örjan
8505.55	Lindbergh, A.M.
8505.6	Lindblom, A.A.F.
8505.65	Linde, S.B.
8505.7	Lindegren, Erik
8505.85	Linder, E.H.
8505.96	Lindgren, Astrid
8506	Lindgren, Waldemar
8506.13	Lindhardt, P.G.
8506.15	Lindman, S.O.G.
8506.17	Lindqvist, Sune
8506.2	Lindsay, Nicholas Vachel
8506.24	Lindsay, Norman
8506.3	Lindsay, W.L.
8508	Linné, Carl von
8509	Linnemann, W.A.
8509.5	Linnik, I.V.
8509.8	Lins, Guilherme Gomes da Silveira d'Avila
8510	Linstead, Sir R.P.
8511	Lintner, J.A.
8511.5	Lipschütz, E.M.
8511.7	Lipsius, Justus
8511.77	Lisboa, Henriqueta
8511.78	Liscano, Juan
8511.79	Lisit͡syna, T. A. (Tamara Arkad'evna)
8511.8	Lispector, Clarice
8511.9	List, Friedrich
8511.93	Lister, Martin
8511.95	Littmann, Enno.
8511.957	Litván, József
8511.96	Litvin, Martin
8511.97	Litvinenko, L.M.
8512.13	Liu, Shaoqi, 1898-1969
8512.15	L͡iubovikov, Ovidiĭ Mikhaĭlovich
8512.2	L͡iufanov, Evgeniĭ
8512.5	Liversidge, Archibald
8513	Livingstone, B.E.
8513.2	Livingstone, David
8513.22	Livingstone, Douglas
8513.26	Ljungberg, L.T.B.
8513.3	Lloyd, H.D.
8513.4	Lobato, J.B.M.
8513.45	Locke, John
8513.57	Lodge, David
8513.58	Lodge, Sir O.J.

L -- Continued

8513.585	Lodge, Thomas
8513.587	Loening, G.C.
8513.58745	Loginov, A.S.
8513.5875	Logstrup, K.E.
8513.588	Lohenstein, D.C. von
8513.5887	Łojek, Jerzy
8513.589	Lőkös, István
8513.5894	Lomer, G.R.
8513.59	Lomonosov, M.V.
8514.6	London, Jack
8514.85	Longepierre, H.B. de Requeleyne, baron de
8515	Longfellow, H.W.
8515.4	Longhi, Roberto
8515.5	Löns, Hermann
8515.7	Loos, Adolf
	Lope de Vega see Z8930
8517.6	López y Martínez, J.L., marqués del Risco
8517.7	Loredano, G.F.
	Lorenzine, Carlo see Z8184.88
8517.8	Lorrain, Jean (P.A.M. Duval)
8517.95	Losskii, N.O.
8518.3	Loth, Julien
	Loti, Pierre see Z8941.2
8519.5	Louis XVII, king of France
8519.7	Louis, Joe
8519.9	Louis, René
8520.3	Louise, consort of Frederick William III, king of Prussia
8520.64	Louw, N.P. van Wyk
8520.9	Lovecraft, H.P.
8520.94	Lovejoy, A.O.
8520.95	Lovejoy, E.P.
8521	Lowell, J.R.
8522	Lowell, Robert
8522.5	Lowis, R.H.
8522.53	Lowndes, R.W.
8522.55	Lowry, Malcolm
8523	Loyola, Ignacio de, Saint
8523.53	Lozano, Pedro
8523.55	Lozoya, Juan Contreras y López de Ayala, marqués de
8524	Lu, Y'u
8524.3	Lubac, Henri de
8524.314	Lubkivs'kyĭ, Roman
8524.4	Lucas, E.V.
8524.5	Luce, Siméon
8525	Luchuk, Volodymyr
8526.5	Luchyts'kyĭ, V.I.

L -- Continued

8527	Lucianus Samosatensis
8527.23	Lucretius Carus, Titus
8527.26	Ludwig, Emil
8527.28	Ludwig II, King of Bavaria
8527.4	Lugones, Leopoldo
8527.5	Luis de Granada
8527.6	Lukács, György
8527.64	Lukash, Mykola
8527.65	Lukevīt͡s, Ė. I͡A.
8527.7	Lull, Ramon
8527.72	Lumley, Brian
8527.73	Lummis, C.F.
8527.75	Lunacharskiĭ, A.V.
8527.78	Lundberg, G.W.
8527.79	Lunde, Johannes
8527.8	Lundstedt, A.V.
8527.917	Luppov, P.N.
8527.92	Luppov, S.P.
8527.93	Luria, I.B.S.
8527.94	Lurye, Note
8528	Luther, Martin
8528.5	Lut͡sevich, I.D.
8528.58	Lutyens, E.L.
8528.6	Lutzky, Aaron
8528.7	Luxemburg, Rosa
8529	Luz y Caballero, J.C. de la
8529.7	Luzzatto, M.H.
8529.8	Luzzatto, S.D.
8530	Lydgate, John
8530.5	Lyly, John
8530.55	Lyn'koŭ, Mikhaś
8530.556	Lyons, Joseph Aloysius, 1879-1939
8530.56	Lyotard, Jean-François
8530.564	Lypa, IUriĭ
8530.57	Lytle, A.N.
8530.58	Lytvyn, Volodymyr

M

8531.017	Maamägi, Viktor
8531.02	Maas, Paul
8531.15	McAdoo, W.G.
8531.2	MacArthur, Douglas
8531.8	McCarthy, Mary Therese
8531.87	McClung, C.E.
8531.88	McClure, Michael
8531.9	McCollum, E.V.
8532	McCosh, James

Z8001-8999

M -- Continued

8532.16	McCoy, Esther
8532.2	McCrae, Georgiana Huntly (Gordon)
8532.23	McCullers, C.S.
8532.25	MacDiarmid, Hugh
8532.28	MacDonagh, Thomas
8532.3	MacDonald, Arthur
8532.38	Macdonald, George
8532.383	MacDonald, J.D.
8532.386	Macdonald, Ross
8532.39	McDougall, William
8532.4	Macedo, J.A. de
8532.6	Maceo, Antonio
8532.8	McFee, William
8533.7	Mácha, K.H.
8533.74	Machado, J.G.
8533.743	Machado, J.J.
8533.745	Machado de Assis, J.M.
8533.747	Machado y Ruiz, Antonio
8533.748	Machal, Jan
8533.749	Machel, Samora
8533.75	Machen, Arthur
8534	Machiavelli, Niccolò
8534.6	Mackay, I.E.
8534.8	Mackaye, Percy
8535.2	Mackenzie, Compton
8535.3	Mackenzie, Sir James
8535.35	McKenzie, W.P.
8535.5	Mackintosh, C.R.
8535.7	Maclean, Ian
8536	McLean family
8536.2	MacLeish, Archibald
8536.9	McMurtrie, D.C.
8537	McMurtrie, William
8537.4	McNabb, V.J.
8537.43	MacNeice, Louis
8537.45	McNeill, J.T.
8538	McPherson, A.S.
8538.1	Macpherson, James
8538.45	McPike, E.F.
8538.5	Macrí, Oreste
8538.6	MacSwiney, T.J.
8538.8	Macůrek, Josef
8538.82	Mączak, Antoni
8538.85	Madgulkar, V.D.
8539	Madison, D.P.T.
8540	Madison, James

M -- Continued

8540.8	Madsen, Carl
8540.85	Madsen, S.A.
8541	Madvig, J.N.
8541.2	Madzharov, Kiril
8541.3	Maekawa, Kunio
8541.8	Maerlant, Jacob van
8542	Maeterlinck, Maurice
8542.35	Magalhães, Basílio de
8542.36	Magalhães, Luís de
8542.42	Magnin, Pierre
8542.44	Magocsi, P.R.
8542.47	Magsaysay, Ramón
8542.48	Magtymguly
8542.5	Mahan, A.T.
8542.56	Mahathir bin Mohamad
8542.58	Mahdī, Muḥammad ibn al-Ḥasan
8542.59	Mahdihassan, S.
8542.6	Mahen, Jiři
8542.7	Maheux, Arthur
8542.73	Maḥfūẓ, Najīb, 1911-
8542.8	Maḥmudov, Ḣ. I. (Ḣikmăt Ismaǐyl oghlu)
8542.9	Maīākovskiĭ, V.V.
8543	Maidment, James
8543.3	Maier, Hans
8543.6	Maĭkov, L.N.
8543.65	Mailer, Norman
	Maimonides, Moses see Z8597.2
8543.7	Main, V.N.
8543.8	Mairet, Jean de
8543.813	Maironis
8543.815	Maiuri, Amedeo
8543.82	Majerová, Marie
8543.84	Major, John
8544	Makarenko, A.S.
8544.2	Makar'ev, L. (Leonid)
8544.25	Maki, Fumihiko
8544.4	Makrygiannēs, Iōannēs
8544.5	Malakhov, G.M.
8544.57	Malamud, Bernard
8544.573	Malaniuk, Evhen
8544.58	Malaparte, Curzio
8544.584	Malaspina, Alessandro
8544.584	Malaspina, Alessandro
8544.6	Malaviya, M.M.
8544.7	Malebranche, Nicolas
8544.8	Maleev, A.K.

Z8001-8999

M -- Continued

8544.815	Malez, Mirko
8544.83	Maliszewski, Dionizy
8544.85	Mälk, August
8544.9	Malkiel, Yakov
8545	Mallarmé, Stéphane
8545.16	Malmeister, A.K.
8545.2	Malmquist, Eve
8545.45	Malone, Kemp
8545.5	Malory, Sir Thomas
8545.8	Malraux, André
8546.2	Mamedaliev, IŪ. G.
8546.3	Mamin-Sibiri͡ak, D.N.
8546.33	Mămmăd Jăfăr, 1909-
8546.35	Mămmădguluzadă, Jălil, 1866-1931
8546.37	Mămmădyarov, Măhărräm Äli oğlu
8546.4	Mañach, Jorge
8546.5	Manasseh ben Joseph ben Israel
8546.7	Manastryrs'kyĭ, A.I.
8546.9	Mandelló, Gyula
8546.92	Mandeville, Bernard
8547.1	Mandeville, Jean de
8547.11	Manent, Marià
8547.12	Manetti, Antonio
8547.2	Manfred, F.F.
8547.3	Mangan, J.C.
8547.32	Manganelli, Giorgio
8547.33	Manger, Itzik
8547.34	Mangurian Robert
8547.345	Maniu, Adrian
8547.35	Manker, E.M.
8547.37	Mann, Heinrich
8547.4	Mann, Horace
8547.405	Mann, Klaus
8547.41	Mann, Thomas
8547.47	Manner, Eeva-Liisa
8547.47	Manner, Eeva-Liisa
8547.5	Mannerheim, C.G.E., friherre
8547.515	Mannheim, Karl
8547.52	Mannoury, Gerrit
8547.525	Manor, Alexander
8547.53	Manousakas, M.I.
8547.57	Manrique, Jorge
8547.59	Mansart, François
8547.593	Manselli, Raoul
8547.595	Mansfield, Alfred
8547.6	Mansfield, Katherine

M -- Continued

8547.8	Mantell, G.A.
8547.9	Mantese, Giovanni
8548	Manzoni, Alessandro
8548.3	Mao, Tŝe-tung
8548.4	Mappouras, Antreas
8548.45	Márai, Sándor
8548.5	Marais, E.N.
8548.76	Marakuev, A.V.
8548.84	Mar'ashī Najafī, Shihāb al-Dīn
8549	Marat, J.P.
8549.6	Marcel, Gabriel
8549.8	March, William
8550	Marchegay, P.A.
8550.05	Marchi, Riccardo
8550.1	Marchlewski, J.B.
8550.12	Marchuk, G.I. (Gurĭĭ Ivanovich)
8550.13	Marconi, Guglielmo
8550.14	Marcus, J.R.
8550.15	Marcuse, Herbert
8550.17	Margerie, Emmanuel de
8550.18	Margolis, ĪŪ. D.
8550.19	Marguerite, Queen, consort of Henry II, King of Navarre
8550.2	Margueritte, Paul and Victor
8550.23	Margulan, A.Kh.
8550.26	Mariátegui, J.C.
8550.3	Marie Antoinette
8550.314	Marie de France
8550.317	Marīīà, mat'
8550.32	Marin, André
8550.325	Marín Rojas, Juan
8550.33	Marinello, Juan
8550.332	Marinetti, Filippo T.
8550.335	Marino, Giambattista
8550.34	Maritain, Jacques
8550.35	Markham, Sir C.R.
8550.36	Markham, Gervase
8550.363	Márki, Sándor
8550.364	Markiewicz, Henryk
8550.365	Markopoulas, G.J.
8550.367	Marković, Svetozar
8550.37	Markovych, M.O.
8550.38	Marlborough, John Churchill, 1st duke of
8550.4	Marlowe, Christopher
8550.43	Mármol, José
8550.45	Marmontel, J.F.
8550.5	Marot, Clément

Z8001-8999

M -- Continued

8550.54	Marquand, John P.
8550.55	Marqués, René
8550.58	Marquet de Vasselot, J.J.
8550.7	Marquez Tapia, Ricardo
8551	Marsh, G.P.
8551.24	Marshak, S. IA
8551.26	Marshall, Alan
8551.38	Marston, John
8551.43	Martí, José
8551.5	Martial (Marcus Valerius Martialis)
8551.56	Martin, Helmut
8551.59	Martin du Gard, Roger
8551.6	Martineau, Harriet
8551.612	Martinet, André
8551.6128	Martínez Capó, Juan
8551.613	Martínez Durán, Carlos
8551.614	Martínez Estrada, Ezequiel
8551.616	Martini, Francesco di Giorgio
8551.618	Martius, K.F.P. von
8551.62	Martynov, A.I.
8551.64	Marulus, Marcus
8551.646	Maruyama, Kaoru
8551.647	Maruyama, Masao
8551.65	Marvell, Andrew
8551.67	Marx, Karl
8551.7	Mary Stuart, queen of Scots
8552	Mary, Virgin
8552.7	Masaryk, T.G.
8553.5	Mascart, Jean
8553.6	Masefield, John
8553.62	Masereel, Frans
8553.625	Mashev, Georgi
8553.63	Mashrykov, K.K.
8553.65	Mašínova, Leontína
8553.7	Mason, William
8553.75	Masperó, Sir G.C.C.
8553.83	Massaie, Guglielmo, cardinal
8553.84	Massignon, Louis
8553.85	Masso Torrents, Jaime
8553.87	Masson, J.P.
8553.89	Masson, Jean-Claude
8553.92	Matelski, Dariusz
8553.95	Mateu y Llopis, Felipe
8554	Mather family
8554.3	Mathurine, Mme
8554.32	Matisse

M -- Continued

8554.34	Matoš, A.G.
8554.343	Matos Moctezuma, Eduardo
8554.345	Matouš, Lubor
8554.35	Matoušek, Miloslav
8554.36	Matsudaira, Sadanobu
8554.365	Matsumoto, Seichō, 1909-
8554.37	Matsuo, Bashó
8554.38	Matsuura, Takeshirō
8554.4	Matthew, W.D.
8554.7	Matthews, Brander
8554.712	Matthiessen, Peter
8554.7123	Mattioni, Stelio, 1921-1997
8554.713	Matylis, Juozas
8554.72	Matz, Friedrich
8554.75	Matzke, Josef
8555.3	Maugham, W.S.
8555.45	Maupassant, Guy de
8555.5	Maurer, Konrad von
8555.65	Mauriac, François
8555.75	Maurois, André
8555.9	Maurras, Charles
8556	Maury, M.F.
8556.5	Mawson, T.H.
8556.7	Maximilianus, Transylvanus
8556.9	Maximus, Confessor, Saint
8557	Maximus, the Greek
8557.6	May, Julian
8557.7	May, K.F.
	Mayakovsky, Vladimir see Z8542.9
8558	Maybeck, B.R.
	Mayekawa, Kunio see Z8541.3
8558.5	Mayröcker, Friederike
8558.6	Mayne, Thom
8559.3	Maza Zavala, Domingo Felipe
8559.5	Mazarin, Jules, cardinal
8559.7	Māzinī, Ibrāhīm 'Abd al-Qādir
8559.75	Mazlumov, A.L.
8559.78	Mazrui, Ali 'Amin
8559.79	Mazur, Jan
8560	Mazzatinti, Giuseppe
8560.3	Mazzei, Filippo
8560.5	Mazzini, Giuseppe
8561	Mazzuoli, Francesco, called Il Parmigianino
8561.13	McAllister, Bruce
8561.15	Mchedlishvili, G. I. (Georgiĭ Iosifovich)
8561.16	McIlvanney, William

Z8001-8999

M -- Continued

8561.17	McIntire, Samuel
8561.18	McKinley, William
8561.3	Mead, Margaret
8561.46	Méautis, Georges
8561.6	Mechev, M.M.
8561.65	Medaković, Dejan
8561.7	Medeiros, Coriolano de
8562	Medici family
8562.12	Medici Tornaquinci, Aldobrando
8562.14	Medina, J.T.
8562.15	Medina, Pedro de
8562.153	Meem, J.G.
8562.156	Meghani, Z.K.
8562.158	Mehmet Âkif
8562.16	Mehring, Franz
8562.17	Meier, H.C.
8562.172	Meier, Richard
8562.174	Meierkhol'd, V.E.
8562.18	Meigret, Louis
8562.2	Meil, J.W.
8562.24	Meireles, Cecília, 1901-
8562.25	Meisel, Nachman
8562.3	Meister, J.H.
8562.33	Meister, Richard
8562.4	Mekhtiev, Sh.F.
8562.5	Melanchthon, Philipp
8562.517	Meletinskĭ, E.M. (Eleaza Moiseevich)
8562.52	Melezh, Ivan
8562.54	Melida y Alinari, J.R.
8562.55	Melikset - Bek, L.M.
8562.56	Mello Moraes, A.J. de
8562.565	Melo Neto, João Cabral de
8562.57	Meltzer, David
8562.58	Melville, Herman
8562.6	Memling, Hans
8563.5	Mencken, H.L.
8563.58	Mendel, Gregor
	Mendele Mokher Sefarim see Z8007.3
8563.6	Mendeleev, D.I.
	Mendeleyev, D.I. see Z8563.6
8563.62	Mendelsohn, Erich
8563.63	Mendes Corréa, A.A.
8563.75	Mendez Pereira, Octavio
8564.2	Mendonca, Lucio de
8564.25	Mendoza, C.L.
8564.3	Menendez Pidal, Ramón

M -- Continued

8564.6	Menéndez y Pelayo, Marcelino
8564.65	Meneses, Guillermo
8564.8	Menezes, Emílio de
8565	Menges, K.H.
8565.4	Menn, Walter
8565.45	Menner, V.V.
8565.5	Menno Simons
8566	Menshikov, A.D., kníāz
8566.34	Menyhért, Hefele
8566.4	Menzel, A.F.E. von
8567	Mera, J.L.
8567.7	Mercantini, Luigi
8568	Mercator, Gerardus
8568.3	Mercer, David
8568.5	Merchán, R.M.
8568.55	Mercier, Louis-Sébastien
8568.6	Merck, J.H.
8568.8	Meredith, George
8568.9	Meri, Lennart
8569.3	Merian, M.S.
8569.6	Merilaas, Kersti
8570	Mérimée, Prosper
8570.3	Merkel, F.H.
8570.4	Merkel, G.H.
8570.45	Merleau-Ponty, Maurice
8570.5	Merrick, David
8570.6	Merton, Thomas
8570.63	Meryon, Charles
8570.65	Mesa, Cristóbal de
8570.66	Mesevrinos
8570.665	Meštrović, Ivan
8570.67	Mészöly, Miklós
8570.675	Metodiev, Dimitur
8570.677	Metreveli, Elene, 1917-2003
8570.68	Mette, H.J.
8570.69	Metternich-Winneburg, C.L.W.
8570.694	Meumann, Ernst
8570.695	Meyer, Augusto
8570.697	Meyer, C.F.
8570.7	Meyer, Eduard
8570.77	Meyer, Otto
8570.91	Meyerhof, Max
8570.93	Meyerson, Ake
8571	Meza y Suárez Inclán, Ramón
8571.4	Mhuiṅʻ, Sa khaṅʻ Kuiysʻ toʻ, 1875-1964
8571.8	Michaux, Henry

M -- Continued

8572	Michelangelo Buonarroti
8572.3	Michelet, Jules
8572.7	Michurin, I.V.
8573	Mickiewicz, Adam
8574	Middleton, Thomas
8574.18	Mies van der Rohe, Ludwig
8574.2	Mieželaitis, Eduardes
8574.24	Migge, Leberecht, 1881-1935
8574.25	Mignault, P.B.
8574.28	Migne, J.P.
8574.3	Migón, Krzysztof
8574.37	Miguéis, J.R.
8574.4	Miguères, Jean
8574.42	Mihailovich, Vasa D.
8574.5	Mik Josef
8574.53	Mikaeloff, Philippe
8574.54	Mikailov, S.I.
8574.547	Mikhaïlov, Ivan
8574.55	Mikhalkov, S.V.
8574.554	Mikheev, V.K.
8574.557	Mikhoėls, Solomon Mikhaïlovich, 1890-1948
8574.56	Miki, Kiyoshi
8574.58	Mikkelsen, Ejnar
8574.59	Mikszáth, Kálmán
8574.63	Mikulski, Tadeusz
8574.7	Milá y Fontanals, Manuel
8574.716	Miladinov, Dimitŭr
8574.72	Miladinović, M.M.
8574.724	Milani, Lorenzo
8574.725	Milankovic, Milutin
8574.73	Milev, Geo
8574.74	Mileva, Leda
8574.8	Mill, J.S.
8574.82	Millar, Kenneth
8574.84	Millares Carlo, Agustín
8574.87	Millay, Edna St. Vincent
8574.876	Milleker, Felix
8574.88	Miller, Arthur
8574.89	Miller, E.M.
8574.9	Miller, G.S.
8574.93	Miller, Henry
8574.95	Miller, M.O.
8575	Miller, Samuel
8575.5	Miller, Susanne
8575.53	Miller, T. N.
8575.56	Miller, W.M.

M -- Continued

8575.65	Millin, S.G. (Liebson)
8575.66	Millionshchikov, Mikhail Dmitrievich, 1913-1973
8576	Mills, C.K.
8576.13	Mills, Robert
8576.2	Milne, A.A.
8576.27	Milosz, Czeslaw
8576.3	Milosz, O.V.
8576.6	Milovidov, V.
8577	Milton, G.F.
8578	Milton, John
8578.4	Mináč, Vladimír
8578.5	Mindszenty, József, cardinal
8578.52	Minghetti, Marco
8578.6	Minio, Michelangelo
8578.7	Minkoff, N.B.
8578.8	Minorskiĭ, V.F.
8578.94	Minulescu, Ion
8579.59	Miquel y Planas, Ramón
8579.65	Mira de Amescua, Antonio
8579.67	Miranda, Francisco de, 1750-1816
8579.7	Miró Ferrer, Gabriel
8579.76	Mirza, S.H.
8579.8	Mirzeev, A.M.
8579.84	Mirzoĭan, L.V.
8579.87	Misawa, Katsue
8579.89	Mishima, Michitsune
8579.9	Mishima, Yukio, pseud.
8580	Mistral, Frédéric
8580.5	Mistral, Gabriela
8581.5	Mitchell, S.W.
8581.55	Mitchell, William
8581.6	Mitchell/Giurgola Associates Architects
8581.7	Mitin, M.B.
8581.9	Mitre, Bartolomé
8582.3	Mitskevich, K.M.
8582.6	Miyamoto, Teru
8582.8	Miyazawa, Kenji
8582.9	Mizner, Addison
8584	Mladenov, Stefan
8584.7	Mo, Ti
8584.9	Mochalov, P.S.
8585	Mockel, Albert
8585.3	Močnik, Franc
8585.4	Moderhack, Richard
8585.5	Modjeska, Helena
8585.54	Moe. O.H.

Z8001-8999

M -- Continued

8585.6	Möhler, J.A.
8585.8	Mokrīīēv, ĪŪ. O.
8585.87	Moldoveanu, Valeriu
8585.9	Molek, Ivan
8586	Molière, J.B.P.
8586.3	Molina, G.I.
8586.5	Molinet, Jean
8586.8	Mollard, Pierre
8586.9	Molnár, Ferenc
8586.94	Moltmann, Jürgen
8586.95	Momigliano, Arnaldo
8587	Mommsen, Theodor
8587.5	Monfette, J.J.
8587.55	Moniz, Egas
8587.7	Monnier, H.B.
8587.75	Monod, Théodore, 1902-
8587.8	Monroe, James
8587.84	Monroziès, Maurice
8587.87	Monselet, Charles
8588	Montaiglon, Anatol de Courade de
8589	Montaigne, M.E. de
8589.216	Montale, Eugenio
8589.3	Montalembert, C.F.R.
8589.4	Montalvo, Juan
8589.5	Montanelli, Indro, 1909-2001
8589.7	Monteagudo, Bernardo
8589.76	Montefiore, Moses, Sir
8589.78	Montégut, Emile
8589.85	Montes de Oca y Obregón, Ignacio, abp.
8590	Montesquieu, C.L. de Secondat, baron de la Brede et de
8590.5	Montessori, Maria
8591	Montgomery, James
8591.2	Montgomery, L.M.
8591.3	Montgomery of Alamein, B.L.M.
8591.5	Montherlant, Henry de
8592.2	Monti, Achille
8592.4	Monti, Vincenzo
8592.42	Montoliu y de Togores, Manuel de
8592.43	Montoro, Rafael
8592.48	Mood, Fulmer
8592.51	Moody, D.L.
8592.52	Moora, H.
8592.53	Moorcock, Michael
8592.54	Moore, Brian
8592.55	Moore, Charles Willard
8592.56	Moore, Clement Clarke

M -- Continued

8592.6	Moore, George
8592.62	Moore, Henry Spencer
8592.65	Moore, Marianne
8592.7	Moore, Thomas
8592.72	Moore, Thomas Sturge
8592.728	Móra, Ferenc
8592.73	Morales, Rafael
8592.734	Morand, Paul
8592.74	Morasso, Mario
8592.75	Moratín, L.F. de
8592.76	Moravia, Alberto
8592.765	Mørch, Dea Trier
8592.77	More, P.E.
8592.8	More, Sir Thomas, Saint
8592.9	Moréas, Jean
8592.94	Moreira, T.M.
8592.95	Moreno, G.R.
8592.96	Moreno, Mariano
8592.97	Moreno Villa, José
8592.98	Moreto y Cavana, Agustin
8592.984	Morettti, Roberto
8592.987	Morgan, D.L.
8592.99	Morgan, F.C.
8592.995	Morgan, Julia
8593	Morgan, L.H.
8593.15	Morgan, T.H.
8593.16	Morgan, W.N.
8593.17	Mori, Ogai
8593.18	Mori, Vittorio
8593.185	Móricz, Zsigmond
8593.2	Morin, Louis
8593.35	Morison, Stanley
8593.36	Morize, Henrique, 1860-1930
8593.5	Morlent, Joseph
8594	Morley, C.D.
8594.44	Morozov, N.A.
8594.5	Morra, Umberto
8595	Morris, William
8595.5	Morrison, Toni
8596	Morse, W.L.
8596.7	Moscati, Sabatino
8597	Moses
8597.2	Moses ben Maimon
8597.23	Moses ben Nahman
8597.26	Moses of Khoren
8597.4	Mosquera, M.J.

Z8001-8999

M -- Continued

8597.46	Moss, E.O.
8597.5	Most, J.J.
8601	Motoori, Norinaga
8602	Mottram, R.H.
8602.17	Mouligneau, Michel
8602.19	Mount, W.S.
8602.194	Mountbatten of Burma, Louis Mountbatten, Earl
8602.2	Mountford, C.P.
8602.3	Mousley, Henry
8602.33	Mövsümov, Zeynalabdin Räsul oğlu, 1925-
8602.35	Mowinckel, Sigmund
8602.45	Mqhayi, S.E.K.
8602.6	Mrstik, Alois
8602.65	Mtshali, O.J.
8602.7	al-Mubashshir ibn Fātik, Abū al-Wafā
8602.86	Mudaliar, A.R.
8602.9	Mudie, Ian
8602.94	Müftuoglu, A.H.
8603	Mühlbrecht, Otto
8603.3	Mühlmann, W.E.
8603.7	Müller, Friedrich
8603.9	Müller, Han, von
8604	Müller, Johannes, von
	Müller, Maler see Z8603.7
8604.4	Müntz, Eugen
8604.5	Münzer, Thomas
8604.8	Muḥammad, the prophet
8604.83	Muḥammad ibn Abd al-Wahhāb
8604.84	Muḥammed, M.R.
8604.85	Muhlenberg family
8604.95	Muir, Edwin
8605	Muir, John
8605.013	Mujibur Rahman, Sheikh
8605.02	Muk, Jan
8605.024	Mukhin, N.S.
8605.026	Mulisch, Harry
8605.028	Müller, K.O.
8605.03	Muller, Pierre
8605.036	Mumey, Nolie
8605.04	Mumford, Lewis
8605.046	Munari, Bruno
8605.05	Munch, Edvard
8605.1	Munch, P.A.
8605.3	Munday, Anthony
8605.34	Munk, Holger
8605.35	Munk, K.H.L.

M -- Continued

8605.36	Munk, K.H.L.
8605.5	Muñoz Gallardo, J.A.
8605.55	Munro, Alice
8605.63	Munro, Manuel
8605.65	Munroe, C.E.
8605.8	Muoni, Damiano
8605.85	Mŭqanov, Săbit
8605.86	Muradov, Sh. M. (Shahbaz Musa oghlu)
8605.87	Muradyan, Suren, 1930-
8605.89	Murano, Tōgo
8605.92	Murasaki Shikibu
8606	Murat, J.E.
8606.1	Muratori, L.A.
8606.2	Muratov, Aleksandŭr
8606.25	Muratova, K.D.
8606.3	Murdoch, Iris
8606.4	Murnane, Gerald
8606.5	Muroo, Asako
8606.6	Murray, David
8606.65	Murry, J.M.
8606.72	Musaev, M.A.
8606.73	Musaev, M.R.
8606.78	Mushanōkoji, Saneatsu
8606.8	Mushketov, I.V.
8606.83	Musil, Robert
8606.87	Mŭsrepov, Ghabit
8606.9	Mussafia, Adolfo
8607	Musset, Alfred de
8607.8	Mussolini, Benito
8607.85	Mustafaev, I.D.
8607.88	Mustelin, Olof
8607.887	Mutafchiev, Petŭr
8607.8875	Muṭahharī, Murtaẓá
8607.89	Mutanabbī, Abū al-Ṭayyib Aḥmad ibn al-Ḥusayn
8608	Myasnikyan, Alek'sandr
8608.17	Mykytenko, Ivan
8608.2	Mylńikov, A.S.
8608.3	Myrdal, Jan
8608.4	Mytropol's'kyĭ, I.O.

N

8608.6	Nabokov, V.V.
8608.9	Nabuco, Joaquim
8608.93	Nachbin, Leopoldo
8608.96	Nádas, Péter
8609	Nader, Ralph
8609.2	Nadirov, A.A.

Z8001-8999

N -- Continued

8609.6	Nafīsī, Sa'íd
8609.8	Nagai, Kafū
8609.85	Nagel, Otto
8610	Nägeli, K.W.
8610.2	Nagy, László
8610.25	Nagy, Miklós
8610.3	Nahman ben Simhah, of Bratzlav
8610.35	Naïdakov, V.TS.
8610.36	Naïenko, M.K.
8610.37	Naipaul, V.S. (Viviadha Surajprasad)
8610.4	Naitō, Torajirō
8610.45	Nakajima, Atsushi, 1909-1942
8610.47	Nakayama, Miki
8610.5	Nakhimov, P.S.
8610.53	Nalbandīān, D.A.
8610.55	Nalbandyan, A.B.
8610.6	Nałkowska, Zofia
8610.8	Nametkin, S.S.
8610.84	Nanak, Guru
8611	Napier, John
8612.5	Napoléon II (F.C.J. Bonaparte, herzog von Reichstadt)
8613	Narayana Menon, Vallathol
8614	Narducci, Enrico
8614.3	Narimanov, N.N.
8614.4	Nariño, Antonio
8614.5	Narymbetov, Ăbdīlkhamit
8614.7	Nash, Ogden
8614.72	Nāṣir-i Khusraw
8614.74	Nasser, G.A.
8614.8	Nathan, Robert
8615	Nathorst, A.G.
8615.4	Natsagdorzh, Dashdorzhiïn
8615.5	Natsumē, Sōseki
8616	Naumann, Friedrich
8616.16	Nava, Pedro
8616.2	Navarro, Tomás, Tomás
8616.4	Nayak, H.M.
8616.45	Nāyaka, Puṇḍalīka Nārāyaṇa
8616.5	Nazarov, I.N.
8616.6	Nazrul Islam, Kazi
8616.8	Neagoe, Peter
8617	Neale, J.M.
8617.2	Nebrija, E.A. de
8617.24	Nedeljković, Dušan
8617.26	Needham, D.M.
8617.28	Negmatov, N.N.

N -- Continued

8617.29	Negreev, V.F. (Vsevolod Fedorovich)
8617.3	Nehru, Jawaharlal
8617.34	Neidus, Leib
8617.35	Neihardt, J.G.
8617.355	Neilands, Ojārs
8617.36	Neilson, J.S.
8617.43	Nejedlý, Zdeněk
8617.45	Nekrasov, N.A.
8617.5	Nelligan, Émile
8618	Nelson, H.N., viscount
8618.2	Némcová, Bożena
8618.3	Németh, László
8618.4	Nemiro, O.V.
8618.5	Nemirov, Dobri
8618.6	Nemirovskiĭ, A.I.
8619	Nerciat, A.R., known as Andrea de
8619.2	Nerman, Birger
8619.28	Neruda, Jan
8619.3	Neruda, Pablo
	Nerval, Gérard Labrunie, known as Gérard de see Z8336.5
8619.37	Nervi, P.L.
8619.4	Nervo, Amado
8619.45	Nesch, Rolf
8619.48	Neshkov, Velichko
8619.5	Nesmeĭanov, A.N.
8619.54	Nestroy, J.N.
8619.7	Nettleford, Rex. M.
8619.75	Neu, Heinrich
8619.8	Neubecker, F.K.
8620	Neugebauer, L.A.
8620.6	Neumann, S.K.
8620.8	Neutra, R.J.
8621.3	Newberry, J.S.
8621.5	Newcastle, Thomas Pelham-Holles, Duke of
8621.7	Newcomb, Simon
8621.73	Newell, L.C.
8621.75	Newhall, Beaumont
8622	Newman, J.H., Cardinal
8622.7	Newton, A.E.
8623	Newton, Sir Isaac
8623.9	Nexø, M.A.
8623.95	Nezval, Vitězslav
8624.5	Ngata, Sir A.T.
8624.56	Ngũgĩ wa Thiong'o
8624.58	Nguyên, Đình Chi'êu
8624.6	Nguyên, Trãi

Z8001-8999

N -- Continued

8624.7	Nguyên Du
8624.8	Ni, L.P.
8624.9	Nicholas II, Emperor of Russia, 1868-1918
8625	Nichols, J.G.
8626.2	Nicklès, F.J.J.
8626.4	Nicolaus Cusanus, Cardinal
8627.5	Nicolet, Jean
8627.7	Nicolini, Fausto, 1879-1965
8628	Niebuhr, Reinhold
8628.3	Nielsen Brovst, Bjarne, 1947
8628.4	Nienaber, P.J.
8628.6	Niepce, J.N.
8628.8	Nieto, David
8628.85	Nietzsche, Friedrich Wilhelm, 1844-1900
8628.856	Nieuwenhuis, F.D.
8628.857	Nieuwenhuys, Constant
8628.86	Nifo, Agostino, ca. 1473-1545?
8628.87	Nightingale, Florence
8628.9	Nīĩāzmukhamedov, B.N.
8628.913	Nīĩāzov, A.M.
8628.915	Niit, Ellen
8628.916	Niitamo, O.E.
8628.917	Nikitin, I.S.
8628.918	Nikitin, Sergeĭ
8628.92	Nikitina, E.V.
8628.923	Nikolaev, Antalolii Vasil'evich
8628.925	Nikol'skiĭ, B.P.
8628.93	Nikula, Oscar
8628.94	Nimuendaju, Curt
8628.945	Nin, Anais
8628.95	Niño, F.L.
8628.98	Ninomiya, Sontoku
8628.984	Nipperdey, Thomas
8628.986	Nishida, Kitaro
8628.99	Nishikawa, Sukenobu
8629	Nissen, Ingjald
8629.25	Niuksha, IU.P.
8629.3	Niven, Larry
8629.4	Nixon, R.M.
8629.5	Niẕāmī Ganjavī, 1140 or 41-1202-3
8629.7	Nkrumah, Kwame, Pres. Ghana
8630.5	Nodier, Charles
8630.75	Nöldeke, Theodor
8630.76	Nohejl, Miloslav
8630.77	Nohl, Herman
8630.84	Nolan, W.F.

N -- Continued

8630.85	Nolen, John
8630.87	Noli, Fan Stylian
8631	Nonaka, Kenzan
8631.4	Nonius Marcellus, 4th cent.
8632	Nordenskjöld, Otto
8632.5	Norlie, O.M.
8632.6	Normann, Regine
8633	Norris, Frank
8633.17	North, Robert Grady, 1916-
8633.2	Norton, Andre
8633.23	Norton, Caroline Sheridan
8633.3	Norwid, Cyprian
8633.4	Nossack, H.E.
8633.45	Notker, Labeo
8633.5	Notredame, Michel de
8634	Nouvel, Jean
8634.3	Novák, Arne
8635	Novi, Giuseppe
8635.3	Novikov, A. G. (Anatoliĭ Georgievich)
8636	Novy, F.G.
8636.6	Nud'ha, H.A.
8636.7	Nunes, Pedro, 1502-1578
8636.8	Nuñéz, E.B.
8637.3	Núñez, Cabeza de Vaca, Alvar
8637.34	Núñez, Jiménez, Antonio
8637.4	Nurpeisov, Abdizhamil
8637.6	Nušić, B.D.
8638.2	Nyberg, H.S.
8638.4	Nyerere, J.K.
8638.6	Nyvall, David

O

8639.4	Oates, Joyce Carol
8639.5	Obruchev, V.A.
8639.8	O'Cadhain, Máirtín
8640	O'Casey, Sean
8640.3	O'Connor, Flannery
8640.5	O'Connor, W.V.
8640.8	Odarchenko, Petro
8641.12	Odassi, Tifi
8641.13	Odets, Clifford
8641.2	Odorico da Pordenone
8641.5	Ōe, Hiroshi
8641.6	Oehlenschlager, A.G.
8641.7	Oeser, A.F.
8641.73	Österlings, Anders
8641.75	O'Flaherty, Liam

O -- Continued

8641.77	Oganesi͡an, N. O. (Nikolaĭ Oganesovich)
8641.8	Ogarev, N.P.
8641.83	O'Gorman, Edmundo
8641.85	Oguri, Füyó
8642.28	O'Hara, Frank
8642.32	O'Hara, John
8642.38	O'Higgins, Bernardo
8642.4	O'Higgins family
8642.415	Oinas, F.J.
8642.418	Okada, Mokichi
8642.42	Okada, Shin'ichi
8642.423	Okáli, Daniel
8642.426	O'Keeffe, John
8642.43	O'Kelly, Seumas
8642.435	Okladnikov, A.P.
8642.44	Ōkubo, Toshimichi
8642.46	Olafsen, Olaf
8642.465	Olavide, Pablo de
8642.47	Olay, Ferenc
8642.6	Olesii͡uk, T.H.
8642.64	Oliphant, Mrs. (Margaret)
8642.65	Olitzky, Baruch
8642.7	Oliva, Anello
8642.74	Oliveira Lima, Manuel de
8642.76	Oliver, Chad
8642.77	Olivier, Rejean
8642.8	Olmedo, J.J. de
8642.9	Olmos, Andres de
8643.3	Olmsted, F.L.
8643.63	Olsen, I.S.
8643.65	Olsen, M.B.
8643.7	Olson, Charles
8643.72	Olson, Elder
8644	Omar Khayyam
8644.2	Omodeo, Adolfo, 1889-1946
8644.3	Omont, H.A.
8644.35	On Pe, U
8644.4	Onats'kyĭ, I͡Evhen
8644.45	Oncken, Hermann
8644.46	Ondrejov, Ľudo
8644.5	O'Neill, E.G.
8644.55	Onofre Júnior, Manoel, 1943-
8644.6	Onufriĭchuk, Fedir, F.
8644.8	Onyshchenko, O. S. (Oleksiĭ Semenovych)
8645.1	Opatoshu, Joseph
8645.14	Opitz, Martin, 1597-1639

O -- Continued

8645.16	Oppenheimer, J. Robert
8645.17	Oppenheimer, Joel
8645.2	Opperman, D.J.
8645.3	Optic, Oliver
8645.47	Orbán, Balázs
8645.5	Orbeli, I.A.
8645.6	Ordubadi, M.S.
8645.69	O'Reilly, J.B.
8645.72	Orfila, M.J.B.
8645.85	Origenes
8645.87	Origuchi, Shinobu
8645.93	Orintaitė, Petronėlė, 1905-1999
8646	Orleans, E.C., duchesse d'
8646.15	Orlīt͡skiĭ, I͡U. B. (I͡Uriĭ Borisovich)
8646.2	Orlov, I͡U.A.
8646.3	Orlowski, Hans
8646.5	Oro, Julius
8646.6	Ors, Eugenio d'
8646.64	Orsi, Paolo
8646.7	Országh, László
8646.8	Országh, Pavol
8646.9	Ortega y Gasset, José
8646.93	Ortelius, Abraham
8646.94	Ortíz Fernández, Fernando
8646.96	Orudzhev, A.A.
8647	Orwell, George
8647.15	Orzeszkowa, Eliza
8647.35	Osaragi, Jirō
8647.5	Osborn, H.F.
8647.54	Osborne, John
8647.6	Oscar II, King of Sweden
8647.63	Oschilewski, W.G.
8647.67	Oshima, Shotaro
8647.7	Osiander, Andreas
8647.72	Osint͡sev, L.P. (Leonid Petrovich)
8647.74	Osiss, Jānis
8647.8	Osler, Sir William, bart
8647.814	Osmańczyk, Edmund Jan, 1913-
8647.815	Osmeña, Sergio
8647.82	Osorgin, M.A.
8647.84	Osorio, M.A.
8648	Ossian
(8648.13)	Ossoli, S.M.F., marchesa d'
	see Z8318.26
8648.15	Osterhout, W.J.V.
8648.155	Ostroĭ, Ol'ga Semenovna

Z8001-8999

O -- Continued

8648.16	Ostroviṭīanov, K.V.
8648.17	Ostrovskiĭ, A.N.
8648.172	Ostrovskiĭ, N.A.
8648.174	Otaka, Masato
8648.175	Ōtani, Sachio
8648.1758	Otero, Lisandro
8648.176	Otfrid von Weissenburg
8648.18	Othón, M.J.
8648.3	Otsuka, Hisao
8648.32	Otto, Frei
8648.43	Oud, J.J.P.
8648.5	Outes, F.F.
8648.76	Ovcharenko, F.D.
8648.77	Ovchinnikov, ĪŪ.A.
8648.78	Ovchinnikov, P.N.
8648.8	Overbeck, F.C.
8649	Ovid (Publius Ovidius Naso)
8649.11	Ovsīānkin, E. (Evgeniĭ)
8649.12	Ovsiĭchuk, Volodymyr
8649.13	Owen, Daniel
8649.2	Owen, Richard
8649.3	Owen, Robert
8649.6	Owen, Wilfred
8649.7	Owings, N.A.
8649.8	Oyarzún, Luis
8649.88	Oz, Amos
8649.89	Ozaki, Hōsai
8649.9	Ozansoy, F.A.
8649.93	Ozerova, Galina Aleksandrovna, 1905-1990
8649.95	Oznobishin, D.P.
8650	Ozols, Alfrēds

P

8650.5	Paaver, Kalju
8650.7	Pacheco, C.M.
8651	Packard, A.S.
8651.7	Padula, Vincenzo
8651.72	Paegle, Leon
8652.78	Pagano, F.M.
8653	Paget, Sir Thomas
8653.5	Pain, William
8653.8	Paine, R.T.
8654	Paine, Thomas
8654.1	Paisiello, Giovanni
8654.2	Paisiĭ Khilendarski, ieromonakh
8654.6	Pal, Bipin Chandra
8655	Palacký, František

P -- Continued

8655.4	Palamas, Kōstēs
8656	Palfijn, Jan
8656.65	Pall, Eduard
8656.66	Palladio, Andrea
8656.67	Palma, Rafael
8656.675	Palme, Olof
8656.68	Palmer, T.S.
8656.683	Palmerston, H.J.T.
8656.69	Palmgren, Raoul
8656.7	Palmieri, Aurelio
8656.73	Paluzzi, Carlo Galassi
8656.75	Pamfile, Tudor
8656.77	Panagiōtopoulos, Iōannēs Michaēl, 1901-1982
8656.78	Panagiōtou, Nikos
8656.8	Panakh, Molla
8656.84	Pancrazi, Pietro
8656.85	Panelakh, V. M.(Viktor Moiseevich)
8656.86	Pani, Mario
8656.87	Panić-Surep, Milorad
8656.88	Panizza, Oskar
8656.9	Pantev, Andreĭ Lazarov
8656.93	Pañzari, Ludmila
8657	Paoli, Cesare
8657.5	Papadat-Bengescu, Hortensia
8657.6	Papadiamantēs, Alexandros
8657.7	Papini, Giovanni, 1881-1956
8657.8	Papkovich, P.F.
8657.9	Papp, Árpád
8658	Paracelsus
8658.12	Pāratiyār
8658.125	Parczewski, Alfons
8658.13	Pardo Bazán, Emilia
8658.14	Pardo de Figueroa, Mariano
8658.16	Paré, Ambroise
8658.17	Pareyson, Luigi
8659.2	Pargamin, M.N.
8659.7	Parini, Giuseppe
8660	Paris, G.B.P.
8660.62	Parker, Eleanor
8660.64	Parker, Theodore
8660.65	Parker, W.T.
8660.8	Parkes, J.W.
8660.9	Parolek, Radegast
8661.24	Parra, Teresa de la
8661.3	Parrish, Maxfield
8661.4	Parronchi, Alessandro

Z8001-8999

P -- Continued

8661.5	Parrott, T.M.
8661.68	Parteli, Carlos
8661.7	Partsch, J.F.M.
8661.8	Pârvan, Vasile
8662	Pascal, Blaise
8662.15	Pascoli, Giovanni
8662.16	Pashnev, E.I.
8662.17	Pasolini, P.P.
8662.2	Paspalev, Georgi
8662.3	Pasquié, Maurice
8662.33	Passfield, S.J. Webb, baron
8662.35	Pasternak, B.L.
8662.4	Pasteur, Louis
8663	Pastorius
8663.5	Pat, Jacob
8663.53	Paṭavardhana, Mādhavarāva
8663.6	Patchen, Kenneth
8664	Pater, Walter
8664.3	Patera, Paul
8665	Pathelin
8665.14	Patin, Charles
8665.2	Paton, Alan
8665.3	Patrick, Saint
8665.35	Patten, Simon Nelson
8665.39	Paty, Michel
8665.43	Paukszta, Eugeniusz
8665.45	Paul, Saint, apostle
8665.49	Paul VI, Pope
8665.6	Paulding, J.K.
8665.65	Paulet, Georges
8665.66	Paulhan, Jean
8665.67	Paulin, Louisa
8665.68	Pável, Ágoston
8665.7	Pavese, Cesare
8665.77	Pavlenko, P.A.
8665.78	Pavlík, Jaroslav
8665.8	Pavlov, I.P.
8665.89	Pavlov, S.D.
8665.9	Pavlov, Todor
8665.93	Pavlovich, Parteniĭ
8665.935	Pavlychko, S.D.
8665.94	Pavlyk, Mykhaïlo
8665.97	Paxton, Joseph, Sir
8666.13	Payno, Manuel
8666.15	Payró, J.E.
8666.2	Payró, R.J.

P -- Continued

8666.3	Paz, Octavio
8666.4	Paz Castillo, Fernando
8666.5	Pazzi, Muzio
8667.35	Pearse, P.H.
8667.38	Pearson, Karl
8667.39	Pedro, Borja de
8667.4	Pedrotti, Pietro
8667.8	Peel, Robert, Sir
8668	Peele, George
8668.3	Peev, A.K.
8668.6	Péguy, Charles
8668.9	Pei (I.M.) & Partners
8669	Peignot, Gabriel
8669.4	Peirce, C.C.
8669.5	Peïve, A.V.
8669.6	Peixoto, Afranio
8669.64	Pellegrin, Jacques
8669.65	Pellegrini, Giovan Battista
8669.66	Pelli, Cesar
8670	Pellicer de Ossau Y Tovar, Jose
8670.3	Pellico, Silvio
8670.5	Pelše, Roberts
8670.7	Pelt, J.M.
8671.2	Penck, Albrecht
8671.3	Penev, Boîan
8671.4	Penev, Pen'o
8671.5	Penfield, S.L.
8672	Penn, William
8672.3	Penttilä, Aarni
8672.5	Pepys, Samuel
8672.56	Peralta, José
8672.57	Peranthes, Michael
8672.596	Perec, Georges
8672.6	Pereda, José María de
8672.7	Peregrino da Silva, M.C.
8672.8	Pereira, J.F.
8672.83	Pereira da Costa, F.A.
8672.85	Pereira da Figueiredo, Antonio
8672.88	Pereﬁs, V.P. (Adrianova)
8672.89	Peretz, I.L.
8672.9	Pereyra, A.I.
8672.93	Pérez, Carlos Andrés
8672.936	Pérez de Ayala, Ramon
8672.94	Perez de Montalvan, Juan
8672.95	Perez Galdós, Benito
8672.96	Pérez Guerrero, Manuel

P -- Continued

8673.25	Perkins, Frances
8673.26	Perlick, Alfons
8673.37	Peron, Eva
8673.42	Perović, Puniša
8673.6	Perrault, Charles
8673.65	Perret, Auguste
8673.67	Perrin-Fayolle, Max
8673.7	Perron, Edgar du
8673.8	Perry, O.H.
8674	Persius (Aulus Persius Flaccus)
8674.5	Persoon, C.H.
8674.58	Perttu, Pekka
	Peshkov, A.M. see Z8357.8
8674.6	Pertuiset, Bernard
8674.7	Perutz, Leo
8674.8	Pessoa, Fernando
8675	Pestalozzi, J.H.
8675.3	Petar II, prince bishop of Montenegro
8675.5	Peter I, the Great, emperor of Russia
8675.6	Peter III, emperor of Russia
8675.65	Peter, Saint, apostle
8675.7	Peter Damian, Saint, 1007?-1072
8675.8	Peters, Hugh
8675.82	Petersen, C.C.M.
8675.83	Petersen, Nis
8675.85	Petkanov, Konstantin
8675.852	Petkov, Liuban
8675.853	Petkov, Veselin
8675.86	Petliūra, S.V.
8675.9	Petófi, Sándor
8675.95	Petr, Jan
8675.96	Petrak, Franz
8675.97	Petranović, Branko
8676	Petrarch (Francesco Petrarca)
8676.3	Petrascu, Gheorghe
8676.35	Petriāev, E.D.
8676.38	Petrītskiĭ, V. A.
8676.4	Petronijević, Branislav
8676.5	Petronius
8676.57	Petrov, B.N.
8676.58	Petrov, Zdravko
8676.6	Petrovíc, Vēljko
8676.8	Petrovskiĭ, I.G.
8676.84	Petrucci, Armando
8676.86	Petrucciani, Mario
8676.9	Petry, A.L.

P -- Continued

8677	Pettigrew, J.B.
8678	Petty, Sir William
8680	Peyriguère, Albert
8682	Peyron, Bernardino
8682.5	Pezoa Véliz, Carlos
8683.3	Pharar, Abraham
8683.5	Philip, John
8683.52	Philipp I, Landgraf von Hessen, 1504-1567
8683.54	Philipp, H.W.
8683.6	Philipson, David
8683.7	Philipz, Dirk
8683.9	Phillips, U.B.
8684	Phillips, W.B.
8684.5	Phillpotts, Eden
8685	Philo Judaeus
8685.6	Piaget, Jean
8685.63	Piano, Renzo
8685.7	Piattoli, Renato
8686	Picasso, Pablo
8687	Piccone, Antonio
8687.5	Pichamurthi, N.
8687.7	Picheta, V.I.
8688	Pichon, J.F., baron
8689	Pickering, E.C.
8689.2	Pico della Mirandola, Giovannii, 1463-1494
8689.4	Picón-Salas, Mariano
8689.5	Pidhora, V.P.
8689.7	Pieper, Josef
8689.9	Pierce, Franklin
8690	Pierce, G.W.
8690.2	Piercy, Marge
8690.4	Piermarini, Giuseppe
8690.6	Pieron, René
8690.7	Pietilä, Reima
8691.2	Pike, Albert
8691.3	Piksanov, N.K.
8691.5	Piliński, Adam
8691.55	Pilinszky, János
8691.58	Piłsudski, Józef, 1867-1935
8691.6	Pimenta, Belisário
8691.8	Pinart, A.L.
8692	Pinchot, Gifford
8692.3	Pindarus
8692.36	Pineda, J.C.
8692.4	Piñeyro y Barry, E.J.N.
8692.5	Pinsker, L.S.

Z8001-8999

P -- Continued

8692.53	Pinsky, David
8692.55	Pinter, Harold
8692.56	Pintner, Rudolf
8692.58	Pinto, Cesar
8692.6	Pinto, Isaac de
8692.62	Piontek, Heinz
8692.63	Piotrovskiĭ, B.B.
8692.68	Pippard, A.J.S.
8693	Pirandello, Luigi
8693.4	Pires, B.V.
8693.5	Pires de Lima, J.A.
8693.55	Pirkheimer, Wilibald
8693.6	Pirogov, N.I.
8693.7	Pisan, Christine de
8693.8	Pisarev, D.I.
8694.3	Pisarzhevskii, L.V.
8694.4	Pissurlencar, P.S.
8694.44	Piterans, A.V. (Alfons Viktorovich)
8694.46	Pitrè, Giuseppe
8694.5	Pitt, William
8694.52	Pitt, William, Earl of Chatham
8695	Pius II, pope
8695.5	Pius XII, pope
8695.6	Placci, Carlo
8695.67	Planck, K.C.
8695.7	Planck, M.K.E.L.
8695.8	Platen-Hallermünde, August, graf von
8695.85	Plath, Sylvia
8695.88	Platner, Warren
8696	Plato
8696.2	Platonov, A.P.
8696.4	Platt, C.A.
8697	Plautus (Titus Maccius Plautus
8697.2	Plávka, Andrej
8697.25	Pláza Salvador de la
8697.5	Plekhanov, G.V.
8697.54	Plenzdorf, Ulrich
8698	Plinius Caecilius Secundus, C.
8698.2	Plivier, Theodore
8698.3	Ploss, E.E.
8698.5	Plutarch
8698.57	Pocaterra, J.R.
8698.6	Pocock, G.N.
8698.7	Počs, K.
8698.8	Podvoĭskiĭ, N.I.
8699	Poe, E.A.

P -- Continued

8699.5	Poel, Johannes van der
8700	Poey y Aguirre, Andrés
8700.5	Poghosian, Hrip'sime
8700.7	Pohorilyĭ, O.I.
8701	Pokrovskiĭ, M.N.
8701.7	Poláček, Karel
8702.2	Polanco Alcántara, Tomás
8702.3	Polanski, Roman
8702.35	Põld, Peeter
8702.37	Poli͡akova, Larisa
8702.374	Poli͡an, P. M.
8702.4	Poli͡uha, L.M.
8702.5	Poliziano, Angelo
8702.6	Polkanov, A.A.
8702.7	Pollard, A.W.
8703	Polo, Marco
8703.49	Polubarinova-Kochina, P.I.
8703.494	Poluéktov, N.S.
8703.5	Pombal, S.J. de Carvalho e Mello, marquez de
8703.6	Pompeia, Raul
8703.63	Pompey, S.L.
8703.65	Ponce Saginés, Carlos
8703.67	Ponti, Gio
8703.7	Pontiac, Ottawa chief
8703.73	Pontoppidan, Henrik, 1857-1943
8703.74	Pontri͡agin, L.S. (Lev Semenovich)
8703.85	Poortinga, Ype
8703.95	Popa, Vasko
8704	Pope, Alexander
8704.14	Pope, C.H.
8704.16	Pope, J.R.
8704.18	Pope-Hennessy, J.W., Sir
8704.2	Popkonstantinov, Khristo
8704.3	Popov, A. Serafimovich
8704.5	Popov, A. Stepanovich
8704.6	Popov, Konstantin G.
8704.8	Popov, Metodiĭ
8704.82	Popov, Pavel
8704.84	Popov, V.I.
8704.85	Popova, D.G.
8704.86	Poppe, N.N.
8704.87	Popper, Karl Raimund, Sir, 1902-1994
8704.88	Poptomov, Vladimir
8704.895	Porietis, Jānis
8704.9	Porphyras, Lampros, pseud.
8704.92	Porphyry

Z8001-8999

P -- Continued

8704.94	Porras Barrenechea, R.
8705.1	Porta, C.A.M.F.
8705.3	Porter, A.K.
8705.5	Porter, C.E.
8705.55	Porter, G.S.
8705.6	Porter, Hal
8705.7	Porter, K.A.
8706	Porter, Noah
8706.14	Porter, Peter
8706.2	Porter, W.S.
8706.8	Portman, John
8707	Portmann, Michel
8707.3	Porto, Luigi da
8707.35	Portoghesi, Paolo
8707.45	Pos, Hendrik Josephus
8707.5	Post, G.B.
8707.6	Postel, Guillaume, 1510-1581
8708.3	Potapov, L.P.
8708.4	Potapov, S.G.
8708.6	Potebnīā, Aleksandr Afanas'evich, 1835-1891
8709	Potgieter, E.J.
8709.15	Potter, Beatrix
8709.16	Potter, P.A.
8709.17	Pottier, A.A.
8709.25	Poumon, Émile
8709.3	Pound, E.L.
8709.4	Pound, Roscoe
8709.45	Povarennykh, A.S.
8709.48	Powell, Anthony
8709.5	Powell, J.W.
8709.52	Powell, L.C.
8709.55	Powell, T.R.
8709.8	Power, F.B.
8710.5	Powys, J.C.
8710.55	Powys, Llewelyn, 1884-1939
8710.6	Powys, T.F.
8710.67	Prabhākaraśāstri, Vēṭūri
8710.7	Prados, Emilio
8710.73	Prajadhipok, King of Siam
8710.74	Prasolov, A.T.
8710.745	Pratolini, Vasco
8710.75	Pravdin, I.F.
8710.77	Praz, Mario
8710.777	Prebelakēs, Pantelēs
8710.78	Preble, E.A.
8710.784	Predock, Antoine

P -- Continued

8710.79	Premacanda
8710.8	Preradović, Petar
8711	Prescott, A.B.
8711.5	Prescott, W.H.
8712	Prešeren, France
8712.3	Prestipino, Giuseppe
8712.5	Preti, Giulio
8712.7	Prévert, Jacques
8713	Prévost, A.F., called Prévost d'Exiles
8713.2	Priakhin, A.D. (Anatoliĭ Dmitrievich)
8713.4	Price, J.C.
8713.44	Price, Richard
8713.45	Prichard, K.S.
8713.53	Priest, Josiah
8713.535	Priestley, John Boynton
8713.54	Priestly, Joseph
8713.55	Prieto, Guillermo
8713.555	Primo de Rivera, José Antonio
8713.56	Prims, Floris
8713.562	Primus, Pearl
8713.563	Prints, I.I.
8713.5635	Prinz, Gyula
8713.564	Prior, A.N.
8713.57	Prishvin, M.M.
8713.573	Prisovs'kyĭ, IEvhen Mykolaĭovych
8713.576	Proclus
8713.58	Profeld, Bedřich
8713.582	Prokopcikas, Arianas
8713.584	Prokudin, IU.N.
8713.59	Propertius (Sextus Aurelius Propertius)
8713.592	Prószyński, Kazimierz
8713.9	Proudhon, Pierre-Joseph
8714	Proust, Marcel
8714.68	Prynne, William
8714.7	Przybyszewski, Stanislaw
8714.8	Przyluski, Jean
8714.9	Przywara, Erich
8714.93	Psellus, Michael
8715	Ptolemy (Claudius Ptolemaeus)
8715.7	P'u, Sung-ling
8715.8	Puccini, Mario, 1887-1957
8715.9	Puchinger, G.
8716	Puckly, James
8716.2	Pugin, A.W.N.
8716.4	Pukhlev, Aleksi
8716.5	Pulaski, Kazimierz

Z8001-8999

P -- Continued

8716.6	Pulci, Luigi
8716.65	Pulver, E. (Evgenii)
8717.2	Purdy, James
8717.5	Puriņš, B.
8717.7	Pushcharovskiĭ, I.M.
8718	Pushkin, A.S.
8718.5	Putnam, Samuel
8720	Pyle, Howard, 1853-1911
8721.4	Pym, Barbara
8721.5	Pynchon, Thomas
8722	Pypin, A.N.
8722.3	Pythagoras

Q

8722.5	Quaife, M.M.
8722.7	Quang Trung
8723	Quarles, Francis
8723.3	Quasimodo, Salvatore, 1901-1968
8723.5	Quazza, Guido
	Queirós, Eca de see Z8254
8724	Queneau, Raymond
8724.5	Quental, Antero de
8725	Quérard, J.M.
8726.9	Quevedo y Villegas, F.G. de
8727.4	Quinault, Philip
8727.5	Quine, W.V. (Willard van Orman)
8727.54	Quiñones, Magaly
8727.6	Quintana, J.M.
8728	Quintilianus (Marcus Fabius Quintilianus)
8728.5	Quiroga, Horacio
8728.55	Quiroga, Vasco de
8728.6	Quisling, Vidkun
8728.7	Qūnanbaev, Abaĭ

R

8728.8	Raam, Villem
8730	Rabelais, François
8730.15	Rabinowitz, Shalom
8730.2	Racine, J.B.
8730.33	Rackham, Arthur
8730.335	Radcliffe, Ann
8730.34	Raddall, T.H.
8730.342	Radev, Ivan Nikolov
8730.35	Radičevic, Branko
8730.36	Radichkov, Ĭordan Dimitrov, 1929-
8730.37	Radion, Stepan
8730.4	Radischev, A.N.
8730.43	Radkova, Rumĭāna

R -- Continued

8730.44	Radlov, V.V.
8730.45	Radnóti, Miklós
8730.452	Radó, György
8730.454	Radoev, Ivan
8730.46	Radványi, Netty (Reiling)
8730.48	Radzhabov, Z.S.
8730.49	Raevskiĭ, V.
8730.5	Raffaele Sanzio
8730.53	Raffles, T.S.
8730.6	Rafikov, S.R.
8730.7	Rafinesque, C.S.
8730.82	Raghaven, V.
8730.83	Ragionieri, Ernesto
8730.85	Ragona, Domenico
8730.86	Rahner, Karl
8730.865	Rahoŭsha, V. P. (Vi͡achaslaŭ Pi͡atrovich)
8730.87	Rais, K.V.
8730.88	Rajberti, Giovanni
8730.92	Rajwade, V.K.
8730.95	Rakette, Egon H. (Egon Helmut)
8730.97	Rakhmannyĭ, Roman, 1918-
8731	Raleigh, Sir Walter
8731.7	Ram, Jagjivan
8731.8	Rama, Angel
8732	Ramakrishna
8732.15	Ramana, Maharshi
8732.2	Ramel, Stig
8732.3	Ramírez Vázquez, Pedro
8732.5	Rammohun Roy, Raja
8732.6	Ramón y Cajal, Santiago
8732.65	Ramos, J.A.
8732.66	Ramos Sucre, J.A.
8732.67	Rampon, Simone
8732.7	Ramsay, Allan
8732.76	Ramsey, I.T.
8732.81	Ramuz, C.F.
8732.82	Ran' 'Oṅ', 1904-
8732.83	Rand, Ayn
8732.834	Randell, Beverley
8732.84	Randolph, John
8732.85	Randolph, Thomas
8732.9	Randwijk, H.M. van
8732.95	Ranjit Singh, Maharaja of the Punjab, 1780-1839
8733	Ranke, Leopold von
8733.18	Ransom, J.C.
8733.2	Ransome, Arthur

R -- Continued

8733.5	Raoult, F.M.
	Raphael see Z8730.5
8733.58	Raposo, P.A.B.
8733.59	Rappoport, Solomon
8733.62	Rascol, Andre
8733.63	Rasmussen, M.P.
8733.634	Rasmussen, Poul
8733.64	Rasmussen, S.E.
8733.67	Raspail, F.V.
8733.675	Rasputin, G.E.
8733.68	Rasputin, V.G.
8733.7	Rastell, John
8734	Rathenau, Walther
8734.3	Raud, Mart
8734.33	Raun, Alo
8734.4	Ravenstein, E.G.
8734.6	Ravina, J.H.
	Ravīndranātha Ṭākura, Sir see Z8857.9
8735.1	Ravitch, Melech
8735.2	Rawidowicz, Simon
8735.23	Rawlings, M.K.
8735.24	Rawls, John
8735.3	Ray, John
8735.33	Ray, Satyajit
8735.34	Raymond, Eleanor
8735.35	Raynal, G.T.F.
8735.36	al-Rāzī, Abū Bakr Muḥammad ibn Zakarīyā
8735.37	Razumov, A.I.
8735.38	Razusova-Martakova, Maria
8735.4	Read, Sir H.E.
8735.46	Reagan, Ronald
8735.49	Rebelo, J.F.N.S.
8735.52	Rebinder, P.A.
8735.55	Rébora, Clemente
8735.6	Redi, Francesco
8735.7	Redouté, P.J.
8736.3	Reed, C.S.
8736.32	Reed, Ishmael
8736.33	Reed, John
8736.4	Reese, L.W.
8736.44	Rēgas, Velestinlēs, 1757?-1798
8736.47	Reginald, R.
8736.5	Regnard, J.F.
8736.6	Régnier, Mathurin
8736.614	Rego, José Lins do
8736.62	Reich, Wilhelm

R -- Continued

8736.7	Reichenbach, H.G.L.
8736.73	Reichwein, Adolf
8736.75	Reid, Whitelaw
8736.76	Reifen, David
8736.78	Reimarus, H.S.
8736.79	Reinach, Salomon
8736.8	Reinach, Théodore
8736.9	Reinacher, Eduard
8736.95	Reinhold, K.L.
8737	Reisch, Gregor
8737.2	Reisin, Abraham
8737.3	Rej, Mikolaj, z Naglowic
8737.66	Remarque, E.M.
8737.7	Remington, Frederic
8737.74	Remizov, A.M.
8737.76	Remizovskiĭ, V.I.
8738	Renan, Ernest
8738.2	Renborg, Greta
8738.3	Rendoing, Jacqueline
8738.6	Renier, Léon
8738.64	Renner, Karl
8738.66	Renoir, Jean
8738.665	Renou, Louis
8738.667	Rensi, Giuseppe, 1871-1941
8738.674	Renwick, William
8738.68	Repessé, Guy
8738.7	Repin, I.E.
8738.8	Rerikh, N.K.
8738.9	Resnick, Michael D.
8739	Restif de La Bretonne, N.E.
8740	Retzius, Gustaf
8740.2	Reubell, J.F.
8740.3	Reuchlin, Johann
8740.35	Reuter, Fritz
8740.4	Reverdy, Pierre
8740.7	Rexroth, Kenneth
8740.87	Rey Pastor, Alfonso
8740.97	Reyes, Alfonso
8740.98	Reyes Baena, J.F.
8740.985	Reyles, Carlos
8740.9852	Reymont, Władysław Stanisław, 1867-1925
8740.9853	Reynolds, Mack
8740.9855	Reznicek, Václav
8740.99	Rhodes, C.J.
8741	Rhodes, E.M.
8741.5	Rhodokanakēs, Dēmētrios

Z8001-8999

R -- Continued

8741.7	Rhys, Jean
8742	Riant, P.E.D.
8742.2	Ribaud, Gustave
8742.22	Ribeiro, João, 1860-1934
8742.23	Ribeiro, Orlando
8742.235	Ribeyro, Julio Ramón, 1929-
8742.25	Ricardo, David
8742.35	Riccoboni, Luigi
8742.5	Richards, T.W.
8744	Richardson, H.H. pseud.
8744.13	Richardson, Henry Hobson
8744.14	Richardson, John
8744.19	Richardson, Samuel
8744.44	Richler, Mordecai
8744.7	Richter, J.P.F.
8745	Richthofen, F.P.W. freiherr von
8745.2	Ricoeur, Paul
8745.25	Ridgway, M.B.
8745.3	Riel, L.D.
8745.35	Riese, Adam
8745.4	Rifberg, Klaus
8745.5	Righi, Augusto
8745.7	Rihani, A.F.
8745.8	Riis, J.A.
8745.83	Riismøller, Peter
8746	Riley, C.V.
8746.2	Riley, J.W.
8746.3	Rilke, R.M.
8746.5	Rimbaud, J.N.A.
8747.12	Rio, João do
8747.14	Ríos, José
8747.15	Ríos de Lampérez, Blanca de los
8747.17	Ripoll, Carlos
8747.19	Ristikivi, Karl
8747.2	Ritsos, Giannēs
8747.25	Ritter, Hellmut
8747.26	Ritter, Johann Wilhelm
8747.3	Ritter, W.E.
8747.44	Rive, Richard
8747.47	Rivera, J.E.
8747.5	Rivera Cambas, Manuel
8747.63	Rivkind, Isaac
8747.65	Rizal y Alonso, José
8747.67	Robbe-Grillet, Alain
8747.7	Roberts, K.L.
8747.74	Robeson, Paul

R -- Continued

8747.82	Robida, Albert
8748.2	Robin, C.P.
8748.3	Robins, Elizabeth
8748.37	Robinson, E.A.
8748.5	Robinson, Mary (Darby)
8748.86	Rocha, Antonio dos Santos
8748.88	Roche, Kevin
8749	Rochefort-Lucay, V.H., marquis de
8749.7	Rochester, J.W., Earl of
8750	Rochette, Jean
8750.3	Rockingham, Charles Watson-Wentworth, 2d marquis of
8750.33	Rocklynne, Ross
8750.5	Rockwell, W.W.
8750.8	Rodari, Gianni
8751.1	Rodenbach, Georges
8751.3	Rodenburgh, Theodor
8751.5	Rodgers, M.C.
8752	Radó, J.E.
8752.3	Rodorea, Mercè
8752.5	Rodríguez, J.H.
8752.53	Rodríguez, Mariano
8752.57	Rodríguez-Alcalá, Hugo
8752.6	Rodríguez Guerrero, Ignacia
8752.7	Rodríguez Martin, Francisco
8752.8	Rodríguez Tizón, Ventura
8752.9	Roebling, J.A.
8753	Röntgen, W.C.
8753.4	Roethke, Theodore
8753.7	Rogala, Stanislaw
8753.8	Rogalski, Aleksander
8754	Rogers, B.R.
8754.3	Rogers, Richard
8754.5	Rogers, Will
8755	Rogoff, Hillel
8755.2	Rohan, A.G.M. de, cardinal
8755.6	Roig, Jaime
8755.7	Roig de Leuchsenring, Emilio
8755.8	Roig y Mesa, J.T.
8756	Rojas, Arístides
8756.1	Rojas, Fernando de
8756.16	Rojas, Ricardo
8756.2	Rojas Zorrilla, Francisco de
8756.7	Rolfe, F.W.
8756.8	Rolfe, W.J.
8756.9	Rolland, Romain
8757	Rolle, Richard, of Hampole

Z8001-8999

R -- Continued

8757.124	Rollins, H.E.
8757.128	Rolnick, Joseph
8757.13	Rolova, Aleksandra
8757.134	Rolt, L.T.
8757.135	Romaniuk, M. M. (Myroslav Mykolaĭovych)
8757.136	Romano, Giulio
8757.138	Romanov, A.A.
8757.14	Romanov, I.M.
8757.143	Romain, J.M.
8757.144	Romein-VErschoor, Annie
8757.145	Romera-Navarro, Miguel
8757.15	Romero, C.A.
8757.16	Romero Quiroz, Javier
8757.18	Rommel, Erwin
8757.23	Ronsard, Pierre de
8757.25	Rooke, Daphne
8757.27	Roosevelt, Eleanor
8757.29	Roosevelt, F.D.
8757.3	Roosevelt, Theodore
8757.35	Roosval, J.A.E.
8757.45	Rosa, of Lima, Saint
8757.46	Rosa, Salvatore
8757.47	Rosalia, Saint
8757.48	Rosas, J.M.J.D.O. de
8757.49	Rosenbaum, Karol
8757.5	Rosenberg, Alfred
8757.57	Rosenberger, F.C.
8757.6	Rosenberger, H.T.
8757.62	Rosenblat, Angel
8757.628	Rosenfeld, Hellmut
8757.63	Rosenfeld, Morris
8757.635	Rosenfeld, Paul
8757.65	Rosenstock-Huessy, Eugen
8757.67	Rosenthal, Feiga Rebeca Tiomno
8757.69	Rosenzweig, Franz
8757.79	Roslik, Galina Mikhaĭlovna, 1946-2002
8757.8	Rosmini Serbati, Antonio
8757.9	Rosny, J.-H.
8758	Rosse, I.C.
8759.67	Rossellini, Roberto
8759.75	Rossetti, C.G.
8759.8	Rossetti, D.G.
8760	Rossetti, G.P.G.
8760.3	Rossi, Aldo
8760.4	Rossi, Vittorio
8760.65	Rössing, Karl

R -- Continued

8760.7	Rostius, Christopher
8760.9	Rotach, Petro, 1925-
8761	Roth, Cecil
8761.12	Roth, Gerhard, 1942 June 24-
8761.15	Roth, Joseph
8761.2	Roth, Philip
8761.5	Rothenberg, Jerome
8762	Rothrock, Joseph T., 1839-1922
8763	Rousseau, J.J.
8763.6	Rowlandson, Mary (White)
8763.67	Rowse, A.L.
8763.7	Rowson, Susanna (Haswell)
8763.76	Roy, Camille
8763.763	Roy, D.N.
8763.765	Roy, Gabrielle
8763.77	Roy, M.N.
8763.78	Royden, A.M
8763.79	Rozanov, M.G.
8763.794	Rozanov, V. V. (Vasiliĭ Vasil'evich), 1856-1919
8763.81	Rozhkov, N.A.
8763.813	Rozova, E.A.
8763.82	Ruban, V.G.
8763.83	Rubens, Sir P.P.
8763.84	Rubincam, Milton
8763.844	Rubió i Balaguer, Jordi
8763.846	Rublev, Andreĭ
8763.85	Rūdakī
8763.855	Rudlovchak, Olena
8763.86	Rudnyts'kyĭ, ĪA.B.
8763.862	Rudofsky, Bernard
8763.8625	Rudolf, von Elms
8763.863	Rudolph, Paul
8763.866	Rudzīte, Marta
8763.868	Rudzītis, Meinhards
8763.87	Rueda, Lope de
8763.875	Ruggeri, Pietro
8763.88	Rugojev, Jaakko
8763.895	Ruiz, Juan
8763.9	Ruiz de Alarcón y Mendoza, Juan
8763.95	Rukuiza, Antanas
8764.3	Rumīānt͡sev, A.M.
8764.35	Rumīānt͡sev, Nikolaĭ Petrovich
8764.5	Rumpf, G.E.
8764.6	Ruppin, Arthur
8764.65	Rurawski, Józef
8764.7	Rusev, Pen'o

R -- Continued

8764.8	Rush, Benjamin
8764.85	Rushdie, Salman
8765	Ruskin, John
8765.3	Rusnac, Gheorghe
8765.48	Russell, B.R.
8765.485	Russell, C.M.
8765.5	Russell, G.W.
8765.7	Russell, Peter
8766	Russo, Luigi, 1892-1961
8766.5	Rustaveli, Shota
8767	Rutgers van der Loeff-Basenau, An.
8767.3	Rutherford, Ernest
8767.5	Ruzh, Ivan
8767.8	Ruzzante
8768.5	Rvhe U Doṅ‘‴
8769	Ryan, H.J.
8769.2	Rybák, Josef
8769.3	Rybakoc, B.A.
8769.4	Rychner, Max
8769.7	Rydberg, Viktor
8770	Rye, Walter
8770.2	Rygh, Oluf
8770.3	Ryleev, K.F.
8770.5	Rylenkow, N.I.
8770.57	Ryl'skyĭ, Maksym
8770.7	Ryōkan
8770.76	Ryskamp, Charles
8770.8	Ryskulov, T.R.
8770.9	Ryzhkov, V.L.

S

8771.6	Sa-Carneiro, Mário de
8771.8	Sá de Miranda, Francisco de
8771.9	Sá Nunes, José de
8772	Saar, Ferdinand von
8772.4	Saarinen, Eero
8772.6	Saat, Joosep
8773.2	Saba, Umberto
8773.45	Ṣabrī, Muḥammad, 1894-1978
8773.7	Sacco, Federico
8774	Sachs, Hans
8774.2	Sachs, Nelly
8774.3	Sachs, Senior
8774.5	Sackville-West, Vita
8775	Sacré, Maurits
8775.13	Sadan, Dov
8775.14	Sade, D.A.F., comte, called Marquis de

S -- Continued

8775.16	Sadhale, Anand
8775.17	Sa'dī
8775.2	Sadoveanu, Mihail
8775.25	Sadovskiĭ, Mikhail Aleksandrovich
8775.253	Ṣadr al-Dīn Shīrāzī, Muḥammad ibn Ibrāhīm
8775.254	Ṣadūqī, Muḥammad, d. 1982
8775.255	Šafárik, Pavel Jozef, 1795-1861
8775.35	Sahgal, Nayantara
8775.36	Sahiba Singha
8775.38	Sahleanu, Victor
8775.44	Said Ahmad
8775.45	Saigō, Takamori
8775.456	Saigusa, Hiroto
8775.46	Saigyō
8775.47	Saijō, Yaso
8775.48	Sainchuk, Gleb Vasil'evich
8775.5	Saint-Amant, M.A.G.
8776	Saint Exupéry, Antoine de
8778.75	Saint-Martin, L.C. de
8778.8	Saint-Pierre, J.H.B. de
8778.84	Saint-Simon, C.H., comte de
8778.85	Saint-Simon, Louis de Rouvroy, duc de
8779	Sainte-Beuve, C.A.
8779.15	Sainte-Hilaire, Auguste de
8779.27	Sakakura, Junzo
8779.28	Sakamoto, Rōro
8779.295	Săkhapov, Ăkhmăt
8779.3	Sakya-mchong-ldan, Gser-mdog Pan-chen
8779.38	Salavat
8779.4	Salazar, A. de O.
8779.6	Šalda, F.X.
8779.64	Salgari, Emilio
8779.66	Salinger, J.D. (Jerome David)
8779.7	Sallander, Hans
8779.75	Sallust (C. Sallustius Crispus)
8779.78	Salmone-Marino, Salvatore
8779.82	Saltillo, Miguel Lasso de la Vega y López de Tejada, marqués del
8779.83	Saltykov, M.E.
8779.86	Saltykov, S.A.
8779.9	Salvadori Adlard, Tommaso, conte
8780	Samaran, C.M.D.
8780.3	Samaritani, Antonio
8780.36	Samāwī, Muḥammad al-Tījānī
8780.47	Samec, Maks
8780.5	Samelson, Adolph

Z8001-8999

S -- Continued

8780.53	Samsonov, A.M.
8780.8	San-Antonio
8781	San Martín José de
8781.2	Sanā Allah Kharābatī
8781.25	Sanabria Fernández, Hernando
8781.29	Sánchez, Diego, fl. 1525-1549
8781.3	Sanchez, Florencio
8781.32	Sánchez, L.A.
8781.34	Sanchez-Albornoz, Claudio
8781.4	Sand, George
8781.45	Sandblad, Henrik
8781.5	Sandburg, Carl
8781.53	Sandemose, Aksel
8781.56	Šándor, Elo, 1896-1952
8781.6	Sandys, George
8781.7	Sanford, H.S.
8781.73	Sanford, John B., 1904-
8781.75	Sangallo, Giuliano, da
8781.76	Šaniże, Akaki
8781.77	Sant'Elia, Antonio
8781.8	Santa Cruz, Andrés de, Pres. Bolivia
8781.84	Santa Cruz y Espejo, Francisco Xavier Eugenio de
8781.9	Santarem, Pedro de
8781.93	Santayana, George
8781.95	Santema, Oepke
8781.98	Santō, Kyōden
8782	Santos Fernández, Juan
8782.2	Santsevych, A.V.
8782.22	Sanukov, K.N.
8782.24	Sanvitores, Diego Luis de
8782.3	Sapori, Francesco
8783	Sappho
8783.34	Sargent, Pamela
8783.344	Sargsyan, D. (Davit' Mkrtch'i), 1957-
8783.345	Sargsyan, G.Kh.
8783.35	Sarkar, B.K.
8783.353	Sarkar, Sir Jadunath
8783.355	Sarkisov, P.D. (Pavel Dzhibraelovich)
8783.68	Šarmaitis, R. (Romas), 1909-
8783.69	Šarmaitis, Romas, 1939-
8783.7	Sarmiento, D.F.
8783.9	Saroyan, William
8784.2	Sarraute, Nathalie
8784.3	Sarrazin, Albert
8784.4	Sarre, F.P.T.
8784.44	Sartre, J.P.

S -- Continued

8784.46	Sarvig, Ole
8784.49	Sasdi, Sandor
8784.5	Sassoon, S.L.
8784.51	Sata, Ineko
8784.53	Satow, Takeo
8784.54	Satpaev, K.I.
8784.55	Sauerwein, G.J.J.
8784.57	Saussure, Ferdinand de
8784.6	Savard, F.A.
8784.7	Savelov, L.M.
8784.8	Savino, Alberto
8785	Savonarola, G.M.F.M.
8786.45	Sawyier, Paul
8786.55	Sayers, D.L.
8786.6	Sayre, F.B.
8786.66	Sbarbaro, Camillo
8786.8	Scaliger, J.J.
	Scanderbeg, Prince of Epirus see Z8460.84
8786.9	Scarcia, Gianroberto
8787	Scarron, Paul
8788	Schaeufelein, H.L.
8788.5	Schapera, Isaac
8788.6	Schapiro, Meyer
8788.67	Schattner, Karljosef
8788.7	Schaub-Koch, Emile
8789.3	Schechter, Solomon
8789.6	Scheerbart, Paul
8791.5	Schefer, C.H.A.
8791.53	Schefer, Leopold
8791.62	Scheiber, Sandor
8791.7	Scheler, M.F.
8791.77	Schellhas, Walter
8791.8	Schelling, F.W.J. von
8791.9	Scherer, Anton
8792	Scherfig, Hans
8792.2	Scheuchzer, J.J.
8792.5	Schiaperelli, G.V.
8792.55	Schiavi, Alessandro, 1872-1965
8792.57	Schickele, René
8792.59	Schillebeeckx, Edward
8793	Schiller, J.C.F. von
8793.14	Schimmel, Annemarie
8793.16	Schindler, Peter
8793.18	Schinkel, Karl Friedrich
8793.2	Schio, Almerico da, conte
8793.3	Schirmann, Jefim

Z8001-8999

S -- Continued

8794	Schlegel, Gustaaf
8794.2	Schlegel, Hermann
8794.26	Schleiermacher, F.E.D.
8794.28	Schlichter, Rudolf, 1890-1955
8794.29	Schliemann, Heinrich
8794.32	Schlettwein, J.A.
8794.34	Schmelz, U.O.
8794.35	Schmid, Christopher von
8794.37	Schmidel, Ulrich
8794.44	Schmidt, Annie M.G.
8794.48	Schmidt, Arno
8794.5	Schmidt, August F.
8794.515	Schmidt, Leopold
8794.52	Schmitt, Carl
8794.53	Schmitt, Jean
8794.535	Schmitz, Ettore
8794.6	Schnell, Robert Wolfgang
8794.7	Schnitzler, Arthur
8794.72	Scholem, G.G.
8794.77	Schönlank, Bruno
8794.8	Schoonover, F.E.
8795	Schopenhauer, Arthur
8795.45	Schou, August
8795.52	Schramm, P.E.
8795.57	Schreiber, Georg
8795.6	Schreiner, Olive
8796	Schroeder, T.A.
8796.65	Schück, Henrik
8796.68	Schuler, Alfred, 1865-1923
8796.69	Schuler, P.J.
8796.7	Schuller, R.R.
8797.2	Schulze-Gaevernitz, Gerhart von
8797.6	Schurek, Paul
8797.7	Schurig, Arthur
8797.73	Schurz, Carl
8797.732	Schuster, Rudolf
8797.733	Schützeichel, Rudolf
8797.738	Schweikert, Rudi
8797.75	Schweitzer, Albert
8797.77	Schwencke, Johan
8797.79	Sciacca, M.F.
8797.8	Scialoja, Vittorio
8797.87	Sciascia, Leonardo
8800	Sclater, P.L.
8801	Sclopsis de Salerano, Federigo
8801.7	Scolari, Massimo

S -- Continued

8801.8	Scotellaro, Rocco
8802	Scott, Sir Walter
8802.4	Scott Brown, Denise
8802.5	Scribanius, Carolus
8803	Scudder, S.H.
8803.3	Scully, V.J.
8803.8	Sealsfield, Charles
8804.5	Sébillot, Paul
8804.6	Sebris, Kārlis
8806	Seckel, Emil
8806.3	Sedmalis, Uldis
8806.37	Seghers, Anna
8806.4	Segre, Cesare
8806.8	Sehsuvaroğlu, B.N.
8806.9	Seidler, Harry
8806.94	Seignolle, Claude
8807	Seike, Kiyoshi
8807.15	Seip, D.A.
8807.2	Seitz, Heribert
8807.3	Sejong, King of Korea
8807.4	Seler, Eduard
8807.5	Selim I, sultan of the Turks
8807.53	Sella, Emanuele
8807.56	Semenenko, N.P.
8807.6	Semper, Gottfried
8807.63	Şemseddin Sâmî
8807.68	Sena, Jorge de
8807.75	Sénancour, E.P. de
8807.78	Sendak, Maurice
8807.8	Sender, R.J.
8807.82	Seneca, L.A.
8807.9	Senthinathan, Kanaga
8807.98	Sepeev, G. A.
8808.2	Sepheriadēs, Geōrgios
8808.4	Serafimov, Kiril
8808.42	Sergeev, A.D.
8808.48	Sergeev, E.M.
8808.49	Sergeev, Mark
8808.5	Sergeeva, V.N. (Varvara Nikolaevna)
8808.53	Sergienko, S.R.
8808.54	Sérgio, Antonio
8808.6	Seriman, Zaccaria
8808.63	Serlio, Sebastiano
8808.65	Serov, A.N.
8808.665	Serra, Renato, 1884-1915
8808.67	Serrão, J.V.

Z8001-8999

S -- Continued

8808.7	Servetus, Michael
8808.713	Service, R.W.
8808.716	Śeśpĕl, Mishshi
8808.72	Sestan, Ernesto
8808.74	Sestrimski, Ivan
8808.85	Setchell, W.A.
8808.88	Settala, Lodovico
8808.89	Settembrini, Luigi
8808.9	Setterlind, Bo
8808.915	Seuss, Dr.
8808.92	Sevak, Gurgen
8808.93	Severn̄ı̄ak, Serafim
8808.94	Seymour, A.J.
8808.944	Seyrânî, 1807-1666
8808.96	Shabazi, Shalem, 1619-1686
8808.97	Shabliovs'kyĭ, Ievhen Stepanovych
8809.4	Shadr, I.D.
8809.5	Shadwell, Thomas
8809.6	Shaffer, Peter
8809.7	Shahn, Ben
8809.8	Shahowmyan, Step'an
8809.82	Shahriyār, Muḥammad Ḥusayn, 1905 or 6-
8809.84	Shaig, Abdulla
8809.85	Shain, G.A.
	Shakespeare, William
8811	General
8812.A-Z	Individual works, A-Z
8813	Other special topics (not A-Z)
	Including folios, quartos, etc.
8813.22	Shakhmatov, A.A.
8813.23	Shant', Lewon
8813.25	Shapiro, K.J.
8813.37	Sharafat Naushāhī, S.A.
8813.4	Sharett, Moshe
8813.45	Sharī'atī, 'Alī
8813.5	Sharofov, N.A.
8814	Shatelen, M.A.
8814.3	Shatzky, Jacob
8814.5	Shaw, G.B.
8814.54	Shaw, R.N.
8814.65	Shchepkin, I.M.
8814.68	Shchepkin, M.S.
8814.7	Shcherbakov, D.I.
8814.72	Shcherbatov, M.M., kn̄ı̄az'
8814.73	Shcherbatskoĭ, F.I.
8814.8	Shea, J.G.

S -- Continued

8814.95	Shelley, M.W.G.
8815	Shelley, P.B.
8815.3	Shemiakin, M.M.
8815.4	Shén, Yen-ping
8815.45	Shennikov, A.P.
8815.5	Shenstone, William
8815.7	Sheps, Elias
8815.8	Sheremetev, S.D., graf
8815.85	Sherff, E.E.
8815.9	Sheridan, P.H.
8816	Sheridan, R.B.B.
8816.5	Sherman, W.T.
8816.57	Sherrington, C.E.R.
8816.62	Shestov, Lev
8816.7	Shevchenko, Taras
8816.73	Shevel'ov, Ūriĭ
8816.75	Sheviakov, L.D.
8816.83	Shiba, Ryōtarō, 1923-
8816.87	Shibli Numani, Muhammad
8816.9	Shiel, M.P.
8817	Shimanskii, ĪŪ.A.
8817.12	Shimao, Toshio
8817.13	Shimazaki, Tōson
8817.14	Shimoda, Utako
8817.15	Shinohara, Kazuo
8817.157	Shirai, Sei'ichi
8817.16	Shiraliev, M.S. ogly
8817.2	Shirley, James
8817.3	Shirokov, V.M. (Vīacheslav Mikhaĭlovich)
8817.37	Shishkan, Konstantin
8817.4	Shishkin, I.I.
8817.42	Shishkov, Georgi
8817.43	Shishkov, V.I.
8817.5	Shishmarev, V.F.
8817.8	Shmelev, I.V. (Ivan Sergeevich)
8817.85	Shneur Zalman, of Lyady
8817.88	Shockley, A.A.
	Sholem Aleichem see Z8730.15
8817.9	Sholokov, M.A.
8817.98	Shores, Louis
8818	Shotman, A.V.
8818.1	Shotwell, J.T.
8818.13	Shovkoplīas, I.H.
8818.15	Shramko, B.A.
8818.2	Shreve, R.H.
8818.27	Shteĭnberg, V.A.

Z8001-8999

S -- Continued

8818.3	Shtern, L.S.
	Shu, Ch'ing-Ch'un see Z8483.24
8818.5	Shufeldt, R.W.
8818.516	Shukhevych, Volodymyr, 1849-1915
8818.52	Shukhov, Ivan
8818.55	Shukrī, 'Abd al-Raḥmān
8818.57	Shukshin, V.M.
8818.6	Shukurov, M.R.
8818.63	Shul'ha, I.H.
8818.64	Shuli̐akovskiĭ, E.G. (Efim Geert̃sevich)
8818.645	Shul't̃s, M. M. (Mikhail Mikhaĭlovich)
8818.65	Shunkov, V.I.
8818.67	Sichirollo, Livio
8818.68	Sichyns'kyĭ, Volodymyr
8818.74	Ṣiddīqī, Rashīd Aḥmad
8818.8	Sidney, Sir Philip
8818.816	Sidorenko, A.V.
8818.82	Sidorov, A.A.
8818.83	Siebold, P.F. von
8818.84	Sienkiewicz, Henryk
8818.85	Sierra, Justo
8818.87	Sierra, M.J.
8818.89	Sierra Bardecia, Fernando
8818.9	Siguenza y Góngora, Carlos de
8819	Sigurðsson, Jón
8819.12	Sikelianos, Angelos
8819.123	Sillastu, Kh.
8819.125	Sillitoe, Alan
8819.128	Silva, António José da, 1705-1739
8819.13	Silva, José Bonifacio de Andrada e
8819.133	Silva, Presciliano
	Silva Leitão de Almeida Garrett, J.B. da see Z8028.8
8819.135	Silverberg, Robert
8819.142	Simak, Clifford D.
8819.143	Simard, Claude
8819.145	Simard, Georges
8819.147	Simenon, Georges
8819.148	Simmonds, Roy S.
8819.149	Simmons, J.S.G.
8819.2	Simms, W.G.
8819.34	Simon, H.A.
8819.37	Simon, István
8819.4	Simone Fidati, da Cascia
8819.43	Simonescu, Dan
8819.44	Simonov, K.M.
8819.443	Simonyan, Babken

S -- Continued

8819.445	Simpson, L.A.M.
8819.45	Simpson, Percy
8819.46	Şimşir, Bilâl N.
8819.47	Sin'" Phe Mraṇ"
8819.5	Sinclair, U.B.
8819.55	Singer, I.B.
8819.553	Singh, Ganda
8819.554	Singh, Puran, 1881-1931
8819.556	Sinka, István
8819.56	Sinkevičius, Klemensas
8819.563	Sinor, Denis
8819.57	Sipos, Gyula
8819.575	Sippaṃ Moṅ' Va
8819.58	Siren, Heikki
8819.6	Sirén, Osvald
8819.62	Sirindhorn
8819.63	Sisakīan, N.M.
8819.635	Sitnikov, Vladimir
8819.64	Situmorang, Sitor
8819.65	Sitwell family
8819.655	Sivananda, Swami, 1887-1963
8819.66	Siza, Alvaro
8819.67	Skards, ĪA. V.
8819.68	Skarga, Piotr
8819.683	Skaryna, Frantsysk
8819.684	Skarzhinskiĭ, Matveĭ Isaakovich
8819.685	Skazkin, S.D.
8819.686	Skelton, John
8819.6865	Skidmore, O. & M.
8819.6866	Skjoldborg, Johan
8819.687	Skovoroda, G.S.
8819.6875	Skuodis, Vytautas
8819.688	Skutil, Josef
8819.68815	Skvorecký, Josef
8819.6882	Skwarczynska, Stefania
8819.6883	Sladek, John Thomas
8819.6884	Slater, F.C.
8819.69	Slaveĭkov, P.P.
8819.692	Slaveĭkov, P.R.
8819.693	Slavītyns'kyĭ, Mykola Andriĭovych
8819.695	Slavici, Ioan
8819.696	Slavík, Jan
8819.7	Slingerland, M.V.
8819.9	Slosson, E.E.
8819.915	Słowacki, Juliusz
8819.918	Smal-Stocki, Roman

Z8001-8999

S -- Continued

8819.92	Small, J.K.
8819.93	Smallegange, Mattheus
8819.94	Smart, Christopher
8819.95	Šmatlák, Stanislav
8819.96	Smedt, Jan de, 1905-1954
8819.97	Smetona, Antanas
8819.99	Smilgis, Eduards
8820	Smirnenski, Khristo
8820.14	Smirnov, B.L.
8820.142	Smirnov, N.P.
8820.143	Smirnov, V.I.
8820.15	Smirnov-Sokolo'skiĭ, N.P.
8820.19	Smith, A.J.M.
8820.2	Smith, Adam
8820.3	Smith, Alfred C.
8820.35	Smith, Bernard
8820.4	Smith, C.A.
8820.43	Smith, Dave, 1942-
8820.5	Smith, E.F.
8820.7	Smith, G.C.M.
8820.73	Smith, Goldwin
8820.83	Smith, J.W.
8820.89	Smith, James
8820.9	Smith, James E.
8820.95	Smith, J.L.
8821	Smith, John
8821.5	Smith, John L.
8821.63	Smith, Joseph
8821.8	Smith, L.E.
8822.15	Smith, Peter
8822.3	Smith, S.I.
8822.32	Smith, Stevie
8822.33	Smith, T.G.
8822.34	Smith, W.E.
8822.37	Smith, William
8822.38	Smith, William B.
8822.43	Smithson, A.M.
8822.45	Šmits, Pēteris
8822.5	Smollett, T.G.
8822.7	Smuts, J.C.
8822.8	Smuul, Juhan
8823	Smyth, W.H.
8823.13	Snegirev, Ivan
8823.16	Sniečkus, Antanas
8823.2	Šnobr, Jan
8823.3	Snodgrass, W.D.

S -- Continued

8823.37	Snow, C.P., Baron Snow
8823.4	Snoy, Reynier
8823.46	Snyder, Gary
8823.48	Sŏ, Pyŏng-sŏl
8823.486	Soares, Mário
8823.49	Sobczak, Kazimierz
8823.495	Sobinnikova, V.I.
8823.5	Sobolev, S.L.
8823.55	Sobolev, V.S.
8824	Sobrero, Ascanio
8824.3	Sochava, V.B.
8824.34	Socrates
8824.343	Södergran, Edith
8824.35	Soffice, Ardengo
8824.36	Sohon, Gustave
8824.48	Sokolov, B.S.
8825.3	Solano, Vicente
8825.48	Soleri, Paoli
8825.55	Solis-Cohen, Solomon
8825.7	Solmi, Arrigo
8825.72	Solomon ben Isaac, called Rashi
8825.723	Soloveitchik, J.D.
8825.725	Solov'ev, S.M.
8825.727	Solov'ev, V.S.
8825.73	Solov'ev, Z.P.
8825.76	Solzheniṯsyn, A.I.
8826.3	Somerville, E.A. OE
8826.4	Sønderby, Knud
8826.45	Sontag, Susan
8826.47	Sontani, Utuy Tatang
8826.77	Sophron
8826.8	Šopov, Aco
8826.85	Sørensen, Villy, 1929-
8826.86	Sorescu, Marin, 1936-
8826.9	Soriano, Raphael
8826.92	Sorokin, Pitirim Aleksandrovich
8826.94	Sorrentino, Gilbert
8827.2	Sosi͡ura, Volodymyr
8827.6	Sottsass, Ettore
8827.8	Soupault, Philippe
8827.885	Sousa, Cruz e, 1861-1898
8828	Sousa Viterbo, F.M. de
8828.4	Southcott, Joanna
8828.43	Southey, Robert
8828.5	Southgate, Horatio
8828.52	Souto Maior, Mário

Z8001-8999

S -- Continued

8828.54	Sova, Antonín
8828.6	Sovrè, Anton
8828.7	Sowerby family
8828.73	Soyinka, Wole
8828.76	Spadolini, Giovanni
8828.8	Spallanzani, Lazzaro
8829	Spano, Giovanni
8829.4	Sparenta, Bertrando
8829.7	Speck, L.W.
8830.2	Spence, Catherine Helen
8830.35	Spencer, Herbert
8830.4	Spencer, J.W.
8830.5	Spender, Stephen
8830.8	Spenser, Edmund
8830.87	Spiegelberg, Wilhelm
8830.89	Spielberg, Steven
8830.93	Spijker, W. van 't
8830.96	Spillane, Mickey
8830.98	Spini, Giorgio
8831	Spinoza, Benedictus de
8831.13	Spir, African
8831.14	Spirito, Ugo
8831.16	Spitsyn, V.I.
8831.18	Spitzer, Leo
8831.2	Spivakovskiĭ, A.O.
8831.3	Spoelberch de Lovenjoul, C.V.M.A., vicomte de
8831.6	Spofford, A.R.
8831.8	Spranger, Eduard
8832	Squier, E.G.
8832.2	Squier, G.O.
8832.5	Squire, J.C.
8832.64	Šramek, Fráňa
8832.65	Srebrov, Zdravko
8832.7	Sreznevskiĭ, I.I.
8832.75	Srivastava, D.R.
8832.78	Sruoga, Balys
8832.8	Ssu-ma, Ch'ien
8832.9	Staden, Hans
8833	Staël-Holstein, A.L.G. (Necker) baronne de
8833.3	Stafford, Jean
8833.5	Stalin, Iosif
8833.7	Stal'skiĭ, Suleíman
8833.72	Stamelos, Dēmētrēs
8833.74	Stanchev, Lŭchezar
8833.745	Stangerup, Henrik
8833.753	Stanislavskiĭ, A.L.

S -- Continued

8833.76	Stanislavsky, Konstantin
8833.77	Stanković, Borisav
8833.8	Stanley, Sir H.M.
8833.9	Stanley, Thomas
8833.94	Stapledon, Olaf
8834.15	Starkey, James
8834.2	Starrett, Vincent
8834.5	Starter, J.J.
8834.6	Startsev, Vitaliĭ Ivanovich
8834.7	Stasov, V.V.
8834.73	Statulevičius, V. A.
8834.77	Staub, J.F.
8834.85	Staviskiĭ, B.ĪA.
8834.9	Stead, W.F.
8836	Stearns, R.E.C.
8837	Stebliĭ, F.I.
8838	Steele, Sir Richard
8838.15	Steenberg, A.S.
8838.18	Stefan Batory, King of Poland
8838.183	Štefanko, Ondrej
8838.185	Stefanov, B.P.
8838.187	Stefansson, Vilhjalmur
8838.2	Stefanyk, V.S.
8838.3	Stegner, W.E.
8838.5	Steiger, J.R.
8838.8	Stein, C.S.
8838.9	Stein, Gertrude
8839.4	Steinbeck, John
8840	Steiner, Rudolf
8841	Steinman, D.B.
8841.3	Stel'mashchuk, H.H. (Halyna Hryhorivna), 1943-
	Stendal' see Z8092.8
	Stenvall, Aleksis see Z8465.74
8841.7	Štěpánek, Čeněk
8841.73	Stepanov, ĪUriĭ Sergeevich
8841.75	Stepermanis, Marġers
8841.77	Stephen, Leslie, Sir
8841.773	Stephen, Voivode of Moldavia, d. 1504
8841.8	Stephens, C.A.
8841.84	Stephens, James
8841.85	Stephens, Suzanne
8841.86	Stephensen, P.R. (Percy Reginald)
8841.88	Stepovyk, D.V.
8842	Sterling, George
8842.17	Stern, Irma
8842.2	Stern, M.A.

Z8001-8999

S -- Continued

8842.26	Stern, R.A.M
8842.3	Sterne, Laurence
8842.4	Sternheim, Carl
8842.6	Steuben, F.W.L.G.A., baron von
8842.67	Stevens, Shane
8842.7	Stevens, Wallace
8842.8	Stevenson, R.L.
8844	Stevenson, T.G.
8844.3	Stewart, D.A.
8844.5	Stewart, I.M.
8845.2	Stickley, Gustav
8845.3	Stifter, Adalbert
8845.83	Stillwell, L.B.
8845.9	Stinde, Julius
8845.93	Stirling, J.F.
8846	Stirling-Maxwell, Sir William bart
8848	Stockton, F.R.
8848.2	Stockhardt, J.A.
8848.28	Stoĭanov, Lŭidmil
8848.3	Stoĭanov, Nikolaĭ
8848.315	Stoianov, Zakhari
8848.32	Stoker, Bram
8848.33	Stoll, Ladislav
8848.335	Stoltze, Friedrich
8848.34	Stone, E.D.
8848.35	Stone, Irving
8848.38	Stone, Robert
8848.4	Stone, T.T.
8848.7	Stopes, M.C.C.
8848.8	Stoppard, Tom
8849	Storer, D.H.
8849.2	Storm, Theodor
8849.3	Stormi, Alfonsina
8849.32	Stott, John
8849.34	Stout, Rex
8849.35	Stow, G.W.
8849.37	Stow, Randolph
8849.4	Stowe, H.E. (Beecher)
8849.54	Strachey, Lytton
8849.55	Stradins, Janis
8849.56	Straka, Georges
8849.57	Strakhov, N.M.
8849.58	Strakosch, Syiegfried von
8849.6	Stránská, D. (Drahomíra)
8849.65	Strashimirov, Anton
8849.69	Stratemeyer, Edward

S -- Continued

8849.7	Stratico, Simone
8849.74	Strauss, Leo
8849.78	Strazdas, Antanas
8849.8	Strazdins, Karlis
8850	Streatfield, Noel
8850.05	Street, G.E.
8850.1	Stresemann, Gustav
8850.2	Strindberg, August
8850.23	Stringer, Arthur, 1874-1950
8850.24	Stritecka, Klementina
8850.26	Strittmatter, Erwin
8850.4	Strnadel, Josef
8850.5	Strods, H.
8850.8	Struiskii, N.E.
8850.814	Strukhmanchuk, I͡Akiv
8850.82	Strumilin, S.G.
8850.824	Struminskiĭ, V.V.
8850.83	Struther, Jan
8850.84	Struve, P.B.
8850.85	Struve, V.V.
8850.855	Strzhel'chik, Vladislav Ignat'evich
8850.9	Stuart, Jesse
8850.95	Stubbins, Hugh
8851	Stubbs, William, bp. of Oxford
8851.9	Studart, Carlos
8852	Studart, Guilherme, barao de
8852.22	Stuparich, Giani
8852.25	Stŭpov, P.I.
8852.3	Štúr, Ľudovĭt
8852.32	Sturgeon, Theodore
8852.35	Sturgis, Russell
8852.355	Sturzo, Luigi
8852.36	Stus, Vasyl'
8852.37	Stylianou, Petros
8852.4	Styron, William
8852.5	Suárez, Francisco
8852.6	Suárez, M.F.
8852.65	Suchodolski, Bogdan
8852.7	Sucre, A.J. de, Pres. Bolivia
8852.8	Sudrabkalns, Jānis
8852.85	Sue, Eugène
8852.9	Süleyman Nazif
8853	Suetonius Tranquillus, C.
8853.125	Sugimori, Hisahide
8853.127	Sugimura, Sojinkan, 1872-1945
8853.13	Sukarno, Pres. Indonesia

Z8001-8999

S -- Continued

8853.14	Sukebatur
8853.15	Sukhomlinov, M.I.
8853.17	Sukhovo-Kobylin, A.
8853.2	Sukiasīān, E.R.
8853.25	Suleĭmenov, Olzhas
8853.3	Sullivan, L.H.
8853.35	Sultanov, Mămmădaga
8853.4	Sulte, Benjamin
8853.5	Sumbatzade, A.S.
8853.9	Summanen, Taisto
8854	Summerall, C.P.
8854.25	Summers, Montague
8854.28	Sumtsov, Nikolai
8854.4	Sun, Yat-sen
8854.43	Sundukyan, Gabriel
8854.45	Sung, Ch'ing-ling
8854.5	Sūradāsa
8854.54	Surguchev, Il'īā
8854.55	Surguladze, Akakiĭ
8854.57	Susini, G.C.
8854.6	Sutcliff, Rosemary
8854.64	Sutzkever, Abraham
8854.7	Suvorov, A.V., knīāz'Italiĭskiĭ
8854.7114	Suvorov, B.V.
8854.712	Suvorov, M.I.
8854.713	Suyūṭī
8854.716	Švabinský, Max
8854.73	Svantner, František
8854.734	Svartz, Nanna
8854.74	Svensson, Sigfrid
8854.75	Sverdlov, ĪĀ.M.
8854.78	Šverma, Ján
	Svevo, Italo see Z8794.535
8854.79	Svidzinskyi, Volodymyr, 1885-1941
8854.8	Svinin, V.V.
8854.82	Svitel'skiĭ, V.A.
8854.85	Swain, G.F.
8854.855	Swanson, H.B.
8855	Swedenborg, Emanuel
8855.4	Swem, E.G.
8856	Swift, Jonathan
8857	Swinbourne, A.C.
8857.3	Swirszcyńska, Anna
8857.4	Sydykov, Zh.S.
8857.5	Symonds, J.A.
8857.6	Symons, Arthur

S -- Continued

8857.7	Symons, Julian
8857.8	Synge, J.M.
8857.813	Sysoíkov, Mikhail
8857.814	Szabó, Dezső
8857.815	Szabó, Ervin
8857.817	Szabó, István
8857.82	Szabó, Lorinc
8857.826	Széchenyi, István
8857.828	Szederkényi, Ervin
8857.83	Szendrei, Janos
8857.835	Szent-Györgyi, Albert
8857.84	Szerb, Antal
8857.842	Szij, Rezsö
8857.845	Szily, János
8857.85	Szirmai, Endre
8857.855	Szönyi, István
8857.857	Sztaudynger, Jan, 1904-1970

T

8857.86	Ṭabarī, 838?-923
8857.87	Tabarov, S.S.
8857.875	Ṭabenḳin, Yitsḥaḳ
8857.877	Tablada, J.J.
8857.88	Taft, W.H.
8857.9	Tagore, Rabindranath
8857.95	Ṭahā Husayn
8857.96	Tāhirulqādrī, Muḥammad
8857.97	Ṭahơtāwī, R.R.
8858	Taine, H.A.
8858.4	Takamatsu, Shin
8858.43	Takamura, Kōtarō
8858.435	Takats, Gyula
8858.437	Take, Motoo
8858.438	Takeda, Izumo
8858.439	Takeda, Rintaro
8858.44	Takeyama, Minoru
8858.45	Takii, Kosaku
8858.46	Takizawa, Bakin
8858.47	Takizawa, Katsumi
8858.48	Talipov, Sh.T.
8858.5	Talleyrand-Périgord, Charles Maurice de, prince de Bénévent
8858.57	Tamaoka, Shoichiro
8858.58	Tamás, Attila
8858.6	Tamminga, D.A.
8858.62	Tammsaare, A.H.
8858.64	Tan, Nail, 1941-

Z8001-8999

T -- Continued

8858.65	T'an, Ssu-T'ung
8858.655	Tanabe, Hajime
8858.657	Tanabe, Seiko
8858.66	Tananaev, I.V.
8858.663	Tandori, Dezső
8858.665	Taneda, Santōka
8858.68	Tange, Kenzō
8858.688	Tan'gun
8858.7	Taniguchi, Yoshirō
8858.727	Taniuk, Leś, 1938-
8858.73	Tanizaki, Jun'ichiroō
8858.75	Tanizawa, Eiichi
8858.8	Tansel, F.A.
8858.84	Tao-fen
8858.9	Tarkington, Booth
8858.95	Tarle, E.V.
8858.97	Tarn, Nathaniel
8858.975	Tarnavs′ka, Marta
8858.98	Tarnavs′kyĭ, Ostap
8859.2	Tartarotti, Girolamo
8859.5	Taruffi, Cesare
8859.7	Tasman, A.J.
8860	Tasso, Torquato
8860.6	Tatarkiewicz, Władysław
8860.7	Tatsiĭ, Oleksa, 1903-1967
8861	Taube, Otto, Freiherr von
8861.15	Tauber, M.F.
8861.17	Taufer, Jiří
8861.18	Taunay, Afonso de E.
8861.19	Taxell, L.E.
8861.194	Tayama, Katai
8861.2	Taylor, A.J.P.
8861.4	Taylor, Edward
8861.5	Taylor, Sir Frederick, bart
8861.8	Taylor, Jeremy, bp. of Down and Connor
8862	Taylor, John
8862.6	Taylor, Meadows
8862.7	Taylor, P.H.
8863	Taylor, Thomas
8863.5	Taylor, Zachary
8863.7	Tcherikower, Elias
8863.73	Tchernichovski, Saul
	Tchernichowsky, Saul see Z8863.73
8863.75	Tchernowitz, Chaim
8863.77	Tecchi, Bonaventura
8863.78	Teilhard de Chardin, Pierre

T -- Continued

8863.785	Teitelbaum, Benjamin
8863.787	Teixeira, Manuel
8863.788	Tejeda, Luis de
8863.8	Tejera, y García, D.V.
8863.9	Telford, Thomas
8864	Tellez, Gabriel
8864.5	Temple, W.F.
8864.6	Teňcík, František
8864.7	Tendriakov, V.F.
8864.8	Tenev, Tenko
8865.5	Teng, Hsiao-ping
8866	Tennyson, Alfred Tennyson, baron
8866.25	Tennyson, Sir Charles
8866.3	Teplý, Bogo
8867	Terence (Publius Terentius Afer)
8868	Teresa, Saint
8868.15	Terhune, A.P.
8868.2	Terpigorev, A.M.
8868.25	Terrera, G.A.
8868.3	Tesarek, Anton
8868.32	Tešić, Milosav
8868.37	Těšitelová, Marie
8868.4	Tesla, Nikola
8868.45	Těsnohlídek, Rudolf
8868.5	Testori, Giovanni
8868.7	Texier, Lucien
8869	Thackeray, W.M.
8869.12	Thälmann, Ernst
8869.13	Thalbitzer, W.C.
8869.14	Thatcher, Margaret
8869.15	Thayer, John
8869.16	Theiler, Willy
8869.3	Thirring, G.A.
8869.8	Thomas, à Kempis
8870	Thomas Aquinas, Saint
8870.5	Thomas, Dylan
8870.6	Thomas, Percy, Sir
8870.8	Thomasius, Christian
8871.07	Thompson, A.H.
8871.1	Thompson, Francis
8871.91	Thomson, C.W.
8872	Thomson, James
8872.5	Thomson, James P.
8872.7	Thomson, S.H.
8872.9	Thomson, William
8873	Thoreau, H.D.

Z8001-8999

T -- Continued

8873.5	Thorez, Maurice
8874	Thorington, J.M.
8875	Thorlakson, P.H.T.
8876	Thoulet, Julien
8878	Thucydides
8878.16	Thünen, J.H. von
8878.2	Thürer, Georg
8878.4	Thurber, James
8878.5	Thurneysen, Rudolf
8878.79	Thyregod, C.A.
8879	Tiberghien, Guillaume
8879.4	Tibullus, Albius
8879.6	Tichelen, Hendrik van
8879.63	Tieck, Ludwig
8879.65	Tiffany, L.C.
8879.68	Tigerman, Stanley
8879.72	Tikhonov, N.S.
8879.725	Tikhvinskiĭ, Sergeĭ Leonidovich
8879.73	Tilander, Gunnar
8879.75	Tillich, Paul
8879.76	Tilliette, Xavier
8879.77	Timasheff, N.S.
8879.8	Timiri͡azev, K.A.
8880.5	Timotijević, Božidar
8881.5	Tingsten, H.L.G.
8881.9	Tiraboschi, Antonio
8881.95	Tirats'yan, Gevorg Artashesi
8882.2	Tiruvalluvar
8882.23	Tischendorf, Constantin von, 1815-1874
8882.25	Tischner, Jósef
8882.3	Tishby, Isaiah
8882.4	Titarenko, M. L.
8882.5	Tito, J.B., Pres. Yugoslavia
8882.6	Ti͡um͡ënev, A.I.
8882.7	Ti͡utchev, F.I.
8882.9	Tkatch, M.Z.
8882.93	Tobar Donoso, Julio
8882.95	Tobi, Joseph
8882.96	Tobias, P.V.
8882.97	Tobilevych, I.K. (Ivan Karpovych), 1845-1907
8883	Tocqueville, A.C.H.M.C. de
8883.15	Todd, Ruthven
8883.18	Todorov, P.I.
8883.19	Togan, Ahmed Zeki Velidi
8883.2	Tōge, Sankichi
8883.3	Togliatti, Palmiro

T -- Continued

8883.35	Toki, Zenmaro
8883.38	Tokugawa, Ieyasu
8883.39	Tokunaga, Sunao
8883.395	Tokutomi, Iichirō
8883.4	Toland, John
8883.45	Tolkien, J.R.R.
8883.5	Toller, Ernst
8883.55	Tolstoĭ, A.K.
8883.6	Tolstoĭ, I.I.
8883.8	Tolstoĭ, L.N.
8883.82	Tolstoĭ, N.I.
8883.824	Tōmadakēs, N.B.
8883.83	Tommaseo, Nicolò
8883.834	Tomov, Toma St.
8883.835	Tönies, Ferdinand
8883.837	Toonder, Marten
8883.84	Topelius, Zakarias
8883.85	Topencharov, Vladimir
8883.86	T'oranean, T'oros
8883.87	Torczyner, Harry
8883.874	Törnudd, Elin
8883.877	Toroev, A.A.
8883.88	Torp, Carl
8883.9	Torralbas, J.I.
8883.97	Torre, Susana
8884.15	Torre Revello, José de
8884.38	Torres Bodet, Jaime
8884.4	Torres-García, Joaquin
8884.44	Torres Naharro, Bartolomé de
8884.5	Torroja Miret, Eduardo
8884.7	Toscanelli, Paolo del Pozzo
8884.72	Tosta, Virgilia
8884.725	Tóth, Béla
8884.726	Tóth, Imre
8884.73	Tourgée, A.W.
8884.75	Tourneur, Cyril
8884.78	Toussaint, Manuel
8884.79	Tovstonogov, G.A.
8884.8	T'owmanian, Hovhannes
8884.85	Toynbee, A.J.
8884.86	Tozzi, Federigo, 1883-1920
8884.87	Trager, G.L.
8884.88	Traherne, Thomas, d. 1674
8884.9	Trakl, Georg
8884.93	Tranøy, K.E.
8884.94	Tranströmer, Tomas

Z8001-8999

T -- Continued

8884.96	Tranven, B.
8884.97	Traub, Hellmut
8884.98	Trávníček, František
8885.1	Trébutien, G.S.
8885.16	Trejos, Juan
8885.2	Trenchard, John
8885.3	Tretíakov, P.N.
8885.4	Trifunoski, J.F.
8885.45	Trillet, Marc
8885.47	Trillin, Calvin
8885.48	Trilling, Lionel
8885.49	Tripāṭhī, G.M.
8885.5	Tristan L'Hermite, François
8885.74	Troeltsch, Ernst
8885.75	Troepol'skiĭ, G.N.
8885.77	Trofimovich, K.K. (Konstantin Konstantinovich)
8885.9	Trollope, Anthony
8885.95	Tron'ko, Petro Tymofiĭovych
8886.5	Trotskiĭ, Lev
8887	Trowbridge, Augustus
8888.5	Trubachev, O.N.
8888.8	Truber, Primus
8888.85	Trubetskoĭ, K.N.
8888.9	Truman, Harry
8888.93	Trumpy, Bjørn
8889	Trushkin, V.P.
8890	Tryon, G.W.
8891	Tsakōnas, D.G.
8891.3	TSamutali, A.N.
8891.4	TSander, F.A.
8891.43	Ts'ao, Chan
8891.48	Tschiżewskij, Dmitrij
8891.52	Tschumi, Bernard
8891.525	Tsimpoukidēs, Dēmētrēs I.
8891.6	Tsirkas, Stratēs
8891.65	TSonchev, Doncho
8891.7	TSonevski, Minko
8891.77	Tsuboi, Sakae
8891.8	Tsubouchi, Shōyō
8891.87	Tsuruda, Takuchi
8891.9	Tsuruya, Namboku
8891.96	Tsuzuki, Keiroku
8891.98	TSvetaeva, Marina
	TSvicić, Jovan see Z8207.8
8891.99	Tu, Fu
8891.995	Tucholsky, Kurt

	T -- Continued
8892	Tucker, Josiah
8892.3	Tuglas, Friedebert
8892.4	Tukārāma
8892.42	Tulasīdāsa
8892.44	Tumanyan, B.E.
8892.45	Tupac-Amaru, José Gabriel
8892.46	Tŭpkova-Zaimova, Vasilka
8893.5	Tur-Sinai, N.H.
8893.53	Turaev, S.V.
8893.54	Turakulov, Talkin Khalmatovich
8893.56	Turati. Filippo
8893.58	Turčány, Viliam
8893.6	Turco, Lewis
8893.7	Turgenev, I.S.
8893.8	Turibius, Saint, abp. of Lima
8893.9	Turner, F.J.
8894	Turner, J.M.W.
8894.2	Tursunzoda, Mirzo
8894.3	Ṭūsī, Naṣīr al-Dīn Muḥammad ibn Muḥammad, 1201-1274
8894.4	Tutkovskiĭ, P.A.
8895	Tuwim, Julian
8895.13	T'valčrelize, Alek'sandre
8895.15	Tvardovskiĭ, A.T.
	Twain, Mark see Z8176
8895.17	Tyard, Pontus de
8895.2	Tyl, J.K.
8895.3	Tyla, Antanas
8896	Tyler, John
8897	Tylor, E.B.
8898	Tyndale, William
8899	Tyndall, John
	U
8900	Ubbelohde, Otto
8900.15	Uchida, Hyakken
8901	Uchimura, Kanzo
8901.3	Udvardi, Erzsébet
8901.4	Ueda, Akinari
8902	Ünver, A.S.
8906	Uhle, Max
8906.3	Ui, Hakuju
8906.4	'Ujayī, 'Abd al-Salām
8907	Ukhtomskii, A.A.
8907.5	Uklonskii, A.S.
8908	Ukrainka, Lesia
8908.8	Ulashchik, N.N.
8909	Ulbricht, Walter

Z8001-8999

U -- Continued

8910	Ul'ianova, Maria Aleksandrovna
8911	Ülken, Hilmi Ziya
8913	Umberto I, king of Italy
8913.3	Unamuno y Jugo, Miguel
8913.5	Unbegaun, B.O.
8913.55	Under, Marie
8913.6	Undset, Sigrid
8913.7	Ungers, O.M.
8913.8	Unna, P.G.
8913.83	Upadhye, A.N.
8913.85	Updike, John
8913.855	Upendra Bhañja
8913.86	Upfield, A.W.
8913.88	Urabe, Shizutarō
8914	Urazov, G.G.
8914.2	Urban, Joseph
8914.3	Urbaneja Achelpohl, L.M.
8914.6	Urdaneta, Rafael
8915	Urechiă, V.A.
8915.5	Urquiza, Justo José de
8916	Urwick, L.F.
8916.4	Urx, Eduard
8916.8	Useĭnov, M.A.
8917	Ushinskii, K.D.
8917.3	Usinger, Fritz
8917.5	Uslar, Pietri, Arturo
8917.6	Usman Awang
8917.67	Utley, R.M.
8917.7	Utzon, Jorn

V

8919.4	Vaarandi, Debora
8919.43	Váchal, Josef
8919.5	Vacheron, André
8919.6	Vachkov, Marko K. (Marko Kolev)
8919.65	Vacina, Ladislav
8920	Václavek, Bedřich
8920.18	Vagnetti, Luigi
8920.24	Värnlund, Rudolf
8920.4	Valcárcel Esparza, C.D.
8920.43	Valdens, Pauls
8920.44	Valdés, Gabriel de la Concepción
8921	Valdivia, Pedro de
8923	Valeinis, Vitolds
8923.3	Válek, Miroslav
8923.5	Valentini, Giuseppe
8923.8	Valera y Alcalá Caliano, Juan

V -- Continued

8924	Valéry, Paul
8924.15	Valeskalns, Pèteris
8924.156	Valiani, Leo, 1909-
8924.16	Valikhanov, Ch. Ch. (Chokan Chingisovich)
8924.18	Valla, Lorenzo, 1407-1457
8924.3	Valle, J.C. del
8924.35	Valle, R.H.
8924.4	Valle-Inclán, Ramón del
8924.42	Vallejo, Cesar
8924.43	Vallès, Jules
8924.53	Vālmīki
8924.75	Vampilov, A.V.
8924.9	Van der Merwe, I.W.
8924.93	Van der Ross, R.E.
	Van Dine, S.S. see Z8986.34
8924.95	Van Rensselaer, Schuyler, Mrs.
8925	Vanags, Gustavs
8925.15	Vanbrugh, John, Sir
8925.17	Vance, Jack
8925.2	Vančura, Vladislav
8925.5	Vanneuville, Guy
8926	Van Vechten, Carl
8926.17	Vaphopoules, G.Th.
8926.18	Vaptsarov, N.I.
8926.2	Varadarajan, M.
8926.25	Varela, F.
8926.27	Varentsov, M.I.
8926.276	Vares-Barbarus, Johannes
8926.28	Varese, Claudio
8926.3	Varga, Eugen
8926.37	Vargas Ponce, José, 1760-1821
8926.4	Vargas Ugarte, Rubén
8926.48	Varma, Siddheshwar
8926.5	Varnhagen, F.A. de, visconde de Porto Seguro
8926.6	Varona y Pera, E.J.
8926.8	Varro, M.T.
8926.85	Varsanof'eva, V.A.
8926.87	Varslavan, A.IA.
8927	Vasari, Giorgio
	Vasconcellos, E.J. de Carvalho e see Z8150.6
8927.05	Vasconcelos, José
8927.1	Vašek, Vladimír
8927.13	Vashchenko. V.S.
8927.137	Vasilev, Ivan
8927.14	Vasilev, Orlin
8927.15	Vasiliev, Asen

Z8001-8999

V -- Continued

8927.16	Vasken I, Catholicos of Armenia
8927.17	Vassilikos, Vassilis
8927.18	Vassoevich, N.B.
8927.19	Vasylenko, Mykola Prokopovych
8927.2	Vaszari, János
8927.3	Vaughan, Henry
8927.35	Vavilov, N.I.
8927.36	Vavilov, S.I.
8927.38	Vaz Ferreira, M.E.
8927.39	Važa-P'šavela
8927.4	Vazov, I.M.
8927.45	Vázquez, Honorato
8927.48	Včelička, Géza
8927.5	Veblen, Oswald
8927.53	Veblen, Thorstein
8927.6	Vecchioni, Mario
8929	Vega, Georg, freiherr von
8930	Vega Carpio, L.F. de
8930.3	Veidenbaums, Eduards
8930.5	Vekene, Emil van der
8931	Velázquez, D.R. de Silvay
8931.13	Velengurin, Nikolaĭ Fedorovich
8931.15	Velez de Guevara ya Duenãs, Luis
8931.17	Velkov, V.I.
8931.25	Venegas Filardo, Pascual
8931.3	Venturi, Adolfo
8931.37	Venturi, Robert
8931.95	Veracruz, Alonso de la, father
8931.96	Verbĭtskiĭ, Vasiliĭ Ivanovich
8931.97	Verdaguer, Jacinto
8931.972	Verdcourt, Bernard
8931.975	Veres, Péter
8931.978	Verga, Giovanni
8931.98	Vergilius, Polydorus
8932	Vergilius Maro, Publius
8932.5	Verhaeren, Emile
8933	Verlaine, P.M.
8933.3	Vermigli, P.M.
8933.4	Vermishev, A.A.
8933.6	Vernadskii, V.I. (Vladimir Ivanovich)
8933.8	Vernadsky, George
8934	Vern, Jules
8934.5	Verney, L.A.
8935	Verseghy, Ferenc
8935.3	Vershigorov, P.S.
8936	Vertès, Marcel

V -- Continued

8937	Vertova, Luisa
8938	Vesalius, Andreas
8939	Veselovskiĭ, A.N.
8939.2	Veselovskiĭ, N.I.
8940	Vespucci, Amerigo
8940.2	Vestdijk, Simon
8940.4	Veuillot, L.F.
8940.5	Vialov, O.S.
8940.6	Viana, Javier de
8940.8	Vianu, Tudor
8941	Viau, Théophile de
8941.2	Viaud, Julien
8941.6	Vicaire, Gabriel
8941.7	Vicente, Gil
8941.8	Vico, G.B.
8942	Vicuña Mackenna, Benjamín
8942.16	Vida, M.G., bp. of Alba
8942.19	Vidal, Gore
8942.2	Vidal, Jacques, docteur
8942.3	Vieira, Antonio
8942.315	Vienuolis, A., pseud.
8942.32	Viera y Clavijo, José de
8942.33	Vierge, D.U.
8942.337	Vigil, J.M.
8942.34	Vignal, Jacques
8942.344	Vignalou, Jean
8942.345	Vigneault, Gilles
8942.347	Vignola, G.B., known as
8942.35	Vigny, A.V., comte de
8942.37	Vila, M.A.
8942.4	Villa Antonio and G.B.
8942.418	Villalonga, Llorenç
8942.42	Villamediana, Juan de Tarsisly Peralta, conde de
8942.426	Villard, de Honnecourt
8942.43	Villavicencio, Pablo de
8942.44	Villon, François
8942.56	Vimba, Ė. K. (Ėdgar Karlovich)
8942.7	Vinay, J.P.
8942.9	Vincentius Ferrerius, Saint
8943.2	Vingedal, S.E.A.
8943.3	Vinogradov, I.M.
8943.5	Virchow, R.L.K.
	Virgil see Z8932
8943.8	Viščakas, Jurgis
8943.9	Vischer, F.T. von
8944	Vischer, G.M.

Z8001-8999

V -- Continued

8944.13	Visconti, Luchino
8944.17	Vitányi, Iván
8944.18	Vitéz, János
8944.19	Vitkauskas, Vytautas
8944.2	Vitry, Gaston
8944.23	Vittorini, Elio
8944.32	Vivas, Eliseo
8944.35	Vivekânanda, swami
8944.39	Vives, J.L.
8944.4	Vladimirovas, L.
8944.42	Vleeschauwer, H.J. de
8944.43	Voegelin, Eric, 1901-1985
8944.44	Vogeler, Johann Heinrich
8944.45	Voghera, Giorgio
8944.454	Vogler, Werner, 1944-
8944.46	Voiculescu, Vasile
8944.5	Voigt, Johannes
8944.54	Voisin, Cyr
8944.56	Volƀerg, G.M.
8944.57	Volf'kovich, S.I.
8944.6	Volk, Paulus
8944.7	Volobuev, V.R.
8944.76	Volov, Panaĭot
8944.9	Volta, A.G.A.A., conte
8945	Voltaire, F.M.A. de
8945.8	Von Mises, Ludwig
8946	Vondel, Joost van den
8946.2	Vonnegut, Kurt
8946.32	Vorob'ev, Vladimir Vasil'evich
8946.34	Voronskiĭ, A.K.
8946.35	Vörösmarty, Mihály
8946.4	Voulliéme, E.H.
8946.5	Voynich, E.L. (Boole)
8946.55	Vrána, Stanislav
8946.6	Vráz, E.S.
8946.65	Vries, Anne de
8946.7	Vulcan, Iosif
8946.72	Vurghun, Sāmād
8946.73	Vvedenskiĭ, N.E.
8946.75	Vvedenskiĭ, S.N.
8946.8	Vybíral, Bohus
8946.82	Vygotskiĭ, L.S.
8946.83	Vykhodtsev, I.V.
8946.84	Vynnychenko, V.K.
8946.85	Vysotky, Vladimir

W

W -- Continued

8946.86	Waaler, Erik
8946.878	Wadström, C.B.
8947	Wadsworth, M.E.
8947.13	Wagenbreth, O.
8947.15	Waggerl, K.H.
8947.17	Waghenaer, L.J.
8947.2	Wagner, H.R.
8947.23	Wagner, Otto
8947.27	Wain, John
8947.3	Waite, A.E.
8947.32	Waite, M.R.
8947.34	Wakoski, Diane
8947.36	Walcott, Derek
8947.37	Waldén, Bertil
8947.4	Waley, Arthur
8947.415	Walichnowski, Tadeusz
8947.42	Walker, Alice
8947.44	Walker, F.D.
8947.46	Wallace, Edgar
8947.5	Wallenstein, A.W.E., von
8947.8	Waller, A.D.
8947.85	Wallin, J.O., Abp.
8947.9	Walpole, Horace, 4th earl of Oxford
8948.2	Walschap, Gerard
8948.3	Walser, Martin
8948.5	Walsh, B.D.
8948.7	Waltari, M.T.
8948.75	Walter, T.U.
8948.8	Walther von der Vogelweide
8949	Walton, Izaak
8949.22	Warburg, Aby
8949.25	Ward, Sir Adolphus William
8949.27	Ward, Arthur Sarsfield
8949.7	Warne, F.J.
8949.715	Warnecke, J.C.
8949.72	Warner, Susan
8949.73	Warren, R.P.
8949.75	Warshawski, Mark
8949.76	Warton, Joseph
8949.9	Washington, B.T.
8950	Washington, George
8950.2	Washington, Harold
8950.5	Wästberg, Per
8951	Waters, Frank
8952	Watkin, W.T.
8952.4	Watson, Ian

Z8001-8999

W -- Continued

8952.5	Watts, Isaac
8952.6	Watzlawick, Paul
8952.7	Watzlik, Hans
8953.5	Waugh, Evelyn
8954.7	Weaver, Lawrence, Sir
8955	Webb, John
8955.5	Webb, P.B.
	Webb, S.J. see Z8662.33
8955.8	Weber, Alfred
8955.9	Weber, Carl Jefferson
8956	Weber, Charles David Maria
8957	Weber, Max
8961	Webster, Daniel
8961.3	Webster, John
8961.5	Webster, Noah
8961.8	Wedgwood, Josiah
8962	Weems, M.L.
8962.17	Wegener, Alfred
8962.2	Wegner, A.T.
8962.23	Weibull, C.H.J.
8962.24	Weichmann, Herbert
8962.26	Weil, Simone
8962.27	Weimar, Robert
8962.29	Weinert, Erich
8962.3	Weinheber, Josef
8962.5	Weinrib, B.A.
8962.8	Weisgerber, Leo
8962.9	Weiss, Ernst
8962.93	Weiss, H.B.
8962.95	Weiss, Peter
8963	Welch, W.H.
8963.8	Wellington, A.W., Duke of
8964.3	Wellman, Manly Wade
8964.75	Wells, Gabriel
8964.8	Wells, H.G.
8964.83	Wells, Malcolm
8964.86	Welty, Eudora
8964.87	Weöres, Sándor
8965.3	Wergeland, H.A.
8965.4	Werin, A.G.
8965.47	Werner, A.G.
8965.5	Werner, Zacharias
8967	Wesley, John and Charles
8967.7	Wesseling, H.L.
8968	Wessely, Carl
8968.3	Wessén, Elias

W -- Continued

8968.36	West, Jessamyn
8968.38	West, Nathanael
8968.4	West, Rebecca, pseud.
8968.44	Westerlund, E.
8969	Wey, F.A.
8969.14	Weyns, Jozep
8969.2	Wharton, E.N. (Jones)
8969.27	Wheat, C.I.
8969.28	Wheatley, Dennis
8969.285	Wheatley, Phyllis
8969.3	Wheeler, H.L.
8969.5	Whistler, J.A.M.
8970	White, C.A.
8970.3	White, E.G.H.
8970.5	White, Gilbert
8970.7	White, Patrick
8970.74	White, Stanford
8970.78	White, T.H.
8970.8	White, Wallace Humphrey
8970.9	White, William Allen
8971	White, William Hale
8971.16	Whitefield, George
8971.2	Whitehead, A.N.
8971.4	Whitman, Marcus
8971.5	Whitman, Walt
8972	Whittier, J.G.
8972.16	Wibbelt, Augustin
8972.17	Wichern, J.H.
8972.2	Wickramasinghe, Martin
8972.3	Widmann, Hans
8972.35	Widukind
8972.37	Wiechert, E.E.
8972.4	Wied, G.J.
8972.5	Wieland, C.M.
8972.65	Wiesel, Eliezer
8972.7	Wiesener, A.M.
8973	Wigglesworth, Michael
8973.7	Wilberforce, William
8974.15	Wilbur, Richard
8974.2	Wilczynski, E.J.
8975	Wilde, Oscar
8975.5	Wilder, B.J.
8975.54	Wilder, Doug
8975.6	Wilder, L.I.
8975.7	Wilder, T.N.
8976	Wilhelm II, German emperor

Z8001-8999

	W -- Continued
8976.2	Willard, DeForest
8976.23	Willem I, Prince of Orange (William the Silent)
8976.25	Willems, Leonard
8976.27	William, of Ockham
8976.28	Williams, A.R.
8976.3	Williams, Charles
8976.34	Williams, Jonathan
8976.42	Williams, Roger
8976.424	Williams, Tennessee
8976.43	Williams, William
8976.44	Williams, William Carlos
8976.45	Williamson, Henry
8976.454	Williamson, Jack
8976.46	Willibrord, Saint, bp. of Utrecht
8976.465	Willis, Bailey
8976.47	Willmann, Otto
8976.48	Wilmot, F.L.T.
8976.485	Wilson, Angus
8976.487	Wilson, Colin
8976.49	Wilson, Edmund
8976.5	Wilson, Edmund Beecher
8976.55	Wilson, Edwin B.
8976.6	Wilson, G.S.
(8976.72)	Wilson, John Anthony Burgess
	see Z8132.2
8976.75	Wilson, John D.
8976.8	Wilson, Richard
8976.9	Wilson, Woodrow
8977.3	Winchell, Alexander
8977.33	Winckelmann, J.J.
8977.35	Windham, Donald
8977.37	Winnicott, D.W. (Donald Woods), 1896-1971
8977.5	Winslow, Anne Goodwin
8978	Winsor, Justin
8978.25	Winters, Yvor
8978.46	Winthrop, Henry
8978.47	Winthrop, John
8978.66	Wirth, Louis
8978.7	Wirth, Zdeněk
8979	Wise, I.M.
8979.17	Wiseman, Adele
8979.2	Wiseman, Frederick
8979.3	Wislicenus, Johannes
8979.37	Wister, Owen
8979.4	Wittgenstein, Ludwig
8979.44	Witvoet, Jacques

W -- Continued

8979.5	Wodehouse, P.G.
8979.6	Woislawski, Zui
8979.7	Wolf, Christa
8979.8	Wolf, Friedrich
8980.12	Wolf, Helmut, 1910-1994
8980.2	Wolf, J.R.
8980.45	Wolfe, Thomas
8980.72	Wolff, E.B.
8980.8	Wolff, Max
8981	Wolfram von Eschenbach
8981.3	Wolfskell, Karl
8981.36	Wolkenstein, Oswald von
8981.4	Wolker, Jirí
8981.45	Wollman, Frank
8981.5	Wollstonecraft, Mary
8982	Wood, H.C.
8982.5	Woodberry, G.E.
8983.3	Woods, Shadrach
8983.4	Woodson, C.G.
8983.6	Woodward, R.S.
8983.8	Woolf, Leonard
8984.2	Woolf, Virginia
8984.4	Woolrich, Cornell
8985	Wordsworth, William
8985.25	Wossidlo, Richard
8985.4	Wouk, Herman
8985.5	Woytinsky, W.S.
8985.6	Wren, Christopher
8985.7	Wren, P.C.
8986	Wright, Sir A.E.
8986.3	Wright, F.L.
8986.315	Wright, G.H. von
8986.316	Wright, H.B.
8986.3168	Wright, J.A.
8986.317	Wright, J.L.
8986.318	Wright, Judith
8986.319	Wright, Lloyd
8986.32	Wright, Quincy
8986.323	Wright, Richard
8986.33	Wright, Wilbur and Orville
8986.34	Wright, Willard Huntington
8986.36	Wu, Shou-li
8986.4	Wulfschmidt, J.P. von
8986.5	Wundt, W.M.
8986.7	Wurster, W.W.
8986.9	Wycherley, William

Z8001-8999

	W -- Continued
8987	Wycliffe, John
8989.5	Wylie, Alexander
8989.6	Wyllers, E.A.
8989.63	Wynar, B.S.
8989.65	Wynar, L.R.
	X
8989.7	X, Malcolm
8989.73	Xenophon
8989.75	Xenopol, A.M.
8989.78	Xerez, Francisco de
8989.79	Xiberta y Roqueta, Bartolomé María, 1897-1967
8989.83	Ximenes, Francesch, bp.
	Y
8990.3	Yaari, Abraham
8990.32	Yaari, Meir
8990.36	Yakobson, Sergius
8990.38	Yamada, Taichi
8990.4	Yamamoto, Kōshō
8990.412	Yamamoto, Shūgorō
8990.4123	Yamanaka, Chiruu, 1905-1977
8990.413	Yamasaki, Minoru
8990.42	Yanagita, Kunio
8990.424	Yanait-Ben-Zvi, Rachel
8990.43	Yang-Shu-ta
8990.7	Yates, E.H.
8992	Yeats, W.B.
8992.45	Yehoshua, A.B.
8992.7	Yepes, J.R.
8993	Yermak
8993.2	Yesha'yahu, Yiśra'el
8993.3	Yevtushenko, Y.A.
8993.37	Yi, Hwang
8993.4	Yi, Hyŏng-sang
8993.5	Yi, Ki-yŏng
8994.3	Yoe, J.H.
8994.7	Yosano, A.H.
8994.8	Yoshida, Isoya
8994.84	Yoshida, Shōin
8995	Young, Edward
8995.3	Young, Ian
8995.4	Yourcenar, Marguerite
8996	Yü, Ta-fu
8996.2	Yuasa, Toshiko
8996.3	Yün, Shou-p'ing
8997	Yule, Sir Henry
8997.22	Yunus Emre

Y -- Continued
8997.223	Yūshīj, Nīmā
8997.224	Yusifzadä, Xoşbäxt Bağı oğlu, 1960-

Z
8997.225	Zabīelin, Ivan
8997.2258	Zabolótskiĭ, N. (Nikolaĭ), 1903-1958
8997.226	Zaborskaitė, Vanda
8997.227	Zadonskiĭ, N.A.
8997.228	Zagorovskiĭ, V.P.
8997.229	Zagrebin, S.I. (Sergeĭ Ivanovich)
8997.23	Zaimov, Stoĭan
8997.235	Zăĭnullin, M. V.
8997.24	Zaĭonchkovskiĭ, P.A.
8997.2438	Zaitsev, B. P. (Boris Petrovich)
8997.244	Zaitsev, Boris
8997.25	Zak, Abraham
8997.26	Zakrevs′ka, ĪA.
8997.3	Zalka, Maté
8997.35	Załuski family
8997.37	Zamīātin, Evgeniĭ Ivanovich
8997.4	Zamīātin, N.N.
8997.5	Zanella, Giacoma
8997.54	Zannovich, Stiepan
8997.57	Zanzotto, Andrea
8997.823	Zápotocký, Antonín, 1884-1957
8997.8233	Zaragoza Pascual, Ernesto
8997.8234	Zarev, Panteleĭ
8997.8235	Zaryan, R.V.
8997.82358	Zaval′nyĭ, A. N. (Aleksandr Nikiforovich)
8997.8236	Zavriev, K.S.
8997.824	Zborovjan, Jvlo
8997.8247	Zea, Leopoldo
8997.825	Zebrowski, George
8997.826	Zech, Paul
8997.827	Zeitlin, Solomon
8997.829	Zelazny, Roger
8997.83	Zeleny, John
8997.834	Zelk, Zoltán
8997.84	Zeman, Kamil
8997.85	Zeromski, Stefan
8997.855	Zesen, Philipp von
8997.86	Zetkin, Klara
8997.866	Zetti, Italo
8997.87	Zhabaev, Zhambyl
8997.88	Zhabotinskiĭ, V.E.
8997.89	Zhdanov, ĪU. A.
8997.892	Zhefarovich, Khristofor

Z8001-8999

Z -- Continued

8997.894	Zhigulin, Anatoliĭ
8997.897	Zhinzifov, Raĭko
8997.9	Zhirmunskiĭ, V.M.
8997.915	Zhivkova, Lĩudmila
8997.917	ZHurba, Kuz',ma
8997.92	Zidarov, Nikolaĭ
8997.925	Zientara-Malewska, Maria
8997.927	Zimin, A.A. (Aleksandr Aleksandrovich)
8997.93	Zimmer, Heinrich
8997.95	Zinny, Antonio
8998.1	Zinzendorf, N.L. graf von
8998.2	Žiugžda, Juozas
8998.3	Zlatarov, Asen
8998.4	Zlenko, Hryhoriĭ
8998.44	Zlupko, Stepan
8998.5	Zola, Émile
8998.513	Zolnay, László
8998.514	Zolotov, ĨU.A.
8998.52	Zorilla de San Martín, Juan
8998.56	Zorivchak, R.P.
8998.58	Zorzi, Giangiorgio
8998.66	Zubiri, Xavier
8998.67	Zuckmayer, Carl
8998.8	Zukofsky, Louis
8998.85	Zul'fugarly, D.I.
8998.9	Zunz, Leopold
8998.92	Żurakowski, Bogusław
8998.93	Zvonkov, V.V.
8998.94	Zweig, Arnold
8998.95	Zweig, Stefan
8999	Zwingli, Ulrich

Information resources (General)
> Class here works on sources of information in general, not limited to a specific topic, format, medium, or provider, as well as general works on how to find information
>
> For works limited to information on a specific subject, see the subject
>
> For technical works on online data processing see QA76.55+
>
> For works on information science as a discipline see Z664.2+
>
> For works limited to a specific format or medium see ZA4050+
>
> Cf. HC79.I55 Information economy
>
> Cf. Q350+ Information theory
>
> Cf. T58.5+ Information technology
>
> Cf. Z667+ Information storage and retrieval systems

3038	Bibliography
3040	Periodicals. Societies. Serials
3045	Congresses
3050	Directories. Catalogs. Lists of information sources
3060	General works
3070	Juvenile works
3072.A-Z	By region or country, A-Z

Research. Seeking and finding information. Information retrieval
> Including information behavior and information literacy

3075	General works
3080	Juvenile works

Information services. Information centers
> Including documentation centers, data libraries, bibliographical centers, etc.
>
> Cf. AG500+ Clipping bureaus
>
> Cf. HD9999.I49+ Information services industry
>
> Cf. Z662+ Libraries
>
> Cf. Z695.93+ Abstracting and indexing services

3150	Periodicals. Societies. Serials
3153	Congresses
3155	Directories
3157	General works
3159.A-Z	By region or country, A-Z

Under each country:

.x	*General works*
.x15.A-Z	*Local, A-Z*
.x2.A-Z	*Individual centers. By name, A-Z*

Information superhighway

3201	Periodicals. Societies. Serials
3203	Congresses
3225	General works
3235	Juvenile works

ZA

Information superhighway -- Continued

| 3250.A-Z | By region or country, A-Z |
| 3270 | Information commons |

Information in specific formats or media

For books and other print media see Z4+

Electronic information resources

4050	Catalogs. Lists of resources
4060	Research. How to use electronic information resources
4065	Electronic information resource literacy

Digital libraries

Class here works on the development and administration of digital libraries

For works on digital libraries on specific topics see the topic

For works on digital libraries as information resources see ZA4150+

4080	General works
4080.5	Collections development
4081.8	Children's digital libraries
4081.86	Institutional repositories
4082.A-Z	By region or country, A-Z

Under each country:

.x	*General works*
.x2A-.x2Z	*By region, state, or place, A-Z*
.x3A-.x3Z	*Individual digital libraries. By name, A-Z*

4084.A-Z	Special topics, A-Z
(4084.A78)	Art
	see N59
(4084.E37)	Education
	see L995
(4084.H85)	Humanities
	see AZ195
4084.M85	Multimedia
(4084.S25)	Science
	see Q224.5 (General); Q182.7 (Science education)

Computer network resources

For computer network resources on specific subjects, see the subject

For technical works on the telecommunications aspects of computer networks see TK5105.5+

| 4150 | General |

Resources of particular networks, online services, etc.

Including works on how to use individual networks or online services

Internet. World Wide Web

Including works on Web sites not limited to a specific topic

Information in specific formats or media
Electronic information resources
Computer network resources
Resources of particular networks, online services, etc. --
Continued
Cf. TK5105.888+ Technology

4195	Bibliography
4197	Web archives
	Class here general Web archives. For Web archives on special topics, see the topic.
4201	General works
4225	Directories
(4226)	World Wide Web (General works)
	see ZA4201
4228	Research
	Class here works on conducting research projects using the Internet
	Searching. Search engines
	Class here works on using search engines to retrieve information
	For works on the engineering and technology of search engines see TK5105.884+
4230	General works
4232	Subject access
4233	Federated searching
4234.A-Z	Individual search engines, A-Z
4234.G64	Google
4234.Y33	Yahoo
4235	Web users. Internet users
	Including web usage mining
4237	Invisible Web
4240	Semantic Web
	Cf. TK5105.88815 Technology
4251.A-Z	Particular online services, etc., A-Z
4251.A5	America Online
4251.C6	CompuServe
4251.D4	DELPHI
4251.E25	Echo
4251.E8	eWorld
4251.F57	FirstSearch
4251.G4	GEnie
4251.I96	iWon
4251.M5	Microsoft Network
	OCLC FirstSearch see ZA4251.F57
4251.P7	Prodigy
	Research. How to use networks, online services, etc.
	For particular networks, services, etc. see ZA4195+

ZA

Information in specific formats or media
Electronic information resources
Computer network resources
Research. How to use networks, online services, etc. --
Continued

4375	General works
4380	Juvenile works
4390	Computer bulletin boards

Databases
Including databases on CD-ROM and other physical media
For databases on specific subjects, see the subject

4450	Catalogs. Lists of databases
4460	Research. How to use databases
4480	Electronic discussion groups
4482	User-generated content

Motion pictures. Video recordings
For motion pictures and video recordings on specific subjects,
see the subject

4550 Lists and catalogs
Class here lists of nonfiction films and video recordings not
limited to a specific topic, as well as general lists that
include both fiction and nonfiction films
For lists of dramatic videos see PN1992.95
For lists of dramatic films see PN1998.A5+

4575 Research. How to use or find motion pictures
Pictures. Photographs
Cf. TR199 Catalogs of photographs (General)
Cf. TR640+ Artistic photographs

4650 Lists and catalogs
Pictures and photographs on specific subjects
see the subject

4675 Research. How to use or find pictures and photographs.
Picture research
Sound recordings
For sound recordings on specific subjects, see the subject

4750 Discographies. Lists and catalogs
Class here lists of non-music sound recordings not limited to
a specific topic, as well as general lists that include both
music and non-music sound recordings
For works limited to music, see class M

4775 Research. How to use or find sound recordings

Government information

> Class here works on government information not limited to a
> specific topic
> For government information on specific subjects, see the subject
> For works on government publicity, see JF1525.P8, JK849, etc.
> For works on public records, see JK468.P76, JL86.P76, etc
> For works on secret and confidential government information, see
> JK468.S4, JL86.S43, etc.
> For bibliographies of printed government publications see
> Z7164.G7

5049   General works

Lists and catalogs of government information resources

5050   General
5055.A-Z   By region or country, A-Z

Electronic government information resources

> For electronic government information resources on specific
> subjects, see the subject

5060   Catalogs. Lists of resources
5065   Research. How to use electronic government information
resources

Computer network resources

> Including government information resources on the Internet or
> on specific online services
> For computer network government information resources on
> specific subjects, see the subject

Lists, catalogs, directories, etc., of government
information resources

> Including government Web portals

5070   General

By region or country

United States

5075   General works
5076.A-Z   By region or state, A-Z
5078.A-Z   Other regions or countries, A-Z
5110   Research. How to use networks, online services, etc., to
retrieve government information
5120   Computer bulletin boards

Databases

> Including databases on CD-ROM and other physical media
> For databases of government information on specific
> subjects, see the subject

Lists and catalogs of databases of government
information

5180   General
5185.A-Z   By region or country, A-Z
5190   Research. How to use or find databases of government
information

ZA

1.A1	Bibliography of bibliography
1.A2	Theory, method, etc.
1.A3-Z	General bibliography
2	Bibliography of early works
2.5	History of bibliography
3	Publishers' catalogs
5	Periodicals
6	Societies
7	Collections. Festschriften, etc.
9	Government publications
	For bibliographies of government publications on specific topics, see the topics in Z5051+
10	Biobibliography
	Literature (General)
	For local see Z1 23+
11.A1	Bibliography of bibliography
11.A3-Z	General bibliography
	By period
12	Early through 1800
13	1801-1950
13.3	1951-
13.5.A-Z	Special classes or groups of writers, A-Z
13.5.A87	Australians, Aboriginal
	Authors in foreign countries see Z1 13.5.E42
13.5.E42	Émigré authors. Authors in foreign countries
13.5.G39	Gays
13.5.I44	Immigrant authors
13.5.J4	Jewish authors
13.5.W6	Women authors
14.A-Z	Special topics, A-Z
	For all forms of children's literature see Z1 14.5
	For local see Z1 23+
14.A5	Almanacs
14.A7	Argot
14.A74	Avant-garde (Aesthetics)
14.B2	Ballads
14.B6	Book reviews
14.C43	Chapbooks
14.C45	Characters and characteristics
14.C53	Chivalry
	Classical influences see Z1 14.C55
14.C55	Classicism. Classical influences
14.C78	Comparative literature
	Cf. Z6514.C7, Comparative literature (General)
14.C79	Country life
14.C797	Criminals
14.C8	Criticism

TABLES

470

Literature (General)
  Special topics, A-Z -- Continued

14.D47	Detective and mystery stories
14.D5	Dialect literature
14.D7	Drama. Theater
14.E76	Erotic literature
14.E8	Essays
14.E93	Expressionism
14.F34	Fantastic literature
14.F4	Fiction
14.F55	First editions
14.F6	Folk literature
14.F87	Futurism
14.G46	Ghost stories
14.H4	Hellenism
14.H58	History
14.H67	Horror tales
14.I8	Italy
14.L4	Letters
14.L45	Librarians
14.L5	Limited editions
14.L66	Lost books
14.M6	Modernism
14.M69	Mozarabic literature
14.M98	Muwashshah
	Mystery stories see Z1 14.D47
14.M985	Mythology
14.N36	Nasreddin Hoca (Legendary character)
	Pamphlets see Z1 27.P3
14.P35	Parodies
	Periodicals see Z1 5
14.P5	Picaresque literature
14.P7	Poetry
14.P79	Popular literature
14.P795	Prose
14.R32	Radio plays
14.R43	Refugees
14.R44	Religion
14.R6	Romances
14.R75	Romanticism
14.S3	Satire
14.S33	Science fiction
14.S45	Sequels
14.S5	Short stories
14.S6	Sonnets
14.S63	Sports
14.S64	Spy stories

TABLES

	Literature (General)
	Special topics, A-Z -- Continued
14.S8	Strambotto
14.T3	Tales
14.T43	Teachers
	Theater see Z1 14.D7
14.T7	Translations
14.U84	Utopias
14.W37	War
14.W54	Wills
14.W65	Women
14.Y68	Youth
14.Z35	Zaragoza (Spain), Siege of, 1808-1809
14.Z44	Zemstvos
14.5	Children's literature. Juvenile literature
	Language. Philology
	For philology and linguistics of African, Australian, Oceanian, Oriental and American Indian languages see Z7046+
15.A2	General
15.A3-Z	Special topics, A-Z
15.A4	Adverb
15.A44	Alphabet
15.D5	Dialects
15.D6	Dictionaries, glossaries, vocabularies, etc.
	Glossaries see Z1 15.D6
15.G7	Grammar
	Letter writing see Z1 14.L4
15.L48	Lexicography
15.L49	Lexicology
15.N34	Names
15.O7	Orthography
15.P43	Periodicals
15.P45	Phonology
15.P47	Phraseology
	Poetics see Z1 14.P7
15.R4	Readers
15.R5	Rhetoric
15.S4	Semantics
15.S55	Slang
15.S66	Spoken language
	Study and teaching
	see Z5818.L35; Z5818.C9; etc.
15.S86	Style
15.S9	Syntax
15.V27	Variation
15.V37	Versification
	Vocabularies see Z1 15.D6

TABLES

	Local
23	General
24.A-Z	Special, A-Z
27.A-Z	Special topics not otherwise provided for, A-Z
27.A43	Americans as an element in the population
	Antiquities see Z1 27.A67
27.A65	Arabs as an element in the population
27.A67	Archaeology. Antiquities
27.A74	Armenians as an element in the population
27.A9	Autobiography
	Blacks as an element in the population see Z1 27.N4
27.B55	Boers as an element in the population
27.B7	British as an element in the population
	Broadsides see Z1 27.P3
27.C5	Chinese as an element in the population
27.C55	Civilization. Intellectual life
27.C58	Cossacks
27.C74	Croats as an element in the population
27.D65	Dolgans as an element in the population
27.D8	Dutch as an element in the population
27.E2	East Indians as an element in the population
27.E85	Ethnology
	Including individual tribes
	For Indians, see Z1209
27.E87	Etruscans as an element in the population
27.E9	Eurasians as an element in the population
27.F55	Filipinos as an element in the population
27.F58	Finns as an element in the population
27.F65	Foreign opinion
27.F74	Friulians as an element in the population
27.G4	Germans as an element in the population
27.G73	Greeks as an element in the population
27.H8	Hungarians as an element in the population
	Intellectual life see Z1 27.C55
27.I75	Irish as an element in the population
27.I82	Italians as an element in the population
27.J3	Japanese as an element in the population
27.K6	Koreans as an element in the population
27.K88	Kushans as an element in the population
27.L42	Lebanese as an element in the population
27.M54	Minorities
27.M87	Muslims as an element in the population
27.N4	Negroes (Blacks) as an element in the population
27.N67	North Africans as an element in the population
27.P3	Pamphlets. Broadsides. Proclamations, etc. Street literature
27.P75	Poles as an element in the population
	Proclamations see Z1 27.P3

	Special topics not otherwise provided for, A-Z -- Continued
27.P87	Psychology
27.R3	Race question
27.R4	Relations with other countries
27.R6	Romanians as an element in the population
27.S24	Samaritans as an element in the population
27.S35	Selkups as an element in the population
27.S42	Sikhs as an element in the population
27.S45	Slovaks as an element in the population
27.S57	Social life and customs
	Street literature see Z1 27.P3
27.T87	Turks as an element in the population
27.U44	Ukrainians as an element in the population
27.W3	Walloons as an element in the population
27.W34	Walsers as an element in the population
27.5	Citizens residing in foreign countries (General)
29	Catalogs

TABLES

1.A1	Bibliography of bibliography
1.A2	Theory, method, etc.
1.A6-Z	General bibliography. Imprints (General)
2	Bibliography of early works
2.5	History of bibliography
2.8	Publishers' catalogs
3	Periodicals
4	Societies, etc.
4.2	Collections. Festschriften, etc.
5	Government publications
	For bibliographies of government publications on specific topics, see the topics in Z5051+
5.5	Biobibliography
6	General bibliography of the country as subject
	Including general history and description
7.A-Z	Local, A-Z
	History and description
	General see Z2 6
	By period
	For local see Z2 7.A+
8.A3	To 1500
8.A35	16th century
8.A39	17th-18th centuries
8.A4	19th century
8.A5	20th century
8.A55	21st century
8.A6-Z	Special topics, A-Z
	For list of Cutter numbers, see Table Z1 21.A+ or Table Z1 27.A+ except those listed here
	For local see Z2 7.A+
	Antiquities see Z2 8.A8
8.A8	Archaeology. Antiquities
	Drama see Z2 8.L5
8.E74	Ethnology
	Including individual ethnic groups
	Geography see Z2 6; Z2 7.A+; Z2 8.A2+
8.H5	Historiography
	Juvenile literature see Z2 8.L6
	Language see Z2 8.L5
8.L5	Literature, language, poetry, drama, etc.
	For philology and linguistics of African, Australian, Oceanian, Oriental and American Indian languages see Z7046+
8.L6	Children's literature. Juvenile literature
	National characteristics see Z2 8.P7
	Poetry see Z2 8.L5
8.P7	Psychology. National characteristics
8.R3	Race question

9   Catalogs

TABLES

1.A1   Bibliography of bibliography
1.A2   Theory, method, etc.
1.A6-Z   General bibliography. Imprints (General)
                    Including general bibliography of the country as subject and
                        including publishers' catalogs
2   Government publications
                    For bibliographies of government publications on specific topics,
                        see the topics in Z5051+
3.A-Z   Local, A-Z
                History and description see Z3 1.A6+
4.A-Z   Special topics, A-Z
                    Subarrange like Z2 8.A6+
5   Catalogs

1.A1	Bibliography of bibliography
1.A2	Theory, method, etc.
1.A3-Z	General bibliography
2	Bibliography of early works
3	Periodicals. Societies
4.A-Z	Special topics, A-Z
5.A-Z	Local, A-Z
6	Catalogs
6.Z9	Sales catalogs

TABLES

1.A1	Bibliography of bibliography
1.A2	Theory, method, etc.
1.A3-Z	General bibliography
2	Bibliography of early works
3	Periodicals. Societies
4.A-Z	Special topics, A-Z
5	Catalogs
5.Z9	Sales catalogs

1.A1	Bibliography of bibliography
1.A2	Theory, method, etc.
1.A3-Z	General bibliography
2	Periodicals. Societies
3.A-Z	Special topics, A-Z
3.V66	Voting
4.A-Z	By region or country, A-Z

    Under each country:

.x	*General works*
.x2A-.x2Z	*Local, A-Z*
5	Catalogs
5.Z9	Sales catalogs

TABLES

1	General works
	Including topics and forms not otherwise provided for
2	Bibliography
3	History
	Arrange histories of individual firms by name of firm, A-Z
	Including histories of individual firms, and including collective and individual biography
	For catalogs, see Publishers' catalogs in national bibliography, e. g. Z1217, United States publishers' catalogs
4	Special lines of business (not A-Z)
5	Directories
6	Handbooks, manuals, etc.
7	Periodicals. Societies. Congresses
8	Collections
	Local
8.3.A-Z	By state or region, A-Z
8.6.A-Z	By city, A-Z

1	General works
	Including topics and forms not otherwise provided for
1.2	Bibliography
1.3	History
	Arrange histories of individual firms by name of firm, A-Z
	Including histories of individual firms, and including collective and individual biography
	For catalogs, see Publishers' catalogs in national bibliography, e. g. Z1217, United States publishers' catalogs
1.4	Special lines of business (not A-Z)
1.5	Directories
1.6	Handbooks, manuals, etc.
1.7	Periodicals. Societies. Congresses
1.8	Collections
	Local
1.83.A-Z	By state or region, A-Z
1.86.A-Z	By city, A-Z

TABLES

.x	General works
	Including topics and forms not otherwise provided for
.x2	Bibliography
.x3	History
	Arrange histories of individual firms by name of firm, A-Z
	Including histories of individual firms, and including collective and individual biography
	For catalogs, see Publishers' catalogs in national bibliography e. g. Z1217, United States publishers' catalogs
.x4	Special lines of business (not A-Z)
.x5	Directories
.x6	Handbooks, manuals, etc.
.x7	Periodicals. Societies. Congresses
.x8	Collections
	Local
.x83A-.x83Z	By state or region, A-Z
.x86A-.x86Z	By city, A-Z

.A1	Catalogs of collections not confined to one region, state, etc.
.A12A-.A12Z	By region, state, etc., A-Z
.A13A-.A13Z	By city, county, etc., A-Z
.A14-.Z	Individual libraries. By place, A-Z

TABLES

.xA1-.xA119	Catalogs of collections not confined to one region, state, etc.
.xA12-.xA129	By region, state, etc.
	Arrange alphabetically
.xA13-.xA139	By city, county, etc.
	Arrange alphabetically
.xA14-.xZ	Individual libraries, A-Z

1   General works
                        Including topics and forms not otherwise provided for
1.2   Bibliography
1.3   History
                        For catalogs, see publishers' catalogs in national bibliography, e. g.
                               Z1217, United States publishers' catalogs
1.4   Special lines of business (not A-Z)
1.5   Directories
1.6   Handbooks, manuals, etc.
1.7   Periodicals. Societies. Congresses
1.8   Collections

TABLES

.xA1-.xA19	Periodicals. Societies. Serials
.xA2-.xA29	History
.xA3	Dictionaries. By date
.xA4-.xA49	Dictation exercises and tests
.xA5-.xZ8	Manuals
.xZ9-.xZ99	Transcriptions of literary works. By author of original works

1   General bibliography
2.A-Z   Regions, counties, cities, etc., A-Z

TABLES

.x   General works
.x2A-.x2Z   Local, A-Z

.x	General bibliography
.x2	Societies
	Universities
.x3	Collective
.x4A-.x4Z	Invididual. By city and institution, A-Z

1   General bibliography
2   Societies
                          Universities
3   Collective
4A-4Z   Invididual. By city and institution, A-Z

Arctic regions
  Bibliography
    Geography: Z6005.A73
  Libraries
    Mechanized bibliographic control:
      Z699.5.A72
Area studies
  Bibliography
    History: Z6208.A73
  Libraries: Z675.A84
    Classification: Z697.A78
    Special collections: Z688.A68
Argentina: Z1611+
  Bibliography
    Botany: Z5358.A8
Argot: Z1 14.A7
Arid regions
  Bibliography: Z6004.A7
Arid regions agriculture
  Bibliography: Z5074.A83
Arid regions ecology
  Bibliography: Z5322.A74
Arithmetic
  Bibliography: Z6654.A7
    Education: Z5818.A7
Arithmetics, Printers': Z245
Armenia: Z3461+
Armenian manuscripts: Z115.5.A7
  Bibliography: Z6605.A7
Armenian paleography: Z115.5.A7
Armenian philology and linguistics
  Bibliography: Z7054
Armenian shorthand: Z58.85
Armenian type: Z251.A7
Armenians as an element in the
  population: Z1 27.A74
Armeno-Kipchak manuscripts:
  Z6605.A72
Arminians
  Bibliography: Z7845.A8
Armor
  Bibliography
    Costume: Z5693.A7
Armorial bindings: Z269.3.A75
Arms control verification
  Bibliography: Z6724.A73

Arms race
  Bibliography: Z6724.A75
Aromatherapy: Z6665.A67
Aromatic compounds
  Bibliography
    Chemistry: Z5524.A75
Aromatic plants
  Bibliography: Z5074.A85
  Medicine: Z6665.A67
Ars moriendi
  Bibliography: Z6521.A8
Arson
  Bibliography: Z5703.4.A75
Art
  Bibliography
    Education: Z5818.A8
    Literature: Z6514.A77
    Manuscripts: Z6611.A7
  Bookplates: Z994.5.A76
  Libraries
    Classification: Z697.A8
    Mechanized bibliographic control:
      Z699.5.A75
    Reference work: Z711.6.A76
Art auctions
  Bibliography: Z5956.A66
Art books
  Libraries
    Special collections: Z688.A7
Art deco
  Bibliography: Z5936.A76
Art industries
  Bibliography: Z5956.A68
Art libraries: Z675.A85
Art museums
  Bibliography
    Architecture: Z5943.A77
Art nouveau
  Architecture
    Bibliography: Z5941.396
  Bibliography: Z5936.N6
Art publishing
  Bookselling and publishing: Z286.A77
Art typing: Z50.2
Art, Visual
  Libraries
    Cataloging: Z695.1.A7

Asparagus
  Bibliography: Z5074.A87
Asphalt
  Bibliography: Z7914.A8
Aspirin
  Bibliography
    Therapeutics: Z6665.A7
Assamese manuscripts
  Bibliography: Z6605.A75
Assaying
  Bibliography: Z6679.A8
Assertiveness
  Bibliography
    Psychology: Z7204.A78
Association libararies: Z675.A87
Associations
  Bibliography
    Political and social sciences:
      Z7164.A85
    Bookselling and publishing: Z286.T7
Assyrians (Nestorians)
  Middle East: Z3014.A77
Assyriology
  Bibliography
    Oriental philology and linguistics:
      Z7055
Asteroids
  Bibliography: Z5154.A85
Asthma
  Bibliography: Z6664.A8
ASTRA (Computer program)
  Word processing: Z52.5.A77
Astrology
  Bibliography: Z6878.A88
    Manuscripts: Z6611.A8
Astronautics
  Bibliography: Z5061.A1+, Z6683.A7
Astronautics in earth science
  Bibliography: Z6033.A8
Astronomy
  Bibliography: Z5151+
    Manuscripts: Z6611.A85
Athapascan philology and linguistics
  Bibliography: Z7119.A9
Atheism
  Bibliography: Z7765
    Literature: Z6514.A85

Atherosclerosis
  Bibliography: Z6664.A79
Athoensen, Fred: Z232.A63
Atlantis
  Bibliography
    Geography: Z6005.A8
Atlases
  Bibliography
    Astronomy: Z5151.5
    Science: Z7405.A8
  Libraries
    Cataloging: Z695.6
Atmosphere, Upper
  Bibliography: Z6683.A8
Atmospheric circulation
  Bibliography: Z6683.A83
Atmospheric radioactivity
  Bibliography: Z5158
Atomic arms control verification
  Bibliography: Z6724.A73
Atomic energy
  Bibliography: Z5160+
  Libraries
    Cataloging: Z695.1.A86
    Mechanized bibliographic control:
      Z699.5.A85
Atomic medicine
  Bibliography: Z6675.A8
Atomic power
  Bibliography: Z5160+
Atomic ships
  Bibliography: Z6834.A7
Atomic warfare
  Bibliography: Z6724.A9
Attitude and attitude change
  Bibliography
    Psychology: Z7204.A8
Aucassin et Nicolette
  Bibliography: Z6521.A92
Auction catalogs
  Booksellers: Z998+
Auctions, Art
  Bibliography: Z5956.A66
Audin, Marius: Z232.A862
Audio players, Preloaded
  Cataloging: Z695.7184
Audio-visual library service: Z716.65+

Cargo handling
  Bibliography
    Navigation: Z6839.C3
Caribbean Area: Z1595
  Libraries
    Cataloging: Z695.1.C32
    Special collections: Z688.C34
Caribbean authors
  Canadian literature: Z1376.C37
Caribou
  Bibliography: Z7996.C28
Caricatures
  Bibliography: Z5956.C3
Carlists: Z1 21.C3
Carmelites
  Bibliography: Z7840.C2
Carnival
  Bibliography: Z5711.C37
Carpal tunnel syndrome: Z6664.C25
Carpathian Mountains
  Bibliography
    Geography: Z6005.C3
Carpets
  Bibliography: Z7914.T3
Carriages and carts
  Bibliography: Z7914.C32
Carrots
  Bibliography
    Gardening: Z5996.C36
Cars
  Bibliography
    Railroads: Z7234.C3
Carter, Will: Z232.C28
Carthage: Z3513
Carthusians
  Bibliography: Z7840.C3
Cartographic materials
  Libraries
    Cataloging: Z695.6
Cartography
  Bibliography: Z6001+
  Libraries
    Mechanized bibliographic control:
      Z699.5.C3
Cartoons
  Bibliography: Z5956.C3

Casa Literária do Arco do Cego:
  Z232.C35
Case
  Linguistics: Z7004.C36
Caseg Press: Z232.C354
Cashew
  Bibliography
    Gardening: Z5996.C37
Casino gaming
  Bibliography: Z7164.G35
Casinos
  Bibliography
    Architecture: Z5943.C34
Cassava
  Bibliography: Z5074.C28
  Libraries
    Cataloging: Z695.1.C34
Cast-iron
  Bibliography: Z6333.C3
Caste
  Bibliography: Z7164.C2
Casting
  Bibliography
    Technology: Z7914.C33
Castles
  Bibliography
    Architecture: Z5943.C35
Castor bean
  Bibliography: Z5074.C3
Catalan
  Bibliography
    Romance philology and linguistics:
      Z7033.C37
Catalan manuscripts
  Bibliography: Z6605.C36
Catalan newspapers
  Bibliography: Z6944.C38
Catalan shorthand: Z59.3
Catalog cards
  Libraries
    Cataloging: Z693.3.C37
Catalog maintenance
  Libraries: Z695.88
Catalog management
  Libraries: Z695.88
Catalogers
  Libraries: Z682.4.C38

Church and state
  Bibliography: Z7776.72
Church architecture
  Bibliography: Z5943.C56
    Manuscripts: Z6611.C58
Church doorways
  Bibliography
    Sculpture: Z5953.D66
Church growth
  Bibliography: Z7776.8
Church history
  Bibliography: Z7777+
    Manuscripts: Z6611.C59
Church libraries: Z675.C5
Church management
  Bibliography: Z7781
Church of Ireland
  Bibliography: Z7845.C52
Church of Jesus Christ
  Bibliography: Z7845.C53
Church of Scientology
  Bibliography: Z7835.S35
Church Slavic
  Bibliography
    Philology and linguistics: Z7044.C4
Church Slavic manuscripts: Z115.5.C57
  Bibliography: Z6605.S62
Church Slavic paleography:
  Z115.5.C57
Church Slavic type: Z251.C56
Chuvash philology and linguistics
  Bibliography: Z7101.C56
Cigarette smoke
  Bibliography
    Chemistry: Z5524.C6
Cinchona
  Bibliography: Z5074.C5
Cinematography
  Bibliography: Z7136.C5
Cingalese manuscripts
  Bibliography: Z6605.S45
CIP
  Libraries
    Cataloging: Z693.3.C38
Ciphers: Z103.5+
Circuit breakers
  Bibliography: Z5834.C5

Circulation
  Libraries: Z712+
Circumcision: Z6667.C57
  Bibliography
    Anthropology and ethnology:
      Z5118.C57
Circumpolar medicine
  Bibliography: Z6664.33
Circuses
  Bibliography: Z7514.C6
Cirsium arvense
  Bibliography: Z5356.C57
CISS System: Z699.4.C2
Cistercians
  Bibliography: Z7840.C5
    Manuscripts: Z6611.C62
Cities
  Libraries
    Cataloging: Z695.1.C63
Cities and towns
  Bibliography
    Geography: Z6004.C5
Cities and towns in art
  Bibliography: Z5956.C55
Citizen participation
  Bibliography
    Atomic energy and power:
      Z5162.C57
Citizens residing in foreign countries:
  Z1 27.5
Citizenship
  Bibliography: Z7164.C57
    International law and relations:
      Z6464.C6
Citrus fruits
  Bibliography
    Gardening: Z5996.C6
City churches
  Bibliography: Z7782
City halls
  Bibliography
    Architecture: Z5943.C563
City maps
  Bibliography: Z6026.C56
City planning
  Bibliography
    Architecture: Z5942

Diplomatics
  Libraries
    Cataloging: Z695.1.D56
Diptera: Z5858.D5
Direct energy conversion
  Bibliography
    Electricity: Z5834.D55
Direction
  Bibliography
    Drama: Z5784.P7
Directories
  Bibliography: Z5771+
    Science: Z7405.D55
  Bookselling and publishing: Z286.D57
  Libraries: Z721+
    United States: Z731
Directors
  Libraries: Z682.4.A34
Disarmament
  Bibliography: Z6464.D6
    League of Nations: Z6475.D5
Disaster medicine: Z6675.E45
Disasters
  Bibliography: Z5772
Discarding
  Libraries: Z703.6
Disciples of Christ
  Bibliography: Z7845.D6
Discipline
  Education
    Bibliography: Z5814.D49
Discographies
  Information resources: ZA4750
Discourse analysis
  Bibliography: Z7004.D57
Discovery of America: Z1212
Discrimination
  Education
    Bibliography: Z5814.D5
Disinfection and disinfectants
  Bibliography: Z6673.1
Displaced persons
  Bibliography
    History: Z6207.D5
Display type: Z250.5.D57
DisplayWrite 3 (Computer program)
  Word processing: Z52.5.D59

DisplayWrite 4 (Computer program)
  Word processing: Z52.5.D6
DisplayWrite 5 (Computer program)
  Word processing: Z52.5.D62
DisplayWrite (Computer program)
  Word processing: Z52.5.D57
Disposal of the dead
  Bibliography: Z5994
Disposition of books on shelves
  Libraries: Z703.5
Dissenters
  Bibliography: Z7845.D62
Dissertations
  Libraries
    Preservation, restoration, etc:
      Z701.3.D57
Dissertations, Academic
  Libraries
    Cataloging: Z695.1.D57
Dissociative disorders
  Bibliography
    Psychiatry: Z6665.7.D57
Distance education
  Bibliography: Z5814.D54
Distance education and libraries:
  Z718.85
Distillation
  Bibliography
    Chemistry: Z5524.D58
Distilleries
  Bibliography
    Architecture: Z5943.B73
Distributing
  Practical printing: Z253+
Divining rod
  Bibliography: Z6878.D6
Divorce
  Bibliography: Z7164.M2
Djibouti (Republic): Z3687
DOBIS System: Z699.4.D62
Document delivery
  Libraries: Z711.95
Documentary photography
  Bibliography: Z7136.D63
Documentation centers
  Libraries: ZA3150+

Dyslexia
  Bibliography: Z6671.52.D97
Dyslexic children
  Books for: Z1039.D94
Dyslexic readers
  Books for: Z1039.D94

E

Eagles
  Bibliography: Z5333.E2
Early Christian fine arts
  Bibliography: Z5933.2
Early drama
  Bibliography: Z5782.A1+
Early printed books
  Libraries
    Cataloging: Z695.3
    Mechanized bibliographic control:
      Z699.5.E16
Earth sciences
  Bibliography
    Education: Z5818.E3
Earth temperature
  Bibliography: Z6033.T35
Earthquakes
  Bibliography: Z6033.E1
  Libraries
    Mechanized bibliographic control:
      Z699.5.E18
Earthworks (Art)
  Bibliography: Z5936.E27
East Africa: Z3516
East and West
  Bibliography
    Civilization: Z5579.15.E25
East Asia
  Libraries
    Special collections: Z688.E25
East Asian libraries: Z675.E22
East Asian publications
  Libraries
    Cataloging: Z695.1.E17
East Germany: Z2250
East Indians as an element in the
  population: Z1 27.E2

East Indians in the United States
  Bibliography: Z1361.E37
Easter
  Bibliography: Z5711.E2
Easter eggs
  Bibliography: Z6153.E27
Eastern churches
  Bibliography: Z7845.E3
Eastern Europe: Z2483+
Eastern Hemisphere: Z1975
Eastern question
  Bibliography: Z6464.E1
Eastern redcedar
  Bibliography: Z5356.E37
Eastern Slavic
  Bibliography
    Philology and linguistics:
      Z7044.E37
Easy reading books: Z1033.H53
EasyWriter (Computer program)
  Word processing: Z52.5.E27
EasyWriter II (Computer program)
  Word processing: Z52.5.E28
Eating disorders
  Bibliography
    Psychiatry: Z6665.7.E28
Eccentric literature: Z1021
Ecclesiastical law
  Bibliography: Z7776
Ecclesiastical maps
  Bibliography: Z6026.E3
Echinodermata
  Bibliography: Z7996.E35
Echo (Online service): ZA4251.E25
Ecology
  Bibliography: Z5322.E2
    Botany: Z5354.E1
  Libraries
    Mechanized bibliographic control:
      Z699.5.E23
    Special collections: Z688.E28
Ecology, Agricultural
  Bibliography: Z5074.E29
Ecology, Human
  Bibliography: Z5861+
Econometrics
  Bibliography: Z7164.E12

Elk
  Bibliography: Z7996.E43
Ellandi, Otto: Z232.E45
Ellis, Richard Williamson: Z232.E47
Elsevier, family of printers: Z232.E5
Elsevier type: Z250.5.E45
Ema Insatsu Kabushiki Kaisha:
  Z232.E56
Embassy buildings
  Bibliography
    Architecture: Z5943.E45
Embezzlement
  Bibliography: Z5703.4.E46
Emblem books: Z1021.3
Emblems
  Bibliography: Z1021.3
Embossed bindings: Z269.3.E42
Embroidered bindings: Z269.3.E43
Embroidery
  Bibliography: Z6153.E42
    Fine arts: Z5956.L2
Embryology
  Bibliography
    Birds: Z5333.A25
    Zoology: Z7994.E7
Emergency medical services
  Bibliography: Z6675.E45
Emergency medicine
  Bibliography: Z6664.34, Z6675.E45
Emigration
  Bibliography: Z7164.I3
Émigré authors: Z1 13.5.E42
Emission
  Bibliography
    Physics: Z7144.E45
Emotions
  Bibliography
    Psychology: Z7204.E5
    Religion: Z7785
Emperor goose: Z5333.E55
Employee fringe benefits
  Libraries
    Mechanized bibliographic control:
      Z699.5.E56
Employee orientation
  Libraries: Z682.35.E63

Employee training
  Education
    Bibliography: Z5814.T4
Employees, Medical care of
  Bibliography: Z6675.E2
Employees, Rating of
  Libraries: Z682.28
Employees' representation in
  management
  Bibliography: Z7164.E55
Employers' associations
  Bibliography: Z7164.E57
Employment
  Bibliography
    Veterans: Z6724.V4
  Libraries: Z682.35.E65
  Women
    Bibliography: Z7963.E7
Empoasca fabae: Z5858.E46
Emser, Hieronymus: Z232.E58
Emus
  Bibliography: Z5074.E48
Enable/OA (Computer program)
  Word processing: Z52.5.E52
Enameling
  Bibliography: Z7914.E5
Encephalitis
  Bibliography: Z6664.E55
Encyclicals, Papal
  Bibliography
    Catholic Church: Z7838.E5
Encyclopedias
  Bibliography: Z5848+
    Political and social sciences:
      Z7164.D53
    Science: Z7405.D5
Encyclopédie, ou Dictionnaire raisonné
  des sciences
  Bibliography: Z6523.E5
End of the world
  Bibliography
    Religion: Z7786
End papers
  Bookbinding: Z271.3.E53
Endangered plants
  Bibliography: Z5354.P73

Examinations
  Education
    Bibliography: Z5814.E9
    Library collections: Z692.E82
    Word processing: Z52.3
Exceptional children
  Libraries
    Cataloging: Z695.1.E93
Exchange of bibliographic information
  Libraries
    Mechanized bibliographic control:
      Z699.35.E94
Exchanges
  Libraries
    Collections: Z690
Excursions, School
  Bibliography: Z5814.E93
Executive departments
  United States
    National Bibliography: Z1249.E9
Exercise (Physiological effect)
  Bibliography: Z6663.E9
Exercises
  Word processing: Z52.3
Exhibition buildings
  Bibliography
    Architecture: Z5943.E95
Exhibition catalogs
  Libraries
    Cataloging: Z695.1.E95
Exhibitions
  Bibliography: Z5883
Exhibitions of books, etc. in libraries:
  Z717+
Existentialism
  Bibliography: Z7128.E9
Exobiology
  Bibliography: Z5322.E95
Exorcism
  Bibliography: Z6878.E9
EXP (Computer program)
  Word processing: Z52.5.E95
Expanded type: Z250.5.E86
Expeditions
  Bibliography
    Science: Z7405.E9

Experimental design
  Bibliography
    Mathematics: Z6654.E9
Experiments in art and technology
  Bibliography: Z5936.E87
Expert systems
  Bibliography
    Computer science: Z5643.E956
  Library science: Z678.93.E93
Expert writer
  Word processing: Z52.5.E97
Expertising of manuscripts: Z110.E9
Explosives
  Bibliography: Z5885
Express publisher
  Desktop publishing: Z253.532.E94
Expressionism
  Art
    Bibliography: Z5936.E9
  Literature: Z1 14.E93
Expurgated books: Z1019+
Extension teaching
  Bibliography: Z5814.E95
Extension work
  Bibliography
    Agriculture: Z5074.E8
Exterior walls
  Bibliography: Z7914.E93
Extra-curricular activities
  Education
    Bibliography: Z5814.S89
Extra illustrated books: Z1023
Extraction
  Bibliography
    Chemistry: Z5524.E9
Extradition
  Bibliography
    International law and relations:
      Z6464.E8
Eye movements
  Bibliography
    Medicine: Z6663.E95
Ezra (Book of the Bible)
  Bibliography: Z7772.C42

F

Fables
  Bibliography: Z5896
Fabrics
  Bibliography: Z7914.T3
Facades
  Bibliography
    Architecture: Z5943.F2
Facial expression
  Bibliography
    Psychology: Z7204.F34
Facial injuries
  Bibliography
    Surgery: Z6667.H4
Facilities, School
  Bibliography: Z5814.F3
Facility management
  Bibliography: Z7914.F25
Facsimile editions: Z1033.F3
Facsimile transmission
  Library science: Z680.6
Facsimiles, Collections of
  Autographs: Z42
Factory and trade waste
  Bibliography: Z5862.2.F32
Factory layout
  Bibliography: Z7914.F3
Factory libraries: Z675.F3
Fair use
  Copyright: Z649.F35
Fairy tales
  Bibliography: Z5983.F17
Falconry
  Bibliography: Z7514.F2
Falcons
  Bibliography: Z5333.F34
Falkland Islands: Z1945
Families
  Library service to: Z711.92.F34
Family
  Bibliography: Z7164.M2
    Anthropology and ethnology:
      Z5118.F2
    Jews: Z6374.F34
Family medicine
  Bibliography: Z6665.3

Family psychotherapy
  Bibliography: Z6665.7.F35
Family violence
  Bibliography: Z5703.4.F35
Fantastic fiction
  Bibliography: Z5917.F3
  Bookselling and publishing: Z286.F3
Fantastic literature: Z1 14.F34
  Bibliography: Z6514.F35
  Libraries
    Classification: Z697.F29
Fantastic, The (Aesthetics)
  Bibliography: Z5956.F34
Fantasy
  Bookplates: Z994.5.F35
Fares
  Bibliography
    Railroads: Z7234.F2
Farm buildings
  Bibliography: Z5074.B9
    Architecture: Z5943.F3
Farm management
  Bibliography: Z5074.F25
Farmhouses
  Bibliography
    Architecture: Z5943.F3
Farming
  Anthropology: Z5118.F27
Farms, Historic
  Bibliography: Z5074.H63
Fascism: Z1 21.F2
  Bookplates: Z994.5.F37
  By region or country
    Europe: Z2000.7
Fashion design libraries: Z675.C78
Fat
  Bibliography
    Medicine: Z6663.F3
Fate and fatalism
  Bibliography: Z7128.F2
Fathers of the Church
  Bibliography: Z7791
Fatigue
  Bibliography
    Medicine: Z6663.F34
Fats and oils
  Bibliography: Z7914.O3

Heteroptera: Z5858.H6
Hevea
  Bibliography: Z5074.H58
Hexateuch
  Bibliography: Z7772.B4
Hieroglyphic Bibles
  Bibliography: Z7771.I3
Hieroglyphic type: Z251.H6
High-fiber diet
  Bibliography
    Therapeutics: Z6665.H54
High-fidelity sound systems
  Bibliography: Z5838.H5
High interest-low vocabulary books:
  Z1033.H53
  Bookselling and publishing: Z286.H47
High pressure
  Bibliography
    Physics: Z7144.H5
High-priced books: Z1022
High school students
  Books for: Z1039.H54
  Library orientation: Z711.25.H54
High schools
  Bibliography: Z5814.H55+
High speed ground transportation
  Bibliography
    Railroads: Z7234.H53
High-speed photography
  Bibliography: Z7136.H5
High technology industries
  Bibliography: Z7164.H54
High temperatures
  Bibliography
    Technology: Z7914.H45
High tension
  Bibliography
    Electricity: Z5834.H55
Higher education
  Bibliography: Z5814.U7
Highlands of Scotland: Z2063.H5
Highway traffic
  Bibliography: Z7164.T81
Highways
  Bibliography: Z7295
Hijar, Gabriel de: Z232.H613

Hiking
  Bibliography: Z6016.H5
Hill farming
  Bibliography: Z5074.H6
Himalaya Mountains
  Bibliography
    Geography: Z6005.H6
Hindi manuscripts
  Bibliography: Z6605.H5
Hindi philology and linguistics
  Bibliography: Z7071
Hindi typewriters: Z49.4.H5
Hindu architecture
  Bibliography: Z5943.H56
Hindu philosophy: Z7128.H55
Hinduism
  Bibliography: Z7835.B8
    Manuscripts: Z6611.H49
Hiring of architects
  Library buildings: Z679.5
Hiring of consultants
  Library buildings: Z679.5
Hispanic Americans
  Bibliography
    Communication and mass media:
      Z5633.H57
  Libraries
    Personnel: Z682.4.H58
    Special collections: Z688.H57
    Library service to: Z711.92.H56
Hispanic civilization
  Bibliography: Z5579.15.H57
Hispaniola: Z1530.5+
Historic buildings: Z1 21.H49
  Bibliography
    Architecture: Z5943.H58
Historic farms
  Bibliography: Z5074.H63
Historic monuments: Z1 21.H49
  Bibliography
    Preservation: Z5133.P73
Historical Books (Old Testament)
  Bibliography: Z7772.B45
Historical fiction
  Bibliography: Z5917.H6

Hungarians in the United States
  Bibliography: Z1361.H84
Hungary: Z2141+
Hunt roman type: Z250.5.H8
Hunting
  Bibliography: Z5994.6, Z7514.H9
Hunting and gathering societies
  Bibliography
    Anthropology and ethnology:
      Z5118.H86
Hunting, Deer
  Bibliography: Z7514.D44
Huon de Bordeaux
  Bibliography: Z6521.H8
Hurricanes
  Bibliography: Z6683.S8
Hussites
  Bibliography: Z7845.H85
Hutegger (Firm): Z232.H87
Hutterites
  Bibliography: Z7845.H86
Hyaluronidase
  Bibliography
    Medicine: Z6663.H9
Hybridization
  Bibliography
    Biology: Z5322.H93
Hydraulic engineering
  Bibliography: Z5853.H9
Hydraulic mining
  Bibliography: Z6738.H9
Hydraulic turbines
  Bibliography: Z5853.H95
Hydrocyanic acid
  Bibliography: Z5524.H9
Hydrodynamics
  Bibliography
    Physics: Z7144.H9
Hydroelectric power stations
  Bibliography: Z5834.P7
Hydrofoil boats
  Bibliography: Z6834.H8
Hydrogen
  Bibliography: Z5524.H94
Hydrogenation
  Bibliography: Z7914.H9

Hydrogeology
  Libraries
    Mechanized bibliographic control:
      Z699.5.H9
Hydrographic maps
  Bibliography: Z6026.H9
Hydrographic surveying
  Bibliography
    Navigation: Z6839.H92
Hydrography
  Bibliography: Z6004.P5+
Hydrology
  Bibliography
    Geography: Z6004.H9
  Libraries
    Classification: Z697.H9
    Mechanized bibliographic control:
      Z699.5.H93
Hydrometallurgy
  Bibliography: Z6679.H9
Hydrometeorology
  Libraries
    Mechanized bibliographic control:
      Z699.5.H95
Hydroponics
  Bibliography: Z5074.H9
Hygiene
  Bibliography: Z6673+
    Infants: Z6673.3
    League of Nations: Z6475.H4
Hygiene, Industrial
  Libraries
    Classification: Z697.I37
Hygiene of children
  Bibliography
    Political and social sciences:
      Z7164.C5
Hygiene, School
  Bibliography: Z5814.H9
Hymenoptera: Z5858.H9
Hymnology
  Bibliography: Z7800
Hymns
  Bibliography
    Manuscripts: Z6611.H95
Hypertension
  Bibliography: Z6664.H9

Hypertext systems: Z678.93.H94
Hypnotism
  Bibliography
    Medicine: Z6675.H9
Hypomycetaceae
  Bibliography: Z5356.H95

I

I AM Religious Activity
  Bibliography: Z7835.I14
I ching
  Bibliography
    Literature: Z6521.I2
Iatrogenic diseases
  Bibliography: Z6664.I28
IBAS System: Z699.4.I13
IBM Displaywriter
  Word processing: Z52.5.I24
IBM PCjr (Computer)
  Word processing: Z52.5.I26
IBM Personal Computer
  Word processing: Z52.5.I27
İbrahim Müteferrika, 1674?-1745:
  Z232.I14
Ice
  Bibliography
    Geography: Z6004.I2
Ice cream, ices, etc
  Bibliography: Z6270
Ice hockey
  Bibliography: Z7514.H73
Ice navigation
  Bibliography: Z6839.I25
Iceland: Z2590+
Icelanders in Canada: Z1395.I43
Icelandic: Z2556
Icelandic manuscripts
  Bibliography: Z6605.I3
Identification
  Bibliography
    Zoology: Z7994.I34
Iglesia Christiana Evangelica
  Bibliography: Z7845.I35
Ilex
  Bibliography: Z5356.I2
Iliazd: Z232.I26

Illegitimacy
  Bibliography
    Political and social sciences:
      Z7164.I25
ILLINET: Z674.82.I52
Illinois Valley Library System:
  Z674.82.I53
Illiteracy
  Bibliography: Z5814.I3
Illiterate, Libraries and the: Z716.45
Illumination of books and manuscripts
  Bibliography: Z5948.M6
Illustrated Bibles
  Bibliography: Z7771.I3
Illustrated books: Z1023
  Libraries
    Preservation, restoration, etc:
      Z701.3.I45
Illustration of books
  Bibliography
    Fine arts: Z5956.I44
Illustrations
  Libraries
    Preservation, restoration, etc:
      Z701.3.I45
Illustrations, Printing of
  Presswork: Z257
Iloko philology and linguistics
  Bibliography: Z7101.I3
Image files
  Libraries
    Mechanized bibliographic control:
      Z699.5.P53
Image transmission
  Library science: Z680.6
Imaginary bookplates: Z995.5
Imaginary books: Z1024
Imaginary voyages
  Bibliography: Z6017.A1+
Imitatio Christi
  Bibliography: Z7803
Immigrant authors: Z1 13.5.I44
Immigrants
  Bibliography
    Modern literature: Z6520.I5
  Library service to: Z711.8

Information display systems
Bibliography: Z5838.I5
Information filtering systems: Z667.6+
Information literacy: ZA3075+
Information networks: Z674.7+
Information organization
Library science: Z666.5+
Information resources (General): ZA3038+
Information retrieval systems
Library science: Z667+
Information science: Z664.2+
Libraries
Cataloging: Z695.1.I56
Information services
Bibliography
Applied science and technology: Z7914.I55
Libraries: ZA3150+
Information storage and retrieval systems
Libraries: Z699+
Information superhighway: ZA3201+
Information technology
Library science: Z678.9+
Informetrics: Z669.8
Infrared photography
Bibliography: Z7136.I5
Infusoria
Bibliography: Z7996.I4
Initiation rites
Bibliography
Catholic Church: Z7838.I54
Initiative and referendum
Bibliography: Z7164.I5
Ink
Penmanship: Z45
Practical printing: Z247
Ink jet printing: Z252.5.I48
Ink, Printing
Bibliography: Z7914.P75
Inland navigation
Bibliography: Z6839.I6
INMAGIC
Automation: Z678.93.I55
INNOPAC
Automation: Z678.93.I56

INNOPAC System: Z699.4.I15
Innovations
Bibliography
Agriculture: Z5074.I55
Inquisition
Bibliography: Z7805
Inscriptions
Bibliography
Classical languages and literatures: Z7018.I5
Greek philology and linguistics: Z7023.I5
Latin philology and linguistics: Z7028.I5
Inscriptions, Slavic
Bibliography: Z7044.I5
Insecticides
Bibliography: Z5858.E2
Toxicology: Z7891.I57
Insects
Bibliography: Z5856+
Insects as carriers of disease
Bibliography: Z6675.I6
Insects (Fossil)
Bibliography
Geology: Z6033.I48
Instant printing: Z252.5.I49
Institution building
Bibliography: Z7164.I6
Institution libraries: Z675.I6
Institutional repositories
Digital libraries: ZA4081.86
Institutions
Bibliography
Political and social sciences: Z7164.A85
Instructional systems
Bibliography: Z5814.I46
Instrument manufacture
Libraries
Cataloging: Z695.1.I57
Instrumentation
Bibliography
Science: Z7405.A6
Instruments
Bibliography
Electricity: Z5834.A6

Instruments
  Bibliography
    Physics: Z7144.I5
    Science: Z7405.A6
Instruments and apparatus, Medical
  Bibliography: Z6675.I7
Instruments for manuscripts: Z112
Instruments for writing (General): Z45
Instruments, Meteorological
  Bibliography: Z6683.I5
Insular possessions: Z1 21.I5
Insulators and insulation
  Bibliography
    Electricity: Z5834.I6
Insurance
  Bibliography: Z7164.I7
  Libraries: Z683.5
Insurance, Group
  Bibliography: Z7164.G83
Insurance libraries: Z675.I7
Insurance maps
  Bibliography: Z6026.I7
Intaglio printing: Z252.5.I5
Integrated library systems
  Automation: Z678.93.I57
Integrating resources
  Libraries
    Cataloging: Z695.35
Integration
  Education
    Bibliography: Z5814.D5
Intellectual cooperation
  Bibliography
    League of Nations: Z6475.I5
Intellectual freedom
  Libraries
    Reference work: Z711.4
Intellectual life: Z1 27.C55
  Asia
    Bibliography: Z3008.C55
  Middle East
    Bibliography: Z3014.C57
  United States
    Bibliography: Z1361.C6
Intellectuals
  Books for: Z1039.I56
  Library service to: Z711.92.I58

Intelligence
  Bibliography
    Military science: Z6724.I7
    Psychology: Z7204.I5
Intelligence tests
  Bibliography
    Psychology: Z7204.I52
Intensive care
  Bibliography: Z6664.34
Intentionalism
  Bibliography
    Psychology: Z7204.I55
Inter-American conferences
  By region or country
    South America: Z1609.I5
Interactive computer systems
  Bibliography: Z5643.I57
Interactive multimedia
  Bookselling and publishing: Z286.O68
  Cataloging: Z695.37
  In library collections: Z692.I57
Interconnected electric utiligy systems
  Bibliography: Z5834.I64
Intercultural communication
  Bibliography: Z5633.I67
Intercultural education
  Bibliography: Z5814.M86
Interest
  Bibliography: Z7164.I78
Interests of special groups, Works on
  reading: Z1039.A+
Interior architecture
  Bibliography: Z5943.I56
Interior decoration
  Bibliography
    Fine arts: Z5956.D3
Interior walls
  Bibliography
    Technology: Z7914.I57
Interleaf publisher
  Desktop publishing: Z253.532.I58
Interlibrary loans: Z713+
Internal security
  Bibliography: Z7164.I786
International agencies
  Bookselling and publishing: Z286.I56

Jesuits
  Bibliography: Z7840.J5
    Manuscripts: Z6611.J46
Jesus Christ
  Bibliography: Z7806
    Literary characters, themes, etc:
      Z6514.C5J47+
Jet cutting
  Bibliography
    Technology: Z7914.J4
Jeweled bindings: Z269.3.J48
Jewelry shops
  Bibliography
    Architecture: Z5943.J48
Jewish art
  Bibliography: Z5956.J4
Jewish authors: Z1 13.5.J4
Jewish drama
  Bibliography: Z5784.J6
Jewish education
  Bibliography: Z5814.J4
Jewish fiction
  Bibliography: Z5917.J4
Jewish libraries: Z675.J4
Jewish literature: Z6514.J48
Jewish women
  Bibliography: Z7963.J4
Jews
  Autographs: Z42.3.J48
  Bibliography: Z6366+
    Manuscripts: Z6611.J48
    Romance philology and linguistics:
      Z7033.J48
  Books for: Z1039.J48
  Libraries
    Cataloging: Z695.1.J48
    Classification: Z697.J53
    Special collections: Z688.J48
Ji (Sect)
  Bibliography: Z7864.J5
Job descriptions
  Libraries: Z682.25
Jōdoshū
  Bibliography: Z7864.J6
Joh. Enschedé en Zonen: Z232.J56

Joint occupancy of buildings
  Bibliography
    Architecture: Z5943.J64
Joint-use libraries: Z675.J64
Joints
  Bibliography
    Engineering: Z5853.J65
Jojoba
  Bibliography: Z5074.J58
Jones, George William: Z232.J72
Jones, Thomas: Z232.J73
Jordan: Z3471+
Jou, Louis: Z232.J78
Journalism
  Bibliography: Z6940
JPTRS System: Z699.4.J18
Juan, Don
  Bibliography
    Literary characters, themes, etc:
      Z6514.C5J82+
Judaism
  Bibliography
    Manuscripts: Z6611.J48
  Libraries
    Cataloging: Z695.1.J48
    Special collections: Z688.J48
Jugendstil
  Bibliography: Z5941.396
Jungle warfare
  Bibliography: Z6724.J8
Junior college libraries: Z675.J8
Junior colleges
  Bibliography: Z5814.J8
Junior high school students
  Books for: Z1039.H54
Junior high schools
  Bibliography: Z5814.H56
Jurisprudence, Medical
  Bibliography: Z6672.J9
Justice, Administration of
  Libraries
    Cataloging: Z695.1.J88
Jute
  Bibliography: Z5074.J8
Juvenile corrections
  Bibliography: Z5703.4.J87

Konkani philology and linguistics
  Bibliography: Z7101.K7
KONKAT System: Z699.4.K2
Konkokyo
  Bibliography: Z7835.K64
Koran
  Bibliography
    Manuscripts: Z6611.K65
Korea: Z3316+
  Bibliography
    Botany: Z5358.K6
  Libraries
    Mechanized bibliographic control:
      Z699.5.K65
    Special collections: Z688.K65
Korean imprints
  Libraries
    Cataloging: Z695.1.K67
Korean philology and linguistics
  Bibliography: Z7074
Korean type: Z251.K65
Korean typewriters: Z49.4.K6
Koreans as an element in the
  population: Z1 27.K6
Koreans in the United States
  Bibliography: Z1361.K65
Kožičić, Šimun: Z232.K7954
Kraszewski, Józef Ignacy: Z232.K82
Ku Klux Klan
  United States
    National bibliography: Z1249.K8
Kühn, Balthasar: Z232.K86
Kuhn, family of printers: Z232.K86
Kurdish manuscripts
  Bibliography: Z6605.K8
Kurdistan: Z3014.K85
Kurds: Z3014.K85
Kuru
  Bibliography: Z6664.K8
Kushans as an element in the
  population: Z1 27.K88
Kuwait: Z3028.K87
Kwa philology and linguistics
  Bibliography: Z7108.K8
Kyōdō Insatsu Kabushiki Kaisha:
  Z232.K94
Kyrgyzstan: Z3421+

L

Labels
  Copyright: Z656.L2
Labor
  Bibliography: Z7164.L1
    Gynecology and obstetrics:
      Z6671.2.L32
    Modern literature: Z6520.L32
    Statistics: Z7553.L2
  Libraries
    Cataloging: Z695.1.L12
Labor and laboring class fiction
  Bibliography: Z5917.L2
Labor economics
  Libraries
    Mechanized bibliographic control:
      Z699.5.L25
Labor, Home
  Bibliography: Z7164.H7
Labor, Library service to: Z711.85
Labor plays
  Bibliography: Z5784.L2
Labor productivity
  Bibliography
    Agriculture: Z5074.L2
Labor unions
  Bibliography: Z7164.T7
  Practical printing: Z242.9+
Laboratories
  Bibliography
    Architecture: Z5943.L2
    Science: Z7405.L3
Laboratory animals
  Bibliography
    Zoology: Z7994.L3
Laboratory animals (Culture)
  Bibliography: Z5074.L24
Laboratory diagnosis
  Bibliography
    Medicine: Z6664.8.L3
Laboratory schools
  Bibliography: Z5814.L2
Laborers
  Books for: Z1039.L3

Lac
  Bibliography
    Technology: Z7914.L15
Lace
  Bibliography
    Fine arts: Z5956.L2
Lactams
  Bibliography: Z5524.L22
Lactobacillus
  Bibliography: Z5185.L3
Ladino
  Bibliography
    Romance philology and linguistics:
      Z7033.L3
Ladrone Islands: Z4741
Lagos State Printing Corporation:
  Z232.L15
Laguna Verde Imprenta: Z232.L17
Laichter, Jan: Z232.L184
Laity
  Bibliography: Z7808
    Catholic Church: Z7838.L34
Lamaism
  Bibliography: Z7864.L35
Lampblack
  Bibliography: Z7914.L2
Land
  Bibliography: Z7164.L3
  Libraries
    Mechanized bibliographic control:
      Z699.5.L28
Land capability for agriculture
  Bibliography: Z5074.L27
Land use
  Libraries
    Cataloging: Z695.1.L19
Landen, Johann: Z232.L29
Landmarks
  Bibliography
    Preservation: Z5133.P73
Lands, School
  Bibliography: Z5814.L25
Landscape architects, Women
  Bibliography: Z7963.L3
Landscape architecture, Women in
  Bibliography: Z7963.L3

Landscape assessment
  Bibliography: Z5863.L35
Landscape gardening and architecture
  Bibliography: Z5996+
Landslides
  Bibliography: Z6033.L3
L'Angelier, Abel: Z232.L313
Language: Z1 15.A1+, Z2 8.L5
  Bibliography
    People with mental disabilities:
      Z6677.2.C66
  By region or country
    British Africa: Z3554.L5
    Great Britain: Z2015.A1+
    Nicaragua: Z1487.L36
    South America: Z1609.L3
Language acquisition
  Bibliography: Z7004.C45
Language and languages
  Cataloging: Z695.1.L2
  Libraries
    Classification: Z697.L37
Language arts
  Bibliography
    Education: Z5818.L3
Language data processing
  Bibliography: Z7004.L3
Language, Origin of
  Bibliography: Z7004.O75
Language planning
  Bibliography: Z7004.L33
Language policy
  Bibliography: Z7004.L332
Languages
  Libraries
    Special collections: Z688.L36
Languages in contact
  Bibliography: Z7004.L34
Languages (Modern)
  Bibliography
    Education: Z5818.L35
Langue d'oc
  Bibliography
    Romance philology and linguistics:
      Z7033.O25

Leadbeater's possum
  Bibliography: Z7996.L43
Leadership
  Bibliography
    Military: Z6724.L4
    Political and social sciences:
      Z7164.L38
Leaf books: Z1033.L4
League of Nations
  Bibliography: Z6471+
Learning
  Bibliography: Z5814.L45
Learning disabled
  Bibliography: Z5814.L492
Learning disorders
  Bibliography
    Pediatrics: Z6671.52.L43
Least squares
  Mathematics
    Bibliography: Z6654.L5
Leather bindings: Z269.3.L43
Leather industry
  Bibliography: Z7914.L27
Lebanese as an element in the
  population: Z1 27.L42
Lebanon: Z3466+
Leers, Reinier: Z232.L398
Leeu, Gerard: Z232.L399
LEFT language
  Computerized typesetting:
    Z253.4.L43
Leg injuries
  Bibliography
    Surgery: Z6667.L44
Leg surgery
  Bibliography: Z6667.L44
Legal aid
  Bibliography: Z7164.L49
Legal novels
  Bibliography: Z5917.L3
Legal publishing: Z286.L44
Legionnaires' disease
  Bibliography: Z6664.L38
Legislative bodies
  Books for: Z1039.L4

Legislative documents
  Libraries
    Mechanized bibliographic control:
      Z699.5.L44
Legislative indexing vocabulary
  Subject cataloging: Z695.Z8L44
Legislative libraries: Z675.L45
Legumes
  Bibliography: Z5074.L3
Leguminosae
  Bibliography: Z5356.L5
Leishmaniasis
  Bibliography: Z6664.L4
Leisure
  Bibliography
    Political and social sciences:
      Z7164.L53
Leisure hours, Lists of books for:
  Z1035.9
Lenin, V.I.
  Bookplates: Z994.5.L4
Lepidoptera: Z5858.L5
Leprosy
  Bibliography: Z6664.L6
Leptospirosis
  Bibliography: Z6664.L63
Lesbian libraries: Z675.L48
Lesbianism
  Bibliography
    Erotic literature: Z5866.L4
    Political and social sciences:
      Z7164.H74
Lesbians
  Libraries
    Personnel: Z682.4.G39
Leslie, Robert L.: Z232.L62
Lesotho: Z3558
Lesser scaup
  Bibliography: Z5333.L47
Lettering
  Bibliography
    Fine arts: Z5956.L45
LetterPerfect
  Word processing: Z52.5.L47
Letters: Z1 14.L4
  Bibliography: Z6490
  Copyright: Z652.L4

Manchu philology and linguistics
  Bibliography: Z7080
Mandaean philology and linguistics
  Bibliography: Z7053
Mandates
  Bibliography: Z7164.M15
Mande philology and linguistics
  Bibliography: Z7108.M35
Manganese
  Bibliography
    Chemistry: Z5524.M2
    Geology: Z6033.M38
Mangrove swamp ecology
  Bibliography: Z5322.M27
Manichaeism
  Bibliography: Z7845.M34
Mannerism (Art)
  Bibliography
    Fine arts: Z5936.M34
Manors
  Bibliography
    Architecture: Z5943.M36
Manpower
  Bibliography
    Military science: Z6724.M3
Manpower planning
  Libraries: Z682.35.M35
Mantels
  Bibliography
    Architecture: Z5943.M37
Manual training
  Education
    Bibliography: Z5814.M29
Manufacturers
  Bibliography: Z7914.M3
Manufacturing engineering
  Libraries
    Mechanized bibliographic control:
      Z699.5.M26
Manufacturing processes
  Bibliography: Z7914.M32
Manuscripts: Z105+
  Bibliography: Z6601+
  Libraries
    Cataloging: Z695.5
    Mechanized bibliographic control:
      Z699.5.M27

Manuscripts
  Library collections: Z692.M28
Manuscripts, Bible
  Bibliography: Z7771.M3
Manuzio, family of printers: Z232.M3
Maori philology and linguistics
  Bibliography: Z7112.M35
Maps
  Bibliography: Z6001+
    Astronomy: Z5151.5
  Bookselling and publishing: Z286.M3
  Copyright: Z656.M3
  Libraries
    Cataloging: Z695.6
    Classification: Z697.M17
    Mechanized bibliographic control:
      Z699.5.C3
  Library collections: Z692.M3
Maps, Early printed
  Bibliography: Z6022
Marathi literature
  Libraries
    Classification: Z697.M18
Marathi manuscripts
  Bibliography: Z6605.M4
Marathi philology and linguistics
  Bibliography: Z7082
Marbled papers
  Bookbinding: Z271.3.M37
Marbling
  Bookbinding: Z271.3.M37
MARC formats
  Libraries: Z699.35.M28
Marcus Ward & Co: Z232.M322
Marfan syndrome
  Bibliography: Z6664.M35
Mariana Islands: Z4741
Marianists
  Bibliography: Z7840.M3
Marijuana
  Bibliography
    Physiological effect: Z6663.C36
    Toxicology: Z7891.C36
Marine algae: Z5973.M3
Marine biology
  Bibliography: Z5322.M3

Memoirs
  Bibliography
    Manuscripts: Z6611.B6
Memorial Day
  Bibliography: Z5711.M4
Memorials
  Bibliography
    Architecture: Z5943.M45
Memory
  Bibliography
    Psychology: Z7204.M4
Men
  Bibliography
    Political and social sciences:
      Z7164.M49
Mennonites
  Bibliography: Z7845.M4
Mennonites in Canada: Z1395.M45
Menopause
  Bibliography: Z6671.2.M46
Menstruation disorders
  Bibliography: Z6671.2.M47
Mental health
  Bibliography
    Pediatrics: Z6671.52.P78
Mental health libraries: Z675.M43
Mental retardation
  Bibliography: Z6677+
Mental tests
  Education
    Bibliography: Z5814.P8
Mental work
  Bibliography
    Psychology: Z7204.M43
Mentally ill
  Library service to: Z711.92.M42
Mentelin, Johann: Z232.M55
Mentha
  Bibliography: Z5356.M37
Mercedarians
  Bibliography: Z7840.M4
Mercury
  Bibliography
    Astronomy: Z5154.M55
    Toxicology: Z7891.M4
Mercury (Computer program)
  Word processing: Z52.5.M47

Mercury pollution
  Bibliography: Z5862.2.M4
Merrymount Press: Z232.M57
Merthyr Tydfil: Z2083.M47
Mesquite
  Bibliography
    Botany: Z5356.M4
Metabolism
  Bibliography
    Medicine: Z6663.M58
Metadata
  Library science: Z666.7
Metadata harvesting
  Library science: Z666.7
METAFONT
  Computerized type founding:
    Z250.8.M46
Metal cleaning
  Bibliography: Z6679.M47
Metal finishing
  Bibliography: Z6679.C7
Metal pollution
  Bibliography: Z5862.2.M44
Metallurgical libraries: Z675.M44
Metallurgy
  Bibliography: Z6333.M47, Z6678+
  Libraries
    Cataloging: Z695.1.M55
    Classification: Z697.M5
    Mechanized bibliographic control:
      Z699.5.M4
Metals
  Bibliography: Z6678+
Metalwork
  Bibliography: Z7914.M5
    Fine arts: Z5956.M5
  Libraries
    Classification: Z697.M52
Metaphor
  Bibliography
    Philology and linguistics: Z7004.M4
Metaxas, Nikodēmos: Z232.M585
Meteorites
  Bibliography: Z6033.M5
Meteorological libraries: Z675.M45
Meteorology
  Bibliography: Z6681+

Meteorology
  Libraries
    Mechanized bibliographic control:
      Z699.5.M45
Meteorology in aeronautics
  Bibliography: Z5064.M47
Method
  Bibliography
    History: Z6208.M5
Methodist Church
  Bibliography: Z7845.M5
Methodology
  Bibliography
    Philosophy: Z7128.M46
    Science: Z7405.M4
Metric system
  Bibliography: Z7144.W4
Metrics
  Bibliography
    Latin philology and linguistics:
      Z7028.M47
Metropolitan areas and libraries: Z716.2
Mexican Americans
  Books for: Z1039.M5
  Education
    Bibliography: Z5814.M48
  Libraries
    Cataloging: Z695.1.M57
  Library service to: Z711.92.M47
Mexican manuscripts
  Bibliography: Z6605.M6
Mexicans in the United States
  Bibliography: Z1361.M4
Mexico: Z1411+
  Bibliography
    Botany: Z5358.M6
Mezinárodní system vĕdeckých a
  technickych informací (MSVTI)
  Library classification system:
    Z696.M596
Mica
  Bibliography
    Mines and mining: Z6738.M5
Mice
  Bibliography: Z7996.M53
Micro CDS/ISIS: Z699.4.C17

Microbiology
  Bibliography: Z5180+
Microcomputer software
  Libraries
    Cataloging: Z695.615
Microcomputers: Z678.93.M53
  Bibliography: Z5643.M48
Microelectronics
  Bibliography: Z5838.M5
Microfilming, Preservation
  Libraries: Z701.3.M53
Microform editions: Z1033.M5
Microform publishing
  Bookselling and publishing: Z286.M5
Microforms
  Libraries
    Cataloging: Z695.62
    Preservation,, restoration, etc:
      Z701.3.M53
  Library collections: Z692.M5
Micrographics
  Printing: Z265.5.M53
Micronesia: Z4501+
  Bibliography
    Botany: Z5358.O3
Micronesian philology and linguistics
  Bibliography: Z7112.M5
Microphotography
  Libraries
    Preservation, restoration, etc:
      Z701.3.M53
  Printing: Z265.5.M53
Microprocessors
  Bibliography: Z5643.M5
Micropublishing
  Bookselling and publishing: Z286.M5
Microscopic editions: Z1033.M6
Microscopy
  Bibliography: Z6704+
Microsoft Access: Z699.4.M226
Microsoft Network: ZA4251.M5
Microsoft Publisher
  Desktop publishing: Z253.532.M53
Microsoft Windows (Computer file):
  Z678.93.M57
Microsoft Word (Computer program)
  Word processing: Z52.5.M52

Microsoft Word for Windows (Computer program)
Word processing: Z52.5.M52
Microsoft Write (Computer program)
Word processing: Z52.5.M53
Microsurgery
Bibliography: Z6667.M53
MicroTeX system
Computerized typesetting:
Z253.4.M53
MicroUSE-WORD (Computer program)
Word processing: Z52.5.M58
Microwaves
Bibliography
Electronics: Z5838.M52
Physiological effect: Z6663.M62
Middle Ages
Libraries
Special collections: Z688.M42
Middle East
Bibliography: Z3013+
Libraries
Special collections: Z688.N43
Middle East libraries: Z675.M48
Middle English manuscripts
Bibliography: Z6605.E5
Middle Hill Press: Z232.M627
Middle schools
Bibliography: Z5814.H56
Midrash
Bibliography: Z6371.M5
Mifepristone: Z6665.M52
Migrant laborers' children
Education
Bibliography: Z5814.M49
Migration
Bibliography
Birds: Z5333.A37
Military
Bookplates: Z994.5.M5
Military art and science
Libraries
Classification: Z697.M6
Mechanized bibliographic control:
Z699.5.M48
Military history: Z1 21.M5

Military history
By region or country
Canada: Z1387.M54
Middle East: Z3014.M55
United States: Z1249.M5
Military libraries: Z675.M5
Military maps
Bibliography: Z6026.H6
Military medicine
Bibliography: Z6672.M6
Military occupation
Bibliography: Z6464.M5
Military post libraries: Z675.M6
Military railroads
Bibliography: Z6724.R2
Military science
Bibliography: Z6721+
Manuscripts: Z6611.M6
Libraries
Cataloging: Z695.1.M6
Classification: Z697.M6
Milk
Bibliography: Z5706.M6
Medicine: Z6675.M64
Millennialism
Bibliography: Z7835.M54
Millet
Bibliography: Z5074.M5
Mills and mill work
Bibliography: Z7914.M6
Mimeographing: Z48
Mind and body
Bibliography
Psychology: Z7204.M55
Mine filling
Bibliography: Z6738.M54
Mine maps
Bibliography: Z6738.M55
Mineral industries
Bibliography
Environment (General and human):
Z5863.M55
Mineral resources
Libraries
Mechanized bibliographic control:
Z699.5.M5

NEPHIS
  Library indexing system:
  Z695.915.N48
Nephropidae
  Bibliography: Z7996.N43
Nerve injuries
  Bibliography
  Surgery: Z6667.N39
Nervous system diseases
  Bibliography: Z6664.N5
Nestorians
  Bibliography: Z7845.N4
  Middle East: Z3014.A77
Netherlands: Z2431+
Netsukes
  Bibliography: Z5956.N37
Networks, Computers
  Bibliography: Z5643.N48
Neural conduction
  Bibliography
  Medicine: Z6663.N48
Neurochemistry
  Bibliography: Z6663.N49
Neurolinguistics
  Bibliography: Z6663.N498
Neurology
  Bibliography: Z6663.N5
  Pediatrics: Z6671.52.N48
Neuropeptides
  Bibliography: Z6663.N52
Neurophysiology
  Bibliography: Z6663.N54
Neuroptera
  Bibliography: Z5858.N4
Neurospora
  Bibliography: Z5356.N4
Neurosurgery
  Bibliography: Z6667.N4
Neutrality
  Bibliography
  International law and relations:
  Z6464.N4
Never Mind the Press: Z232.N54
New Age movement
  Bibliography: Z7835.N48
New Caledonia: Z4805
New Guinea: Z4811+

New Hebrides: Z4820
New Jersey Library Network:
  Z674.82.N48
New Jerusalem Church
  Bibliography: Z7845.S9
New literates
  Books for: Z1039.N47
New literates and libraries: Z716.45
New South Wales: Z4041+
New states
  Bibliography: Z7164.N4
New Testament
  Bibliography: Z7772.L1+
New Thought
  Bibliography
    Psychology: Z7204.N47
New towns
  Bibliography
    Architecture: Z5943.N48
New Year's Day
  Bibliography: Z5711.N48
New York Public Library
  Bibliography
    Manuscript collections: Z6621.N56+
New Zealand: Z4101+
Newari philology and linguistics
  Bibliography: Z7101.N48
News libraries: Z675.N4
Newsletters
  Bibliography: Z6944.N44
  Bookselling and publishing: Z286.N46
  Graphic design: Z246.5.N49
Newspaper articles
  Copyright: Z652.N4
Newspaper libraries: Z675.N37
Newspaper office libraries: Z675.N4
Newspapers
  Bibliography: Z6940+
  Bookselling and publishing: Z286.N48
  Conservation and restoration:
    Z701.3.N48
  Libraries
    Cataloging: Z695.655
    Mechanized bibliographic control:
      Z699.5.N47
  Library collections: Z692.N4

North America
  Bibliography
    Botany: Z5358.N86
North Atlantic Treaty Organization
  Bibliography: Z6464.N65
North Korea: Z3321+
Northern fur seal
  Bibliography: Z7996.N67
Northern Ireland: Z2043.N6
Northern Rhodesia: Z3579
Northern Territory: Z4161+
Northern Thai manuscripts
  Bibliography: Z6605.N67
Norton Textra
  Word processing: Z52.5.N67
Norway: Z2591+
  Bibliography
    Botany: Z5358.N88
  Libraries
    Classification: Z697.N66
Norwegian press (United States)
  Bibliography: Z6953.5.N7
Norwegian shorthand: Z61
Norwegians in the United States
  Bibliography: Z1361.N67
Nosology
  Bibliography
    Medicine: Z6675.N6
Notation
  Libraries: Z696.A1+
Notes
  Libraries
    Cataloging: Z693.3.N68
Nubian language: Z7108.N82
Nuclear arms control verification
  Bibliography: Z6724.A73
Nuclear bomb shelter construction
  Bibliography: Z7914.N83
Nuclear counters
  Bibliography: Z7144.N77
Nuclear energy
  Libraries
    Cataloging: Z695.1.A86
Nuclear engineering: Z5160+
Nuclear magnetic resonance
  Bibliography
    Medical diagnosis: Z6664.8.N83

Nuclear magnetism
  Bibliography: Z7144.M3
Nuclear physics
  Bibliography: Z7144.N8
Nuclear reactors
  Libraries
    Cataloging: Z695.1.N78
Nuclear warfare
  Bibliography: Z6724.A9
    Fiction: Z5917.N83
    Medicine: Z6675.N65
Nuclear warfare and the environment
  Bibliography: Z5322.N83
Nuclear winter
  Bibliography: Z5322.N83
Nucleic acids
  Bibliography: Z5524.N8
Nucleotides
  Bibliography
    Medicine: Z6663.N85
Nude
  Bookplates: Z994.5.N8
Nude photography
  Bibliography: Z7136.N83
Nudism
  Bibliography: Z7514.N8
Number work
  Bibliography
    Education: Z5818.A7
Numbers
  Type and type founding: Z250.25
Numerals
  Type and type founding: Z250.25
Numerical analysis
  Bibliography: Z6654.N8
Numerical integration
  Bibliography: Z6654.N84
Numismatics
  Bibliography: Z6866+
Nuns
  Books for: Z1039.N76
Nurse-physician joint practice
  Bibliography: Z6675.N67
Nursery rhymes
  Bibliography: Z6514.N8
Nursery schools
  Bibliography: Z5814.N97

Nursing
  Bibliography: Z6675.N7+
    Education: Z5818.N8
  Libraries
    Cataloging: Z695.1.N8
    Classification: Z697.N77
    Mechanized bibliographic control:
      Z699.5.N7
Nursing homes
  Bibliography: Z6675.N85
Nursing libraries: Z675.N8
Nutrition
  Bibliography: Z6663.N9
    Home economics: Z5776.N8
    Pediatrics: Z6671.52.N86
  Education
    Bibliography: Z5814.F7
  Libraries
    Cataloging: Z695.1.N84
Nutritional aspects
  Pregnancy
    Bibliography: Z6671.2.N87
Nuts
  Bibliography
    Gardening: Z5996.N9
Nyanja philology and linguistics
  Bibliography: Z7108.N93
Nyasaland: Z3577
Nyaya
  Bibliography: Z7128.N93

O

Oak
  Bibliography
    Botany: Z5356.O2
Obesity
  Bibliography: Z6664.O34
Object teaching
  Bibliography: Z5814.O2
Oblates of Mary Immaculate
  Bibliography: Z7840.O2
Observatories
  Bibliography: Z5154.O27
Obstetrics
  Bibliography: Z6671+

Occitan
  Bibliography
    Romance philology and linguistics:
      Z7033.O25
Occultism
  Bibliography: Z6876+
Occupational health in pregnancy
  Bibliography: Z6671.2.O33
Occupational health libraries: Z675.O22
Occupational therapy
  Bibliography
    Therapeutics: Z6665.O2
Occupational training
  Libraries
    Cataloging: Z695.1.O29
Occupations
  Bibliography: Z7164.V6
  Libraries
    Cataloging: Z695.1.O3
Occupations in fiction
  Bibliography: Z5917.O25
Ocean
  Bookplates: Z994.5.O28
Ocean currents
  Bibliography: Z6004.P66
Ocean engineering
  Bibliography: Z5853.O6
Ocean waves
  Bibliography: Z6004.P67
Oceania: Z4001+, Z4501+
  Bibliography
    Botany: Z5358.O3
Oceanian philology and linguistics
  Bibliography: Z7111+
Oceanic Bibles
  Bibliography: Z7771.O3
Oceanographic libraries: Z675.O23
Oceanography
  Bibliography: Z6004.P6+, Z6004.P6
  Libraries
    Classification: Z697.O2
    Mechanized bibliographic control:
      Z699.5.O3
Ocharte, Pedro, ca. 1532-1592:
  Z232.O18
OCLC Cataloging Subsystem:
  Z699.4.O29

Palm leaves
  Bibliography
    Manuscripts: Z6603
Palms
  Bibliography
    Agriculture: Z5074.P27
    Botany: Z5356.P28
Paltasîchis, Andreas de: Z232.P154
Palynology
  Bibliography: Z6033.P76
Pamphlets: Z1 27.P3
  Bibliography: Z6895
  By region or country
    Ireland: Z2047.P3, Z2049
    Scotland: Z2067.P3
    Wales: Z2087.P3
  Libraries: Z691
Pan-Africanism
  Bibliography: Z3508.P35
Pan-Pacific
  Bibliography
    Foreign relations: Z6465.P2
Panama: Z1500
Panama Canal
  Bibliography: Z5452.P2
Pancreas diseases
  Bibliography: Z6664.P27
Paneling
  Bibliography
    Technology: Z7914.P17
Panjabi imprints
  Libraries
    Special collections: Z688.P35
Panjabi manuscripts
  Bibliography: Z6605.P3
Panjabi philology and linguistics
  Bibliography: Z7084
Panoan philology and linguistics
  Bibliography: Z7122.P34
Pantomimes
  Bibliography: Z5784.P3
Papacy
  Bibliography: Z7838.P53
Papaver
  Bibliography: Z5356.P3

Paper
  Libraries
    Preservation, restoration, etc:
      Z701.3.P38
  Penmanship: Z45
  Practical printing: Z247
Paper bindings: Z269.3.P37
Paper industry
  Libraries
    Cataloging: Z695.1.P364
Paper work
  Handicraft: Z6153.P35
Paperbacks: Z1033.P3
  Bibliography
    Fiction: Z5917.P3
  Bookselling and publishing: Z286.P35
  Library collections: Z692.P37
Papermaking
  Bibliography: Z7914.P2
Papua New Guinea: Z4811+
Papyri
  Bibliography
    Manuscripts: Z6604
  Museums: Z110.P36
Papyri, Egyptian, manuscripts
  Bibliography: Z6605.E35
Papyri, Greek, manuscripts
  Bibliography: Z6605.G7
Parachutes
  Bibliography: Z5064.P3
Parachuting
  Bibliography: Z5064.P3
Paraguay: Z1821+
  Libraries
    Cataloging: Z695.1.P366
Paralysis
  Bibliography: Z6664.P3
Paramedical education
  Bibliography: Z5818.M43
Paraplegia
  Bibliography: Z6664.P33
Parapsychology
  Bibliography: Z6878.P8
Parasites
  Bibliography
    Fishing and fisheries: Z5973.P3

INDEX

Prayer
  Bibliography: Z7825.5
Prayer books
  Bibliography: Z7813
Pre-Raphaelites
  Bibliography: Z5948.P9
Pre-Socratic philosophers
  Bibliography: Z7128.P83
Preaching
  Bibliography: Z7826
Precious stones
  Bibliography
    Geology: Z6033.P83
Precipitation
  Bibliography: Z6683.P7
PRECIS
  Library indexing system:
    Z695.915.P73
Precursors of modern printing: Z126.A2
Prefabricated buildings
  Bibliography
    Architecture: Z5943.P7
Prefaces
  Printing: Z242.P7
Pregnancy
  Bibliography: Z6671.2.P73
  Complications of
    Bibliography: Z6671.2.C66
  Diabetes in
    Bibliography: Z6671.2.D53
Prehistoric man
  Bibliography: Z5118.A6
Preller, Carl: Z232.P94
Preloaded audio players
  Cataloging: Z695.7184
Premenstrual syndrome
  Bibliography: Z6671.2.P75
Premonstrants
  Bibliography: Z7840.P9
Preparation of reports
  Bibliography
    Political and social sciences:
      Z7164.R38
Prepositions
  Bibliography: Z7004.P74
Prepress
  Practical printing: Z244.64+

Presbyterian Church
  Bibliography: Z7845.P9
    Manuscripts: Z6611.P74
Preschool children
  Bibliography: Z5814.P6
Prescribed burning
  Bibliography: Z5074.B94
Preservation
  Antiquities
    Bibliography: Z5133.P73
  Historic buildings: Z1 21.H49
  Libraries: Z700.9+
  Selection for
    Library materials: Z701.3.S38
Preservation, Digital
  Library materials: Z701.3.C65
Preservation microfilming
  Libraries: Z701.3.M53
Preservation of monuments
  Bibliography: Z5940
Preservation photocopying
  Libraries: Z701.3.P48
Preserving and canning
  Bibliography
    Home economics: Z5776.C3
Presidency
  United States
    National bibliography: Z1249.P7
Presidents
  Autographs: Z42.3.P7
Press and the government
  Bibliography: Z6944.G68
Press at Colorado College: Z232.P945
Presswork
  Practical printing: Z256+
Prevention
  Bibliography
    People with mental disabilities:
      Z6677.2.P74
Preventive medicine
  Bibliography: Z6675.P7
Prices
  Bibliography: Z7164.P94
Primaries
  Bibliography: Z7164.R4
Primates
  Bibliography: Z7996.P85

627

INDEX

Protection
  Bibliography
    Birds: Z5333.A42
Protective clothing
  Bibliography
    Military science: Z6724.P57
Protective coatings
  Bibliography: Z7914.P8
    Metals: Z6679.C7
Proteins
  Bibliography
    Chemistry: Z5524.P83
Protestant churches
  Bibliography: Z7845.P93
Protestant missions
  Bibliography: Z7817
Protozoa
  Bibliography: Z7996.P9
Provençal
  Bibliography
    Romance philology and linguistics:
      Z7033.P8
Provençal manuscripts
  Bibliography: Z6605.P9
Proverbs
  Bibliography: Z7191
    Fine arts: Z5956.P74
Proverbs in literature
  Bibliography: Z6514.P76
Provincial libraries: Z675.S7
PS
  Shorthand system: Z56.2.P18
Psalms (Book of the Bible)
  Bibliography: Z7772.I1
Pseudonyms: Z1041+
Psychiatric nursing
  Bibliography: Z6665.7.P76
Psychiatric rating scales
  Bibliography: Z6665.7.P78
Psychiatry
  Bibliography: Z6665.6+
    Pediatrics: Z6671.52.P78
Psychical research
  Bibliography: Z6878.P8
Psychoacoustics
  Bibliography: Z7204.P79

Psychoanalysis
  Bibliography: Z7204.P8
Psychoanalysis and the arts
  Bibliography: Z5936.P74
Psychohistory
  Bibliography: Z6208.P78
Psychological aspects
  Printing: Z244.4
Psychological aspects of architecture
  Bibliography: Z5943.P77
Psychological aspects of communication
  and mass media
  Bibliography: Z5633.P79
Psychological aspects of sports and
  recreation
  Bibliography: Z7514.P79
Psychological tests
  Bibliography: Z7204.P85
Psychological warfare
  Bibliography: Z6724.P6
Psychology: Z1 27.P87, Z2 8.P7
  Bibliography: Z7201+
  By region or country
    Africa: Z3508.P8
    Criminology: Z5703.4.P8
    Education: Z5818.P75
    Literature: Z6514.P78
    Manuscripts: Z6611.P78
    Military science: Z6724.P65
  By region or country
    British Africa: Z3554.P7
  Education
    Bibliography: Z5814.P8
  International relations
    Bibliography: Z6464.P9
  Languages
    Bibliography: Z7004.P8
  Libraries
    Cataloging: Z695.1.P7
    Mechanized bibliographic control:
      Z699.5.P72
    Personnel: Z682.35.P82
  Typewriters: Z49.A2
Psychology and medicine
  Bibliography: Z6675.P78
Psychometrics
  Bibliography: Z7204.P88

Race relations
 British Africa: Z3554.R3
 Libraries
  Cataloging: Z695.1.R32
Racket games
 Bibliography: Z7514.R32
Radar
 Bibliography: Z7215
Radiation
 Bibliography: Z7144.R17
Radiation chemistry
 Bibliography: Z5524.R25
Radio
 Bibliography: Z7221+
 Libraries
  Classification: Z697.R25
Radio and libraries: Z716.7
Radio astronomy
 Bibliography: Z5154.R3
Radio broadcasting
 Copyright: Z655.5
Radio frequency identification systems
 Libraries: Z699.75
Radio in aeronautics
 Bibliography: Z5064.R2
Radio in education
 Bibliography: Z5814.R2
Radio meteorology
 Bibliography: Z6683.R3
Radio plays: Z1 14.R32
Radio programs
 Libraries
  Cataloging: Z695.7196
Radio stations
 Bibliography
  Architecture: Z5943.R33
Radioactivation analysis
 Bibliography: Z5524.R27
Radioactive pollution
 Bibliography: Z5862.2.R3
Radioactive substances
 Bibliography
  Mines and mining: Z6738.R3
  Toxicology: Z7891.R3
Radioactivity
 Bibliography
  Physics: Z7144.R2

Radiocarbon dating
 Bibliography: Z7144.R3
Radiochemistry
 Bibliography: Z5524.R3
Radioecology
 Bibliography: Z5322.R2
Radiography
 Bibliography: Z5834.R7
Radioisotopes
 Bibliography
  Agriculture: Z5074.R2
Radiology, Medical
 Bibliography: Z6671.7
Radiotherapy
 Bibliography: Z6665.R2
Radium
 Bibliography
  Therapeutics: Z6665.R2
Raeto-Romance
 Bibliography
  Romance philology and linguistics:
   Z7033.R7
Railroad libraries: Z675.R15
Railroad maps
 Bibliography: Z6026.R3
Railroad stations
 Bibliography
  Architecture: Z5943.R36
Railroads
 Bibliography: Z7231+
  Manuscripts: Z6611.R3
  Military science: Z6724.R2
 Libraries
  Cataloging: Z695.1.R34
  Mechanized bibliographic control:
   Z699.5.R3
Rails
 Bibliography
  Railroads: Z7234.R2
Rainmaking
 Bibliography: Z6683.W35
Raised characters, Books in
 Libraries
  Cataloging: Z695.72
Rampant Lions Press: Z232.R17
Range management
 Bibliography: Z5074.R27

Rule of the road
  Bibliography
    Navigation: Z6839.R8
Rulers
  Autographs: Z42.3.K5
Rummonds, Richard-Gabriel: Z232.R94
Runic: Z2556.A2
Running
  Bibliography: Z7514.R85
  Physiology
    Bibliography: Z6663.R86
Rural areas and libraries: Z716.25
Rural crimes
  Bibliography: Z5703.4.R87
Rural development
  Bibliography: Z7164.C842
Rural electrification
  Bibliography: Z5834.R8
Rural geography
  Bibliography: Z6004.R55
Rural libraries: Z675.V7
  Books for: Z1039.R8
Rural medicine
  Bibliography: Z6675.R9
Rural schools
  Bibliography: Z5814.R9
Rural sociology
  Bibliography: Z7164.S688
Russia
  Bibliography
    Botany: Z5358.R9
  Libraries
    Special collections: Z688.R8
Russian Germans in America:
  Z1211.R87
Russian Germans in the United States
  Bibliography: Z1361.R86
Russian imprints
  Libraries
    Cataloging: Z695.1.R85
Russian language and literature
  Bibliography
    Education: Z5818.R8
Russian manuscripts: Z115.5.R8
  Bibliography: Z6605.S6
Russian Orthodox Eastern Church
  Bibliography: Z7842.A3+

Russian paleography: Z115.5.R8
Russian Revolution, 1917-1921
  Bibliography
    Modern literature: Z6520.R87
Russian type: Z251.R9
Russian typewriters: Z49.4.R8
Russo-Japanese War, 1904-1905
  Bibliography: Z6207.R8
Russo-Turkish War, 1877-1878
  Bibliography: Z6207.R85
Rustic type: Z250.5.R87
Ruth (Book of the Bible)
  Bibliography: Z7772.J2
Ruthenian manuscripts
  Bibliography: Z6605.S675
Ruthenian press (United States)
  Bibliography: Z6953.5.U37
Ruthenium
  Bibliography: Z5524.R8
RVK
  Library classification system:
    Z696.R43
Rwanda: Z3721

S

Sa-skya-pa (Sect)
  Bibliography: Z7864.S27
SAB classification: Z696.S24
Sabbath
  Bibliography: Z7843
  Judaism: Z6371.S29
Sabbatical year
  Bibliography
    Jewish religion: Z6371.S3
SABINI (Computer system):
  Z678.93.S32
Sabin's Bibliotheca Americana: Z1201
Sabotage
  Bibliography: Z7164.S3
Sacred Heart, Devotion to the
  Bibliography: Z7838.S3
Safety
  Bibliography: Z7914.S17
Safety engineering
  Bibliography: Z7914.S17

Safety, Industrial
  Libraries
    Classification: Z697.I37
Safety measures
  Bibliography
    Aerospace technology: Z5064.S3
    Electricity: Z5834.S3
    Mines and mining: Z6738.S3
    Motor vehicles: Z5173.S2
    Navigation: Z6839.S2
    Railroads: Z7234.S17
  Library science: Z679.7
Safflower
  Bibliography: Z5074.S2
Saga-ken (Japan). Insatsukyoku
  Imprensa: Z232.S15
Sage grouse
  Bibliography: Z5333.S24
Sahara: Z3709
Sahel: Z3515
Sailing
  Bibliography: Z7514.S2
Sailor (Computer network):
  Z674.82.S24
Saint Helena: Z1946
Saint Thomas Christians
  Bibliography
    Manuscripts: Z6611.S26
Saints
  Bibliography: Z7844
Salaries
  Bibliography
    Railroads: Z7234.S2
  Education
    Bibliography: Z5814.S2
  Libraries: Z682.3
Salesians
  Bibliography: Z7840.S34
Salishan philology and linguistics
  Bibliography: Z7119.S1
Saliva
  Bibliography
    Medicine: Z6663.S3
Saliva philology and linguistics
  Bibliography: Z7122.S3
Salmon: Z5973.S24

Salmonella
  Bibliography: Z5185.S3
Saloons
  Bibliography
    Architecture: Z5943.B37
Salt
  Bibliography: Z7335
  Effect on plants
    Bibliography: Z5354.S35
Salt-tolerant crops
  Bibliography: Z5074.S25
Salvage
  Bibliography: Z7914.R2
Salvation Army
  Bibliography: Z7845.S24
Samaritans as an element in the
  population: Z1 27.S24
Sami (European people
  Religion: Z7835.S25
SAMKAT System: Z699.4.S12
Samna (Computer program)
  Word processing: Z52.5.S25
Samoan Islands: Z4891
Samoan philology and linguistics
  Bibliography: Z7112.S25
Sampling
  Chemistry: Z5524.S35
Samurai Press: Z232.S184
San Marino: Z2371
Sancha, Antonio de, 1720-1790:
  Z232.S186
Sanctions
  Bibliography
    International law and relations:
      Z6464.S2
Sand
  Bibliography: Z7914.S2
Sanitary municipal engineering
  Bibliography: Z5853.S22
Sanitation, Household
  Bibliography: Z5776.S2
Sankhya
  Bibliography: Z7128.S25
Sans serif type: Z250.5.S24
Sanskrit linguistics
  Bibliography: Z7090

Schools and libraries: Z718
Schools Catalogue Information Service
  Subject cataloging: Z695.Z8S35
Schools in fiction
  Bibliography: Z5917.S34
Science
  Bibliography: Z7401+
    Education: Z5818.S3
    Manuscripts: Z6611.S4
  Bookselling and publishing: Z286.S4
  Libraries
    Cataloging: Z695.1.S3
    Classification: Z697.S5
    Mechanized bibliographic control:
      Z699.5.S3
    Special collections: Z688.S3
  Women in
    Bibliography: Z7963.S3
Science and industry
  Bibliography: Z7405.S34
Science and religion
  Bibliography: Z7844.5
Science and technology librarians:
  Z682.4.S35
Science fiction: Z1 14.S33
  Bibliography: Z5917.S36
    Communication and mass media:
      Z5633.S34
  Bookselling and publishing: Z286.F3
  Libraries
    Classification: Z697.F29
    Special collections: Z688.S32
Science indicators
  Bibliography: Z7405.S36
Science publications
  Libraries
    Mechanized bibliographic control:
      Z699.5.S45
Scientific libraries: Z675.T3
  Libraries
    Preservation, restoration, etc:
      Z701.3.S35
Scientists
  Bibliography: Z7405.P7
Scientology
  Bibliography: Z7835.S35

SCIS
  Subject cataloging: Z695.Z8S35
Scoliosis
  Bibliography
    Surgery: Z6667.S36
Scolytidae: Z5858.S3
Scorpions
  Bibliography: Z7996.S36
Scots' colony: Z2067.D2
Scots in Africa
  Bibliography: Z3508.S35
Scots-Irish
  By region or country
    United States: Z1361.S35
Scouts and scouting
  Bibliography: Z7164.S33
Scrapie
  Bibliography: Z5074.S35
SCRIPSIT (Computer program)
  Word processing: Z52.5.S37
SCRIPT (Computer file): Z52.5.S39
Script type: Z250.5.S4
Scripts, Radio
  Bibliography: Z7223.S3
Sculpture
  Bibliography: Z5951+
Sculpture gardens
  Bibliography: Z5953.S37
Sea birds
  Bibliography: Z5333.S4
Sea breeze
  Bibliography
    Meteorology: Z6683.S4
Sea stories
  Bibliography: Z5917.S4
Seals
  Bibliography: Z7421
Search engines
  Computer network resources:
    ZA4230+
Searching
  Computer network resources:
    ZA4230+
Searchlights
  Bibliography: Z5834.S4
Sears list of subject headings:
  Z695.Z8S43

Subways
  Bibliography: Z7234.S9
Success
  Bibliography
    Political and social sciences:
      Z7164.S92
Sudan: Z3665
Suffrage
  Bibliography
    Manuscripts: Z6611.W6
  Women
    Bibliography: Z7963.S9
Sufism
  Bibliography
    Manuscripts: Z6611.S84
Sugar
  Bibliography: Z7609+
Sugarcane
  Bibliography: Z7610.S8
Suicide
  Bibliography: Z7615
Sukkoth
  Bibliography: Z6371.S9
Sulfur
  Bibliography
    Chemistry: Z5524.S93
Sulfur and the environment
  Bibliography: Z5322.S84
Sulfur cycle
  Bibliography: Z5322.S84
Sulfur dioxide
  Effect on plants
    Bibliography: Z5354.S94
Sulfur drugs
  Bibliography
    Therapeutics: Z6665.S9
Sulpicians
  Bibliography: Z7840.S9
Sun
  Bibliography: Z5154.S9
Sundanese manuscripts
  Bibliography: Z6605.S84
Sunday opening
  Libraries: Z708
Sunday school libraries: Z675.S9
Sunday schools
  Bibliography: Z7849

Sunflowers
  Bibliography: Z5074.S9
Suomen Ortodoksinen Kirkko
  Bibliography: Z7845.S86
Superconductors
  Bibliography: Z7144.S8
Superexlibris: Z993.4
Superintendent of Documents
  Classification: Z696.S92
Superintendents of schools
  Bibliography: Z5814.S95
Supermarkets
  Bibliography
    Architecture: Z5943.S77
Superscripsit (Computer program)
  Word processing: Z52.5.S94
Superstition
  Bibliography: Z6878.S85
Superstudio (Group)
  Bibliography: Z5942.5.S94
SuperWrite
  Shorthand system: Z56.2.S94
Supplies
  Bibliography
    Military science: Z6724.S9
  Libraries: Z684
  Printers: Z249+
Supply and demand
  Libraries
    Personnel: Z682.35.S95
Supreme Court
  United States
    National bibliography: Z1249.S9
Surface chemistry
  Bibliography: Z5524.S95
Surface hardenings
  Bibliography
    Metals: Z6679.S9
Surgery
  Bibliography: Z6666+
Suriname: Z1801+
Surrealism
  Bibliography: Z5936.S8
Surveying
  Bibliography
    Engineering: Z5853.S89
    Mines and mining: Z6738.S8

Surveys
  Education
    Bibliography: Z5814.S96
Surveys, Health
  Bibliography: Z6673.5
Sustainable agriculture
  Bibliography: Z5074.S92
Sūtrapiṭaka
  Bibliography: Z7862.7.A2+
Swahili manuscripts
  Bibliography: Z6605.S85
Swahili philology and linguistics
  Bibliography: Z7108.S8
Swamps
  Bibliography: Z6004.S94, Z7405.W48
Swans
  Bibliography: Z5333.D8
Swaziland: Z3560
Sweden: Z2621+
  Bibliography
    Botany: Z5358.S9
Swedenborgians
  Bibliography: Z7845.S9
Swedes in the United States
  Bibliography: Z1361.S9
Swedish Bibles
  Bibliography: Z7771.S9
Swedish press (United States)
  Bibliography: Z6953.5.S9
Sweet potatoes
  Bibliography: Z5074.S94
Sweynheim, Konrad, d. 1477:
    Z232.S965
Swimming
  Bibliography: Z7631
Swine
  Bibliography: Z5074.S96
Swiss in the United States
  Bibliography: Z1361.S94
Swiss press (United States)
  Bibliography: Z6953.5.S92
Switzerland: Z2771+
  Bibliography
    Botany: Z5358.S92
Symbolism
  Bibliography: Z7660
    Architecture: Z5943.S88

Symbolism
  Bibliography
    Fine arts: Z5936.S9
    Modern literature: Z6520.S9
    Psychology: Z7204.S9
Synagogue architecture
  Bibliography: Z5943.S9
Synchrocyclotrons
  Bibliography: Z7144.S94
Syndicalism
  Bibliography: Z7164.S98
Syntax: Z1 15.S9
  Bibliography: Z7004.S94
Syntax-Antiqua type: Z250.5.S95
Synthetic rubber
  Bibliography: Z6297
Syria: Z3481+
Syriac manuscripts
  Bibliography: Z6605.S9
Syriac philology and linguistics
  Bibliography: Z7094
Syriac type: Z251.S97
Syrups
  Bibliography: Z7914.S96
System analysis
  Bibliography: Z7671+
System failures
  Bibliography
    Engineering: Z5853.S94
System tezaurusów Biblioteki Sejmowej
  Subject cataloging: Z695.Z8S74
System theory
  Bibliography
    Science: Z7405.S94
Systems engineering
  Bibliography: Z7671+
Systems librarians: Z682.4.S94
Szántó, Tibor: Z232.S976
Szondi test
  Bibliography: Z7204.S94

T

Tables
  Bibliography
    Mathematics: Z6654.T3
    Science: Z7405.T3

Treebus, K.F.: Z232.T853
Trees
  Bibliography
    Botany: Z5356.T8
    Gardening: Z5996.T73
Trees in cities
  Bibliography
    Gardening: Z5996.T74
Trentino-Alto Adige, Italy
  Libraries
    Classification: Z697.T73
Triangle
  Bibliography
    Mathematics: Z6654.T7
Trinitarians
  Bibliography: Z7840.T8
Trinity
  Bibliography
    Religion: Z7851.5
Tripiṭaka
  Bibliography: Z7862+
Tristan
  Bibliography: Z6521.T7
Tristan de Cunha (Islands): Z1946
Tritium
  Bibliography: Z5524.T7
    Toxicology: Z7891.T7
Triumphal arches
  Bibliography
    Architecture: Z5943.M45
Tropical architecture
  Bibliography: Z5943.T75
Tropical conditions
  Libraries
    Preservation, restoration, etc:
      Z701.3.T75
Tropical crops
  Bibliography: Z5074.T84
Tropical fruit
  Bibliography
    Gardening: Z5996.T76
Tropical medicine
  Bibliography: Z6664.7
Tropics
  Bibliography
    Geography: Z6004.T7
  Library reports, etc: Z730.5

Trucial States: Z3028.U54
TrueType
  Computerized type and type founding:
    Z250.8.T78
Trusses
  Bibliography
    Engineering: Z5853.T78
Trustees
  Library science: Z681.5+
Trusteeships (International)
  Bibliography: Z6464.T84
Trusts
  Bibliography: Z7164.T87
Trypanosomiasis
  Bibliography: Z6664.T8
Tschichold, Jan: Z232.T863
Tsutsugamushi disease
  Bibliography: Z6664.T84
Tuber crops
  Bibliography: Z5074.R58
Tuberculosis
  Bibliography: Z6664.T9
Tubes
  Bibliography
    Engineering: Z5853.T8
Tumors
  Bibliography: Z6664.T93
Tuna fish: Z5973.T9
Tunicata
  Bibliography: Z7996.A8
Tunisia: Z3685.2
Tunnels
  Bibliography
    Railroads: Z7234.T85
Tupi philology and linguistics
  Bibliography: Z7122.T9
Turbulence
  Bibliography
    Meteorology: Z6683.T8
Turf management
  Bibliography
    Gardening: Z5996.T8
Turfgrasses
  Bibliography
    Gardening: Z5996.T8
Turkey
  National bibliography: Z2831+

Writing systems
  Bibliography
    Philology and linguistics:
    Z7004.W69
Written communication
  Bibliography
    Philology and linguistics:
    Z7004.W69

X

X-rays
  Bibliography: Z5834.R7
Xenon
  Bibliography: Z5524.X4
Xeriscaping
  Bibliography: Z5996.3.W37
Xerox 860
  Word processing: Z52.5.X47
Xerox Ventura Publisher
  Desktop publishing: Z253.532.V45
XML (Document markup language):
  Z678.93.X54
XyWrite (Computer program)
  Word processing: Z52.5.X94

Y

Ya' Ityoṗyā 'ortodoks tawāḥedo béta
  kerestiyān
  Bibliography: Z7845.Y32
Yachts
  Bibliography: Z6839.Y2
Yahoo
  Search engines: ZA4234.Y33
Yakut philology and linguistics
  Bibliography: Z7101.Y3
Yards
  Bibliography
    Railroads: Z7234.Y3
Yaws
  Bibliography
    Internal medicine: Z6664.Y3
Yearbooks
  Bookselling and publishing: Z286.Y43

Yeast
  Bibliography
    Home economics: Z5776.Y4
Yellow fever
  Bibliography: Z6664.Y4
Yellowback books: Z1033.Y44
Yemen (People's Democratic Republic):
  Z3028.Y39
Yemen (Yemen Arab Republic):
  Z3028.Y4
Yew
  Bibliography
    Botany: Z5356.Y48
Yiddish literature
  Libraries
    Cataloging: Z695.1.J48
    Special collections: Z688.J48
Yiddish manuscripts
  Bibliography: Z6605.Y5
Yiddish philology and linguistics
  Bibliography: Z7038.Y53
Yiddish press (United States)
  Bibliography: Z6953.5.Y5
Yoga
  Bibliography
    Philosophy: Z7128.Y64
Yogācāra (Buddhism)
  Bibliography: Z7864.Y64
Yorkshire: Z2024.Y6
Yoruba philology and linguistics
  Bibliography: Z7108.Y8
Young adult librarians: Z682.4.Y68
Young adults' libraries: Z718.5
Young Christian Workers
  Bibliography: Z7838.Y6
Young Men's Christian Association
  libraries: Z675.Y7
Youth: Z1 14.Y68
  Bibliography: Z7164.Y8
Youth and architecture
  Bibliography: Z5943.Y68
Youth movement
  Bibliography: Z7164.Y8
Youths' periodicals
  Bibliography: Z6944.Y68
Yugoslavia: Z2951+

Yugoslavs in the United States
  Bibliography: Z1361.Y8
Yuruks (Turkic people): Z3008.Y87

Z

Zainer, Johannes: Z232.Z18
Zaire: Z3631+
Zalewski, Teodor: Z232.Z25
Zambia: Z3579
Zanzibar: Z3589
Zaragoza (Spain), Siege of, 1808-1809:
  Z1 14.Z35
Zarotto, Antonio: Z232.Z37
Zebras
  Bibliography: Z7996.Z43
Zebus
  Bibliography: Z5074.Z4
Zein
  Bibliography: Z5524.Z5
Zemstvos: Z1 14.Z44
Zen Buddhism
  Bibliography: Z7864.Z4
Zenger, John Peter: Z232.Z5
Zeolites
  Bibliography: Z6033.Z46
Zimbabwe: Z3578
Zinc
  Bibliography
    Medicine: Z6663.Z5
    Metals: Z6679.Z5
Zinc peroxide
  Bibliography
    Therapeutics: Z6665.Z7
Zines
  Bookselling and publishing: Z286.Z54
Zionism
  Bibliography: Z6374.Z5
    Manuscripts: Z6611.Z54
  Libraries
    Cataloging: Z695.1.Z55
Zirconium
  Bibliography: Z5524.Z8
Zohar
  Bibliography: Z6371.Z8

Zone melting
  Bibliography
    Metals: Z6679.Z6
Zoo animals
  Bibliography: Z7994.Z65
Zoological gardens
  Bibliography: Z7994.Z66
Zoological libraries: Z675.Z66
Zoology
  Bibliography: Z7991+
    Manuscripts: Z6611.Z65
  Libraries
    Mechanized bibliographic control:
      Z699.5.Z66
Zoonoses
  Bibliography
    Internal medicine: Z6664.Z66
    Medicine: Z6675.A54
Zoroastrianism
  Bibliography: Z7835.Z8
Zulu philology and linguistics
  Bibliography: Z7108.Z84

GPO U.S. GOVERNMENT PRINTING OFFICE: 2009–350–024/60037